THERE IS ONLY ROOM FOR HOPE

THERE IS ONLY ROOM FOR HOPE

A woman's battle with cancer

ANOURADHA BAKSHI

PARTRIDGE
A Penguin Random House Company

To order additional copies of this book, contact
Partridge India
000 800 10062 62
orders.india@partridgepublishing.com

www.partridgepublishing.com/india

For Ranjan with Love

TO THE READER

What makes the corpus of this book is my personal three-year tryst with Cancer. It is a journey I never anticipated let alone wish. It was a relationship that imposed itself on me suddenly and mercilessly, like someone who walks into your bedroom with bag and baggage and thrusts itself into every waking and sleeping moment of your existence, taking your life over and forcing you to have to live with it in a sort of 'till death do us part' way. It happened twice to me earlier when I lost my mother and father to the big C. That was two decades ago when I was no match at all. I lost both times.

When it dared enter my life again, this time with the audacity to attack my life partner, I was ready to face it head on. The reason I was sort of prepared was because being a child of two cancer patients, the medical fraternity was quick to try and seduce me into a life of prophylactic remission! In 1993 in Paris a routine medical visit could have been the trigger for a lifetime of fear punctuated by yearly investigations. I was not ready to live that way so I began my research on cancer and alternative options. It was pre Google days and ferreting information in every which way possible was a herculean task. I did manage to scour some information and I changed my diet and lifestyle and banned the 5 whites from my daily fare: sugar, milk, salt, white rice and white flour. It just felt right to do so.

On my return to India, when I faced a scare that probably would have been detected as cancer by the medical fraternity, I went to a Tibetan doctor. When she suggested investigations more for my comfort than her need, I burst into tears. She never suggested them again. I have been to her for more than a decade now. She is huge part of the motley crew that has healed R's cancer, and I use the word heal with full responsibility.

I could not have fought this battle without one main weapon in my eclectic arsenal: my writing. The Internet and blogging were my saviours. Being an only child and a recluse, I needed to combat loneliness and fear and blogging was just what the doctor ordered.

The reason I have decided to publish this blog in a book form is because I feel that there are many out there who must be going through what I have been. I would feel blessed if my battle would help them in theirs.

I first thought I would rewrite the blog posts in a book form but then realised that they would lose credibility and poignancy as what I need to share is the way things happened, the way the emotions were felt, the way the war was fought battle after battle. I wanted the words to retain their candour and honesty, even when they did not make me look good. However I had to make a few changes and perhaps even deletions as the blog was interspersed with pictures and images that were commented upon and sometimes spoke for themselves.

I also needed to write about the year before the blog which is the genesis of R's ailment and which is needed to comprehend the desperation, pathos and ensuing joy of this unique journey where there was and is only room for hope

ANOURADHA BAKSHI

PREFACE

It was in early July 2013 that R was diagnosed with lymphoma. I still remember the warm and humid evening when I got the results of the CT scan and saw the word lymphoma appended with the customary question mark (?) as is always the case. Pathologists never commit to a diagnosis, they only suggest. Mercifully Doctor's Paul'[1]s clinic was not as crowded as usual and I did not have to wait too long clutching the large envelope to my breast. Though I knew the verdict, I needed the confirmation from someone I trusted implicitly. When my turn came, I slid out the report and slipped it across the desk. No words were exchanged. The question was in my eyes, and the answer came in the form of a hand that extended and held mine.

My eyes welled up and tears were threatening to spill out. I instinctively knew that the choice was mine, and that once it was made, there was no coming back. If I let a single teardrop fall, the tone for the battle to come would have been set. Tears spell defeat and this was a battle I had to win, so the tears would have to wait. I squeezed the hand that still held mine and gave the brightest smile I could muster given the circumstances.

Again no words were needed. A brief hug to the one that had been and would be on my team and clutching the large envelope I left the room for the 3-minute auto-rickshaw ride that would take me home where my family waited for the verdict. I was not just carrying the result of a test, I was also the one chosen to set the mood and spirit of the times to come and conduct the yet unwritten last symphony of our lives.

---

[1]   Dr Ravi Paul, our family doctor.

As I alighted from the flimsy vehicle, I realised that I was no longer clutching the envelope but simply holding it as I would another and that the steps I took as I entered my home were strangely confident and purposeful.

I had sounded the battle cry!

BEFORE THE BLOG

It was in May 2012 that R started feeling unwell. For those who do not know him, R is your regular guy. He is rarely sick and when he does have a cold or a touch of flu, like most men he behaves as if the heavens have fallen! He is such a bad patient that when I hear the slightest sniffle, I pray to all the Gods in heaven to make me ill instead, as caring for him is a nightmare. The numbers of: 'come and sit by me', 'I am dying', 'take my temperature' are enough to drive the most patient soul mad, and I do not fall in that category. Mercifully R has rarely been ill and so my role as Florence Nightingale has been limited.

R relishes good food, enjoys his two sundowners, loves his weekend golf games and can laugh till he cries if told a good earthy joke. He is the perfect counterpoint to the introvert recluse I have turned into in my twilight years. We complement each other perfectly.

In June 2012 whilst on yet another of his golfing trips this time to the US, R complained of a recurring low-grade fever. This would be followed by a loss of appetite and weight. We consulted our doctors, the conventional and the alternative ones. They both asked for blood counts and the results showed a drop in haemoglobin and a high CRP[2] but nothing to be worried about.

R like all men of a certain age had a benign enlarged prostate, but as that was kept in check by both my trusted doctors, so I was not unduly worried.

---

[2]   C-Reactive Protein; test used to evaluate an individual for an acute or chronic inflammatory condition.

He was running on the treadmill, golfing every weekend, playing his piano and was quite happy about the weight he was losing. In hindsight I should have caught the warning signs but I guess my fear of cancer made me a fit case for the Ostrich Syndrome.

Things started going from bad to worse with the blood counts dropping in spite of everything we did. R always sees the brighter side of life and was quite kicked about his weight loss in spite of the bananas and condensed milk – a childhood treat – he was eating unabashedly.

Slowly the appetite started waning and the weight and blood counts where in free fall. But all investigations were inconclusive. We were at a total loss.

In August 2012 a volunteer from the US came and stayed with us. She was a lovely person we all took to immediately. When she left she gifted us a stay at the most luxurious spa in India and R and I spent three glorious days there. The fresh air and serene surroundings worked their magic and R enjoyed massages, meditation classes and gourmet food. This was not your strict and austere Ayurvedic spa. Here you could drink the best on offer and relish a sliver of *foie gras,* another one of my high maintenance man's guilty pleasure. I too enjoyed my stay. Little was I to know that this would be the last moment of respite for a long-long time.

I am not going to subject you to a blow-by-blow account of the next few months. They were by far the worst and most harrowing months of my life. R's weight tumbled down to a mere 65 kilos (his normal weight hovers around 80); his haemoglobin plummeted to 6 necessitating a blood transfusion. Every single test in the book and out of it was done and came inconclusive.

Not satisfied by the conventional and logical route, I also ventured on more arcane ones be it the long lost astrologer friend that was ferreted out of his peregrinations in some remote jungle in Kerala, or the innumerable star and crystal ball gazers I knew directly and indirectly. The common denominator in all their answers was: that too shall pass! I must admit it gave little comfort as things on the ground were turning from bad to worse.

Everyone seemed to be running in circles and doing the best they could, given the circumstances. When I told my Tibetan doctor about what a particular astrologer had said, she ordered the entire gamut of tumour markers but once again the results were negative.

Having always known that nutrition is the best medicine, I crawled the net with all my symptoms in hand and worked out a diet plan for R. The counts and weight continued their downward slide. R was looking like death warmed up. The golf games stopped as he was too embarrassed by his game, the piano was silent and bed seemed to be the preferred place.

At one point we all thought that perhaps the problem was in the head as he had gone through a bad emotional patch and that he was depressed so off we went to a psychiatrist and to counselling sessions. In hindsight it was not a bad decision as it allowed him to voice his hurt and anger, something he never did. It also filled time and broke the cycle of tests and waiting for results.

The husband of the psychiatrist was an MD and she suggested we consult him for a second opinion, which we did. He suggested some more tests, one of them being a serum ferritin as he thought that perhaps the problem was related to iron deficiency. The result was shocking as the ferritin was way too high. The man was not absorbing his iron.

There was one more humiliation the poor man had to suffer: incontinence. Everyone thought it had to do with the prostate but nothing helped. He asked for diapers. I would never have dared suggest them. The only saving grace was that my grandson was with us then and we could joke about both the boys in their Poko Pants! I was devastated but kept a brave face.

One morning, it must have been in May 2013, R came to me after weighing himself and whispered words that seared my heart: *help me, I am falling apart*! His weight had plummeted below 65 kilos @ of 500 grams a day!

I was shattered and totally helpless. It was time to get off my Cartesian cloud and knock at the Almighty's door. I had seen women in the slums going to the Kalka Temple[3] for 40 days, each day marked by a red string attached to their wrist, to seek a boon and laughed at their gullibility. I could have never imagined myself doing that but the rank despair in R's voice and the utter failure of all my efforts triggered the unthinkable: I decided to knock at God's door in the most humble way and do what I had

---

[3] A temple located in Kalkaji dedicated to the Goddess Kali

seen those women doing. I too would perform a 'chalisa'⁴. I would go to the Kalka Temple for 40 days and seek the Goddess's help to get the diagnosis we were craving for.

For the next 40 days, I went to the Temple and everyday I murmured the same entreaty. Forty days went by. There was no improvement, no diagnosis. Nothing. On the last day as I stood in front of the deity I asked her whether she was testing me and where had I failed. My parting silent words were: *I will now come to you the day R's haemoglobin reaches 13 and I will crawl from the entrance to your sancto-sanctorum.* I did not look back. Only time would tell if we were to meet again.

The next results were worse than ever. By now I had a huge file of blood investigations, X Rays, ultrasounds, MRIs, scans and what not.

One fine day a dear friend asked me if he could show the papers to one of his Doctor friend to have his opinion. I had reached the point where I would clutch every straw that came my way. A few days later my friend called to say that the only organ that seemed not quite spot on was the liver and his friend suggested a liver scan. When I sought Doctor Paul's advice he felt that as we were going for a liver scan, why not scan the whole abdomen.

We did just that. The result revealed the well concealed lymphoma.

We had a diagnosis!

---

⁴   40 day pilgrimage

LA SPIRALE INFERNALE

Today's post is personal. Maybe it is because I am at this very instant faced with a challenge that requires me to take a decision I am weary of taking. I do not know if there is a translation for the French expression '*la spirale infernale*'. The best would be a 'vicious circle' or maybe 'downward spiral'. I feel like I am at the edge of a precipice and need to make the decision to jump or not. I did start by saying that this post was personal but realise now that nothing in my life is purely personal anymore. From the day I began my Project Why⁶ journey, I have been compelled to look beyond the obvious in more ways than one. Nothing is what it seems anymore. I have written many posts on health and the medical situation over the past few years. I have been privy to the state of medical care available to us Indians on both side of the spectrum and did not like what I saw. From quacks to super docs, it is all a matter of extorting as much money as possible from people who are at their most vulnerable. The Hippocratic oath is well forgotten. Maybe one should revisit it.

Today medicine is the new commercial kid on the block. Just like education! Hospitals look like 7* hotels if you are rich. A well-rehearsed sales pitch awaits you when you go to seek help and you get drawn into that

---

5   The posts below were part of my main blog projectwhy.blogspot.in but are the precursors of the Last battle! I thought I would include them to set the stage.

6   The charity I run www.projectwhy.org

downward spiral even if you think you are well prepared. I have seen the game from far many a times. Playing on our desperation, we find ourselves drawn into a vortex from which there is no escape.

I have known many who fell in the trap and got landed with surgeries and other interventions that cost a bomb and were not really needed. The arrival of medical insurances has been a boon for such outrages. My own cousin brother was probably DOA, but kept alive and several surgeries performed on him before they finally declared him dead. You would have guessed that the bill amounted to the sum he was insured for!

In 1992, I too fell into this trap though at that time it was not an insurance issue. My father who was in no pain and in good health was taken to a 'specialist'. This happened on the 30th of October. On the 29 of November he breathed his last. In between these two dates, complex surgeries that should not have been performed on an 81 year old were done. In medical terms they were successful! I guess this was because he came out of them. For me they stripped him of his dignity. I still wonder if he would have been with us for some more time had we not visited the specialist. My mother refused all conventional treatment. She lived and died, her dignity intact. She simply followed her instinct.

I also know of people who did not fall for the carefully laid trap that includes dramatic scenes worthy of the best playwright. They sought a second opinion from the still honest medical practitioners who unfortunately work in hospitals where it is quasi impossible to get in, unless you have 'contacts'. In all these cases, people who had been told that they were 'about to die' and needed 'immediate bypass surgeries' were simply advised a change of lifestyle. They are around and in good health! One of my relatives was kept on a ventilator after a car crash for one month. We all knew in our hearts that he would not make it but fell for the well-written scenes that were enacted in front of us every day.

This is not about the poor! Theirs is another story. This is about you and me. And it is not about money. One would be willing to spend the last dime in one's pocket if we could get our loved one the right help. But the problem is that one knows that the advice you get is loaded! I am sure there are honest doctors but I do not know where to find them.

I am lucky to have a wonderful GP who is everything a doctor should be. For the past decades he has treated us of all our ailments and donned every specialist cap possible. I prayed that this would continue till we all breathe our last.

That was not to be. Yesterday I was asked to get a second opinion for the one I love the most. It is true that we have been battling with his health issues for some time and not being able to nail the problem. So my doctor asked for the dreaded 'second' opinion. Sadly he did not know anyone in the field and gave me some names and numbers. I do not know why, but I did not rush to fix an appointment and did some web search. The results were not great. I do not know why again, instinct perhaps, but my mind zoomed back to what happened to papa. My blood ran cold. I found myself at the edge of the precipice that I know will take me down the dreaded spiral from where there is no way up. What is strange is that though I know the game and thus should not fall for it, I also know that when it comes to a loved one, your reason vanishes and your heart takes over. You are sure to make all the wrong decisions.

I am now at the edge of the cliff, fighting to hold my balance. I will give myself some time to explore possible options and also take hold of myself and not act in haste. Love will have to be harnessed, and reason given all the space it needs. I will not jump in the void without a parachute but develop the wings I need to fly.

Wednesday, June 26, 2013

A LITTLE BOX FROM
WAY DOWN UNDER

It was hot and humid and I had survived a rough morning. The mood was definitely not the best. Things were not getting better as no one was answering the doorbell. Someone finally did. But before I could vent my annoyance my eyes fell on a packet lying on the table near the entrance door. I picked it up and tried to look for the addressee as the rains had done their job of smudging the writing. It was indeed for me and came from way down under from a lovely person I so loved. She and her darling man had come twice as volunteers and spread love and joy across Project Why and had somehow crept into my heart in a place that lay empty till then. The more than half a century was well worth the waiting. Each time they came, they had bags full of surprises for the children and I somehow thought that they were sending something for the Project Why kids. I was in for huge surprise: this time the kid was me!

The last months have not been the best for me personally. The pain of a loved one is by far the worst ache in your heart, and not being able to heal it is agony. Trying to keep a brave and happy face in the wake of all odds is undoubtedly a piece of acting worthy of an Oscar! Anyway I went to the kitchen to get a knife to cut the parcel open and imagine my surprise when I realised that it was all for me! Well not quite me, as there were things for others in the family, but I would like to believe it was just for me. The box had a book for me, one I had been longing to read, and one for my golf mad partner. There were other things: a soft toy, a key chain, and trick moustaches as well as two beautiful cards and lots of little stars. One card was from people one had never seen but felt had always known.

That was the visible elements, but that was in no way what that box contained. Like the Little Prince you had to look with your heart and out came truck loads of love, joy and happiness; countless prayers that could in no way go unheard and the feeling that the miracle I have been seeking would materialise. It was just a matter of time.

I was moved, speechless, transfixed. Then from I do not know where the smile I had lost for so many months reappeared and joy filled my heart.

It is always the unspoken words, the unseen things and the invisible articles that say more than any perceptible ones. Long after the box was emptied of its contents, it is still radiating joy all over the house.

I have another confession to make. From the time people who love me know I am going through a rough phase, I have been receiving little indulgences; another loving soul has been sending me boxes of chocolates that I greedily eat alone, too ashamed to let the world know my péché mignon. Each mouthful is again another burst of joy!

That my two guardian Angels share the same name cannot be mere serendipity.

HEALTH A LA CARTE

Blissfully till now my trysts with the medical mafia were few, far apart and often second hand. The stories were often recounted by people I knew, and sometimes by my Project Why family for whom private - commercial - modern medicine is a sine-qua-non to social mobility. Just like for weddings, they will beg, borrow and steal to get their dear ones admitted to one of the top medical five star facilities. I feel appalled and angry when I see people paying tens of thousands of rupees for nothing.

Just like public schools mushroomed a few years back, private hospitals, some obscenely grandiose, are proliferating at every corner of our city. They come as a counterpoint to the avalanche of private health insurance companies that promise the world and more. Somehow the whole symphony sounds extremely false and is the absolute opposite of the spirit of the Hippocratic oath! You even have a modern version [7] now!

I have never been one to plan life with logic and good sense. I am more the one who leaves everything in the hands of the one residing above and takes life a day at a time. So I am not the one who took time reading the fine print of a loved one's insurance cover. A simple query that was answered by a short: *everything* was enough to satisfy my fleeting need. I must confess that there are moments or rather issues that I deal with hubris.

---

[7] http://www.pbs.org/wgbh/nova/body/hippocratic-oath-today.html

Someone had other plans as my carefully crafted world got a blow that almost knocked me out. In spite of all my careful orchestrating I forget that life's symphony is composed by one we have no hold on. I who had clamoured with misplaced confidence that I would never - never say never again- allow myself to be caught in the vortex of private and commercial healthcare suddenly found myself in the midst of it!

Following the first diagnosis with it's forbidding (?), a biopsy was needed and there was no way even I could conjure one on my terms. We were compelled to cross the proverbial Rubicon, in this case enter the portals of big business medicine and medical insurance.

The never read lines revealed their truth. The *everything* so easily accepted turned out to be a maze best typified as illogical. It turned out that the post and number of years toiled in a PSU[8] entitled you to a double room. I wanted a single one. Naive as I am, I thought that paying the difference would be sufficient! Not at all was what I was about to discover in a well -staged and acted play.

Twenty years ago, when my father needed a surgery there were no super speciality hospitals. You either went to a state run one or chose a nursing home. I selected the later. I was given a price list with different items, one of them being rooms. I chose the best. The rest of the items were fixed! But that is not how it goes now. It is the room that defines the price of the rest of the items be it the OT charges or the nursing ones. I wanted a single room for many reasons and tried to dig in my heels. I was sent from pillar to post, as I kept asking why this could not be. I was met by a series of people whose nomenclatures seemed more appropriate to a corporate house than a home of healing. I got the whole enchilada from the kind and polite PRO, to the less kind and polite God knows who; from the seemingly understanding secretary of the Doctor to the most supposedly humane Doc who sent me back to another set of people whose kindness and politeness differed. After having been swung from here to there I was ready for the kill: a meeting with the head of finances, Cerberus herself, devoid of kindness and politeness who barked at me that there was no way I could get that single room, and if I did want it my bill would grow at an exponential rate. And that any way there were no single rooms available. And anyway you are a

---

8   Public Sector Undertaking where R worked

book judged by its cover and I was not wearing the right shoes, carrying the right bag and dripping with the right jewels.

I came back licking my wounds and trying to rearrange my head in accepting that my poor partner would have to be subjected to the snores of another. Trying to come to terms with the fact that we would not be able to be with him as a family was upsetting but what could we do. So alternate plans were drafted and it was decided that we would admit him as late in the day as possible and get him out as soon as possible. I did not know then that the 'protocol' - a word with a whole new meaning for a diplomat's daughter - was to keep a patient in ICU one whole night even if the surgery is minor. Actually in state run hospitals they would send you back in a few hours. We got our open-heart surgery kids back in three days! But we are now in the realm of commercial health and the meter has to keep running for as long as possible. Makes me sick when I see the millions who cannot and do not get access to any form of humane treatment.

So as per plan we shipped the husband to the hospital late in the night! Imagine my surprise when I was told that he had been given a single room! Was it an answer to my entreaties or to my prayers? I do not know. But I feel a little better knowing I beat the system, or so I thought.

Friday, July 12, 2013

THE LAST BATTLE AND
A WALK DOWN MEMORY LANE

My very first encounter with the word 'cancer' was circa 1957. My grandmother was diagnosed with 'cancer'. I was five. All I remember is mama's silent tears as she read a letter that was delivered to her through the weekly diplomatic bag. We were in Rabat where my father was posted. In those times there were no international dialling facility let alone the Internet. News from India came once a week in the 'bag'. Sometimes later I was told my Nani had 'cancer'. I did not know what 'cancer' was. I only knew it made my mama sad and sometimes made her cry. Cancer was a bad word. That is what the little five-year-old thought and went on with her life. On July 13th 1958 a telegram arrived. Telegrams were often bearers of bad news. My Nani[9] had died. 'Died' was also a bad word as it made mama cry and papa sad. She had died of cancer. Now the little girl was sure that 'cancer' was a very bad word! I did not know then that it would become my greatest enemy with many battles lost!

Life went on. Between postings across the globe, we always spent time in India in Meerut where my grandfather lived. For the little girl it was her Nana and Nani's house but this time there was no Nani. She had died of cancer. I had memories of her, memories that still linger in my mind today

---

9   Maternal grandmother in Hindi

and bring a smile on my face; memories of baths taken together, of mangoes eaten under the mango tree, of delicious food my Nani use to cook sitting on a *charpoy* under the same mango tree. As I grew up, my mama told me many stories about my Nani and I realised what a special woman she was, and again the word cancer seemed to be the party pooper.

The word cancer would reappear in my life as I grew up from child do adolescent. Mama had a lump in her breast and needed surgery and a biopsy. But then all would be well when the results came in. Cancer was always a fear that kept cropping in and out of our lives. But mercifully till 1989 it remained just that: a fear quickly allayed.

Things were to change forever. On a sunny afternoon in the summer of 1989 a phone call from my father would turn my life upside down. We were in Prague on a posting. My parents were in Paris and had promised to visit us. We were all excited at spending some time together in the city where I was born. The call was from papa. Mama had been diagnosed with an opacity in one lung and had suffered a dizzy spell after which she seemed to have lost her recent memory. I rushed to Paris and was shocked to see a woman who in no way looked like my mama. She was lost in her own world and frightened like a child. In hindsight that was the day I lost my mother. The last year of her life was hijacked by the said opacity, as we were not allowed to use the word 'cancer'. I do not know whether it was instinct or vanity but mama never visited a doctor, never wanted any treatment, never agreed to pain management. She bore it all with rare dignity and great courage. She died in my arms living life to its very end.

It was hard on papa and I, but we respected her decisions even though our hearts broke each time we saw her smile through the deep lines of a pain she tried to hide. I wish I had known about alternative therapies, about nutrition, about the many ways the beast could be fought. But papa and I were clueless, and only knew about medical treatment that shred every ounce of dignity you had. We had ignored the beast as that was what mama wanted and he took her away.

As papa and I sat licking our wounds and missing her smile, the beast decided to strike again, this time it was papa. Had he somatised the ailment that snatched away the love of his life? I do not know. What I know is that one fine morning papa complained of a bleed. It was the beast again, the one who had kept me in fear for half a century. This time we went for the medical 'protocols' that translated into a mutilating surgery that robbed my father of his dignity and will to live. It took just 29 days.

I was told that I was high risk, and that I needed to be checked every year. This was unacceptable to me. I would not live my life in fear of the beast but instead of trying to avoid it by not naming it and letting it run wild, I would learn every thing about it. I read books and more books, survivor stories, alternative therapies, different options. I learnt about nutrition that could prevent it from attacking and put myself on a diet. I began to exercise, meditate, and do yoga, qigong. I had to take the bull by its horns and rid myself of the fear I had nursed far too long. I was ready for it should it attack.

But it had other plans. Surreptitious and insidious ones. It again attacked a loved one in the most unexpected manner. But what it does not know is that I am prepared. First of all I am going to give it a name of my own and address it directly. Zozo is what comes to my mind and Zozo it will be! So Zozo, you want a fight, you will get one and remember David conquered Goliath.

I do not know why you have been given an exalted status. People suffer a myriad of illnesses but no one says a malaria survivor, a leprosy survivor or a dengue survivor. Death comes at a given time, and you are just the chosen bearer. Maybe you serve the interest of pharmaceutical businesses and commercialised health care. Too many fall into that trap. I too did once, but not anymore.

I am ready for you in every which way possible. I will make informed decisions; I will use an arsenal you cannot even begin to imagine. I will chose each and every weapon I have mastered over the years. I will starve you giving you all the things you hate. I will hit you with targeted bullets of all shapes and sizes. I will not leave you a moment of peace. This is a battle where if needed David will die before allowing Goliath to win.

Let the battle begin!

THE UNADULTERATED BLOG
Tuesday, 16 July 2013

HI EVERYONE

I think the coming months will be difficult and writing will be my main catharsis. Till date I have written about my loved one's ailment on the Project Why blog but I think I need another space to share the day-to-day fight that has begun, not only so that those who love me are aware of the progress, but also because I need somewhere to rant and rave and find an outlet for the tears I have frozen.

Welcome to my last battle.

Wednesday, 17 July 2

A LITTLE BACKGROUND AND THE
BEGINNING OF A ROADMAP

It is official. After almost a year of investigations and running in circles, R has been diagnosed with Classical Hodgkin's T-cell histiocyte-rich large B-cell lymphoma. In a few hours I will be meeting two oncologists and get to understand what it means in a vocabulary I am familiar with. I want to know the stage, the kind (galloping or not), the prognosis, the treatment protocol list, the side effects, the best case and worst-case scenarios. I am mentally prepared for it. I have done some advance study of support therapies and put R on a special diet that will help boost him up. Some is quite nasty tasting but he is extremely cooperative.

After getting all the answers I seek and processing it all, I intend to take some time and decide what course of action we will take. I would like the treatment to be humane and respectful of R's dignity. It is a sort of crossroads for me as I know that once the decision is taken my life will change forever. The person that will write the next post will never be the one who is writing today. It is a coming of age of sorts. Quite frankly I thought I was done with those. From what I have heard, chemotherapy, as I guess that what awaits us, is ugly and nasty. R and I have talked about it and one of the topics that came up was hair loss. He has very short hair, and so do I, but I guess the thought of being bald is not an easy one. I remember when he had a lovely mane of curly hair he would laugh at his friends with baldpates and call them moonshine. I guess it is sunshine days. I have decided to shave my head the day his hair starts falling. I guess we will be the Baldies! The only way to beat this beast, that I call Zozo, is to learn to laugh in whatever way possible so that Zozo does not commandeer all the space in our lives. So there are many things on my to do list. I intend getting a punching bag and boxing gloves and have convinced R to give me a few boxing lessons. The punching back will have Zozo written all over it. I will also get a dartboard and vent my anger and rage on it I already walk 4 km at 6 km an hour and, with every step I take I will trample Zozo. And as Norman Cousins[10] says if negative thoughts bring illness then positive ones should keep then at bay. So we will laugh at our baldheads and at every blow Zozo tries to give.

We will laugh all the way.

We want people to come, though we are quite happy the both of us. But we do not need commiserations, advice and any such nonsense.

Would love to have you on board. Will you jump on the wagon!

---

[10] Norman Cousins, (June 24, 1915 – November 30, 1990), Anatomy of an illness 1979

Wednesday, 17 July 2013

AFTER THE SHOW

Went to see the two doctors, one recommended by my lovely family doc P, humane, and willing to listen and the other the one who till now was all smiles, the one who performed the biopsy but then today looked through me as if I did not exist. His lackey told me I was no more 'his' patient as he was 'surgery' and I would have to meet 'medical oncology'. Pass the parcel, seduce it again and then let it fall in the trap. I am no parcel that has to be passed. I had gone there to find out the way forward and expected the doc who had treated us till then to at least explain what awaited us. Had I chosen to be a 'parcel' I would have gone to a State run hospital. This one was one of the best in town. It was definitely my final OK Tata to them! Exit this show! But my family doc had already gently told me what we needed to do and helped me understand each step, taking time to explain and giving me the time to process. There were no interruptions and the false sense of hurry that I had encountered earlier. So here goes. We must do a bone marrow biopsy. Ouch. He did tell me it hurts a little. And then we start the chemo. It will not be the CHOP I thought, and quite liked the acronym, as it could have been the line of a new song: CHOP ZOZO but ABVD: 1 cycle every 15 days for 2 months. A quick search on the net showed it had the same side effects. We have no choice.

Earlier in the day I had gone to an Ayurvedic Doctor with old friends or rather should I say the closest I have to MY family (my mama and papa) to get a magic powder called Ashwagandha. It would help boost the immune system and mitigate the side effects. It is quite a precious powder and my friend had to trudge to the boonies to get it for us. I was moved to tears but remember these are frozen! How wonderful people can be. I remember how this very person's wife held my father's hand whilst ma was dying of cancer. I know she is there for me and that makes things easier.

We have but a handful of days to feed R so that he can withstand the first poisoning session, then I will have to find out how to sustain him during the bad days.

I have work to do. Thank God for that.

Thursday, 18 July 2013

A SAMPLING OF WHAT AWAITS

This morning we went to the nursing home close to my home to get R's biopsy stitches removed. They were actually staples. The nurse was smiling and as gentle as could be but removing staples does hurt a little. I have had lots of stitched removed but do not recall staples. I was surprised to see R wince and then even let out a cry while the stitches were being removed. I held on to his hand to see him through the ordeal. As I have written before in our almost 40 years together I have practically never seen R sick. The odd cold or stomach upset did occur. I must confess he has never been a very good patient!

His absolute loathing for needles even made him miss the mandatory vaccinations. Poor chap. The last year made up for a lifetime with the amount of pokes he had with blood tests and other investigations. He bore them bravely, I guess because he more than anyone else wanted to know what was wrong with him and why he was wasting away.

I shudder as he will have to undergo a bone marrow needle biopsy and though the doctor assured him it does not hurt 'much' I am sure it will be agony for R. And then the chemotherapy. I will try and make it as easy as I can.

Thursday, 18 July 2013

IN HINDSIGHT... A LULL IS NOT ALWAYS WELCOME

The past weeks have been hectic. One did not have time to think, to hurt, to feel angry, to rant and rave, to question, to cry. A tidal wave swept upon us when results of a scanner came, and then it was a slew of other investigations, visits to doctors, waiting in queues, battling with uncaring hospital administrations, waiting for results, understanding the results, comprehending the options and realising one had none, or at best few. Then the devastating responsibility of taking a decision you know is right but you have avoided all along, desperately looking for some alternatives your heart wants to find but your exhausted mind knows do not exist. Pouring over the net hope in your heart while you peep at the options you so want to avoid because you are aware of the consequences. As someone said: your lives will change the day you cross the line. The line here is the first step to what is known as cancer management. You are told the 'protocol': a bone marrow biopsy and then chemotherapy. You know that once you are in the loop there is no coming back.

The decision has been taken, barring a miracle I know will not happen. Even the Gods cannot conjure it. It all begins in 96 hours. Till then there is a lull, a cessation of all activities and the quiet is scary as you are compelled to look at the road that brought you to this fateful day. Did you make any mistakes; play any delaying tactics borne out of your own fears, procrastinated for far too long? In hindsight if I were to be honest and candid, there were signs that one could have seen. But one was so desperately trying to find anything but the C word, one got lost along the way, and the three Fates - Clotho, Lachesis and Atropos - were not one my side as they spindled a series of results that did not show that the cells had gone berserk. And so in spite of the reality staring at us as the blood counts refused to climb and the weight went into a downward spiral, we kept clutching at straws. And so it went. Prayers and rituals, visits to the temples with pledges taken, everything one could imagine.

Today as I sit next to the man I have loved for more than two thirds of my life, I wonder if I somewhere let him down because of my own fears. But I cannot change what has gone by. I can only make sure that the ordeal that awaits him is alleviated by choosing the most humane conditions for his treatment, tempered with as much love as I can give, and palliated by every thing I can come up with however absurd. I hope I will have the strength to do it.

Thursday, 18 July 2013

TO BE TRUSTED IS A GREATER COMPLIMENT THAN BEING LOVED

This is the nth sleepless night I have had. I can feel R sleeping soundly next to me. For the past month and for the one to come a little Angel sleeps between us. Our grandson whose preferred place to sleep is his Nana and Nani's futon! He has been sleeping with us from the time he was 8 months old. He is now 4. Both these gentle and guileless souls have one thing in a common: they trust me implicitly and to be trusted in far greater and scarier than to be loved.

In a few hours we embark on a terrifying and uncharted journey. The decision to travel that road is mine and mine alone. A friend said that our lives would change forever in days to come. He meant these words kindly and only wished the best. Yet I know that the journey is fraught with pain, indignity and an uncertain outcome. And true it will change our lives forever, as we will live with a Damocles sword hanging on our heads till death do us part.

Some years back, must be almost two decades ago I was given that option, in my own interest of course by a man in white in the city[11] I love so much. I chose not to heed his advice. I did not want to live that way, come

---

[11]   Paris

what may. I was meant to be genetically[12] 'high risk. I was willing to take the risk and my gamble paid. But how was I to know that I would have to make the decision for the one I love most again! Only this time the sword is not simply hanging, it is threatening to fall.

A friend who has gone through the same nightmare and lost her battle wrote to me telling me to scream my pain out. Maybe she is right. Repressing my pain, not expressing it, hiding it behind masks that threaten to crack every minute and need quick fixes is not the approach that will see me through the coming times.

I have been at these crosswinds earlier but there was always someone else to take the decision. In my mother's case she took it herself exonerating papa and I from the burden of it. Her tactic was to become a stubborn little girl. Many believe she had lost her mind. Today I know it was a game she invented and played by the rules she set. Then in papa's case things went so fast that decisions were taken without due diligence. Or so it seemed. Today I know that it was willed by him as he had become a 'hindrance' to the life of his only child all set to fly away to the country he loved most. He flew away and joined his loved one, leaving me to live with mine unhindered by guilt.

Today the script is different. No stubborn child, no man who willed his destiny by making a pact with his God. Today the decision is for the most gentle and wonderful man who has put his entire trust in me. I will be responsible for each and everything that he will have to face: the pain, the indignity, the demeaning side effects and I will feel each and every one of them and know at every moment that I and I alone am culpable and to be blamed. And what makes it all worse is that it is a one-way street with no option of turning back.

I have tried from the time the news befell upon us to put up a brave face and demystify the adversary, giving it a pitiful name, finding out his dislikes, laughing at him and wowing to take him on. And I will. But I have demons to face, demons who haunt me every night and sneer at my foolishness. At dawn they disappear to come back again night after night.

---

[12]   Kamala my mother dies of lung cancer and Ram my father of colon cancer

Do I have choices? Logically no! There are too many people, some well meant and some simply irking, with success stories that proffer hope and straws to clutch at in our despair. And the options are not mine to give, as they are untested or too chilling. If it was for me, I know the road I would take but it is one I do not have the right to suggest. I pray for a miracle, an impossible miracle, one that God alone in his mercy can bestow.

THE FIRST TEARS

I shed my first tears this morning. It was not the tears or anger, rage and frustration I had thought would break the dyke I have carefully built since I heard the one news I did not want to hear. These were silent, quiet tears that streamed gently as I sought forgiveness from R, forgiveness for not having found a way to escape all the pain that awaits him, forgiveness for all the humiliation and ignominy that chemotherapy brings, forgiveness for not being able to share all that he would have to go through alone, though watching him will be far from pain free. His eyes welled too, but I did not want to tell him I had seen his tears though it broke my heart into million pieces. I would have liked to take him in my arms and hold him tight, but I knew that were I to do this, we would both be sobbing uncontrollably. And this we could not afford to do. Not today. Not in the days to come. I guess we both held back our tears. We made some crazy plans that were nonsensical but needed to ward the moment of weakness. We would sell the house and blow all the money; we would buy an island, go to the Caribbean. He even said to forget the treatment and see what happens. He did not know I had searched the web for this possibility and it was one we could not take. Neither of us is brave enough. It is only one like my Mom who could go down that road. We had to tread the other one.

What is gnawing at my soul just as the illness is gnawing at his body is my total sense of helplessness. I have always been called a power freak, but today all power has been taken away from me. If God were on my side, he would take my Angel in his sleep. I would not grudge him that. But that is not to be.

Friday, 19 July 2013

REMISSION

Remission. I hate the word. I discovered today that it is a synonym for forgiveness. Remission is only used for cancer and not for other maladies. Why should I seek forgiveness from an illness? I seek cure, healing, recovery. Who are doctors to talk in terms of months, years, the maximum being five! The time of death is not in our hands. It is has been decided by some bigger force and nothing can change that. I could slip on a banana peel in the next minute and die. Or be run over by a car. Or I could live way beyond the five years that men in white give me.

Friday, 19 July 2013

SOME GOOD NEWS

We had R's blood counts done today and for the first time in almost a year the haemoglobin showed an upward trend. I hope this is a sign of things to come. It also makes me wonder whether our body starts healing itself once it knows we have heard it?

Friday, 19 July 2013

IF I WERE A RICH MAN

If I were a rich man[13] sang Topol in Fiddler on the Roof. I sing the same song today replacing man by woman. If I were a rich woman, I would be able to chose the roadmap I want and treat my loved one the way I want. Maybe it would not be the best in the world, but it would be the best I could find. Anyway all this to say that 'another one bites the dust'.

It is all matter of insurances and what they give. And once again you have to follow their diktats. And that means big commercial hospitals. The new nexus on the block! I was hoping to have R's chemo done in smaller and more humane conditions but no way. Insurance says fancy soulless giant. And so though I had said never again I have to bite the dust and follow the system.

So slight modification: today CECT blissfully at a place I like, as blissfully it makes the mark with the Big Insurance! Then bone marrow biopsy on Monday, my way, am rich enough for that and then consult in the big medical business house on Thursday, big man not available till then and then chemo as he decides.

I know it makes better sense, or should say better financial sense. Will take some time to get used to. I must admit hours and hours in those

---

[13]   **If I Were a Rich Man**" is a popular song from the 1964 musical *Fiddler on the Roof*. It was written by Sheldon Harnick and Jerry Bock

corridors, coffee at the branded fast food counter and having to pay 35 rupees for a bottle of water as you cannot take your own, though I sneak in mine, is not what I look forward to. But what the hell, will do it.

It I were a rich woman ya ba dabba....

Saturday, 20 July 2013

SOME COMFORTING NEWS

We got the results of the CECT scan of the chest that was done to determine the 'stage' of Zozo and whether it has not spread above the diaphragm.

Yippee it has not! Whatever that means, but I know it is good news

Tomorrow bone marrow biopsy... R is scared of the pain

And I am working on my brave, smiling face...

Sunday, 21 July 2013

A QUIET DAY

It was a quiet day before the journey really begins. R's school friend P and best pal came by and it was really nice to see them joke and laugh. Crazy plans were made like holidays in faraway lands. I cannot yet imagine uprooting the banyan tree I have become but who knows the fantastic and uncharted voyage that we embark on in a few hours may have some strange mutations in my cells and make me want to travel again. Guess the cancer buddy also gets zapped by weird after effects!

My grandson ensured that P meet Zozo the punching bag and give it some good punches. But there is an elephant in the room, though only for the next 22 hours. R is really terrified by the pain he will have to endure tomorrow when he gets his bone marrow biopsy. I can understand him, as I am a big coward in the face of physical pain. I have been trying to tell him not to worry and have even decided to hold his hands through the procedure but am not looking forward to it. Tomorrow will be a long day. I intend taking a little time off and wander around a bookshop.

Talking of books, I picked the Emperor of all Maladies [14] and am reading it. I had not done so when it came out as I had thought I would never have to encounter this Emperor again in my life, save for me but I have my roadmap

---

[14] ***The Emperor of All Maladies: A Biography of Cancer*** Siddhartha Mukherjee an Indian-born American physician and oncologist. Published on November 16, 2010 by Scribner it won the 2011 Pulitzer Prize for General Nonfiction

and will stick to it no matter what. Anyway the biography of cancer, I have read 150 pages, is quite interesting and demystifies some of the beliefs we hold. Will try and finish it by tomorrow.

R is now busy playing scrabble with the daughters of his other best friend - these are the only true real friends he has, the rest I can do without -. I can hear the laughter coming from the room where the match is going on. It is heart-warming. I hope there will be many more such moments.

So today has been a hiatus in the hectic times we have had for the past months. I guess the fact that we finally have a diagnosis, however brutal and unfair has changed things in many ways. No more groping in the dark and praying for the impossible. Just processing, accepting and surrendering.

LET US GET THE SHOW ON THE ROAD

Let us get the show on the road only there is a hitch: I need to write the script, chose the music and the props as we go on. My packing list is ludicrous and somewhat surreal and my travel bag will have to be filled as we go along. In my make up kit is a ton of super glue to keep the brave face and smile intact. My repertoire of funny lines is rather thin so have to get some help from people who will be hired along the way. I still do not know the lines and I guess neither does my partner in this *pas-de- deux* we have to perform. The uniqueness of this show lies in the fact that we have to produce and enact it even if we do not want to. It may be a comedy or a tragi comedy or even turn into a sombre play. We just hope that the last scene will be an Ode to Joy.

Sunday, 21 July 2013

RAIN SWEAT AND TEARS

I was waiting for the rains
The dark clouds to gather
The skies to open
I waited and waited
Holding on to the tears I needed to shed
I wanted to take a long walk
Stomping in the rain
My face turned up to the sky
So that the tears would mingle with the raindrops
And no one would know I cried
But the clouds blew away
And the tears remained unshed
Choking my very soul
Crushing my spirit
Whilst the smile, the brave one, remained
Stuck to my face
Let us not forget
It is show time
But how long would the tears
Remain unshed
I knew they would swell

Into a torrent
And come gushing out
Ruining the carefully scripted play
And revealing to one and all
The agony I am so painfully trying to hide
I could not wait for the rain Gods
I needed to find another outlet
To mask the tears I so needed to shed
Blissfully I found the way
The daily walk on the treadmill
And the humidity soaked air
Would provide the domino
I so desperately sought
All it would need was a little extra push
Of the ageing body that
Would bring the sweat that would hide the tears
So every morning
For the time it takes to complete four kilometres
The tears spill unabashed and freely
Mingle with the sweat that conceals them so well
Providing the relief needed to carry on
Putting up a stellar show for the world to see
There are tears of regret for things of the past
Tears for the fears of things not yet come
Tears for the prayers not answered
Tears for the dreaded reality that brings you full circle
And makes you stand at a place you stood before
Holding the morrows of loved ones in your shaking hands
Knowing your words will seal the fate of all to come
And as the tears spill out ceaselessly
You find yourself in a spinning time machine
That takes you on a ride you never wished
And all the times gone by
All wounds you had thought cured
All hurts you had hoped healed

All you failures and blunders
Come back to haunt you seeking answers
You know you do not have.
The flood gates are opened
There is no going back

Sunday, 21 July 2013

REVISITING THE WORD PROTOCOL

As a diplomat's daughter the word protocol entered my lexicon at a very early age. My parents often used the word whatever language they were speaking in. As I grew from a toddler to child I realised that the word could be associated to many things: a person (Chief of Protocol) - the man who use to come to our house to escort my father to the head of state of the country we were posted in to present his Credentials -, to a situation - when mama used to flitter around the dressed dining table with a list, place cards in hand as everyone was to be seated according to protocol and so on. Everything had to be done following protocol and every thing was spelt out in a hard cover book called: *Manuel Pratique du Protocole.* [15]

I remember once way back in the mid sixties during a rather choppy journey between Marseilles and Algiers where we were posted, having the fat book fall on my hand as the boat pitched and rolled. When my parents asked me what happened they went into hysterics. I do not know why it sounded funny, as the book had hurt my head, but since that day the mention of the name of the book always brings a smile on my face.

My first job too was linked to this word too as I was the Social Secretary of the Ambassador of Belgium for more than 2 years. This meant I was in charge of protocol and it was a pain in the you know where! I had hoped that it would be last time but not quite as I chose conference organisation as

---

[15]   Manuel Pratique du Protocole Jean Serres

a career and protocol was a huge part of it and how can I forget that I was chief of protocol for the Asian Games 1982. One should write about this experience, as some of them are rib tickling!

When I decided to make a huge career change and chose the slums as my beat, I truly thought I would never hear the word again. But my friend the Fates had other plans. I was to discover a whole new meaning of the word, one that I wished I never had discovered.

The meaning I am referring to is: course of medical treatment, most often used for cancer. Actually I am in the midst of reading about its origin in The Emperor of all Maladies. I am in the middle of the book reading about how chemotherapy came to exist and how protocols were first established. It is scary as the drugs used are nothing short of poison. I guess it is far better than the initial ablations and surgeries done without anaesthetic! I still have to read about the progress made in administering poisons but I am not sure I will learn to accept let alone welcome it.

It is easy to decide for yourself. You can either go the mama way and turn into a stubborn child pretending to have lost her memory, or maybe she actually did as a way of dealing with the situation, or like my pa who accepted everything suggested as he knew he had to go so that I could fly. He needed an excuse and found one.

We have made a decision and I will stick by it as R has to get the best available. I will sit by him as he is slowly poisoned. I can understand now why one of the side effects of chemo is nausea. It is the intelligent response of an intelligent and wise body to any form of poisoning. I can understand why the hair falls, as all growing cells including the healthy ones will have to die. The blisters and ulcers are because the healthy cells of the digestive tract will also. I will watch all this with a smile on my face as I see him lose weight and become weaker and try and remember that all will be well one day, some day...

I hate this new protocol business. I find chemo too brutal. If cells go haywire there must be a reason. Why not find the reason and reverse it.

Monday, 22 July 2013

BONE BIOPSY OVER

Yippee. The bone marrow biopsy is over. I do not know how it went as he went alone with the doctor for the biopsy like a brave man. It took a 15 minutes and R said it was not painful. Dr Bansal was very gentle and kind. He has promised to be with me throughout the journey though we cannot have him as our doctor, Insurance oblige!

This is a big step and I hope the rest goes as easily!

I prayed for miracles that could not happen. Now I pray for small things and they are happening. Maybe this is the right approach.

Tuesday, 23 July 2013

SHADES OF GREY

R has been sleeping a lot. His face looks like a little child's. Trusting, at peace. He can sleep for hours at an end and right through the night. Not a line of worry on his face. Strange for someone who has just been diagnosed with Hodgkin's disease. Or maybe it just his way of coping with the news. Staying awake is scary even terrifying. For the past days he has had his share of advice, counsel, shared experiences all given in good spirit and faith but I guess all the images muddle in his brain and become incoherent and confused. So Morpheus's arms is a safe and secure option. His time out till he can process things better.

I asked my good doc why this was happening. His answer was that for the past year or so we had been drifting through shades of grey (not the mommy porn kind). What he meant was that as the diagnosis had not been confirmed, anything was possible: the good, the bad and the ugly. And like all humans we hoped, prayed and petitioned one and all. In the back of our minds was the dreaded word C, but every investigations done pushed it away But now we have a diagnostic and whether we like it or not, the road map lies ahead and a new C word has taken over all our fears: Chemo. No more shades of grey to comfort you, just black and white and either very scary.

Each one of us is dealing with it in her or his way, and R has taken the withdrawal way: sleep your fears away, and when you are awake then switch on the idiot box so that its drone becomes your new lullaby. For the rest meekly follow the leader. Get up and dressed, walk down the stairs, get in the car and allow your self to be driven to whatever horror awaits you, scared to death but hiding it by remaining in your 'état second', - the trance you have chosen to keep the nightmares away. So sleep sweet child. I will not awake you.

For me the story is different. Morpheus has decided to desert me. I lie awake in the night, thoughts crowding my mind. I spend the day reading as much as I can on this new C companion that has taken over my life. Adrenaline pumps at an accelerated rate. The over 400 pages of the Emperor of all Maladies have to be finished. Diet charts worked out. The anger and tears now take the shape of febrile and almost delirious words that fill an empty screen. Some to be shared now, others awaiting their cue.

There is no long term any more. The good doc told me not to expect any changes before 3 months. 90 days. 2160 hours. Days that will coalesce into one big day of seeing my loved one destroyed as C destroys before it condescends to make you better. There is no other way. The side effects are terrible. I cannot imagine how C will first ravage and already devastated body. I know I will have to conjure all the tricks in my repertoire to keep a brave face and find the words to soothe, the games to fill time that will get truly Bergsonian, and appear almost still. In between I will have to find ways of shedding frozen tears, releasing suffocating anger and above all finding the strength not to say ENOUGH!

It is all black and white now. No more shades of grey!

Tuesday, 23 July 2013

CONQUERING THE OTHER C

In a few hours we will be meeting the oncologist who will lead the team that will administer the chemo to R. Most probably the 'protocol' followed will be ABVD (Doxorubicin, Adriamycin, Bleomycin, Vinblastine and Dacarbazine). They are all poisons of sorts that stop the growth and destroy cancer cells. On the way the also destroy healthy cells hence the terrible and unpleasant side effects. The story of these lethal drugs makes an interesting read and shows how allopathy actually works. In the *Emperor of all Maladies*,[16] Siddharta Mukerjee traces the life of this age-old disease in a fascinating way. I am more than half way through and have witnessed the birth of the 4 drugs that will soon become an intrinsic part of my life.

I always feel that one of the best ways to conquer an enemy is by getting to know it as best you can. And that is what I am doing no. Knowing the enemy is also getting the better of your fears and learning how to deal with them. In this journey we will have to make friends at least temporarily.

I was reading a book *called Cancer: 50 essential things to do* [17]and one of the earliest is to take the lead in the therapy and ask all the questions you need to know about the proposed treatment and never accept to be bullied

---

[16] *The Emperor of All Maladies: A Biography of Cancer* Siddhartha Mukherjee an Indian-born American physician and oncologist. Published on November 16, 2010 by Scribner it won the 2011 Pulitzer Prize for General Nonfiction

[17] Cancer: 50 Essential Things to Do: Greg Anderson

by the doctor. I had selected such a doctor but because of Insurance Oblige have to settle for an overcrowded hospital where doctors give you scant time. I am armed with my list of questions and also prepared to read every line of the consent form and score out the one I do not like. Before the biopsy we were made to sign a form and I crossed out the line that asks for permission to use filming and pictures for commercial purpose. Believe it or not there was such a line and so I do intend to look at every line carefully before consenting to anything! I also intend asking every question that disturbs me from what would happen if we did nothing at all, to what the line of therapy will be, its schedule, the short term effects, the long term effects, the signs to watch out for in between chemo sessions and I expect ANSWERS. I do not want to be pushed around. I want a telephone number that will always be answered should I have a question or some unexpected reaction.

So today goes like reading my book to end if possible before 3.30pm. I think I should be able to as I read fast and even in a moving auto rickshaw!

Wednesday, 24 July 2013

MY PREVIOUS BRUSHES WITH THE NEW C

Chemotherapy and I have had some fleeting trysts. My mother Kamala gave us a few scares as before she actually was attacked by cancer, she had a few lumps that needed to be excised and then the ensuing biopsies. Thankfully they were all clear with no malignancy but in hindsight I think they did one big damage to Kamala's mind and spirit: they made the fear of cancer take over her life. By that time chemotherapy was talked about a lot and its side effects were almost commonplace. Along the way they surreptitiously embedded themselves in her mind and instilling a fear that I guess she did not even understand but triggering a response and a road map that she would follow when the time came.

When the opacity in her lung was diagnosed in the summer of 87, she had a small stroke, or so one thinks. She fainted for a few minutes and when she came out of the faint she behaved as if she had lost her recent recall memory and travelled in the past to happier times. Each time we would suggest any form of conventional investigation, a stubborn little child appeared and threw a tantrum no one could control. Once she had won her game, she would retreat back into the past. In hindsight again I am convinced that it was more of a crafty game she would play when needed: refuse a CT scan, run out half clad of the one she was coaxed into, refuse any medication and so on. We only guessed she had cancer of what we quite do not know what but which gnawed at her slowly in front of our helpless eyes. The pains did come. Horrible and excruciating but she bore them telling us that when she screamed she felt better. How could we tell her it was killing Papa and I?

She bore it all with rare dignity and grit. At one point she stopped anyone from helping her bathe. She did not want anyone except Papa to see her ravaged and emaciated. Once she was partially dressed, I took over combing her hair, applying her make up - she had to every day till the last - and then come out to take on the day. As in her game she had to be the one who had lost her recent memory, she would go along with the ploy papa had come up with: write a daily diary under his dictation so that if someone came she could find an excuse to pop into her room and read the previous day' entry and engage in a normal conversation.

Till the moment she breathed her last, the word C was not mentioned in the house. And as far as any treatment was concerned it was a big no-no! Kamala did not want to loose her hair. Actually I think she knew that there was much more at stake and she had somehow decided that she had paid her tithe over and over again to the medical fraternity and the world of allopathy. Now she wanted to live on her own terms. Without hospitals and people in white, and needles in her arms and tubes down her throat. When Papa mentioned Sloan Kettering she answered Habib Sahib! The noted Habib was her coiffeur and believe it or not he use to come and do her hair at home. She had a beauty session every day: her feet, her hands. An aunt who had done aromatherapy came daily to massage her. Papa took her out to lunch and they discovered all the new restaurants that opened. She went to plays, impeccably groomed and enjoyed herself. It was only in the last few weeks of her life that she suffered pain. But she refused any palliative care as she wanted to LIVE aware till her least breath.

She died in my arms. She had won her battle against chemotherapy in her own inimitable way.

As I said earlier, Mama played a game she invented and set the rules of. And she duped us all. Hers was a star performance. How could I have not guessed it, as there were moments when she showed her legendary lucidity and wisdom? Was she not the woman who had taken her life in her own hands at a time when young girls simply followed set rules? She studied when no girl did, decided not to marry till her country was independent;

drove trucks into the boonies to give women their rights; lived alone in a big city when girls barely stepped out of the house. Then how could she have succumbed to simple fear! No she once again wanted to live and die on her own terms.

She once told me that she would have borne all the ills of chemo had I been a child and needed her, but she has seen it all: her son-in-law, her grandchildren and she had extracted a promise from her beloved husband on the first day of her marriage: she would go before him and dressed as a bride. She did.

The C word appeared again in my life 16 months later. We had been posted to Paris but I was bound by a promise I had given my mother on her dead bed: to look after papa till his last day! Papa was in good health and our departure was scheduled a month ahead. I shared my angst with him and he told me to leave it to Guru Maharaj[18]. I was surprised by his words but said nothing. A day later he told me he was bleeding but felt it was his old piles. We went to the doctor. It was cancer of the colon and I was caught in the vortex of medical protocols: surgery, chemo... He was operated upon and died 29 days later. Chemo never entered my life. He too had willed its exit! Now in 3 hours I will again be caught in the same eddy but this time it seems I have no escape. Only time will tell how the battle goes.

---

[18] Ramakrishna Parmahans

Wednesday, 24 July 2013

THE JOURNEY BEGINS

Friday 26th July is the first chemo. It will be preceded by a PET scan (Positron Emission Tomography), which I believe is absolutely imperative! I am not happy as these scans necessitate injecting a radioactive substance through your body and that has the risk of radioactive exposure. But I agreed because the Doctor we met was extremely nice and just the kind of Doctor I had prayed for. He explained every step taking his time to answer my most inane questions. So my prayer for the right Doc was answered. With the present investigations we have in hand he confirmed a stage 2 B. But we still await the bone marrow results. If these are good then it is 2B. If not it is 3 or 4. In the better case the chances of cure are 60%, in the worst they are 50%. The other 50% is in the hands of God.

There will be 12 chemo sessions over the next 6 months so the journey ends on 26 January 2014. According to Dr V, the worst sessions will be the last 2 when one is fed up of the whole thing. We plan to place a line at the next session, as it will make things easier. That will be a minor surgery. I really hope they do, as R is very fidgety when he has an intravenous line in his arm. We saw that when we did the first transfusion. In this case we cannot have him move and run the risk of the medicine spilling out. Must find a way of sorting this one!

The side effects are there: nausea that can be controlled, extreme fatigue and weight loss and of course the dreaded hair loss. I intend to shave my head when his hair falls and keep it that way till his comes back.

So this is the news.

The processing has not begun, neither in my head nor his.

I guess the next blog will have the anger, pain and the rest.

Wednesday, 24 July 2013

FIRST SLEEPLESS NIGHT AND COUNTING

I spent a sleepless night. Just like I had 21 years ago on the eve of papa's operation. Once again I carry the burden of a decision the consequences of which a loved one will have to bear. This is something no one can understand, as it is deeply personal and would probably be miffed at by one and all. But I need to share this as it is perhaps my way of seeking absolution or rather getting one step further on the road of forgiving myself as I am likely to carry this to my grave. Forgiving yourself for any hurt caused to another is quasi impossible. But as we are about to start a battle for life, I feel it is important to be brutally honest.

For one year and even more we tried desperately to find out why R was ill. He was losing weight, had intermittent fever and cold sweats. We went though every investigation imaginable and never could get a satisfying diagnosis. Today when I look at the symptoms of Hodgkin's or any other lymphoma they stare at me with a wicked sneer almost saying: Got you! And they did, maybe also because of my petrifying fear of the word Cancer! So what we were doing is looking for all other causes possible. In my pathetic defence I can say that R's lymphoma was well hidden and not in the usual more visible places. And while we ran this scary 'treasure' hunt, R was fading away. Finally we got the results and because of its delay he has B cell lymphoma, which is probably 2nd stage or more.

I spent the night going through the last year and trying to see whether I had missed out on something; whether there had been some indication that we failed to understand. Whether we could have caught it earlier. It is no point on crying on spilled milk. But I know I will carry this feeling of culpability all along my life and each time I look at R.

I also realised in the course of my white night that though R has been with me all the time, I always see him with the eyes of my heart. Yesterday evening as we sat in the drawing room listening to Tom, one of our volunteers play some haunting classical music on R's piano, I caught a glimpse of him as he really has become. For the first time I saw the 75-kilo man weigh 61 kilo. It was a rude shock and a new guilt choked me. Could I have stopped this? And then the dreaded: Oh my God, he will loose more after his chemo. I have to master the art of seeing him with my heart and not as he is. It would kill me.

And then the whole guilt trip all over again.

It has to stop.

Thursday, 25 July 2013

ETAT SECOND

Etat second. I have always liked this expression. One of the meanings found in the dictionary is: *the state of mind into which some writers go when writing short stories. It mixes abstraction and concentration at the same time, ironically telling sometimes more facts than in conscious writing.* Others translate it as: *trance!*

I have used the expression in a slightly different way all through my life. To me *Etat Second* means a period of time when you step off the planet for some reason, and enter a parallel zone when your life is dictated by extraneous reason. It could be something as mundane as an examination, as credulous as your first heartbreak or as is the case now as harsh as chemotherapy.

Stepping into *an Etat Second* means giving up life, as you know it and following the strict and inevitable regimen of the cause that sent you in this state. Your life is then dictated by a set of dates separated by a fixed number of days with each having its own diktats. One thing is certain you cannot change the protocol and anything else your normally do from caring for yourself, to pursuing your coping strategies, to completing your work responsibilities, to finding your 'alone' time, to having a cup of tea with a friend, to just taking a break has to be sneaked into the little moments where your loved one sleeps, or is having a better moment.

The first 15 days will be a learning experience for everyone. R will have to learn how is body tolerates and reacts to the deadly cocktail that will be pumped into him and I will have to deal with each of these finding the right strategy to counter the side effect: be it nausea, blisters in the mouth or exhaustion. We will need to conjure meals he can ingest and then hopefully enjoy. They will have to be presented in diverse ways to break the monotony as how inventive can you get with soup and smoothies!

Normal activities like bathing and dressing will also have to follow a new pattern. Bad days and good days will have to be carefully noted and numbered so that the next cycle is better organised and less exhausting. And this for the next six months, day after day after day.

Today is the last day of life as I have lived it. Tomorrow I enter my état second.

Wish me luck!

Friday, 26 July 2013

NIGHT ONE

Ok Zozo aka Goliath you caught me unawares today. But this is the last time I assure you. I have a terrific team in my corner of the ring. Not only friends the likes of which you can NEVER have as who would love you, be there for you, care for you, pamper you and above all reveal all your secrets. But I have them starting from a wonderful doc who knows you better than you can ever imagine and above all has an arsenal to beat all you wily tricks. I have friends who are there 24/7 to stand by me and ensure your machinations and surprises are countered with laughter and joy. Then I also have a bag of ruses you do not know and master.

True I thought I knew everything about the side effects of chemo. So lesson 1: do not think you know all and be prepared for anything and everything. You will not be caught unaware again. I admit that the state R was yesterday when we brought him home was scary to say the least. I was taken aback when I saw him in a state I have never seen him in. He was aggressive, babbling away - that is my prerogative alone - confused, lost in time and space, uncooperative, and the exact opposite of who he is. But my wonderful doctors guided me through the episode and I beat it without having to resort to any medication. He slept and is still sleeping and I know he will wake up exorcised of you.

You are right when you say I am breaking inside and can have a meltdown. But you do not know of what steel I am made, you cannot begin to imagine my coping strategies where tears turn to ice and anger to cold hate!

You will have to break me before you can get him!

Saturday, 27 July 2013

EVERYTHING HAS A CAUSE

I have always believed that everything has a cause. Maybe it is because of my having studied Philosophy! So cancer too has a cause. I am reading the Emperor of all Maladies, which is, as its author states a biography of cancer. I have not yet finished it so I do not know what remains in its last hundred or so pages but down 300 pages I am not in total agreement with the causes espoused. Cancer is not like other diseases where a series of tests reveals the cause and defines the treatment. In cancer one fine day your own cells which have been following a rigid pattern, decide to talk a walk and go free, multiplying at an exponential speed and hence causing havoc in the well-regulated system they have followed till date.

Our brain is undoubtedly the most complex, intelligent and wondrous machinery you can imagine and would not change an iota. Its logic is faultless. But there is another part of our being, let us called them emotions that play an important role that people often do not comprehend. Let us say that if the brain is the reason, than the emotions are the heart.

However strong our mind and brain are, they are not infallible and sometimes emotions can give them a shock they cannot withstand. That shock in my humble and laywoman's opinion is sometimes sufficient to jolt the well planned machinery into total disarray and start the inexorable march of cancerous cells. I know for certain that Papa's cancer was caused by mama's death.

ANOURADHA BAKSHI

It was heart warming to hear that R's oncologist shares my view, in spite of its not being 'scientific'. I know why his cells took a life of their own. There is only that much anyone can take. When those you loved unconditionally let you down, not once but over and over again in ways that no sane human being can fathom; when they hurt your near and dear ones unabashedly and with impunity; when each step you take to heal backfires and brings more hurt then it is expected that something will shatter. Being a man you have been 'taught' not to cry, not to scream, not to express your hurt, then it is but evident that your body will 'talk' for you and your cells will go on a wild ride.

That is what happened.

Saturday, 27 July 2013

DAY 1 WITH CHEMO... ALL YOU NEED IS FRIENDS

First things first! The chemo needs a name, what about chemchow! What do you all think? Any better ideas? So the first day living with chemchow was to say the least astonishing! In all the good ways possible! Before I go on further I must share something personal. It was the first time in my life that I cursed my nomadic life however privileged. My dotting and dotty parents gave me everything except the possibility of having life long friends. Yesterday I understood the true value of friendship.

Here I was on day 1 with chemchow dreading nausea, loosies, lack of appetite, extreme fatigue (R was always sleeping before he was diagnosed) and all the gory things that I had read about on line and in the file given by the hospital and I was imagining having to create 3 star Michelin food within the parameters of what is allowed. But let me tell you the best recipe for battling chemchow: a brew made of your best pals, a basket of jokes and reminiscences, and laughter. When friends left, thanks to one of them, R discovered the magic of iPad in Zozo mode! You need an iPad, earphones and access to the movies and shows that made you laugh. It was pure unadulterated pleasure to see him laugh. Those who know his laughter will understand. So to recapitulate R had a good day! Ate all I gave him that was far from 3* Michelin. Laughed and had a great time in between he had 2 loosies and was a little tired so had to take iPad away so that he could sleep. On the flip side guess who had nausea, loosies and anxiety: ME!!!!

Sunday, 28 July 2013

DAY 2 WITH CHEMCHOW

Today was a sort of annoying day. None of the expected side effects you read about or are told bar two bouts of the loosies. R was restless the entire day. He felt *fidgety in the legs* was how he put it and thus could not do anything like watching a funny show or read a page. Called his doctor who prescribed some medicine but that made him sleep an hour or so and he is back to his restless self. Wonder what else is in store for me.

Sunday, 28 July 2013

LOVE IN THE TIME OF CANCER

Till date I have had three trysts with cancer.

In the first one, it was my mother who was targeted. Her absolute and unequivocal defiance resulted in a strange drama played over 11 months. The protagonists were mama, papa, me and of course Cancer that actually set the tone. When you are dealing with someone with a terminal disease who refuses any form of known treatment believe me things are not easy. Conventional medicine with its set protocols does provide you with set milestones that you follow blindly. These protocols fill your spatio-temporal reality and provide mechanical props to make you feel your are doing something. Whether the something works or not is not in your hands but you feel you are giving the best available. Papa asked mama if she wanted to go to Sloane Kettering. Her answer was a candid no! So how would we fill the hours, days and months when we saw her fading away, wincing in pain, and slowing dying?

She had her answers ready: hairdressers, beauticians, plays, outings, shopping etc. And she had her way. You did not argue with Kamala Goburdhun née Sinha! What was being put to test was a husband and daughter's love. I guess I fared poorly in comparison to papa. Watching him for those 11 months showed me what true love really was. He put his life on hold to attend to each and every whim she threw his way. If he was ready to go out for an important errand and she wanted him with her, he simply took off his hat (papa was of the generation that did not leave the house without a head gear) and sat with her. The most poignant demand she made was towards the end. As she did not want to die in a drugged sleep and thus had refused any form of medication, there came a time when she decided not to sleep. A deal was made: she would sleep in spurts of 45 minutes provided papa sat next to her on a stool and held her hand and woke her every 45 minutes. He did. Night after night till her very last night. When I asked him to rest and that she would not get up, his brusque answer was *I gave your mother my word*! It broke my heart to see my 80-year-old father who was portly to say the least sit on that tiny stool and stroke his loved ones hand fulfilling the promise he had made. He past the test magna cum laude. I came a poor second as I was torn between my love for my mother and for my father. She had beaten all the protocols and won her battle her way and papa had fulfilled another inane promise she extracted from him on their first day of marriage: that she would die before him.

I know when the first cell in my beloved father's body went awry. It was when Kamala breathed her last, and I thought papa would break down and weep. He did not and took me in his arms and said softly *I am here for you*! But those words came with an unsaid caveat: *as long as you need me*! His pain had taken another road. That is when his cells began their morbid march. He was there for me all the time I needed him. But then came the day when R was posted to Paris. It should have been a moment of elation but two promises came in the way of a father and a daughter. I had promised mama to never leave papa and he had promised me to be there till I needed him. But who would define the term "needed"? The march of the cells became deathly and though protocols were followed, the end had to come as otherwise the pledges would be broken. It took 29 days. He too had beaten protocols in his wise way.

In both cases Love was the main protagonist though none of us realised it. Cancer was just a sidekick.

So the question I ask myself today as Cancer has taken hold of another one I love, what is the real motive this time. The dying, as a bride does not apply, no real pledges have been made and need to be fulfilled. I still believe that Love again is the main lead. So whose love is being put to test? Or is it that our love that had been hijacked by others for so many years has finally come centre stage? Is it the only way to catch up for lost times as Cancer has catapulted us in a tiny orbit where all else has to be put on hold. And will the big C leave my loved one so that we can enjoy some peaceful and quiet twilight years?

Monday, 29 July 2013

DIVINE JUSTICE

We often or should I say always remember God at times of need, what ever shape it may take - the hungry will pray for just a meal whilst the businessmen for a new contract- or at times when we feel - erroneously or selfishly - that justice has been denied to us. In those times we tend to forget our failings if any. We pray and petition that powerful entity to grant us justice in the manner we wish to see it granted, often blinded by our own hubris. We think we know all, and know best and are often blinded by the moment and its magnitude not able to see the *big picture,* a phrase my father use to pronounce whenever I was hurting, no matter what age I was.

Divine justice is fair, equitable and sometimes difficult to fathom. What makes it different is that unlike us, God also remembers all the other petitions and prayers we forget along the way and hands out His judgement at the times he thinks best. In his final pronouncement he also deals a blow to all our hubristic moments and puts us back in place. All your never say never are taken care of.

The first time I really felt the power of divine justice was when he took my father away. When mama died I had promised her to look after my dad till his last breath. When a few months later my husband was posted to Paris, a dream posting for us as both my daughters studied in the French system, the promise I made to my mother came into the way of my going. At that time my father was in excellent health and no one could have ever imagined he would die within 29 days. I had been freed of my promise and he could be united with the woman he loved. God had intervened.

The past years have been clouded by a series of emotional upheavals of the worst kind drawing battle lines impossible to cross. In the middle of it all one person who took all the blows. On both side contradictory petitions to God and prayers and supplications. No human judge however wise could have found a way out. It was an imbroglio needing divine intervention. I suppose it was a tough one for God too! But the verdict has fallen taking care of all the past prayers and supplications, taking into account all our wrong doings and failings not to forget the never say never.

I had always prayed to have the full attention of my beloved who for too long was torn between two sides and bore too many blows that finally affected his entire being. For month and months we knocked at every door possible to find out what ailed him. My worse nightmare happened when the diagnosis was the one word I hated most: cancer! Bye-bye hubris. Cancer it was. And this time, the whole enchilada. I was terrified of chemotherapy. Well this time I had to live with it and conquer my fears. I wanted my husband 24/7. Well wish granted as my life is put on hold and for the next six months R and I are destined to live in a bubble! Just the two of us.

What the future holds, I do not know. Only He knows the whole picture.

Tuesday, 30 July 2013

WAITING FOR GODOT BUT THIS ONE WILL COME

As this is my first and hopefully last encounter with chemo I feel a bit like the Beckett's protagonists in Waiting for Godot. Only in my case Godot will come. Being a total neophyte in the matter, I did arm myself with all the knowledge possible about the side effects of chemo a.k.a. chemchow (to make it less scary) and for this post Godot. The nausea, the weight loss, the hair loss, the blisters in the mouth, the fatigue, the tingling, the loss of sensation, the loss of appetite, the fever and God knows what else. And just like Vladimir and Estragon[19], I too need to divert myself to hold the terrible silence at bay! I do not have a pal to swap hats[20] with and will not in anyway consider suicide, but I sleep, argue, stomp on the treadmill, listen to loud music, browse the shelves of my favourite book shop, peruse the net for more information: will Godot come on the 4th, 10th or whatever day.

The waiting is endless and killing. I even find myself puling at R's hair to see if it will come in my hands. I meticulously record all he eats, and how he feels in carefully designed charts. Helps pass time. But time drags its feet. There are 175 more days to go. 4200 hours. 100 080 minutes! True they will be interspersed with visits to doctors and hospitals, tests and

---

[19]   Protagonists of Waiting for Godot Samuel Beckett 1953
[20]   Waiting for Godot Act II

more waiting for results, moments of celebrations when things look good, stellar performance when things look bad so that the face does not show the disappointment. The list is endless but still does not fill the hours and minutes when you are left with just waiting. I guess I will have to be prolific during these days and not have a writer's block!

Tuesday, 30 July 2013

DAY 4

Day 4 with chemo. Waiting for side effects but none as yet. Or just some anodyne ones: a few loosies, some restlessness. Tomorrow is the blood test that will chart the next days after we visit his oncologist on Friday. I am concerned about his blood counts that were low when we began. I am taking all precautions and ruses to keep the side effects away or at least minimise them. The poor man has to eat strange brews that I concoct. Some are quite horrid.

I am the anxiety ridden one as R keeps his legendary calm. I have confirmation on my theory that his cancer is man made or rather women made! A friend sent me some pages of Gary Null's Encyclopaedia[21] on natural healing where he says that suppressing anger can make you more prone to cancer. I think the easy tears and rages we women are legendary for are a good way to release all repressed feelings. I wonder why boys are told not to cry. One should cry, scream, rant and rave, bang doors and vent our rage.

R had a reasonably good day that ended on a high. A visit from his best friend P that turned out into a photography class for grandson Agastya with R as the subject!

Must cherish all these moments. They may help us go through the bad ones

---

[21] The Complete Encyclopedia of Natural Healing Gary Null, Kensington Books 2005

Wednesday, 31 July 2013

DAY FIVE…. GODOT STILL NOT WITH US

Day 5 went on well. Godot has not appeared. I guess he is making his vile plans but I am ready with my arsenal. Just loosies for the moment. Appetite OK. Spirit high. Did some work, played the piano after months, watched some funny shows, read his historical novel. Slept. Ate all the food he was given, even the yucky tasting juice. But the piece de resistance of the day was learning a new way of playing chess. It is called the Agastya[22] way! Lots of laughter! Hope it lasts.

---

[22] My grandson

Wednesday, 31 July 2013

LIFE IN THE TIME OF CANCER

Since the day we discovered that R had a lymphoma, life has taken a surreptitious 180-º turn. Everything is on hold and I must learn to discretely weave the bits of my life I cannot give up. There is an elephant in the room. Whether we like or not. At best we can befriend it and accept as gallantly as possible that it will stay in our lives for the next 6 months. The problem with this elephant is that it takes all the space possible leaving you barely enough to exhale and do all the others things you need to. Whether I like it or not, I have to put my life on hold for the next 174 days.

The elephant in the room is chemo and the arsenal I have chosen to counter makes a very stringent timetable. It starts at 6am and ends when R goes to sleep. So it covers at least 15 hours of my day. This timetable necessitates stick adherence. Everything that goes down R's throat has to be freshly prepared, never reheated so nothing can be made in advance. Vegetables and fruits need to be organic and thus sourced in different parts of Delhi. Calls need to be made to know when they will be delivered. Then R has to be coaxed to do things he does nor feel like: read, laugh but what is more important to make him do: talk and vent all that is bottled inside.

An eminent advocate of alternative medicines states that: people who tend to suppress anger are more prone to cancers than others. I know for certain where R's cancer stems from. I also believe that if he gets it out, screams in rage, sheds angry tears and lets it out of his system by ultimately forgiving he will improve by leaps and bounds. So some time of the day is earmarked to help him talk. Not much success there. Now in between all this, I have to sneak time to do the minimum needed for Project Why though my team is incredible, find some alone time to write and even to take a break and leave the house and the elephant. Not easy.

Must work on my coping strategies.

Thursday, 1 August 2013

CHEMO ATTACKS!

The first week of chemo ends today. Though R looks OK and feels OK and eats OK and laughs OK, works, and reads OK, the nth descendant of mustard gas has begun its terrible attack on his body. A perusal of the history of chemotherapy [23]is scary reading.

R's first blood test results were terrifying. In one tiny week, and we have 26 weeks to go, his WBC have tumbled from 9000 to 4000 leaving him open to all infections and viruses. And this is only the beginning.

The modus operandi is suspect. Kill all cells that divide, the good, the bad, the ugly and hope for the best.

The adversary is lethal. How do I counter it? Am at a loss! Must regroup my troupes.

---

[23]   http://en.wikipedia.org/wiki/History_of_cancer_chemotherapy

Thursday, 1 August 2013

SCALING DOWN AND REPHRASING PETITIONS

For the last 15 months or so, since R's problems began, I have been petitioning the Lord in all ways possible. From a big ritual puja with over 12 priests chanting to my daily prayers at home. As his health slowly dwindled, my prayers intensified. My petitions were vague and in hindsight quite inane. Before every test I prayed for the results to be good not realising that the quicker we had a diagnosis the better it was. And I got my wishes: every test was OK, even the tumour markers. I rejoiced not realising that what I actually should have prayed for was a DIAGNOSIS!

For over a year we fell into a strange loop. R's symptoms aggravating, my prayers multiplying and every investigation revealing nothing. I kept asking for his counts to go up, his weight to stop falling and so on, not realising that this could not be possible without knowing what is wrong.

I now realise that I should have adopted my papa's gratitude mantra. His prayers went something like this: *Thank you for all the good things you send my way and thank you for all the bad ones. I accept both with deep gratitude. I lay them at your feet and know that you will get me out of my troubles as I have surrendered everything at your fee*t. I wonder why I had forgotten this.

Two months ago I started a 40-day pledge to visit the Kalka Temple every morning. I did not miss a single day and battled the crowds to get a glimpse of the deity. I simply asked for R to be well. Nothing. On the last day I made a pledge stating that I would crawl to the deity the day his haemoglobin crossed 13. Soon after we had our diagnosis even if it was the one I dreaded.

I still pray every day. I may also decide to visit a temple for another 40 days but this time my petitions will be scaled down to the need of the moment: make his chemotherapy side effects minimal, make his TLCs multiply, make his haemoglobin increase, make his nausea stop, bring his appetite back! I will not succumb to hubris.

Like papa I accept R's cancer and place his health at the feet of God. I will continue to pray and know that He will get me out of this trial.

Thursday, 1 August 2013

WHY I ABHOR CHEMOTHERAPY

It is not quite politically correct to write a post on my repugnance towards chemotherapy particularly as I have allowed it to enter my beloved's body. Was I seduced by medical glib? Was it the constant repetition of friends and dear ones stating that this cancer - Hodgkin's - responded well to chemo? Was it that even my Tibetan doctor reiterated the same? Was it because the decision I had to take would have to meet the aspirations of others who were chemo believers? I do not know. All I know is I said yes to the one thing I never wanted in my life. Cancer had taken my parents not chemo!

The primogenitor of chemo was mustard gas[24] the very gas that killed millions in the Second World War. The logic is that if chemo kills cells that divide then it will kill cancer cells. Now it will also kill cells in your bone marrow, intestinal tract and so on. We hope the good cells will resuscitate and proliferate. Mustard Gas was a weapon of mass destruction. When such weapons are used they destroy everyone: soldiers, children, women, old people etc. But we know that all will die. It is not as if the innocents will rise from the dead.

---

[24] The Immortal Cell, Dr Gerald B Dermer, Avery Publishing Group, Garden City Park, 1994

Chemo is a choice. But not an easy one as it is a sort of lie[25]. Disraeli once stated that *'there are three kinds of lies in the world: lies, damn lies, and statistics.'*[26] Chemo falls in the third category. Statistics are often presented in a somewhat false way and you get *'statistic-ed.'*!

The first oncologist I met at the hospital where R was being treated first told me that Hodgkin's was 80% curable! By the time we began chemo the odds were 60/40! 60 for cure and 40 for what cancer specialists call remission.

Now hang on. We are all on remission from the instant we are born. I there is one thing we can be sure of if we are born is that we will die. So cut out the remission bit.

So to me a drug whose objective is to poison the system makes little if no sense.

---

[25] Chemotherapy, An Interesting Choiceby Jon Barron

[26] This quotation is often attributed to Benjamin Disraeli, the 19th century British Prime Minister. The source for this view is the autobiography of Mark Twain, where he makes that attribution. Nevertheless, no version of this quotation has been found in any of Disraeli's published works or letters. An early reference to the expression, which may explain Twain's assertion is found in a speech made by Leonard H. Courtney, (1832-1918), later Lord Courtney, in New York in 1895:

Friday, 2 August 2013

JUMP FOR YOUR HEALTH

A large part of my awake time, and there is quite a lot of it, is spent either thinking or browsing the net to find ways to beat the ill effects of chemo. The first results did show a deep drop in WBC and hence the importance of keeping the lymphatic system on the move.

I just came across an interesting blog of a lymphoma survivor who found that rebounding is one of the best exercise for the lymphatic system[27]. Rebounding not only exercises the lymphatic system, but his also kind on your joints and allows the lymphatic fluid to travel 15 to 30 times faster then when the body is at rest. A real spring cleaning!

So off to buy a rebounder tomorrow so that R can start jumping to perfect health!

---

[27] http://changeforcancerwellness.blogspot.in

Friday, 2 August 2013

MY NEW NORMAL

For the past 13 years and 3 months my life was dictated by the incessant needs of Project Why, which came to be on May 7th 1998. From a small idea and a personal mission '*repay back a debt*' it has grown over the years to become a vibrant organisation that reaches out to over 1000 beneficiaries. This did not happen over night and the years long learning curve had many ups and downs. It put me to the test many a times, challenging me as nothing else had ever done and making me discover aspects of myself I did not even know existed. And more than anything else it filled the huge well of loneliness that engulfed me after my parents' death. The orphaned only child had found more than a family.

For the last 13 years I have worn so many caps that I have lost count. I think some God decided to put to test all the abilities I had shunned or found infra dig! From one who barely balanced a house budget I was made to take charge of financing an organisation that today is worth almost 10 million rupees a year and employs 50 persons! I discovered shocking realities that slowly turned me into an activist. I fulfilled the long forgotten dream that probably took seed in a cafe in Paris: that of writing! I published a book[28] and now have blogs many read and like. I had unpleasant altercations with politicos and learnt to wear them down. The list is endless. Let me

---

[28] Dear Popples, Anouradha Bakshi, Undercover Productions; http://www. amazon.in/Dear-Popples-letters-unlikely-mother/dp/0979811651

just say I became someone who did not have to turn away when she saw her face in the mirror every morning.

Project Why became my way of life. It was normal for me to give it all the time it needed and slink in the rest of my life in the tiny time slots I could find. Till a few months back life ran on an even keel. I had found my comfort zone and hoped it would last till my final curtain call. I often found myself calling Project Why my magnum opus and my swansong!

Even when R showed his first sign of illness, I was convinced that it would be a passing ailment that would be dealt with as everything else was dealt with. It was only a matter of time. How wrong I was. Project Why would not be my swansong. R was diagnosed with cancer and I soon realised that what had been my 'normal' life till just a few days ago would not do anymore. I had to define a *new normal*. Everything would now have to be worked out around R's treatment. Cancer is not the kind of ailment that gets better as soon as you pop the first pill or take the first shot. Once you let chemo into your life you have to accept that it will take all the space around you and in you and leave very little time for other pursuits. One part of your life will have to be put on hold. I am on forced leave!

From what I have read, heard and understood, the first chemo is a dream and it gets worse, as toxic drugs suppress the immune system every 15 days. In between those days you have to live one day at a time, as you do not know what will transpire. You just have those 15 days to work your magic and boost the immune system, the sagging spirit and all else without losing your smile or venting your anger at least in front of others. You also need to continue looking for ways to alleviate the side effects and select the options you feel are right. I never thought that at age 60+ I would have to learn to be Florence Nightingale. So this is my new normal. Ms Nightingale who also has to keep the home in order and run Project Why by remote control. Not an easy task!

Saturday, 3 August 2013

JUMPING TO BOOST IMMUNE SYSTEM

Believe it or not jumping on a rebounder or trampoline is an excellent way of boosting your immune system when you have Hodgkin's disease[29]! So got R his trampoline and we began jumping. The idea is to jump for a few minutes, even 1, many times a day so that your lymphatic system which unlike your circulatory system does not have a pump is jolted into moving. If you walk for a few miles after a while your lymphatic and circulatory systems will be back to where you began. A survivor[30] says that having a trampoline at home and jumping on it a few times a day get all systems going: blood and lymph! So R will be doing a lot of bouncing.

---

[29] http://www.greendrinkdiaries.com/detox-jump-around/

[30] http://changeforcancerwellness.blogspot.in

Sunday, 4 August 2013

DAY 9

A quiet day though some family folks (mine) came by. I was touched as being the recluse I have become, I have not been very good at maintaining relationships but as my cousin D said, no matter how often we see each other, we are there when we need each other. Just my kind of approach. I hate the formalities mode that many adopt: all smiles when they see you and blasting you as soon as they turn the corner. I was touched by the fact that my Aunt who can barely walk came too! And another sister in law brought the picture of her Guru and kept it under R's pillow. These things mean so much and give one hope.

R was feeling well today. He jumped on his trampoline and ate his food and laughed and read! Makes me so happy to see him like that, but I know it is not going to be like that for long. I dread the 2nd, and the 3rd and the nth chemo.

But life goes on. It has to!

I do not know why, but feeling blue today.

Sunday, 4 August 2013

SCREAM, TEARS AND FEARS

A new week starts. The first one went on well. Could not have hoped for a better one. This makes one apprehensive after all the horrific side effects one has been told and one has read about. It was a sleepless night for both of us. R is giving a stellar performance of taking it all in his stride, but having known him for almost 40 years I know it is a facade, a domino he wears to hide his feelings. We are like two old souls trying to perform in a play the lines of which are written as we go on. The degree of fear and apprehension of the exit lines are a mystery. It is too scary to plan. The only way to make it is one day at a time, like the good old AA guys! But I guess that is the only sensible way to go.

This week is busy: doctor, placing of port and the next chemo! And then the learning curve of week 3 and 4 till 12. The coping strategies will also have to be fine-tuned as we go on. Maybe bottling everything and freezing tears is not the sensible way. I will need to let out the silent scream and let the tears flow. My papa never cried when mama left. I guess his unshed tears became the cancer that took him away. So will have to find a way to scream without anyone knowing.

Another coping strategy is to fill your day with a busy timetable that does not leave you much time to wallow in self-pity or other such inane feelings. The fact that R's food cannot be cooked in advance and conveniently put into Tupperware boxes and frozen is a boon. So planning all his meals and brews and executing them takes time. The new kid on the block is the trampoline and watching him jump is good for our endorphins too. What else? The Internet for new chemo support potions makes good reading. In between all this, writing gives the much-needed outlet for all screams, tears and fears.

But then there is the night. The time you cannot fill up with your mundane activities. The night that comes every 12 hours, when silence falls, the little baby sleeps soundly and barring from covering him, you have nothing to do if Morpheus has not kept her tryst. That is when you feel alone and scared. That is when time weighs like Baudelaire's proverbial lid.[31]

I know every day cannot be perfect, some will go awry, some will bring laughter whilst others pain. The pain another goes through and you remain helpless feeling it tear your heart. Maybe then, when the loved one is soothed and lulled to sleep, will I seek a space where I can scream, cry and assuage my fears.

---

[31] Charles Baudelaire Les Fleurs du Mal. Spleen. http://fleursdumal.org/poem/161

Sunday, 4 August 2013

SOURSOP BENEFITS

My doctor friend sent me an SMS about a fruit called soursop[32]. I believe this fruit helps cure cancer and fight low immunity. I am going to find out more. Maybe R will have to bounce on the rebounder while sipping soursop tea!

---

[32] Soursop is the fruit of Annona muricata, a broadleaf, flowering, evergreen tree native to Mexico, Cuba, Central America, the Caribbean islands of Hispaniola and Puerto Rico, and northern South America,

ANOURADHA BAKSHI

Monday, 5 August 2013

QUICK UPDATE

Went to the oncologist for a review and to chart the next steps. The good news he has downgraded the cancer to 1B! Yippee! And we place a port on Wednesday 7/8 so there will be no needles at the next chemo on the 9/8. I have booked a BED, as the so-called recliner was a sure recipe for back aches.

Monday, 5 August 2013

SOMETHING DOES NOT SOUND RIGHT

For the past week I have been feeling a little uneasy. I guess that has been the cause of the sleepless nights! What seems to be the reason is that after receiving the worst news I could have wished for, till date I always thought I would be the one diagnosed with the big C courtesy by genetic imprint, the shock of getting to know that it was R who was the chosen target, should have led to a slew of tears, rants, raves and so on. I am normally good at that. I must admit that for the past months when we were trying to identify the cause of R's symptoms, and I was foraging the Internet for some logical explanation to the symptoms, the fear of Cancer was in me, but I would quickly push those away and would go seeking for something I was more comfortable with. However I did every test or investigation suggested and all results, even the tumour markers, were within norms. R showed no sign of improvement and that should have been a red flag. But we are so scared of our demons that we easily bury them rather than face them.

This is not a mea culpa post. We did catch the slimy lymphoma in Stage 1, confirmed by the specialist yesterday but it is 1B, which means it had the symptoms we were battling. But as I said, this is not "I should have..." post. What has happened has happened and we need to count our blessings and take the battle head on!

What is worrying me is my reaction. I normally deal with the worse situations, and I have had my share, in a totally different way, and that since childhood. I bang doors - so much so that when I was 18 or so my mom bought a whole set of earthen pots and placed them in the back yard and told me I could break as many as I wished if I spared the doors of our new house alone -. Felt sheepish and I do not think I banged a door since. I cry buckets. Scream. In a word I let the world know I am upset.

On July 4th at around 7.30 pm when I got the news that it could be a lymphoma, I was with my family Doc. I normally have cried many times in front of him for far less serious matters. This time my eyes remained bone dry. My voice did not quiver, my throat did not constrict. In a cold voice I could not recognise, I simply said: what next? The answer to the question charted the next years of my life. Something on that day froze inside me and has still not begun to thaw.

In the beginning I thought I was just being brave. I had to. I thought it was a brave face and the tears would come at some point. I worked out coping strategies that seem to be doing their job. But something does not sound right. I have become impervious to everything, the good news, the not so good one. It almost seems as if something had left my body and is hovering somewhere waiting for the right moment to take back its place. Could be a good strategy if it was not that I feel I am missing the most important part of me!

Tuesday, 6 August 2013

UPDATE AND CHANGE OF PLAN

I thought we had it planned to the T but my pal chemo wants to give me a good fight. So though R's haemoglobin is up and 8.5 now, the first upward trend since MAY 2012 his TLC has tumbled down: from 9000 when we began chemo, to 4000 last week and to 2000 yesterday! The silver lining as a dear friend says is that it shows the chemo is working. Rather radical in my humble opinion. But this means a slight change in the plans.

By the time I got to know this it was 9.30 pm. Sent my man Friday to the chemists in the area but could not find the Grafeel injection. But God is on my side because Parul and Jef[33] had gone to see a movie in Saket and could then buy the injection from the hospital itself. It is sitting in the fridge and we will give it to R at 9 am. Then on Friday morning we go to the Hospital at about 7. 30 am then grab a bed as there are few and it is first come, first served, then an blood test, then if the TLC have climbed up then chemo through the veins!

After this post, I am back on the net to see how to improve the TLC counts naturally. I know the jumping works, so R will have to jump some more; then there is green tea, shitake mushrooms and let me what else.

Another day!

---

[33]   daughter and son-in-law

Wednesday, 7 August 2013

INCARCERATED OR RATHER
INCANCERATED

In his prison diaries Jeffrey Archer's [34] recounts how he had to fit his writing schedule within the prison schedule. Seems to fit me to a T with a few additions or modifications. First I have been *incancerated* and not incarcerated, and then have little or no control over when or if I can write but also on when and if I can run on the treadmill, read a book, go for a loaf etc. There is more, prison life is fairly monotonous and orderly. *Incanceration* is not quite the same as you are entirely at the mercy of things like blood counts, which bamboozle any plans you have made at the drop of a result. So we had planned to have a port fixed today and a comfortable chemo (meaning without needles) on Friday. I had organised my programme around that. But come 6pm yesterday the TLC counts were 2000 and everything had to be reviewed and organised.

The port would not be placed and if all went well then there would be a chemo on Friday after another blood test to be done at 7.30 am at the hospital. So chemo or no chemo would be decided around 8 am on Friday. But there is more. An injection had to be conjured in the middle of the night to be given to R this morning. After rushing to many chemists and

---

[34] Jeffrey Archer A prison diary, Volume I Hell Page 150

founding none, the injection was bought at the hospital around midnight. Now we wait for Godot again.

Incanceration is not for the cancer patient. He just has cancer and earns the privilege of becoming the centre of everyone's world. The cancer buddy, yours truly in the occurrence, is the one *incancerated!* Not only do I have to live one day at a time, which would be luxury, but one moment at a time.

Now for a person who likes a routine to the point of eating practically the same thing every day for 365 x n days, living in on the edge is a new experience I am finding difficult to adapt to. But I know I will have to if I want to survive *incanceration*!

Wednesday, 7 August 2013

JUST THINKING ABOUT YOU

Every cloud has a silver lining! If anyone would have asked me a few weeks back if Cancer could have the proverbial silver lining I would have yelled out a big NO! How wrong I would have been. Being *incancerated* has huge silver linings that warm you and dazzle you more than the brightest ray of sunshine! It took me some time to share with the ones that make my world the terrible news that had befallen on me. First it was a few friends, then a blog restricted to those very few friends, then some understated allusions on my main blog and to my Project Why family: loved one, not well etc. Then one fine day I decided to say it loud and clear: my husband had cancer.

That day the clouds parted and my world was filled with sunshine. I was humbled by the amount of goodwill, love, positive thoughts and support that engulfed me like the softest and yet strongest real and virtual avalanche. From every corner of the world people reached out to me, even people I had never met but knew because of Project Why. It almost seemed like Project Why had been created more than a decade ago by the big picture God my father had introduced to me when I was a child and was hurt in some way or the other. Pa always said that the hurt was for good reason in the big picture that God only sees. And as a little girl I believed in that God with all my heart. That God did not have a face, or a name. Today I call it the big picture God!

So this big picture God must have seen R's cancer and got busy filling the orphaned only child's world so that she would not be alone when cancer struck. And it was not just the Project Why family, but a new family that took seed the moment the news was known. My A team!

When I get up every morning at some unearthly hour as sleep deludes me, I switch on my computer and am always greeted with mails from all across the world. What is extraordinary, is that many of the people who send these mails, I have never met. One of today's mail was most touching: *Hi Anou, Just thinking about you. How is hubby doing? Love.*

Then before everything else I have to send an update to two wonderful people who normally sleep late and thus wake up late, but wake up at the ping of my mail and send me a message filled with love. Were it not for my incanceration I would have never been blessed by the love of these exceptional souls!

As the news spread, my extended family which had become estranged for some reason or the other, more so I guess because my only child status made me a sort of a self sufficient happy recluse, came from every part of the city and across the world. Every single one from the oldest (90+) to the youngest offered their blessings, love and support. We recalled old memories, those that had made us laugh till we cried and realised that in time of need all was forgotten.

The big picture God, the one that has no colour, no religion, no form and no prescribed rituals is a great chap. I know that he has charted the next months with the same spirit as he charted the past years.

I can only say: Chapeau Bas!

Thursday, 8 August 2013

CHEMO OR NO CHEMO THAT IS THE QUESTION

Chemo or no chemo; that is the question. This does not mean we are giving up. It is just that today's chemo depends on the blood count results this morning. If the WBCs are up then chemo, if they are not up then I guess it will have to be postponed and we will have to go in *Waiting for Godot* mode: jumping, eating, waiting! Hope the WBCs are up so we can tick one more box and just have a maximum of 10 chemos left! And all this also means that the port was not placed so it is needles and more needles. Just one more hurdle in the race.

To crown it all have a crick in the neck that entailed another sleepless night so mood is not at its best. R too did not have a great night. Hope he can sleep a bit during his chemo. It is just that he moves a lot and the darned needle comes out. Will have a hand holding roster.

Thursday, 8 August 2013

UP, UP AND FLYING

The counts are up! Yippee. The WBCs were 2.2 two days back and are up to 4.2! So the chemo is on. I guess it will be a few annoying hours and I hope and pray that he will have no side effects. Have all the brews boiling in my magic cauldron to counter the evil potions. Have put my best foot forward! I also have proof that jumping works and so there is going to be a lot of jumping in between chemo sessions. The diet prepared with care laced with love also seems a winner, so we are on the right track!

Friday, 9 August 2013

ROUND 2

After small hiccups, we have begun Round 2 of my 12-round battle. The odds on both sides: mine - 9.2 haemoglobin and 4.2 WBCs; new brews, and an indomitable will to win; Zozo's; track record of hitting harder each time and not winning all the times! Gloves on! Let the fight begin. Results at the end of week1, and week 2! We have spent the first week watching each other's moves and finding counter moves. I guess it will be the same next week and the one after.

My arsenal is growing each day and will keep growing. I have a wide basket to choose from ranging from the different brews and concoctions and the moves I keep discovering as if someone was guiding my hand. But what really makes all the difference is the team in my corner who stuff me with something my adversary will never get: support, love and the feeling that I am not and will not be alone.

I am ready for the gong!

Saturday, 10 August 2013

OR AT LEAST TEAR UP!

Just wanted to tell all of you who are part of this journey with me and definitely my A team, a little about this blog and the reasons I write it. First of all writing is the only way I know of getting rid of my demons and sharing my inner most feelings. So apologies for all the rants and raves and even the sometimes not politically correct diatribes. Writing this blog is my way of coping with what I never asked for and yet have to face. Writing is my way of keeping the happy and composed face I have to keep 24/7 and not screaming, or crying. It is in no way a diary tracing R's cancer. It is the diary of what I am going through, the story of how my life has changed, the story of how I am living almost symbiotically R's fight with Hodgkin's disease.

It would make it better to know that you are there sharing this with me, that the orphaned only child is not alone because God knows how I miss Ram and Kamala[35] and even 2 day old demised brother. So write a comment, a smiley or just a word. It will make me smile or at least tear up!

---

[35]   My parents

Saturday, 10 August 2013

A DEBT I WAS UNAWARE OF

For the past weeks, since the diagnosis of R's cancer I have been spending a lot of what would be called 'alone' time and found myself looking back at the 39 years R and I spent together. Somehow this turned out to be a selective walk down memory alone, as all the so-called difficult moments vanished or at least made themselves so tiny that they became invisible.

It is in these stolen moments, that I came to realise what R means to me and how he made every single wish, dream and even idiosyncrasy of mine possible. I stand guilty of having taken all this for granted. In hindsight I realise that every success of mine was seeded and lovingly watered by him. He stood by me in my career choices never standing in their way even though some were quite inane. Anyone glancing through my bio data would realise that I am a bit of a rolling stone. My first job was a midnight one at the radio station, something not quite appropriate for a married lady 40 years back. But worse was to come. After a seemingly quiet and sedate period as Assistant Professor at JNU and the IAS story played to please a demanding mom who always looked in me for her dead son, it is he who introduced me to the senior bureaucrat who would transform my career path for some years. One conference for the Young Congress set me on a semi political course and as a conference organiser. Midnight became several nights be it Asian Games or Non Aligned summits. I was barely home. I was convinced I was the ultimate emancipated woman who led her life the way she wanted!

Today I realise that I could have done none of all that without the quiet and strong support of my life partner who had to put up with a so-called modern woman. Today I know he did all that out of love. I was told much later how proud he was of me. I wish he had said it to me but R is a man of few words when it comes to emotions.

If Project Why exists it is again because R not only did not stand in the way, but nudged me gently to live this dream. He was always there when I needed him and never complained when I took the house over for some extravagant folly like making soap out of Pongamia seeds or bringing hordes of slum kids to the house. He may have grumbled a bit, but I would have screamed had the roles been reversed.

Today I am taking time off from Project Why and I am doing so without guilt. Because I have come to my senses and realised that if not for R nothing would have been possible. There is a huge debt to pay, a debt I was unaware of, a debt I would have never been asked to repay had things been the way I wished.

For the next months, till he is back to his old self, I will do all in my power to make things better than the best for him, and try and repay a tiny bit of the debt I owe him.

Sunday, 11 August 2013

UPDATE LONG OVERDUE

This battle is for R and I realise that I often forget to update his status regularly. That is perhaps because all is going as well as one could hope and better, but I do not dare make the God jealous. So we had our second session of chemo on Friday last. We got a bed and not what they (the hospital) call a recliner but is at best an uncomfortable sofa that would kill even a good back. R has a weak one and was in agony for the first few hours till I got him a bed! So bed it was, then in spite of many messages to the good doctor to leave instructions so that time would not be wasted, as we first needed a blood test to make sure the blood count was high enough to take on chemo. So it was 2 hours before all this was done, then the chemo began post noon. An excellent nurse placed the cannula properly and we did it all through one vein and not the 5 and more pokes he went through the last time. We were home by 6pm and then the wait for the side effects began. Till date we have had a few strands of hair coming out and nothing else except constipation. The wait is on.

In the meantime R is having fun with his grandson who leaves a week from now, jumping on his trampoline a few times a day, eating fairly well and not making grimaces at my side effect fighting brews and concoctions.

As I said all well till now.

This week 3 injections for the next 3 days to boost the WBCs, a blood test on 16th and then visit the Doc on 19th. In between all this, on the 14th he celebrates 64 years on this planet!

Sunday, 11 August 2013

SMOOTH SEDUCTION

I have been seduced. I guess that in this case the only weak defence I can put forward is that the decision I succumbed into talking was reinforced in every which was possible: by doctors of course but they are always suspect (I have been reading that the very doctors who badger you into chemo would never prescribe it for themselves of their loved ones), by friends I love and trust implicitly; by my Tibetan doctor whom I had gone to hoping to hear she had a cure but who said that in this cancer chemo worked well and she would take care of the side effects; by articles carefully perused on the net. Every one said: HODGKIN'S RESPONDS TO CHEMOTHERAPY!

So I opened the tightly shut door and let the deadly brew in. (Apologies to someone I love a lot and who has been trying to convince me of the need of chemo. Just to let her know that I will follow all the protocols prescribed.) However this whole approach really disturbs me.

Finished reading the Emperor of All Maladies[36], a biography of cancer. One would have thought that it would have answered the questions that plagued my hazy mind and helped me make my peace with chemo but far from that: it validated all that I had instinctively felt and ma had also intuited and shunned even if it meant losing her mind. The approach to cancer cure

---

[36] The Emperor of All Maladies: A Biography of Cancer is a book written by Siddhartha Mukherjee, an Indian-born American physician and oncologist. 2011 Pulitzer for General Non Fiction

seems totally illogical from a healing point of view and eminently logical from the business angle. And everything was done to obliterate the former to the point of ridiculing it and banning it, and everything was done to 'prove' the kill to heal approach as the only one with often outrageously low statistics to validate success.

Anyway the harm is done. But thanks to the Internet you can access all the 'banned' and 'hidden' information. Wish the world-wide-web existed when my mother was fighting her cancer. The only choice she had was chemo or nothing. I am sure she would have jumped at the juice therapy, the bitter decoctions and even accepted coffee enemas.

There are many alternative cures, tested by few but that work: eating 17 apricot kernels a day till the biggies accept the benefits of vitamin B 17; drinking soursop tea or juice; eating ashwagandha or popping Tibetan medicine pills. Thankfully all these alternatives also have brews to minimise the effects of chemo.

Yes I have been seduced this time but this unwilling seduction has made me wiser and more knowledgeable to alternatives. I cannot accept this approach that was again validated when the oncologist refused that a port be placed for R 3 days after his chemo. Can you guess why? Because it would be too dangerous not for the poor poisoned patient but for those operating on him. One needed at least a week to allow our wonderful body to flush the poison!

Need I say more?

Tuesday, 13 August 2013

TIME OFF

For all of those of you who worry about me, I took some time off today and indulged in some retail therapy. R's birthday tomorrow was a good excuse for me to hit the shops. Also needed a bedside lamp that would allow me to read and work in the bedroom without disturbing anyone. So found myself in Lok Nayak Bhavan and the Decon lamp shop. Brought back so many memories, some more than 40 years old. It is from the Decon shop, that we bought lighting for this very house with mama and also some furniture that is still there. Must say the experience was not as friendly as the old days when we had long chats with the owners! It was a rather cold reception but I got the lamp I wanted. Then went to Meher Chand market, which is now becoming the new Khan market. In the old days there were just a few shops, one of them being a south Indian one that sold real coffee and where my father went often. I also hit the good old Tantra T shirt outlet and smiled at some of their zany T-shirts and picked up 2 for the birthday boy.

On the same road, pass the red light are a whole lot of new shops and eateries that I never knew existed. The reason I found them was that there is also an organic food store called Altitude that has a wide range of foodstuff including quail and duck eggs! I stuck to hen eggs and also got some nice vegetables that had just arrived. I was hoping to stop by a bookshop and

ANOURADHA BAKSHI

indulge in some browsing but it was time to get back to the drill. Must say I enjoyed my time off. Must do it more often.

R spent a quiet morning, sleeping and reading and bar a few hairs that came off, he seemed in a good mood.

Tuesday, 13 August 2013

WHEN I'M SIXTY FOUR

Today R's turns sixty-four. But I have been hearing this number from the time we met almost 40 years ago! R is a Beatles fan; all his Doon School pals would remember the famous Logarithms, the band he and three buddies created and which was a clone of their idols John, Paul, George and Ringo! When I'm sixty-four was not part of their school repertoire as it was released post 66, and R is class of 66! But when I met him in 1974 it was one of the songs he often strummed on his guitar and sang with a glint in his eyes. We were young and 64 seemed so far away. The lyrics[37] made us smile. The losing your hair part seemed almost impossible when one looked at R's mane! The song made us happy.

Today the lyrics have taken a poignant meaning. Not the one we could have dreamt of when we laughed and sang, when we were young. Today my husband turns 64 and yes he is losing hair, in chunks. I need him more than ever and feed him, as I have never done before. R's 64th year turned out to be the one when he was diagnosed with cancer. The fear of losing him is real though I hope we will make it and he will be with me when I am 64 and losing my hair! Not that I have much.

R often played this song when he sat at his piano every day. I realise I should have known something was terribly wrong when he stopped playing, a couple of months before his diagnosis. It is then that I realised how much

---

[37] When I am sixty-four Lennon-Mc Cartney 1966

his music meant to me and was part of our lives. The deafening silence of the past months has been unbearable. I am just waiting for the day when the house is filled with his music again.

R is 64. The big party we had envisaged and dreamt of will be a small get together of dear friends and two unwanted ones: cancer and chemo!

But we will overcome.

Happy Birthday R.

Wednesday, 14 August 2013

THE TWO MEN IN MY LIFE'

Two men have influenced my life. Their birthdays follow each other. Mu husband's is on August 14th and my Pa's on August 15th, of course they were born 38 years apart. There is another thing they share, something I did not really ask for: cancer! Maybe this is the cross that I was destined to bear. But in the last weeks when every bit of me has been on edge, when every nerve raw and exposed, when each of my senses have been subjected to the harshest test and when my travels down memory lane have taken unknown detours, I have come to one realisation: every cloud, however dark and threatening has a silver lining or as Pa would say only God knows the Big Picture of your life. You get stuck in dark corners not knowing what awaits you at the bend. So instead of moaning and wallowing in self-pity, I need to figure out why the crab struck again.

Yes Pa's cancer was a difficult reality to accept, however pious or Cartesian one tried to be. Ma had succumbed to the beast just a few months earlier and there it came lurking again. Today I see the big picture. It all began on a hot day in May in 1949 when a not so young bride asked her not so young rotund husband for a promise. The groom was quite besotted with his new bride and accepted to honour the promise without knowing what it was. Poor man! What Kamala wanted that day was the promise that she would die before him and travel her last journey in her bridal attire. I am sure pa must have felt the weight of this promise he had no control on but the Big Picture had already been created and the promise was kept. A cancer took her away when she was barely 70. But before she left, she extracted a promise from me and I too gave it to her without a thought. She asked me to look after Pa till his last breath and never leave him alone. At that time it all seemed eminently feasible. R was posted in Delhi and my daughters were both studying. I had a job I liked and all seemed on track. But then disaster struck. R got posted to Paris, a city ideally suited for a family imbibed in French culture. But there was a promise to keep. Papa was in perfect health and I was in a quandary not knowing how I would keep the promise made to my mother on her deathbed.

Pa, the Big Picture believer simply told me to leave it to God, whoever that God was. I would have given him a mouthful were it not my father! But he was right as always and the crab was again spot on! He died in 29 days and freed me from a promise I could not have broken.

I spend many hours in the dead of the white nights that have been my fate these past weeks and wondered what the Big Picture could be this time as the BP is always meant to be blessed. And then it struck me. This time the beast had surreptitiously crept into our lives to bring us together in the most unexpected yet closest way. Every thing had to be put on hold. It was just the two of us battling to save our love. There were no excuses: be it Project Why or golf! God was giving us the time to share all we had never shared, say all the things left unsaid, clear all the issues if there were any and be there just for each other. All else was on hold! Maybe it was also a promise that needed to be redeemed, the one we made on our wedding day and that somehow got lost along the way as we chased empty dreams or simply fought the battles of life losing sight of the essential.

In 4 *sleepies* (this is Agastya's way of counting time and means the number of nights) Agastya and his family will be gone for a long-long time. There will just be the two us, and the strict regimen that Mr Hodgkin's has imposed on us. In between there will be tender moments, reminiscences, laughter and maybe also the tears that need to be shed. We will walk gently towards the day when we resume our old life after bidding a final farewell to the lymphoma - let us called it by its name - which came with a purpose and was part of the Big Picture.

Friday, 16 August 2013

THE HEAT IS ON

After a great week when R celebrated his 64th and had a relatively easy time after his second chemo, ate well and was in good spirits, had a haircut, and felt good, the chemo was surreptitiously at work within his body, killing the good and the ugly. Yesterday was blood test day and looking at him I thought: all is well. Imagine my fright when I received a cryptic SMS from the lab stating that the counts were out of limits and I should contact the doctor ASAP! The 15 minutes or so that it took my chap to get the results were pure hell! What had happened! Well the cat was soon out of the bag as I got the result. His WBC had dipped to 1900 well below the minimum 4000 needed to fight any infection.

An SMS to his oncologist was promptly replied with the usual: wait and let us do another count on Monday and take it from there. He is scheduled for his next chemo on next Friday. So now we have less than a week to get is WBC to a 'respectable' 4000 so that the toxic brew can kill again.

So this week was as is said in medical parlance: a false positive! The darned chemo lulled us into a false sense of well being and made me forget for a bit that the battle was on, even if outwardly all seemed on track. So now I have 2 days to conjure a miracle with few tricks up my sleeve: food, jumping on the trampoline, my special brews and as much laughter as I can muster. There is a problem though and a big one that may make my task more difficult. Agastya my grandson leaves on Monday night and though every one of us, especially R, are trying to put a brave face, some scary questions do fleetingly cross our minds. Keeping the WBC in these conditions is no easy task.

So my adversary won this round as it lulled me into a false sense of complacency. The war is still on with many battles to come. I am determined to win the next round and the war!

Saturday, 17 August 2013

THE ELEPHANT IN THE ROOM AND DOREAMON'S MAGIC DOOR

My darling grandson will leave tomorrow. For the past two months he has been romping around the house with his *great one-liners* that could solve any problem that came our way. His *to infinity and beyond*, or *how about we*, or *why is this happening to me*, kept us going through the difficult two months he was here and made *cancer, chemo, side effects, WBC counts* take a back seat. His hugs at the time you needed them most made everything possible. For 60 days the little bloke slept between R and I and having him there was the best cure possible for R's illness and my nerves. But tomorrow he will fly away and God only knows when we will see him again!

For the past days there has been a huge elephant in the room. No one has dared acknowledge it. Yet I know that R has asked himself the question. I can see it in his eyes that moisten a little when he holds the little fellow, or strokes his face when he is asleep or just looks at him surreptitiously while I pretend not to see. As for me, I have to rehearse my act that much more and not show my feelings while I mouth answers to silent questions. Cancer does that to you. Even if millions tell you they have made it! The elephant in this case is too big to get rid off.

For the past two months a pair of grandparents have been willingly compelled to watch a lot of Doreamon, Agastya's favourite cartoon for some years now. But this time he is four and a half and understands the story line. For the past week or so he has been asking me why we cannot have Doraemon's magic door that allows you to travel in space and time. You just pick it up and set it in your room and walk across and reach the place you want. Agastya would like one that would allow him to walk from his room to ours and vice versa. And I must admit I too want one.

But all we have is Skype and our crossed Good Mornings and Good Night as St Louis and Delhi have an 11.30 hours difference. So the two of us - Nani and Agastya - have been working out how we will communicate, send each other kisses and hugs across the screen.

I know that in a few weeks, I will hear the *I do not want to talk to Nani*, the little fellow often says when he is busy playing with his cars or doing something far more interesting than talking to an old granny! Children have the ability to adjust to any situation in a jiffy. For R and I, it will take longer if at all. We will have to content ourselves with a glimpse of the little one somewhere in the background of a screen.

I cannot but remember my communications with my grandparents when I was his age. We were posted in Rabat I think and mama use to make me write a letter every week to my Nana and Nani. My English was almost non-existent and all my letters began with: Dear Nana and Nani are you well or not. I use to get long replies that mama read me. We are blessed to have Skype!

I know we will miss Agastya more than I can imagine, but I also know that we will soon be overtaken by the strict regimen and time table that Mr Hodgkin demands. But every morning and evening we will switch on our screen - the best alternative to Doraemon's door - and a glimpse of our beloved angel will help us ignore the elephant in the room.

Sunday, 18 August 2013

BERGSONIAN RHAPSODY

The notion of time has always been a philosophical query that has fascinated me. Though mathematical time is always the same, the perception of it by us mortals is different and according to Bergson[38] intuitive. The time waiting for a loved one will feel far longer than the one spent with the loved one, even if in both cases the minutes on the clock remain the same. I remember how long a year looked when I was small; one birthday to another seemed an eternity! Today it seems to move so fast that one does not realise where time has gone. But within the 365 days that seem to fly, as you get older, there is a Bergsonian Rhapsody being played. Sometimes time *weighs like a lid* as Baudelaire so beautifully wrote in his famous poem entitled Spleen[39] For the past 4 years or so the movements of our rhapsody were punctuated by waiting for Agastya and then waiting for the day he left and then waiting again for him to come back. All this waiting was interspersed by other activities. For R it was his work, his weekly and sometimes morning Golf, his few trips abroad for work and golf; for me it was my work at Project Why, my writing reports and when I could find time my creative writing. But all changed on July 4th 2013 at exactly 7.20

---

[38] Henri-Louis Bergson was a major French philosopher, influential especially in the first half of the 20th century

[39] Charles Baudelaire, Les Fleurs du Mal, Spleen http://fleursdumal.org/poem/161

pm when a scan report landed in my hands with the? lymphoma written on it. All our carefully scripted lives keeled over as an unwanted guest forced itself on us, hogging all the space. Everything else had to fit around its non-negotiable demands. Agastya's presence made things easier as it brought the much-needed laughter and joy as he wrestled for his place and always won. But there is a flip side. His presence made me push away all the elephants in the room and in my head. Come to think of it the 'R has cancer' I find myself mouthing to people enquiring about his health, does not seem to have sunk in. It still feels like saying 'R has the flu'! And that is because the presence of a little child makes you want to hope and live.

I dread tomorrow when the house falls silent and little things strewn here and there - a pair of tiny Crocs, a small car, a cricket bat in the garden, the Odomos tubes that his mom seems to place in the most unlikely of places, his favourite chocolate drink in the store room, his clothes folded neatly on the ironing table - will be heart wrenching reminders of the little chap's presence. It will take time for the house to get out of Agastya mode and get back to its usual shape. Somehow no one, even the staff, likes putting things back and everyone delays the task as much as possible. But inevitably, things will fall back in place.

Time that seemed to run at the speed of light while the child was here, will now take on new perceptions in true Bergsonian style, seeming so incredibly slow at times and quicker at others. This time it is not the demands of a child that will trace our day, but the ones of the unwanted guest and his impositions that have to be met. And there is no routine here as one bad blood test can alter everything else. It is strange but true that somehow this will help us fill the empty space and time of our lives. We have another timetable to follow and this for quite a few months to come.

There is yet another side to this Rhapsody. I do not when or how the *cancer* will replace the *flu* in my mind but I know it will. The tears will have to be shed. Tears of sorrow. Tears of rage. Tears of helplessness and even tears of fear. Till now a little Angel kept them all at bay.

MY HEAD IS TAKING ME EVERYWHERE

For the past few days we all have been dealing in our own way with another elephant in the room, one so big that it overshadowed the other one. I refer to Agastya's departure. Yes he left late yesterday night. As I said we each had our coping strategies: R smothered him with kisses and hugs; I made several trips with him to the toyshop looking for the tiniest cars so that his mom would not give me another mouthful. She did but we hid the cars in his bag! His cricket team - the gardener, the auto driver and his pal Deepak - gave their best, in spite of the rain. Geeta made his favourite food. None of us admitted to being sad. How could we? We are adults. But children are different. They have not learnt deceit and guile. They say what they feel in the best way they know. So did my little fellow.

He stood at the bottom of the staircase and knowing how much we all were upset simply said: *My head is taking me everywhere?* He just knew we all wanted to be with him. His nana upstairs, his cricket pals outside and I ready to take him out. I just hugged the little bloke and told him to do what his heart wanted. He stood a while, picked up his bat and went out. A few instants later we heard his giggles and laughter. All was well. The moment had passed.

As I sit in an empty house I wonder where my head will take me today. For now, I am just numb!

ANOURADHA BAKSHI

Monday, 19 August 2013

RECLAIMS ITS SPACE

The little boy has flown away. He is still in the air, somewhere between Delhi and Paris where his Bapu awaits him and then will fly again back to St Louis and his life. For the past 2 months or 60 sleepies - sleepie being the way Agastya counts time - he was with us. I realise this morning that he and only he was able to push away the other elephant in the room aka Zozo aka Hodgkin and make all of us forget the Damocles sword hanging on our heads. However, even before the little chap could pack his bag and fly, Zozo reclaimed its place, lest he be forgotten. Yesterday a visit to the good doctor charted at least the week to come.

For those of you who are always asking for updates on the chemo here is the latest bulletin: WBCs dropped to an alarming 1.9 - I say alarming because I even got an SMS from the lab - on Friday. Monday morning the WBCs were up to 2.9 but the haemoglobin dropped one point. Two Grafeel injections today and tomorrow, blood test on the next day and if all goes well and the counts behave then on Friday the 23rd the port will be placed first and then the third chemo. In between R will have to visit the hospital for a PAC (pre anaesthesia test). Then more waiting for Godot, Godot being here the side effects of chemo, and more injections and blood test. So that is the situation today! It can all change if the counts don't behave.

I have my life charted for the next 4 months at least.

Tuesday, 20 August 2013

IT'S NOT SO DIFFICULT WHEN
YOU ARE COMPLETELY NUMB

Before I go on I need to introduce you to the two new inhabitants of our room sitting on R's favourite chair! For those of you who have kids or grandchildren who are allowed TV time you would know the funny little cat robot Doreamon and the mighty Chota Bheem! These were the farewell gifts Agastya got from his teachers at Project Why. Of course mom was quick to decree that they were too big for the suitcase and needed to be left behind in the toy bins that get filled to the brim every time the little bloke flies back to his home. But this time was different. Agastya had other plans. On the day he was laving he came up with these two and very seriously declared: *I am leaving Doreamon and Chota Bheem for Nanou so that he gets well soon* and then sat them on the chair and marched off! That night he flew away. In his little mind he had left a little of himself in the space he shared with us for so many days and nights.

Agastya is a very mature little bloke and in spite of his young age he thinks! His favourite opening line when he is about to say something serious is 'How about...!' So this time his *how about...* was his way of knowing that Nanou having Zozo in his tummy needed someone to take care of him. The two soft toys were the best idea in his little mind. I cannot begin to tell you how many episodes of both these cartoons we have seen in the past two months. Sometimes, when we really miss him, R and I often say: *did you watch Doreamon*! Chota Bheem is the other option. I realise that God works his magic through children. Let me tell you why. When we first saw the Chota Bheem rag doll we all commented on how ugly it was, how badly made etc. But Agastya had his plan. The rag doll is so badly made that when you see it you laugh. And that is what its role is: to make us laugh! As for Doreamon he has a magic pocket full of gadgets that take care of all problems. So when next problem appears, we have to peep into the magic pocket and voila! Well done little bloke.

Yesterday was the first day without him in the house. I had imagined I would miss him, shed a few tears, and walk around the house mournfully. But I just felt numb. I did all that I had to: took R for his injection, held his hand when he winced in pain, booked the blood test for tomorrow and smiled when needed, talked when needed, answered the phone, gave updates about R's health but it was as if someone else was playing the script of the day, I was just numb, my fake smile in place.. As I wrote in an earlier post, saying *R has cancer* is the same as saying *R has the flu*. To that I can add saying Agastya is gone St Louis is the same as Agastya has gone to the park! It seems like nothing can break the walls I have erected within me. I am unable to process anything that could break the barriers I have built.

The *fake smile*, which in my case means all the correct things I need to do in the months to come, is well in place. I must admit it is a little scary. Maybe it is the coping strategy I have opted for. It takes care of terrifying things like Cancer; of heart breaking things like a grandson's departure and perhaps of all that is to come.

Tuesday, 20 August 2013

I LOVE YOUR HOUSE

There are positive sides to cancer coming into your life in whichever way it chooses. I would have never believed I would be writing these lines, and had someone suggested the idea, I would have socked her/his face! And yet here I am writing about the 'good' that cancer brings along. Here is how the story goes. A few blogs ago I posted a picture to remember the good old days, the ones before Mr Hodgkin decided to move in with us. A dear friend, I consider her so though we have never met, wrote the following words after seeing the picture: *As much as I love this picture, it is the background that draws me – what a warm home you have; much lived in, slightly worn, each piece with a story to share. I love your house!* How true she was. I could never truly understand let alone express why I flew into a rage, or almost, when some suggested we redo the house, and make it 'modern' or whatever other word used. When anyone, even those close to me, suggested we break the house down and make flats and thus money, the only excuse I could come up with was that this was the legacy of my parents, and for me it kept them alive. True there have been moments when I too have been infuriated by the cost of maintaining this house, but those were short lived.

My friend's words and the elephant in the room that cancer brings along, do make you conscious of the fact that your time on this planet is not infinite and that death is lurking somewhere in the future. It is time to make your bucket list and tick the items as soon as you can. I can never thank my friend enough for making me see my house with my heart instead of looking at the cracks, the faded paint or the water leaks that come each monsoon. As I looked at the picture I see baby photographs of my kids, a picture of my parents in their prime, books that are an intrinsic part of who I am, the Dali ashtray a maid broke but that we quickly glued together as best we could. I can also see part of the blind that is quite tattered but still plays its role and yes each one has a story, some maybe innocuous but others that need to be told as in our world where the written world has almost disappeared, stories die with you unless you tell them.

Yes this house is much lived in. I built it with my parents. We faced unbelievable obstacles and even litigation. I remembering moving in with my mother when it is was still half built. And even when it was sort of finished we barely had money to furnish it. But it was home and we loved it. It was a place where my parents could finally settle after years of the nomadic life that comes with being a diplomat. It is the place where my parents could finally display all they had bought in the places we were posted and never mind if a Chinese Celadon plate sits next to a Greek Amphora, it looked just right! It is the house where I got married and so did my daughter, the place I brought my grandson to when he came to India for the first time. It is replete with memories that give it the warmth and comfort of a home. It is time I walked through it and let my memory run wild. I know it will be a treat where all the senses will come alive.

True there will be sad memories and happy ones but, is that not what life is all about.

Thank you Saras for opening my eyes and allowing me to fall in love with my home again, and thank you Mr Hodgkin for reminding me that time is short!

Wednesday, 21 August 2013

A SMILE IN CUSTODY

There must me some God, whatever shape, colour or gender, who works in mysterious ways and makes you feel better, specially when you are down. I have talked a lot about my fake smile, and the domino I conceal my feelings under to be able to carry my battle. Imagine how it felt to read this: *As for us – we are sitting here on the other side of the world and we are imagining your real smile. We just want you to know that your real smile still exists (we will keep it safe for you until you want to use it again).* This comes from the most wonderful souls I have met in my life. Two big children who smile all the time and more than that can conjure miracles, as one of them is really a magician. I am talking of Alan and Em! Their words remind me of who I really am and I know my smile is safe with them till I feel the courage of reclaiming it without the fear of other emotions that I need to keep at bay for the moment. Somehow Mr Hodgkin aka Zozo has turned my life on its head.

I entrust my smile to all of you who have reached to me with so much love and affection. I promise you to smile and laugh again without fear of breaking down. But at this moment I am still in learning mode, and a bit on a roller coaster. I have never been on one but I guess it must be quite akin to what my life is. The good old AA pals teach one to live one day at a time. Life with Mr Hodgkin is one minute at a time. You feel all is well and then a touch of sniffles sends you flying. For someone who likes planning things in advance it is a tough lesson to master and I am trying to be a good first time learner, just like my Project Why kids!

To all of you out there who take time to read these words, I would like to say that your messages and comments is what is making it possible for me to fight this battle that has too many bad memories. The fake smile and dark cloak is my coping strategy till I feel stronger. Please be there. I need you to able to remember who I really am.

Thursday, 22 August 2013

NEEDLES AND PORTS

Zozo a.k.a Mr Hodgkin is an unwanted guest. We all know that. He is a real pain in the ****! The main reason is that nothing and I mean NOTHING can be planned in advance. Not even a day in advance. For the past month we have been trying to get a chemo port placed, as R hates needles. Poor chap I have lost count of the number of pokes he has had in the past year! But two chemos down and we have not been able to place the port. It is all a matter of numbers and their vagaries. They go up or down at their own sweet will, sometimes in the span of a few hours. If the haemoglobin is up -- hurray - as is the case today, the white blood cells that were fine two days back have slumped. And the saga goes on. So till 5pm today we had it all planned: chemo port placement at 7am and then 3rd chemo. But at 5 10 pm I got today's blood results and the white cells are down. Call to the oncologist who says that we go ahead with the port and then we shall see about the chemo. Damn!

So another night wondering how tomorrow will go. Just the port and back home by 10 am or chemo with a low level of WBCs and home by the evening and then dreading the next blood result. And then fixing another day for chemo 3 and so on.

Each time the counts dip, I find myself trying to look for new brews that could do the trick. I must say R does not complain and swallows everything I give. I guess my concoctions are better than needles.

Friday, 23 August 2013

MAGICAL MYSTERY TOUR

Living with Mr Hodgkin is nothing short of Magical Mystery Tour, or should I just say a Mystery Tour, as Magical seems a bit out of place here. But mystery it is as you really do not know what will happen at the next bend. So we went to sleep yesterday with the certitude that we would have R's chemo port placed today. As for the ensuing chemo it was still a mystery as the blood counts were low and the Doc would decide after the port was placed and I guess after yet another blood test but no poke this time as the port would be in place. I must admit I had a bad night as I normally only sleep well when I am in control of things. No wonder my elder one calls me a 'control freak' and even a 'nag'! I prefer to say I am organised.

So with Zozo's arrival into our lives the 'control freak' has taken a lashing. I suddenly realise that my place has been taken by a new 'freak' who is the one to set the rules. However this one is temperamental, capricious and deadly. When we did not know of his existence, and that was for quite a few months, it manifested itself with symptoms that were similar to so many mundane ailments that we did not even begin to imagine the havoc inside R's body. We finally found him tucked behind the aorta in the abdomen. Once we identified him there was no turning back. The mystery tour had begun and would end only when the intruder would be annihilated. But this guy has game plans of his own and one is left with few choices. No choice, in the life of the one who is perceived by her own nears and dear ones as a 'control freak' though as I say, I prefer thinking I am organised to a fault, is unthinkable! To win this battle, I needed to feel in control. Not easy when the adversary is someone who has already beaten you twice. In hindsight I think this happened because when we met earlier I was poorly armed. To fight an adversary you have to know him, his strengths and his weaknesses. Only then can you stay a step ahead and hope to win. In the 90s there was no Internet, no search engines and social networks; you fought alone or simply conceded defeat. But today that is not the case and my so called desired to 'control' may well turn out to be my greatest asset. In this case 'control' means getting to know all that I can about Cancer and particularly Mr Hodgkin a.k.a Zozo!

You may wonder why I decided to call this journey a mystery one. Let me elucidate. Cancer has many avatars and forms and you need to recognise and master the one you are dealing with. That is step one. Then you need to ferret out the possible treatment and chose the one you want. If you chose 'chemo' as is the case with us, you have to comprehend how it works and more importantly accept that it is lethal, toxic and poisonous. Hence all the dreaded side effects. You have to come to terms with the fact that you are poisoning the one you are treating. That is a toughie for me but in this case, and this one alone, I have accepted it with my head if not my heart. That is the mystery bit.

So what does the heart do? Well it goes on looking for magic tricks that will counter the side effects and heal and not kill. There is one caveat. All your tricks should not interfere or counter the chemo. A difficult one but believe me if you have the patience and the passion then there are hosts of trick in the magician's hat. Diet for one. Then alternative medicines - I chose Tibetan and one Ayurvedic plant that complements the Tibetan pill -, then the right exercise regimen - in our case yogic breathing as the cancer cells hate oxygen, and the trampoline to keep the lymphatic system moving. So you can imagine what a tight timetable this is. Does not leave much time for anything else. However if you want to survive the drill that is interspersed with chemo sessions and blood tests, you have to be able to remain that control freak whose regimen was as strict and well planned. Ah ha! The clash of the Titans. But there is a way out. It is a choice you need to make. Which one takes the front seat? R's cancer of course! Then you take the back one and accept a little flexibility and juggling and fit your regimen in the tiny and ever changing spaces that are available. This, my friends is my Magical Mystery Tour!

Friday, 23 August 2013

THE PORT... A DRAMA
IN SEVERAL ACTS

The famous chemo port has been placed but what a drama it was. We were asked to reach the hospital at 7 am. We did R, Dharmendra and I. The place was eerie. Not a soul, dim lights: a perfect setting for the play to unfold. At 7.15 all the lights came on. We just sat there waiting for the protagonists. They sauntered in one by one: the guards (there were none till then), the cleaning staff and then the reception staff. By 7.45 we could begin act one. The paperwork. As usual it took forever but by 8.30 we had a room. Then after some more waiting a nurse peeped in. She came back a few moments later and took BP and vitals. Around 9 there was some activity: the OT staff was there. R was made to change and was wheeled out to the OT floor. We were told the procedure would take one hour. So for the next hour we waited quite happily. 10, 11! I started agitating and ask D to find out what was happening. He was told it would take 'a little time'.

At 11. 36 am I get a phone call from some Doc on the surgeon's team asking me if I am R's attendant. I say yes! She then tells me that R is scheduled for a chemo port placement. I again say yes! But I start getting concerned. She goes on to say: is he coming? I am totally zapped. I tell her he is here and has been taken to the OT floor more than two hours ago! Talk of efficiency.

124   ANOURADHA BAKSHI

I guess they 'located' him, as there is no call after that just some more waiting. At about 1pm or so they bring him back to the room. In the mean time I have been busy getting in touch with the oncologist to ask him if we do the scheduled chemo or postpone it for a day. He answers by saying that we go ahead if it is not too 'late'. I try to imagine what 'late' in this case means. The last time we started 'late' after his PET scan we reached home well past 9pm. True it was pouring that night. I finally locate the good Doc and he tells me that we should be able to begin by 2pm as there is no place in the chemo day care and chemo cannot be given any where else. Remember chemo is lethal poison! The toxic brew can only be brewed in a special well–isolated cabin.

Shamika[40] has come in so I decide to take a break and have some lunch at home, the food available in the hospital is all 'fast' and I need a slow cooked meal. I am quite confident that we are on track and the chemo would be on the way soon. But this a play with a lot of action and we are not through. I have a bath, and have just begun to eat - it is 3 pm - when a call informs me that R is still 'waiting' for a bed in the chemo ward. He has been brought down but no bed has yet been vacated. I look at my watch and wonder when this rather laborious and now annoying play will end. By 3.30 he has a bed and after the usual weighing and measuring - this was done earlier one floor up; why can't things be computerised and shared - and the BP, and temperature and pulse routine all seems set for the chemo. A quick mental calculation and I figure we should be done by 7.30 now that there is a port and no need for needles. I plan on getting back by 5pm. At 4 I get another call from Shamika saying that nothing has begun. They are apparently making R's cocktails. Normally 4 of them. I again wonder why, when they knew that he was coming in for chemo at 2pm and was simply waiting for a bed, did they not prepare the mixes. But it is all about protocols! I will not get into that.

When I reach the hospital at 5.10, the actual chemo has not begun. Some shouting and ranting gets things moving and the first of the 4 lethal brews arrives. R who has been in the hospital from 7am, starved till 1 pm and had a port inserted and hence a raw wound is exhausted. All he has had are some bad sandwiches and an 'upma' that Shamika and Dharmendra

---

[40] My second daughter

said looked 'foul'. But the ravenous man gulped it all hungry as he was. He even had bad coffee! When I hear all this, my heart stops. How would his body react to all this bad food when for the past months now he has been on a very healthy and organic diet? React it did. But that is for later. Let us finish this act. Finally the real chemo began at 5.15 and I think they rushed the drips a little as we were through by 8.15pm. After final instructions about the port and the next steps we left at 8.30 to be stuck in the mother of all traffic jams!

That is when all reactions began. R went pale, started feeling nauseous and strange. When we got home he was listless, refused anything to eat and just lay down disoriented and in pain. I was really worried as this was a first for me. I knew he had to take some medicines no matter what - antibiotics and pain killers - but he would not budge. After gentle coaxing he ate a banana and two pieces of chocolate. I gave him the minimum medication and hoped for the best. Finally, after much tossing and turning, whining and moaning he fell asleep. I feel into a light slumber, my ears attuned to his every movement and sound. Thankfully he slept and woke up looking more like himself.

I am ready with my arsenal!

Sunday, 25 August 2013

SERGEANT ANOU'S DAILY DRILL

I could a write song on the lines of Sgt Pepper's Lonely Hearts Club band but I am no Lennon or Mc Cartney. Those were R's avatars. I have been more of a book worm. However let us have some fun whilst giving you a peep at the daily drill R is subjected under the unrelenting and stern eyes of Sgt Anou! But let me try to come up with something one could sing to St Pepper's tune! So let's go:

It was fifty days ago today
Mr Hodgkin's came to stay
Threatening not to go away
But not knowing what would come it's way
So let me introduce to you
The one who will steal the show
Its Sergeant Anou's daily drill!

Its' waking up at six sharp
And swallowing the five pills
It's drinking the juice of the soursop
And eating the oat meal
Its Sergeant Anou's daily drill!
Then come the pills, the juice and slush
And the jumps
And more soursop

Followed by a healthy meal
Of vegetables and cereal crops
Its Sergeant Anou's daily drill!

I know you may be bored
But there is still more to go
A bowl of fruit and protein shake
Make the afternoon easier to take
Till the evening falls and more pills come
Before the soursop
And then the healthy soup
And fish and treats
And sweet meats
Before the bitter brew
Its Sergeant Anou's daily drill!

Its Sergeant Anou's daily drill!
It's made to make Hodgkin's go
Its Sergeant Anou's daily drill!
I hope you will join the show!
That will make Hodgkin go
Its Sergeant Anou's daily drill!

Sunday, 25 August 2013

A DAILY DOSE OF GAYATRI ON!

When I decided to share the news of R's cancer with friends and family, I received a mail from someone very dear and in it he said: *you are going to be buffeted by commiserations that will irk, advise, questions and interrogations sage as well as malicious.* I must admit that I was pleasantly surprised by the number of people who reached out to me from every corner of the planet. Most of them were persons that came into my life through Project Why and in some cases people I had never met face to face. I was also touched by the reaction of my family members, many of whom I rarely meet or talk to for varied reasons. Everyone of those alive, ranging from 90+ to 20 called in person or on the phone and offered to help should the need arise. Each one of them sounded sincere and let us leave it at that. I do not think it will go further but it was comforting. A cousin even went to the extent of reaching out to R directly - they have been to the same school - and convinced him to meet some healer who would help him. I was completely stunned when R accepted to do so, and has been in touch with the said healer on his own. It is really a first, as he has always been cynical or at the very best tolerating and non -interfering when I decide to perform some religious event. He often takes off for a game of golf. I guess cancer changes your attitude to things. But let us get back to the point of this post.

There is a part of the 'family', not mine, that has, for reasons I will not go into as they are hurtful and negative and I have no place for such feelings in this fight, cut me off altogether. However following the news of R's cancer one of them has decided to send an SMS a day, written in that most irritating new age way of 'c u' for 'see you' that gets my goat. Each message has the phrase 'Gayatri on'. It took me some time to decipher the fact that it meant that the person was chanting the Gayatri Mantra for him. It felt irksome. If I do something for the well being of someone I profess to care for, I do it discreetly without reminding the person concerned every single day that I am doing something for him. The whole purpose and sanctity of the prayer or pledge is lost. Why the hell do you want the world to know, and most of all why do you want the person you are doing it for to be reminded every day that you ARE doing something for him/her!

In this time of strife this daily dose of Gayatri on is the only irritant I have to face. So help me God. Or wait, as in everything else these days, is there a silver lining of sorts? Difficult to figure out at first as this irritant emanates from a corner that has left no stone unturned to hurt me and those I love.

The Gayatri itself comes to us from the Rig-Veda and asks us in its purest form to beseech the Absolute Creator to *stimulate our intellect and bestow upon us true knowledge* or in other words to open our third eye. Many benefits have been attributed to it from removing obstacles to lead us to eternal truths. I guess it all depends on where you are on the road to the eternal. Each one can us can derive the depth of the meaning we want to attach to it. Many have forgotten this. Today the Gayatri has become the mantra you loop on your music device every morning for a stipulated time in your shop be it in a small market or a mall; or the one you chant at every havan or prayer meeting; the one you learn at school just as we as convent kids learnt the Lord's prayer. Being reminded of it every day, even in an annoying way, gently nudges me to remember its true meaning and correct my attitude to the inevitable. It is a process I probably have begun. Perhaps it is time to go deeper and cleanse myself of the negativity I hold on to unnecessarily. Easily said than done. But will give it a go!

Sunday, 25 August 2013

COUNTING MY BLESSINGS

When Cancer enters your life, no matter how strong you are, your life inevitably changes. No matter what statistics are thrown your way, no matter if the Doc you trust tell you it is the 'best' cancer to have, no matter if your alternative medicine doctor reiterates that 'this' cancer responds well to the poisoning of chemotherapy, no matter if your astrologist friend who has always been bang on comforts you by saying it is a bad patch but you will come out of it - the worst months are still to come - the reality of dying stares you in the face as never before. For whatever reason Cancer is always associated with words like remission, abeyance etc. Your life changes because you realise your own ephemerality, more so if you are in your seventh decade. This is bound to happen. There are several ways of handling this brutal realisation.

Being born has only one certainty and that is that you will die. But when the going is good everyone forgets this inevitability. We humans fall prey to hubris far too often. Cancer is a sure way of bringing you back to earth. As I have oft repeated in this blog, so please forgive my rambling iterations, I have encountered cancer three times in my adult life. The first time we chose to ignore it and look the other way. The second time I fell hook line and sinker for the then available medical treatment but never reached stage 2 of the said treatment. This time not only do I want to face it with all the arsenal available, even ludicrous ones like jumping on a trampoline, but I also want to deny it of all the space it usually hogs, and consign it to a tiny corner of our lives.

I want to demystify it and find all the positive that it does and can entail if we look at it in the correct perspective. True I would never say this if it were a child or a young person who was afflicted. I am talking about those who have passed the prime of our lives and are in our twilight years, when every extra minute you get is a blessing. When my mother was asked why she refused treatment she simply said I have lived my life. What she meant was that she had seen her child grow, succeed, marry, have children and so on. My take is a little different.

Cancer that comes into your life at a later stage and at a time where information technology is so advanced that you can find out everything you want and make informed choices, should not have the terrifying connotation we still give it. And you should not make it the centre of your existence. Deal with it yes, but be ruled by it no! Yes it requires a lot of your time; give it generously and ungrudgingly. So you may ask, and rightly so, what do I mean by its positive side?

When something hits you where it hurts particularly when nothing warranted it, you are shaken, and the reason you are shaken is because you always felt in charge of your life. You can rant and rave and feel anger and cry. That is what some or many do.

It has been almost two months since I came to know that R had Hodgkin's disease. I have often wondered why I did nor cry, scream, curse whomever and above all feel let down. I thought it was my coping mechanism to freeze my feelings to deal with the crisis, as I thought it was a crisis. But for the past few days I have realised that I have not frozen any feelings, on the contrary I feel strangely serene, as if many puzzles yet unsolved have fallen into place. Somehow cancer has solved my crossroad dilemma and shown me my priorities and the way I had lost. There will be no angry tears as this too is part of the big picture and the wise accept that.

For the past two months I have been travelling down memory lane more than ever and what is extraordinary is that all the things that seemed ugly, hurtful and mean seem to hold tiny spaces that makes them almost invisible and unworthy of any attention. What I need to do is count my blessings and spend my time being grateful!

Tuesday, 27 August 2013

SERENDIPITY

R's cancer seems almost like a fortunate stroke of serendipity! Gosh what am I saying! How can cancer be fortunate! The Three Princes of Serendip according to Walpole[41]'were always making discoveries by accident and sagacity of things they were not in search of. Accident and sagacity seem key words in my journey too! I was certainly not searching for cancer but sagacity was what made me see this setback with new wisdom. Everything in life is for a reason. We can keep believing that we are in control of our lives, but the truth is that everything happens only because (S)HE- whoever that is - and (S)HE only knows the big picture.

For almost two months I was beating myself for not shedding the tears one is presumably supposed to when you hear the words: *your husband has cancer!* I was wondering why the rage and the anger that again presumably should have come did not. The quick explanation was that I had frozen my feelings, as I was afraid that they would weaken me in my resolve to fight this battle. But then why did I not cry when I was alone. The beginning of an answer to these silent questions came via the comment of a friend to a picture I had posted. She looked beyond the happy faces to the backdrop of the picture and her words: *what a warm home you have; much lived in, slightly*

---

[41]   The Three Princes of Serendip. Persian Fairy Tale; Serendipity word coined by Horace Walpole.

worn, each piece with a story to share – were like the proverbial penny that drops and makes you see with your heart instead of just your eyes.

In hindsight I remember that when my dear family Doc confirmed that lymphoma means cancer, I was filled with quietude I had never experienced before. I wrongly interpreted it as bravado. Saras's words helped me look at life with brand new eyes, twilight eyes. This cancer, that I know will be cured, was a gentle nudge that made you understand that it was time to slow down, to look at life gone by, to give up regrets and fill your life with peace and serenity. It was also time to remember and consign your memories to paper so that your progeny have a unique legacy that is not counted in figures but in feelings. It was time to look beyond the picture.

The most touching 'side effect' of this cancer had been rediscovering my love for R and his for me, a love that got lost for far too many years wasted in unnecessary and futile pursuits made to please others and hence hurt each other. How foolish we were. But had cancer not entered our lives we would have probably continued being fools. In the time we have left, we will be able to make up for all the lost years and not leave anything unsaid before one of us exits this world.

Cancer has also made me give up my anger towards things that did not happen when one so wanted them to. Projects close to both our hearts that never materialised in spite of yeoman efforts. Today I understand why they did not come true.

Another 'side effect' has been to look at my warm and much lived in home and remember the stories that every corner has to tell. And God there are so many of them, how will I tell them all.

Of course there is the need to make that famous bucket list though I do not know where to start. Maybe the first step is to look at those who depend on me and have still not found their wings. It is time to be that wind beneath their wings.

Tuesday, 27 August 2013

SOME GOOD NEWS

I know many of you want to know how R is doing, as many of my blogs I realise are becoming soulful reminiscences. So here is some Breaking News. Something has to be working right though I will not celebrate too much as the Gods might get jealous but R has put on 2 kilos and that is great as he is undergoing chemotherapy and we are fighting a battle to keep his immunity in control. This has been the best news for me in a long time. Let us see how short lived this elation is as tomorrow is the blood test and the counts saga. However I am allowing myself to savour this day by taking some time off.

Wednesday, 28 August 2013

FULL CIRCLE

Someone wrote about how everything comes full circle back to the way it was always meant to be. At this moment of my existence I must say life and love have come full circle as they were always meant to be and I am filled with boundless gratitude. And believe it or not coming full circle was a 'side effect' of cancer! It was all a matter of changing one's way of looking at things and in my case walking the talk as am I not the one who always 'swears' by the Fox's maxim in the Little Prince when he urges him to always look with his heart. So even if what you are looking at is as terrifying as cancer, look with your heart and you will find things you could never imagine. For me it is a journey into the forgotten and the yet unknown. So bear with me as I travel this uncharted course.

It is only very recently that I changed the nameplate at the gate though Papa's name and thus my maiden name is still prominently displayed. There will be many stories about the house but today I just want to share one that shows how life does come full circle.

The first one that comes to mind is the day when R, after an inane and unnecessary argument the cause of which I forget, had declared one day: *I will never set foot in this house* (the one we all live in now!).

I had completely forgotten about this incident till recently when my elder child suggested we start looking at options to 'redo' the house, which meant break it down and replace it with flats. One would have expected me to react violently as this is all I have left of my parents and every corner is replete with memories that come alive with very little prompting. But imagine my surprise when R reacted with unexpected passion and said *he wanted to live in this house till his last breath*. Wow! Had we not come full circle?

For those who have never been to my home, let me try to give you a quick walk around. Seen through the eyes only it is a two and half storeys building built in the style of the late sixties initially (one and a half a floor) and then added upon most illogically following needs and idiosyncrasies: mom's and mine. Before I change mode to heart mode, let me reiterate that this house was never rented! The first addition was after my marriage and the birth of my second child. Papa thought it silly for us to pay rent and thus added two rooms on the first floor. Then much to everyone's horror I discovered Vastu[42] and resorted to additions and deletions that made no sense to many. So the house has 2 staircases but is still not rentable, as you cannot divide it into units. You have to come and see it. At some point after my parents' deaths, someone suggested I make more changes to stop looking at it as a mausoleum and refusing to end my mourning. Yes there was a time when I threw a fit if someone dared change the place of a chair. But it was time to move on, at least for the kids. I wanted a big kitchen so my old bedroom and mama's room after my marriage became a big kitchen. And when my in laws moved in to stay, I built a den on the second floor for the much needed isolation and space to keep my sanity. It does get a coat of pain now and then but the costs are prohibitive and the house being old, damp patches are here to stay as well as cracks and peeling paint. As for the interiors if you look only with your eyes, you cannot find any adequate word do define the eclectic blend of styles. You see my parents were also people who functioned in heart mode so everything they bought was never an 'investment' but something they liked. And then arrived R who has strong likes in particular for old furniture and crystal. So the house is filled with chinoiseries that my parents bought, crystal and porcelain that we have in abundance as both Ram and R were posted to Prague. Paintings often bought by Papa to help struggling artists, some have become famous, and all kinds of odds and ends from the countries we lived in. The prize possession

---

[42] The traditional system of **Vaastu** Shastra serves as India's version of Feng Shui, influencing town planning, architecture, and ergonomics.

of my parents was an ugly ceramic cat that I made when I was four, and our prized paintings are two works executed by the grandson.

As you see the move from eyes mode to heart mode was surreptitious. This house defies logic, style and above all practicality. It is worn out, even a bit jaded but yet warm and welcoming. One does not see the cracks and patches but the lives of the people who built it and lived in it. People often ask me why I have given up travelling altogether. The answer is simple. I just want to stay home. I guess R feels the same. We have come full circle.

Thursday, 29 August 2013

THE HOUSE I AM GROWING OLD IN 1

One of the 'side effects' of R's lymphoma has definitely been looking at life past and present with brand new eyes. –

{Before I go further a quick update on R as many of you read my ramblings to get to know how he is. The weight dropped by a kilo today but no worries; the blood counts have been taken; he is feeling well and has gone out for some work; and we see the oncologist tomorrow.}–

One of the things that has come to the fore is our house, the only asset we have and seeing how one could 'use' it better. The obvious solution keeping in mind the size of the structure would be to say: rent it! Well if you have seen the house you would know that is not possible. This house is more like someone's folly and was extended for 'emotional' reasons. The other option is of course break it and make it into flats. Reason says that is the way one should go but before you can plan further, the heart takes over and floods you with memories of the past and alarming images of what is to come should we chose that option. R and Mama seem to have had the same reaction: how can we share our space with people we do not know (future). How can we empty it (future) and where will we stay for the time it takes to build. And now with R not being well, the idea of uprooting him is inconceivable. But I guess if push came to shove, all this would become possible.

But what do you do with the memories that suddenly crowd your mind, memories you had forgotten, some sweet, some bittersweet and some sad.

Let me start at the beginning and you will understand why giving up this rambling folly is quasi impossible. When my father was still in post, they decided to settle in Delhi and thus bought this piece of land. At that time visiting the land was a real expedition as it was situated in the boonies. But it was ours. An architect was found, a plan designed and one of my uncles given the responsibility to supervise the construction. If all had gone well we should have had a built house by the time papa retired in 1969. But that was not to be.

By the time he retired, what we had was a shell with walls and a roof and unpolished floors. There were no doors, no windows, no toilets, no water connection, no electricity, no nothing! The estimated money had been spent and the contractor, who was a crook, had further claims and had taken possession of the ground floor. We went to court but that was another nightmare. Papa was shattered as he was a scrupulously honest man who was lost in the reality of India and its corrupt ways. We won the case, and the police vacated the contractor's material but the next day he had put it all back and this time occupied the ground floor with a bunch of goons. To cut a long story short, Mama packed papa to Mauritius and she and I 'moved' into the half finished first floor. Mama was a real trouper and a woman of steel. Everyone was shocked as I was 17 and the both of us not truly equipped to take on drunken goons. But then you did not know Kamala Goburdhun née Sinha! She stood her ground and in the winter of 1970 mother and daughter began living in the house I am today growing old in.

The situation was burlesque initially. The bedroom was freezing, as all we had were curtains on doors and windows. We slept on two charpoys. There was one tap in the unfinished kitchen that also became the bathroom with one of us guarding the door or should I say curtain. Pooing was the biggest issue. Well we pooed on newspaper that was then packed and thrown away later. I do not remember if we ever had Delhi bellies at that time! We had a cook who cooked us meals and candles to light our dinners which were rarely tête a tête as many friends joined us for dinner and sing-song sessions, mostly bhajans, meant to irritate the goons. The local tea stall man who was a young boy then and still runs the street tea shop, would bring us hot tea every morning and after getting ready, quite a saga, and eating two toast grilled in a frying pan I set off to college. Mama stayed put guarding the fort.

One day when I came back from college, I found myself locked out. The contractor was at the gate and would not let me enter. Mama was on the terrace telling me not to worry and go get help. There were no phones in the vicinity, actually there was nothing! I ran across empty grounds to what you all know as R Block Greater Kailash I where a friend of the family lived, barged in and phoned everyone I could think off: my lawyer uncle, 100 for the flying squad and my father's friend who headed RAW[43] at that time. By the time I got back the police was there in all shades and hues, I was allowed to go to mama and the matter was sorted for the time being. But that incident scared us and we realised that we had to find a solution as courts and law would take an eternity and we would remain on the 'streets'. Before anything, Mama decided we had to have a phone and she moved heaven and earth again and we got one. I still remember the number: 78678. Strange how much one's memory keeps safely inside our heads.

All our money had been sunk in these unfinished walls and unless the contractor did not get out we too were stuck. Going to court did not seem the right option so we were forced to into 'arbitration'. An 'arbitrator' was appointed by the court and again to cut a long story short we were stuck between the devil and the deep blue sea, the arbitrator and contractor were hand in glove and ultimately we had to pay a little less than what had been demanded. Appearances had to be kept you see!

We had our house! By that time papa's famous Provident Fund had been released and that is all we had to finish the house. The few months that ensued were strange yet comforting. Mama and I remained put in our palace without walls while the ground floor was completed. We had a tight budget so quality had to be compromised. The goons had left and in their place came in the workers. This was my first contact with people I would work with half a century later: the migrants! When I look back at those forgotten years I realise how close I felt to them. I spent hours watching them work and chatting with them. I felt a strange empathy for them but could not understand why. How could I begin to imagine that one day I would be working with and for their children. Another full circle I guess.

Anyway there are million of stories about those fateful months waiting to be told. I really do not know whether I will have the time and energy to

---

43   Research Analysis Wing

write them but there is one I have to share. As I recounted earlier we always had someone to cook and 'clean' for us. One of them whose name I forget now, was elderly and used to spend hours cooking though I can recall his food never tasted great. Since my childhood I have never spend time eating and still do not, and get impatient when others take forever. This irritates R no end as I am always wanting to leave the table once I am done specially if it is only family. Anyway in those days when we did not have a dining space, I use to eat my meal in a jiffy and get on with other things, this use to annoy the said cook. One day, in front of all the workers, he threw an ultimatum to my mom: he did not like the little time I took eating the meal he had spent so much time preparing and hence either mama threw me out or he would leave. Everyone burst out laughing and you can well imagine who stayed!

The ground floor was finally ready. It was time to call Papa back home. It had been almost a year since he had left. It was lovely to have a room with doors and windows and above all a bathroom. I was given the first choice and chose the room that is now our kitchen. But now came the hitch: where was the money to furnish the house. There was only one-way to do it and that was selling all the things we had bought and brought back. Many of you do not know the days when one got practically nothing in India so people like us brought back cooking ranges, air conditioners and loads of other appliances not to forget a car! Ours was a Mercedes Benz that was later sold to pay for my wedding. Anyway we furnished the house as best we could. It took time but things were better when Papa decided to take up legal consultancies. There was no looking back.

So even if my head says that this almost crumbling and irrational house should be brought down and made into sensible flats, the heart says no, or at least no until it becomes an emergency. This was not the house I was born in, or the house I grew in but it is definitely the house I would like to grow old in!

Friday, 30 August 2013

THE GODS DO GET JEALOUS

I celebrated too fast. Three chemos down and none of the usual side effects was great encouragement particularly for Sgt Anou and her drill. But the Gods do get jealous and this morning R told me had ulcers in his mouth. Now the question that is bothering me is if this is the only side effect we will see or will the others follow meaning all the brews and drills simply did not work. Only time will tell. The blood results were not too bad: WBCs at 3000. But there is a week to go till the next chemo and one more blood test a day before.

I guess the blisters are also a gentle reminder that Mr Hodgkin should be taken more seriously than we have. Maybe he just wants more space. Maybe we need to alter/change arsenal and tactics. Maybe I had sunk into a comfort zone. Time to regroup and resume the attack. Wish me luck!

Friday, 30 August 2013

NO PAIN BUT LOTS OF WAITING AND CRAWLING

Someone - you know who - was very happy when he was told that the stitches he was dreading to get removed were the soluble kind! So no pain...

Doctor's visit went well though we had to wait for more than an hour and a half for our turn and then it took us one hour to crawl back home in horrible traffic jams. Left home at 4pm got back at 8pm!

All seems on course. Next chemo on the 5th!

Friday, 30 August 2013

SIDE EFFECTS AND SURVIVAL KIT

When Mr Hodgkin comes knocking at your door and then decides to squat uninvited in your home, he does not only change the life of the one he inhabits, but also the lives of all those around. Most of all the life of the spouse who becomes the cancer buddy. And believe it or not the 'side effects' of the buddy are as numerous if not more than the one who is affected. In this case the 'buddy' is me. For those who may be going - God Forbid - through similar conditions and for all others too, I thought it would be fun and useful to list my 'side effects' and the survival kit I have put together. This kit has to be flexible and responsive to all challenges that can come any time. The 'side effects' I have had till date are insomnia, readjusting my work life; giving up a well ordained existence to a one day at a time, or even one minute at a time mode; worrying every time I open an envelope containing the latest blood counts; making trips and sojourns to the kind of hospital I never wanted to have to enter; browsing the Internet every time a new challenge appears - this time it is oral ulcers - and above all spending more time than I ever did with my husband. There may be more 'side effects' but let us just look at the survival kit to counter these.

I must start by admitting that I have not found the item in my survival kit for the biggest 'side effect': insomnia. I do not want to take sleeping pills. I want to figure out why my body clock is behaving this way. I do not feel unduly tired though I get an average of 5 hours of sleep max! Mostly it is sound sleep and I get up refreshed so maybe it is my brain that realises that I have less time than before to pursue my preferred activities and gives that extra hour or more in the early hours of the day to write, but there are nights, thankfully a few, where I cannot sleep at all and lie awake. These are the ones I need to dissect and figure out. Maybe there are some questions that still need to be asked and are not easy to formulate. Must work on that.

If I were to select the one most important personal survival tool in my kit it would be undoubtedly writing about each and everything, the good, the bad, the ugly, as honestly as possible, as loud as possible and to the world at large. This has been why I began this blog the day R's illness had a name. It is my catharsis and emotional release. Without this platform I would already have had a meltdown.

The second, or actually it could share the place with the first, 'tool' for want of a better word is the support I have got from so many people, known and unknown, from across each and every continent. To know that people spend a moment of their precious time reading what I write and reaching out to me is priceless. You cannot begin to imagine how humbled and grateful I feel. I know that I can send out a mail and seek help. I have done so to get medicine not available in India! I have two wonderful friends I wake up every morning at some unearthly hour and if I fail to do so, I get a mail or SMS asking me if all is well. That is not all, I know that they are an SMS away should any need arise 24/7. God bless them all.

The next one is trickier. For a control freak (my daughter's words) or organised person (my words) it is very difficult to readjust your life, particularly when you were devoting all your time to your work and living and breathing Project Why every minute of the day. Well here the survival kit is in the shape of four wonderful people who have taken my worries and run the ship spot on! For me, I have learnt to change priorities and accept to live life a minute at a time. It can be bothersome but exciting as well. I am discovering a new me!

I am also discovering the fact that hospitals that look like five stars hotels do not run like them! Each time we have a 'surprise' package that now makes us smile rather than brood. It also is meat for this blog.

When a challenge appears the Internet is the saviour. Did you know that if you suck ice while the chemo is being done or at least for the first hour, you are less likely to develop ulcers? You have guessed right the next item in my kit on chemo days will be a flask of ice.

The last item I will share today is the importance of alone time (an expression my grandson uses a lot). I have worked out mine. I have to switch off or get off the Hodgkin's spinning wheel. First and foremost my 40 minutes on the treadmill at 6 km an hour with loud music blaring in my ears, music that takes me on a rapid space and time defeating tour of my life. For those 40 minutes I travel in my time machine. One caveat though: my knees! Then there is a sort of retail therapy, which consists in browsing at my favourite bookshop or walking through the market. It is better done with an empty pocket. Then there is my weekly cuppa with the dearest people on earth and last of all locking myself in my cockpit, as that is what my office looks like and writing!

Voila. Any more ideas?

Saturday, 31 August 2013

THE WARRIOR OF LIGHT

You are a *Warrior of Light*[44], wrote my dear friend and soul mate Mrinal in a recent comment to one of my posts! A quick Google search reminded me of Paulo Coelho's book: *Manual for the Warrior of Light*[45] and Wikipedia, gave me the definition I think Mrinal has in her mind when it comes to me: *those in pursuit of their dreams and who appreciate the miracle of life.* The dream bag is rather small at this very moment with one main dream: get rid of Mr Hodgkin. Mrinal also sent me a link[46] that tells you how to protect yourself to add to my survival kit. The aim is to protect yourself while helping others, as it seems we attract people in need. I know some of you out there who worry about me, so I will try and follow the advice! The article ends with these words that could seem a little pompous but are actually true, as I too believe that we do not love ourselves, as we should. It says: *Most importantly. Even if no one thanks you for all of the amazing light that you are shining in this world please, take time to appreciate yourself!*

So I guess I will add the tourmaline and the convex mirror to my kit and pray to my Angel to protect me. I guess I need all the help I can get, even the one that may sound esoteric to some.

---

[44]

[45] Manual of the Warrior of Light is a 1997 collection of Paulo Coelho's teachings summed up into one volume.

[46] http://www.lightworkersworld.com/2013/04/protection-for-lightworkers/

Saturday, 31 August 2013

THE SUB INSPECTOR AND I

The Sub Inspector and I, strange title for a post in a blog that is dealing with R's cancer and my battle. Wait till your hear the story. It is a proof yet again that nothing happens fortuitously in this life that we love thinking we control, even if we are not control freaks. One more reminder of Papa's: *no leave moves without His will!* Here its how it goes.

It was about 4pm when the bell rang twice. Now in my house if anyone, barring my darling grandson, rings the bell more than once, we all jump and rush to the door to normally chide the person. I was in my office, hence near the main door and I went out ready to pounce when I saw a tall man of a certain age that did not look like your courier man. He introduced himself as Sub Inspector Singh, CID. What had I done now! It transpired that he had come for passport verification for Parul, my elder daughter, who of course had got her passport and flown away across many seas. The man was polite, soft spoken and though I asked if there was anything I could do, he said that he needed Parul's signature on his form that now would have to be returned and revived when she came. I guess we are all a little in awe of authority of any kind, even though it could be because of their nuisance value, though in my case it was another parental lesson, I felt the need to explain to him why everything had been rushed and thought that the best thing would be to play on his emotions and mention R's cancer. I guess this was the operative word the man upstairs wanted me to pronounce.

The SI told me his wife had cancer too, blood cancer and she was in a poor state because of the side effects of the chemotherapy. So here I was telling him about my entire arsenal, showing him soursop leaves and Tibetan medicine. I asked him if he had an email and he sheepishly confessed that he has not much knowledge of computers but would send me his son's id.

He was true to his word and in the evening I got a call and talked to his son and promised him to send all the information. This is the first ting I did this morning. I hope it helps relieve the awful side effects of the poor lady. I must say I feel good and maybe should like my grandson loves doing add a middle name to mine. What about - another favourite expression of the grandson - Anouradha Side Effects Bakshi!

Sunday, 1 September 2013

NO UPDATE TODAY

No update today is the message I got this morning at 6.37 am. This from a dear friend who normally sleeps late and wakes up late, but never fails to respond to my early morning update about R. Normally my update beeps on his mobile between 5 and 6 am or sometimes even earlier. This little ritual, that may seem insensitive to some who may wonder why I do not wait for an earthly hour to send my message, is my lifeline. I send my message, get my reply and somehow I know that all will be well for the day. Today the Internet let me down and hence this message. Will remember to send an SMS if ever the same situation occurs. Though I am somehow net savvy, I am a creature of habits and thus like to sit at my computer in my den/cockpit and communicate with the world.

But maybe this also was ordained by the one upstairs that sees the big picture and sends messages in her/his amazing ways. This simple message opened my eyes to yet another positive and wonderful 'side effect' of Mr Hodgkin's stopover. I have never been a formality person and loathe commiserations and duty and visits that ring fake. To me any relationship that is true and valued does not need stand on formalities. If I am your friend, then I need not visit you or call you to prove it. You just need to know that I am there for you. These morning exchanges are proof of that and validate my way as I have often been accused of not being good at keeping appearances. One of the incidents that really took the cake was when in our early marriage days I rarely or almost never attended R's official parties, as we each had our professional life and I did not expect him to tag along with me, people started thinking that all was not well in our marriage! I cannot remember if I did make a few appearances. Knowing me I do not think so.

In the last months, I have been overwhelmed by the number of people who have come into my orbit to extend help and support. This has been the best 'side effect' I could have ever hoped for. Thank you all who read this blog, leave a comment, send a mail and above all wait for the beep of a message that comes when sane people sleep. I am a little insane!

Monday, 2 September 2013

AND THE LADY

After the Sub Inspector, here comes the lady. Cryptic? Read on. One of the tools in my survival kit is getting out of the house either to shop as with R's diet one needs to shop often, as there is always something missing, or to spend some time browsing in my favourite book shop. Yesterday however I had a real errand. R's treasures almost 25-year-old glasses needed to be repaired. So off I went to my one and only favourite optometrist[47]. I have been going to that shop for the past almost 40 years and it is always a pleasure to spend time in the shop with its owner and his now well grown up sons. I knew them when they were just kids. As they know about R's cancer we began talking on the subject. A lady who was walking down the stairs suddenly stopped and came back. She apologised for butting in but told us she was interested in our conversation as her husband had cancer too.

It is funny how cancer has become a conversation piece in my life. The lady had overheard me talking about all the alternative therapies I had embraced to support R's ailment and wanted to know more. So we talked sour sop, apricot kernels, Ashwagandha and diets. I took her email details and promised to send her all the information I have. I did that as soon as I got home as I can now empathise with all cancer buddies. I hope this helps her and her husband.

---

[47] Seventeen Arcade, M Greater Kailash I

I know many of you who read my blog may have dear ones who are battling cancer and chemotherapy. So maybe it is not a bad idea to share all the therapies I am using as of now. R is going to have his 4th chemo on Friday and till date the only side effect we have seen is loss of hair on his head and limbs. Frankly none of us care about his hair but there maybe some who would not want to loose their hair and there is a solution: scalp cooling! You need to wear a scalp-cooling helmet[48] during chemo! We have not got there yet!

Exercise is something that always helps but a cancer patient is not always willing to put on her/his shoes and run. But jumping on a trampoline also know as rebounding[49] is a great and easy exercise that gets all systems going, particularly the lazy lymphatic system responsible for our immunity. I advise it strongly and there are many articles on the net that you can read. A trampoline is easily available on line or in any good sports shop. I try to make R jump has often as possible.

Sour sop leaves tea and apricot kernels (vitamin B17) are also great cancer fighters. There is a lot of information on the net, just Google it. These two can be bought in India. You can read the benefits and place an order if you are convinced at this link[50] I give R Sour sop tea thrice a day and make him chew 3 to 4 apricot kernels before each meal.

A friend and cancer survivor who swears by it suggested pure Ashwagandha Root Powder to us. Sloan Kettering[51] has published information on this herb. I source mine from the Arya Vaidya Sala's Delhi Branch [52]The dose is 5 grams twice a day with honey. You have to insist that you want pure root powder and not the churanam. Over and above all these, R is on Tibetan Medicine under the care of Dr Dolkar[53].

None of the above requires stopping any treatment you may be talking.

---

[48] http://www.cancernet.co.uk/hairloss.htm

[49] Rebounding: A defence against cancer. Linda Brroks; http://www.wholife.com/issues/9_4/01_article.html

[50] http://soursopindia.com

[51] http://www.mskcc.org/cancer-care/herb/ashwagandha

[52] http://aryavaidyasala.com/

[53] http://www.buddhistchannel.tv/index.php?id=7,8270,0,0,1,0#.VR9ClLpCP8t

R's chemo protocol is ABVD (Doxorubicin, Bleomycin, Vinblastine and Dacarbazine.) This protocol has many side effects but till now, and I keep my fingers, toes and all else crossed we have had none or very few: hair loss and drop in TLC.

And last but not the least R's diet is almost vegan and organic. It is high on protein with two protein shakes a day (silken tofu based), and his diet includes all shades of berries one can buy frozen at many shops. His meal includes a protein, a vegetable, a salad and a dessert. He also drinks two glasses of vegetable juices (broccoli, cabbage, beetroot, carrot, ginger etc.). I source all my organic vegetables, rice and pulses in Delhi where many stores deliver at home.

As I said we are three chemos down and have not encountered many side effects. There is a caveat though and that is that you have to really follow a Sgt Major drill, as everything has to be given at specific times if you want to do it all. The biggest side effect is that the cancer buddy has to give up, or at least put her/his life on hold! A little price to pay for the health of the one you love.

Tuesday, 3 September 2013

THE NOSE AND THE HAIR

The nose and the hair, sounds like children's classic fable the *turtle and the hare*[54]! But mine is no fable or moral story but a real one. Now R has a big nose many say; for me it is part of his charm. R has, or should I say had, abundant nose hair that often needed clipping. With all that is happening I did not realise that the hair once visible had vanished and completely forgot a friend of Parul's who had cancer recounting how losing the hair in her nose was a nightmare as the nose kept dripping. So here I am with a new unexpected 'side effect': a dripping nose. The first line of defence is obviously stocking the house with loads of packets of tissue paper. But there is one more worry: nose hair is also our first line of defence[55] against harmful environmental pathogens such as germs, fungus, and spores, and with someone with low immunity that is a big one. So what now. Help Mr Google!

I have been busy searching the net because I really do not care about a dribbling nose, but the germs and spores frighten me to death as we live in a land where these abound and with the clogged rainwater drain in front of my house it becomes a real nightmare. And it is one of the side effects no one talks about! Some patient chat rooms talk about nose filters. I guess

---

[54] The Tortoise and the Hare is one of Aesop's Fables and is numbered 226 in the Perry Index.

[55] http://www.wisegeekhealth.com/what-is-the-purpose-of-nose-hair.htm

it looks like a good idea particularly when he decides to go out to crowded places. I have just discovered they are available in India so let me see how to get them!

I guess the next hurdle is the lashes. They protect the eye from debris. I guess a woman could use false eyelashes for cosmetic purposes but I do not see R doing that! And there seems to be no other option. I guess wearing his glasses would help with the dust, debris and insects. Will see when it happens!

Tuesday, 3 September 2013

I HEAR IT IN HIS VOICE

I must admit that the last months have been very difficult. Actually I should say the last year as R started feeling unwell in June 2012 and for a year we ran from pillar to post trying to find out the cause of his poor health. All possible tests and investigations were done, but they all remained inconclusive, which made things harder as we were really groping in the dark. The only constants were his losing weight and his tumbling haemoglobin counts. It is only in early July this year that the beast was finally identified as Mr Hodgkin. Quite frankly this was the last thing I wanted but to finally know what it was, was a huge relief as it allowed us to plan and start the best treatment possible.

I must admit that chemotherapy was not my first or come think about it my last preference, but a series of circumstances made me reluctantly agree to it. I did. I however decided to turn heaven and earth to find out how I could control the terrible side effects of chemotherapy because I could not have seen him in the throes of any of those. There had to be support therapies that worked. I did my homework better than I have ever done and worked out my brews and potions. We are down 3 and ready for 4, and it seems to be working. I keep vigil and am ready for any unexpected side effect, was it to happen.

The title of this post, *I hear it in his voice*, would not make sense if I were not to give you some background. In the past year as R's health dwindled, he sunk into depression and often use to ask me if he would make it. One of the worse moments for me was when this man of a few words, told me one day: *I am falling apart; help me.* His entire persona changed and from an always cheerful and carefree man, he became sullen and withdrawn. One of the few persons he talked to was his favourite uncle. I was not privy to his phone chats.

Imagine my delight when this morning my aunt - said uncle's wife - called me and told me that she knew R was doing better as she *heard it in is voice*! She was kind enough to compliment me on this as she felt it was my doing. I am humbled but accept her accolade. I needed that pat in the back just to know that I am moving in the right direction. My mission is undoubtedly to give Mr Hodgkin the boot asap, but also to give back R his *joie de vivre* even if Mr H is still around. I have pushed him into a tiny corner of our lives and will not allow him to mar our happiness!

Wednesday, 4 September 2013
MY SPACE AND TIME MACHINE

Almost everyone who enquires about R's health has always some kind advice for me: take it easy, look after yourself, eat well etc. I know they mean well and are spot on as were anything to happen to me, God forbid, then the entire yet fragile support structure that I have crafted with great pain to counter Mr H would fall apart and R split wide open to all the vile side effects of chemo. The problem is that as always, much of the structure is in my head. So I guess the first thing that should be cared for is my head! In normal times, when I need to restore things in my brain, I slink into some corner of the house with a book and travel in time and space. For those few hours I get off the spinning wheel of the day and forget about things around me, specially the annoying or irritating ones. When I feel I can once again face life, I emerge rested and ready to take on the world. Books are so important to me that I have to always have on my shelf a fair amount of unread books should an emergency arise.

With the arrival of Mr Hodgkin and the upheaval in my life, the old and tested reading did not give the needed relief. Even the best thriller or most touching novel that normally would have kept me glued to it for hours fails to do so as I find myself fidgety and keyed up. So for new times new ways had to be found. Something that would allow me to travel in space and time and get my system going and happy hormones up. It was time to put one's thinking cap on and I did. The solution was the treadmill + my iPod with a compilation of songs that I had loved since my early teens. French songs, favourite bands, crooners of the past, a mixture of genres, songs I had grown with in the four corner of the world, songs that could become my unique space and time machine!

So every day, except chemo days, I change into my gym attire, put on my barefoot running shoes, set my iPod on shuffle and the volume at maximum level, set the treadmill to 6km an hour and take off on a 40 minutes travel in time and space. For those 40 minutes I am no more the 61 year old woman living in Delhi. I become a 16 year old dancing in a club in Ankara, the 22 year old in love sitting pillion on the scooter of the one who would become her life partner, then the 40 year woman cooking in her kitchen in Paris, the 13 year old listening to the top of the pop song in her room in Algiers, the 10 year old dancing with her papa in Rabat. Each day is a surprise journey that brings back fond memories, some sweet, some bittersweet, but each one bringing a smile on my face. I wonder what I look like to those who pass by, as I am unaware of anything happening around me. When the 40 minutes are over I am charged and happy to be me, and grateful for every moment of my existence.

So for the buddy survival kit you absolutely need a way to get off this planet for some time everyday!

Thursday, 5 September 2013

THE HOUSE IN WHICH I AM GROWING OLD 2

My den is a tiny room. Tiny by choice as I never wanted it to become a space that could be shared. It was for my alone time. It is a warm place, flooded with pictures of times gone, happy times that bring a smile on my face every time I look up from my computer. This is where I come every morning before the crack of dawn and spend time writing. This is also the HQ of my on going battle. Many changes have occurred since the fateful day I discovered I had to deal with an unwanted guest for some time at least. But this unwanted guest has been a strange stroke of serendipity as it has made me stop and look again at my life and the times gone by. Just this morning as I sat at my computer I realised that this little room did not exist in the house I shared with my parents. It was added when I remodelled the house on the gentle advice of a dear friend who realised that I was sinking into a morbid depression and turning my home into a mausoleum not wanting to move a single object. When I finally understood what she meant I went all out to make drastic changes: the room in which mama died and which was the room where I lived in before my wedding is now the kitchen and this little den was carved from the erstwhile drawing room.

Today is chemo day and though the three that are over were not bad, I always feel a little anxious on chemo morning. Part of what I call getting into chemo mode which often begins the evening before and ends two days after when I am convinced that the dreaded side effects will not appear. I always try to write something before we leave. This morning I allowed my memories to run free and wondered where they would lead me. They took me back several decades to this very spot that happened to be the place where mama had placed her main sofa on the day of my wedding and this is roughly where I sat in my bridal gear just before and after the ceremonies. God what a day. People would think you are over the moon but all I was thinking was when I could take out all the pins from my hair and all the jewels I never wore and stop looking like a Xmas tree. And then I had to keep smiling at all the people I did not know and then posing for pictures. There were no stages and thrones in those days. People sat beside you on the sofa or perched themselves on its the arm while the photographer clicked away. That was on October 20th 1974 when the whole house had been transformed into wedding mode. Yes those days we got married in our homes, and the empty plot next door was where the dinner was held under a tent. Those where the days!

However when the house was in normal mode the place where I am sitting was where the TV set was. What memories that brings back. Papa sitting in his armchair, with his pipe and watching TV almost religiously and often alone as TV was so boring then barring 2 days: Wednesday with Chitrahaar that was half an hour of film songs and Sunday evening when a Hindi film was aired. Then the whole room was full, as many people from neighbouring homes would come. That was sacrosanct time where even the phone, there were no mobiles at that time, was attended grudgingly and if visitors came then it was a disaster. How we cursed them! Dinner was on the table at 8.45 as the film was stopped for the news. By 9 we were back in our places glued to the box.

Today I sit alone in this spot that has seen so many things, witnessed good and bad times, hosted kings and paupers, as that was the way we lived. It was a space filled with the silly giggles of a teenager and the tears of a woman. But somehow it was the happiest place you could imagine and the best ever to wage my last battle from.

I could go on and on and will when I have the time to take a walk down memory lane again.

Friday, 6 September 2013

CHEMO FOUR

It was chemo day, the fourth one! This is either half way through or one-third way through. Pet scan after chemo six holds the key to the question: 8 or 12! Chemo days are always bad, not so much because of side effects as they are not too bad. As I write these words an exhausted R sleeps by my side. Slightly nauseous but I think it is more the car drive and also the fact that he has to eat the rubbish served at the hospital. Now for someone who has been on an organic food diet for over two months, any chemical is quickly detected by his body and rejected. I had hoped to be back for lunch as we were on the hospital bed at 8 sharp, so normal maths would say we should have been home well before 1pm. But that was not to be. We got home at 3.30! The reason: the total lack of efficiency of this super speciality hospital. As one who has managed events professionally, this makes me see red.

Here is how it goes. We reach at 8 am and wait. At 8.20 or so a nurse comes in with a cannula. I am puzzled as R has a port and the last chemo was given through the port. In these days of technology why are records not kept on a computer? Anyway she is surprised and then turns to me and asks me for the tube. I am zapped, as I do not know what she means by tube, and more than that why should I have it! Is it a rubber tube kind of thing I saw one hanging from the port last time, or a tube of medicine? A mystery to all. She then mutters something and leaves. After another 30 minutes we go looking for her and discover that the tube in question is a tube of anaesthetic ointment. I offer to run down and purchase it from the pharmacy but she says that someone has already left. Needless to say that someone must have made many stops on the way as the tube finally appears at 10am. The chemo begins at 10.30 or so. Two hours and ten minutes for nothing. At about 1pm we finally see the end of the last drip and start agitating for our discharge as past experience has shown it is worse than a marathon and tests the limits of your patience. I check with the doctor on duty and she informs me that she has cleared everything and it is the nurse who will give us the papers.

When we ask the nurse she again mutters something unintelligible and says she is waiting for a clearance from upstairs. Now what does upstairs mean? God! Even he would take pity on us. When I ask her how long it will take, I am told five minutes. When I ask again I am again told five minutes. The five minutes become an hour. And we still do not know what the problem is. Apparently the nurse has made a mistake on the file that had to be Okayed by the lab or else we would have been charged double for the test. Quite frankly I would have rather paid double or even treble than wait for almost 1.30 hours. The price to pay was far higher.

R was in great spirits when we set off in the morning and we all hoped that this time we would beat the system and get home early and in a merry mood. But that was not to be. First the *waiting for the tube,* nothing short of an absurd play had a terrible side effect. Breakfast arrived and as there was nothing to do, R did what each of us do when bored: ate! There was some poor quality bread, a boiled egg, certainly not organic and some instant coffee. I knew it would have its reactions, but nevertheless hoped not. And anyway he would not have to have lunch here, as we would be back home. He had even planned his menu!

Now of the 4 toxic brews that ABVD, D aka Dacarbazine, is the longest and the one that seems to be the nastiest. I wonder why they do not give it first so that any side effect could be dealt with in the hospital. So the Dacarbazine drip that takes 90 minutes and then a 10-minute flush ends the chemo saga. Had we been able to leave soon R may still have come home in a better state. But the long wait when you are ready to go was enough to zap him and then the drive back in the heat and the fumes, in spite of the AC made him nauseous and feverish as well as listless. He sleeps fitfully, mumbling some incoherent words. And I watch helplessly, mad at a hospital that can never get its act together! I would forgive an overworked Government hospital, but find it difficult to do so for a hospital that almost charges you for the air you breathe!

Friday, 6 September 2013

SETBACK

I have always held that the Gods do get jealous. Or maybe it is their way of reminding us that we are not really masters of our destiny. Maybe we fall prey to our hubris too easily! I guess I stand guilty at this moment. Till this morning I was so proud of the fact that we had gone through 3 chemotherapy sessions without significant side effects, so happy to see R looking better and thrilled beyond words when the hospital scales showed he had gained 2 kilos! In spite of some annoying occurrences chemo 4 went reasonably well. I was looking forward to a relaxed afternoon and evening, reading or watching some TV with R next to me.

We do spend such tender moments together when words are not necessary. But that was not to be. R was feeling uneasy when we got back and went into a fitful sleep. I touched him and found him warm. The thermometer confirmed my worst fear: he had fever. Not a very high one, but high enough to slam my hubris and presumptions. Over and above that his uric acid was up so the doctors had advised to cut down his protein intake. The two put together shook my, I guess fragile, confidence once for all.

Now what! Would I have to review my regimen? Change what seemed to be going so well? I guess I do, but I must admit at this moment I am lost and feel helpless and all my earlier confidence is shaky to say the least. Mr H has won another battle.

I know I have to garner my troupes and mount an attack. But tonight I am stunned and distressed. I just hope this fever is just a small rap on my knuckles.

Tomorrow is another day[56]! But I am no Scarlett.

---

[56] The last line of the American Civil War novel *Gone With The Wind:*, Margaret Mitchell 1936

Friday, 6 September 2013

WHITE (K)NIGHT

A white night next to my white knight! Sounds terrible but at 3 am the brain does not work as one would like it to and I needed something' brilliant' to begin this post! It is 3.30 am and yes you guessed right I have not slept a wink. Kept vigil on my knight as he has fever and the rather forbidding discharge papers given to you post every chemo in an ugly green cardboard file (what a waste of paper and trees. I have six such files) states that if the fever goes above 101 then you need to press the panic button. It is hovering around 100 and may it stay like that. But how can one not think dark thoughts in the dead of night when one lies awake and time takes on a Bergsonian quality and slows down in sync with your mood. The mind follows suit and imagination goes wild.

I kept vigil on the fever and dread could not be kept bay. The 'what ifs' were numerous and terrifying. What if it is the flu, or dengue or an infection? True as a friend said this is a race with many unknown obstacles that you have to overcome and yes I will, but how can I not worry.

As the night progressed with leaden steps, I almost savoured the slow hours as I lay next to my knight who had temporary lost his shining armour. The mood mellowed as a host of memories meandered by, each one bringing warmth and comfort and making me realise how much the man lying next to me meant to me, and how incomplete I was without him. Every thing I achieved in the last four decades was because he stood in his shining armour behind me making sure I never fall. He fulfilled all my caprices and idiosyncrasies and there were many, believe you me. He ensured I never fall and loved me without conditions. True he is a man of few words and I missed the meaningless 'I love you' or holding hands, but tonight as I travelled our love story I heard all the unsaid I love you and felt his hand on me at ever step.

I cannot see him like this. I want my knight in shining armour back as he was. I will settle for nothing else.

Monday, 9 September 2013

PINK HAPPY GLASSES

I need pink glasses. Saw a pair on the Internet that even hide a pen! So you put them on, take the pen out and write happy thoughts. In these difficult times I would like to have a pair of such glasses that I could put on each time things felt a little too much to handle. So rather than brooding one would just perch the glasses on ones nose and think happy thoughts. But all this is chimera and these glasses are out of reach so one has to invent ones' own happy pink glasses. That is what I am trying to do.

Life is a blend of good and not so good - do not want to use the word bad - occurrences. The good ones we accept as our due, but the not so good ones trigger off a slew of negative feelings: hurt, disappointment, anger and even resentment. This happens all along our lives. It could be a childish whim not fulfilled, poor marks in an exam, a love story gone wrong, an unfair dressing down at work, a friend's betrayal, a loved ones health: the list is endless. We feel upset and let down.

Each of us has our own coping strategies, which can vary from time to time. When I use to get hurt as a child and even later, my father always recalled his 'big picture' theory. Life was a big picture full of hues some dark and some bright and colourful. Only God, whoever that was, saw the picture in its entity; we only saw little pieces of it and sometimes those bits were the dark blotches. One simply had to remember that life was movement and that these dark patches would pass. He would also sometimes add that even the dark speckles had a reason we could not see or know so we had to accept them with the same gratitude as we accepted the colourful ones. It was a bit difficult for a child to think of having to thank that someone for unhappiness but somehow papa's words were soothing and always made things better. I must admit that I have often resorted to the big picture theory it times of strife.

One other coping strategy I have adopted sometimes is trying to imagine the worst-case scenario and ask myself if I have the strength to withstand it. If I do, then the rest becomes easy. It has worked many times for me in the past and got me out of difficult impasses.

Happy pink glasses are not glasses that make you see life in a rosy hue, but ways of making things easier knowing that nothing is static. Life is a dynamic process where each experience makes you a better and perhaps wiser being.

The past days, months and even more than a year must be an enormous dark smear on my big picture, one that I still cannot see the end off, though I must admit that it has cleared a little bit since we have been able to identify the cause of R's ill health. And even with all odds on our side, it will still be a while till we can see the sun shine again in our lives. As for the worst scenario theory, I will not venture in that direction this time.

My happy pink glasses simply show me the day we would have moved out of the dark into the light.

Monday, 9 September 2013

CELEBRATING GANESH

Every morning I sit at the small alter outside my room to say my prayers. The alter is the same one my parents prayed at. It is an eclectic mix of idols that have grown over time, each one of us adding their own. If you look carefully you would also realise that some are of different faiths. Among them, and maybe one of the oldest ones is a soapstone Ganesh. This morning it being Ganesh Chaturthi, I chanted a special prayer to this idol. It is only much later in the day that I realised that this idol and I shared a 'birthday'. It is strange how memories are coming back these days. Though I prayed everyday in front of this idol, I had completely forgotten how we were linked and how special it was in my life. I would like to share this story.

When Mama was pregnant of me, things were very tense as two years earlier Mama had lost her first born, my brother. She had a special statue of Goddess Parvati[57] and use to pray to it every morning and every evening. A day or so before my birth, when she went to touch the feet of the statue it fell apart. Probably a maid had broken it and just put it back together. But for mama it was a bad omen and she was in tears and devastated. Papa did not know what to do. We were in communist Prague and finding a Hindu idol was not the easiest of things. But his love for mama was so intense and irrational that he promised to find her a Parvati before the end of the day.

---

[57] Hindu Goddess, Shiva's consort

Papa went from antiquary to antiquary looking for the Goddess. After a very long search he found a soapstone Ganesh in the back room of a small shop, lying on the floor and covered with dust. He brought it back and told my mother that he could not find Parvati but found her son and that He would protect the unborn child.

I was born some hours later and though there were some problems, both Ma and I survived. Mama placed a small coral pendant of Ganesh around my neck and I wore one for many years. I was simply told he was my brother and would protect me always. Today, after many years I remembered this link. Serendipity at work again! I must admit that I had forgotten it as life took its course. I would like to believe remembering my Ganesh Bhaiya[58] on this blessed day is a sign that all will be well.

---

[58] Brother in Hindi

Tuesday, 10 September 2013

AFTER THE SILENCE.... IS MUSIC

After silence, that which comes nearest to expressing the inexpressible is music wrote Huxley[59]. Imagine my delight when I heard the sound of the piano waft through the house yesterday late afternoon. Though the notes were a little hesitant the touch was R's undoubtedly. He had had a visitor during his visiting hours (5 to 7pm) and I was discussing some office work with the girls downstairs. After his visitor left he decided to sit at his piano and play. I ran up not believing my ears. But there he was struggling with one his favourite tunes. I was overjoyed, as he had not touched the piano for many months. It was nothing short of a miracle for me.

Music has always been part of our lives, the only bone of contention being how loud it should be played! But yesterday nothing mattered but the fact that R was playing again. There was a time when you could not stop R playing. I sheepishly recall the times when I almost resented it. How foolish I was. I only understood this when he stopped playing and the silence in the house was eerie particularly during the hours he normally played. In the morning before setting out to work and in the evenings. The hesitant yet magical notes that floated throughout the house expressed everything I wanted to hear.

One thing is certain: I will never stop R playing his beloved Piano!

---

[59] Aldous Huxley Music at Night 1931

Tuesday, 10 September 2013

MEMORIES AREN'T STORED IN THE HEART OR THE HEAD

Jodi Picoult[60] wrote about memories being stored in spaces between two people. I guess this is the very first time in my life I have been housebound in my home with my loved one. I told you cancer has its good 'side effects'! I never spent so much time ambling around rooms and actually looking at things that have lived in this space for decades. Somehow the house talks to me and I listen and write everything down, as I know this is a onetime experience.

I spent time in the dining room today, just imbibing memories. I think it is grand enough to be called that. Actually it became our dining space circa 1994 when we remodelled the house after my parents' demises. Today it is the place where we sit every evening to share a meal. The room is again an eclectic mix of objects and things gathered during many lifetimes and put together as best possible. From mama's larger than usual dining table, to her old sideboard (bought circa 1969 when we had little money and sun mica was the flavour of the time); from R's two precious antique cabinets to his almost regal chandelier; from family pictures to paintings bought in Cambodia circa 1962; from a Meissen fruit bowl to golf shaped salt and pepper cellars; from Prague crystal objects to poor quality candles that did

---

60   Jodi Picoult; Vanishing Acts

not withstand the Delhi summer and look more like a Dali creation then regular candles in an antique silver candle stand, this space has it all. The cabinet also has our wedding picture where I look so different that someone even asked once if it was R's fist wife!

But when the house was just built or I should say completed after a long protracted set of problems this space was an open terrace and did remain one for quite some time. Before my marriage, we often slept on the terrace in summer and it was a unique experience that one has had to give up. Every evening the terrace was watered (there was no water shortage then) to cool it and then beds were place dorm style with one standing fan to blow some air should the night become too still. My cousin sisters use to live with us and we were quite a merry lot. Papa preferred sleeping indoors. He was quite 'formal' in certain ways. Would you believe me if I told you that it took Mama and I years to convince him that Delhi summer was not quite the place to wear a three-piece suit and a bowler hat. If anyone dropped by to visit, Papa would immediately rush to his room and don his suit that always hung on his dumb butler. Slowly he would graduate to the then in fashion safari suits and kurta pajamas. So sleeping out was a no- no even if it was scorching in the room. At that time coolers did not exist and we did not own an AC as they had all been sold to complete the house.

But the rest of us girls loved our night under the stars. We would have our transistors (no Walkman or MP3s those days) and tune it to our favourite programmes. Mondays and Fridays were the two nights when All India Radio aired western pop music request programmes, which were my favourites; otherwise it was Vivid Bharati and Radio Ceylon. In the morning it was the flies that woke you up and you would get off the cot and rush to your respective room to finish the night. Those were some days!

Then came my wedding, which took place in this very house. You would not believe me if I told you that R spent the first night after our wedding ceremony sleeping on this very terrace with Ma, as the bidai (the ceremony when you officially leave your parental home) was scheduled for the next morning. I slept with my friend in my room. R always loves telling this story. After marriage R and I lived on the first floor of the house and the terrace saw many merry moments when friends dropped in or we had a party. R had is hole in one party here! But then we moved out after Parul[61] was born, as the flat was too small.

Some years later, Papa built us two extra rooms and we moved back after Shamika[62] was born. The girls had a great time splashing in their inflatable pool. The terrace remained one till we came back from our posting in Prague. That is when R decided to cover the terrace with a slanting roof and have a circular wooden staircase climbing up to a TV cum music room. It was very beautiful but somehow the energies did not feel right and I was never comfortable and happy in those days. R must have cursed the day when I met someone who told me about Vastu[63] and fell hook line and sinker for this ancient science. The slanted roof had to be broken and the spiral staircase removed. That is when the terrace took its final shape and an extra room was added upstairs. I felt better but R took a long time forgiving me for my rather expensive idiosyncrasy. There would be more alterations after Papa's death but those were needed. The once open terrace became our dining room! Space does not change per se but time gives it life and thus memories.

There was a time when this space got invaded and I found myself consigned to the tiniest corner possible. The house lost its heart and I found myself roaming aimlessly, avoiding certain spaces and feeling an outsider. I think that for those few years even my parents' souls took leave of absence. I will not delve on the reason at this moment. The hurt is not healed enough to write about it dispassionately. I left it to the one upstairs to set things right because I had given up.

He or She heard the unsaid prayer or petition and the trespassers left and slowly the house smiled again. But it would take a terrible blow or should I say another intruder a.k.a Mr Hodgkin to open my eyes and soul to the poignant and moving memories every corner of the house concealed, memories that needed to be told as my legacy to my children.

When I look at the dining space today, I realise that there is not a single object that I have bought and placed. Everything is either my parents' or chosen by R or a gift. R asked me recently why I had never added my

---

[61]   My firstborn

[62]   My younger daughter

[63]   **Vastu** shastra is an ancient science of architecture and construction.

imprint on the house and I had no answer. But I have one today. My trace is impregnated in each brick of the house, and is not any physical object but an almost ethereal bouquet of feelings that can only be sensed by those who see with their hearts.

Wednesday, 11 September 2013

THE OBSESSIVE COMPULSORY PLANNER AND THE TUMBLING NUMBERS

R is doing great and I just pray it continues like this. Scared to say more lest the Gods get jealous again. I am simply busy being grateful!

Now let us carry on. I wrote to a dear soul, and one who knows me almost better than I know myself that I had sort of settled into a pattern and she wrote back saying that *as an obsessive compulsive planner and scheduler, I am happy to hear that you have found a rhythm, it must make the difficult tasks a little easier.* She did hit the nail on its head. It has been two months and 7 days since we came to know about R's cancer. The previous 12 months had gone by running like a chicken without a head trying to figure out what was wrong and that was exhausting as there was no way even a planner like me could conjure any kind of pattern or structure. I guess the reason why I was so drained out was that for those 12 months I had to live out of the box.

But now since treatment has begun I have finally managed to conjure a kind of structure in my life though it is tenuous and somewhat erratic. My life moves in segments of 15 days. If day one is chemo this is how it goes: day 1 chemo each one has had different side effects so one has to be prepared for every thing possible (rambling, fever, nausea etc.), day 2 to 5 are quieter and we follow the time table I have worked out that starts from 6 am and ends at 9 pm. We follow this to the T, as it seems to be working. My only role is to ensure that all elements and ingredients are available. It gives me a break as it takes me out of the house. This of course is followed from day 1 to 14 so I do not really mind if the staff 'forgets' to tell me something is missing. Day 6 is blood test and playing the tumbling number games that requires you to wait the whole day to get the results of the blood counts. These are often scary. In the last case the WBC which were at 19000 one day before chemo tumbled to 3800 yesterday evening. So you know that immunity is at its nadir. We have even had them at 1400! Day 7, 8, 9 are back to the timetable. Day 11, 12, 13 are the ones when the booster injections have to be given and on day 14 we have the blood tests and the day long wait for the numbers. Day 15 is chemo again! And every day there is the constant vigil: touching the head to see if there is no fever, asking questions and more questions. And in between all this I have to fit in scraps of my old life.

THE UGLY LITTLE CAT AND THE BUDDING ARTIST'S NATURE MORTE

On the shelf in the drawing room, amidst a plethora of valuables, sits a strange looking ceramic object. It is actually a cat - I call it ugly - but to my parents it was the most precious of their possession and always had a place of honour in the drawing rooms of all the grand homes we lived in till it landed in its final resting place on the wall display of the drawing room of this house. The mystery is that it is the first piece of pottery I made when I was five years old. When they left this world I did not have the heart to put it away. Somehow I feel it to be the most poignant reminder of how much mama and papa loved me. When I look at it, I remember the extent of their love and feel their comforting presence around me. Strange how those who love you express their feelings in unique ways. This is all you have left when they leave. I wish one had the ability of understanding this when they were still around and giving them the biggest hug I could. But all you have left are memories, and it is impossible to keep those alive no matter how hard you try. I guess my kids will throw this ugly cat when I am gone! This cat came to life in 1956 in Paris

Fast forward to 2013 St Louis, Missouri. A child made a painting or drawing for his Nanou and Nani and the painting was mailed all the way to Delhi. It has a place of honour on the wall of our bedroom. It is the work of art of my darling Agastya and is a nature morte. The theme is a plate of food. We went gaga over it when it came and it took me no time to get it framed. I then removed what was hanging at that place and hung this treasure worth all the Picassos and Monet in the universe. We look at it R and I when we miss the little bloke though thanks to the magic of Skype we see him often. But I know that it will remain hung there till we breathe our last. I also suspect that many other paintings will be removed from the walls of this house and to be replaced by Agastya's masterpieces much to the horror of his mom. It is all again a matter of seeing with your heart and I am a master at that.

Wednesday, 11 September 2013

IT HAD TO BE TOLD

I met someone today, an acquaintance of sorts. I had not met her for a long time and of course in the course of conversation I told her about old Mr Hodgkin. Imagine my utter surprise when her whole demeanour changed and she held both my hands and with almost teary years told me how sorry she was. It was almost as she was presenting her condolences. I beat a quick retreat! Gosh it was eerie! On the way back in my famous three-wheeler I did not pick my book up as usual but let my thoughts run wild. Why is it that certain medical conditions entail almost bizarre reactions? If you say cancer people think death; if you say AIDS people think loose character. Such are social stigmas! I refuse this kind of reactions and will shun anyone who proffers them. I do get phone calls when I realise people are surprised at the matter of fact way with which I answer as I would if R had had flu or any other ailment. This I know is the only way we will come out of it. Whatever the outcome, I want our lives to be flooded with good energies and laughter! Anything else is verboten!

As I have promised to be honest to a fault in this blog, I have to share something that happened to me a few years back. I think catharsis is needed here if I truly want to walk the talk. This must have been around 2007. I found a white patch on my inner arm and showed it to my doc who initially thought it was some fungus kind of a thing and gave me some ointment to apply. But the patch refused to go away. Finally my doc persuaded me to have a biopsy and it turned out to be Hansen's disease better known as leprosy. I was mortified. I had visions of the Middle Ages and bells and white crosses. I refused to share it with anyone and withdrew in a shell till I got an all clear 8 months later. What a great and relieving feeling to have it our in the open. A true cleansing process for me. I am sure that if I had taken it in my stride, as leprosy is a bacteria much like TB I would saved myself and my family a lot of pain and maybe we would have healed quicker as I would have been free of negativity.

One cannot expect to have a life free of any problem. Time and again certain diseases are given a larger than life status that they do not deserve. Is it the medical fraternity who is to blame or the society? A question that begs to be answered. But one thing is certain: a positive attitude that minimises any problem is bound to help in healing.

That is the way I want to look at R's cancer. A minor irritant that has come our way and that we will deal with as best we can. And rather then zeroing on the negative effects we will count the positive ones and there are many. The biggest one is the bonding of us as a couple and as a family. Next is the abundance of love we have got from the world over. Then comes friendships that have been cemented, friendships that would have just passed us by had this fellow not landed in our lives. Come to think of it there has been far more good things than bad ones!

Thursday, 12 September 2013

WHAT THE STARS HAVE FORETOLD

Some of you may or may not believe in astrology. I did not for a long time and even found it ludicrous when my mom dared suggest R and I get our astrological charts matched. It is one of the rare times I must have told Ma to shut up and leave us alone. I had decided to marry someone because I had fallen in love and no stars would make me change my mind. When my elder child was born she fell extremely ill and we feared for her life, I think Ma must have surreptitiously gone to her pet astrologer and found out that all would be well; it was just a bad moment that would pass. Then I forgot all about as(s)trology as it never concerned me and anyway in mind it was akin to mumbo jumbo. But then, I think something happened. I don't quite remember what and I was extremely worried. A friend suggested I go and see her 'astrologer'. When she saw my reaction she quickly added: *he is just a regular guy like us!*

I did go and meet him and almost fell of my chair when I saw one of the most handsome men I have come across wearing a pair of jeans and a T-shirt. I think I had expected a dhoti-clad person with a turban! This 'astrologer' had studied at St Stephens, got umpteen gold medals and then studied Sanskrit and Astrology in Benares (no one says Varanasi). He could quote Baudelaire and Rimbaud, and was engaged to a lovely French girl. He spent a lot of time explaining that astrology was a science and if one was able to draw someone's chart, then one could predict anything, even as trivial as a car breakdown! But for this you had to view the 'astrologer' as

ANOURADHA BAKSHI

a doctor and be willing to answer precise questions with utmost honesty. Many viewed astrologers as 'magicians' or 'star gazers' and wanted to be dazzled. So this young man, he must be a couple of years younger than me, worked out my chart and calmed my worries. I would meet him years later in Paris when I was again going through a very bad patch after my parents' deaths and he again told me how long it would take to get out of the dark. Somehow when you know that your worries are for a limited time, even a longish one, you have something to look forward to. That is the way my friend looks at astrology. He does not prescribe 'remedies' like many do, at best a mantra to be chanted or a small puja performed. Since, whenever we have been going through rough patches and thanks to the Internet, I have always been in touch and got my worries allayed.

So you will not be surprised if I told you that when R became sick I got in touch with him. He has never sugar coated anything and this time he told me that R was going through a very bad patch but would come out of it. I was relieved but what still worries me is that according to him, the worst months are October to December 2013. When I asked him what to do, he told me to try and build up R's immunity to the maximum before October.

So even as I marvelled at the fact that R is doing great, the next three months loom large and I am truly worried. So much can go wrong, a simple infection, flu, anything can come our way and how on earth does one keep these at bay. What the stars have foretold is not what I would have prayed for, but I also know that it is only a matter of three months and the sun will shine again, bright and warm. It is just a matter of taking it one day at a time, one week at a time and we will see the light at the end of what looks today like a very long dark tunnel.

I also know that there is a Little prince who lives on a star and sees with his heart, who will sprinkle his magic dust and conjure a miracle.

Saturday, 14 September 2013

THAT CAN SCARCELY BE CONTROLLED

For the past days an old forgotten song by Simon and Garfunkel has been ringing in my ears. I do not know how many of you remember Patterns.[64] But in this song S & G talk about the defiant side of our existence.

That is exactly the way I feel. The orderly, well-planned life of a control freak has surreptitiously mutated into a maze full of surprises, some good, some not so good and some frankly manic. Every time the control freak in me heaves a sigh of relief and dares to think that things have fallen into place, a vicious little troll who seems to have made it its life mission to ensure I do not have a moment of rest springs up from his dark cave with another dare. I can almost see him laughing away at my discomfiture as I run helter-skelter picking up the pieces of my still tenuous new seemingly orderly life and fitting them back in the boxes I have created whilst thinking of new boxes to contain the new challenge.

As if Mr Hodgkin was not enough we have Ms Dengue to please. No it is not R who has the crazy fever but a lovely young volunteer who is staying with us at home. My heart goes out to this child who came to volunteer with our kids at Project Why and finds herself in bed with this ghastly ailment. So more blood test for this child, more Googling to find ways to make it easier and of course the fear that it may affect R. So tons of mosquito repellent has been bought and R now smells like a citronella garden!

---

[64]   Patterns; Paul Simon 1966

As I key in these words I am wondering what my little troll is planning to startle me with next. The only way to deal with all this is to laugh because otherwise I would be ready to jump without a chute and see if I have the wings to fly.

Monday, 16 September 2013

BUSY BEING GRATEFUL

The last few days have been peaceful. Blissfully so. R has been well and except for his wincing during his booster shot today, which seemed more painful than usual, he has been in good spirits and almost looking life his old self. The only difference is that there is an elephant in the room, however much we would want to ignore it, and we are all in our own way waiting for chemo 6 as it is only after that that a scan will be done to see if things have improved. But though it is chemo week, we have sort of fallen into a routine, and if there are no bolts out of the blue, the ship is cruising on calm waters. However there is no way of jumping back into your old routine as one would have imagined, as till the ship lands on safe shores these lulls will have to be filled in novel ways.

So for the past two days I have been in deep thinking mode. Somehow at moments like these you tend to look at things with bright new eyes. I am quite amazed at the fact that my reaction to this 'terrible' occurrence in our lives has been quite mind blowing for all the good reasons. I would have expected tears, anger, recriminations and self-pity. The *why me* syndrome. But what did happen was the exact opposite. For some time I had thought I had frozen my tears and put them on hold for some time, but the some time seems to be everlasting making me believe that this is it, and there will be no tears as this time I have chosen my individual way of handling the situation. This Zen like attitude is totally the opposite of who I have been for the first six decades of my life: mercurial, moody, banging doors and shedding tears - the only child syndrome. So what has changed?

If I look deeply at things and at lessons from the past, it seems that I have finally understood and accepted papa's gratitude approach. For years I could not truly understand what he meant when he said in prayer: *I am grateful for the bad things you have sent my way and know you will steer me out in the best way possible.* Would you believe me if I said: I am grateful for Mr Hodgkin's temporary stopover. But as I write these words I am truly grateful and accepting. I know He will drive Mr H away. I also know that He sent him for a reason. So today let us forget the bad side effects like losing hair and tumbling blood counts and look at all the things I am busy being grateful for.

To begin with, this is the FIRST time in four decades that R and I have had time together, even more than in our courting days. The courting days were filled with the passion and exuberance of the young; these are gentle and tranquil ones, when words are not needed and just holding hands is sufficient to say it all. This is also the first time we have shared the hurt and pain we inflicted on each other and begged for forgiveness that was given without a word. What was tragic is that this hurt was not because our love had diminished, but because of others who demanded their pound of flesh creating an unnecessary and hurtful action reaction situation. How foolish we were. But then we also realised that it was time to bury the past and look at the twilight of our lives hoping it will be an Indian summer. I guess without Mr H this may not have happened or happened too late. For this I am ever grateful.

The other wonderful side effect of this unwanted guest had been discovering friends that one had not bothered to keep in touch with, because we did not have the time, or felt there was still so much of it (time) left. Today there are people I wake up at 5 am or even before, people who unlike me like to sleep late. And if by a case of force majeure - no Internet, no electricity- the mail does not go, I get a SMS asking what happened. One of the most precious side effects of Mr H has been forging a new bond with someone I had met long ago and immediately warmed up to. But life took over and we lost touch though we lived barely a mile away. Today we exchange mails and SMSs at the drop of a hat and meet for our weekly cuppa of cha. Never mind if it is at noon! It makes it unique.

Mr H has also made me aware of the innumerable number of people who have reached out to me once they knew of my present plight. Some I have never met and yet I get comments to my posts (I really appreciate them and they are a lifeline) and an abundance of hugs, virtual ones, but nonetheless hugs! I never knew there was so much goodwill in the universe. I again feel humble and grateful.

But there is more. Mr H has made me stop and take a pause from my earlier life, much of which was crafted to meet emotional needs that had slowly disappeared leaving earlier defence mechanisms and coping strategies in place. One is a creature of habits. I now realised they had become obsolete. I did not need to slink down stairwells or lock myself in my little office that had become the only space I could call mine in my own home! How ludicrous it sounds but it was true for more years than one could imagine. It is a friend who looking beyond faces to the wall behind made me aware of *my much lived in, slightly worn*, with *each piece with a story to share* house. I cannot begin to tell you what this meant. It felt like a caged bird whose door had been opened and who could now fly free from room to room and look with her heart at all that she had obliterated for so long. This was a precious gift not only for me but for my progeny as otherwise all the stories would have been burnt on my funeral pyre. I am deeply grateful for this serendipitous freedom.

Between all this, Mr H looks more like an ant than an elephant in the room. An ant that will die its natural death sooner than one imagines! But it brought with it so many wonderful side effects that I find myself having to say that I am grateful for his coming as otherwise the best part of my life would have never happened and I would have remained locked behind the almost impregnable walls I had built to protect myself against foes that had vanished long ago.

So I can I not be busy being grateful!

Wednesday, 18 September 2013

8 TO GO....

When Agastya[65] and Utpal[66], my two boys, were home this summer, Utpal, who is quite a skating star, participated in a skating race and his pal and bro Agastya went to cheer him and root for him. Utpal won the race and got his gold medal, Agastya clapped the loudest. But this is not the point of this post! The race was organised by a small club and the MC was a funny man with sort of orange hair and a singsong way of speaking. The track being small, the contestants had a certain amount of rounds to take that varied according to the age. The funny MC use to shout or rather sing these numbers that could go from 7 to go to none to go. Both the boys found that very amusing and for the remaining days of their stay with me used the 4 to go with glee for almost anything they did.

I find myself in a similar position though I am totally at sea about the number of rounds I need to take before I can hear the *one to go* or better the *none to go*. And I do not how many falls I will have before the last round of this race which is actually very close to a roller skate race as you need to be a master in balance to survive! If we go by the oncologist then we have 8 to go as of today and 7 to go after tomorrow's chemo! I must admit that the

---

[65] My grandson

[66] a.ka Popples, my legal ward and Little Prince, the subject of my book Dear Popples

last 4 have been long haul and just the thought of two times that is nothing short of daunting. But does one have a choice?

After chemo 6 there will a PET Scan to assess how well it has all gone.

Today's news is another side effect: nails! R's are turning blue. A quick search on the net said it was 'normal'. Nails may not only change colour but become brittle and can also become a source of the much dreaded infections. The only solution offered is something called 'cooling gloves' but I cannot find any in India so maybe will carry a few bags of frozen peas in an ice box and put them on his hand during chemo. I do not care about his nails becoming blue or red or whatever colour, but the infection is a no-no. The last time I made him suck on ice throughout the chemo and he did not get any blisters or mouth sores. So let us hope the frozen peas helps with the nails.

Gosh I hate chemo. I hate the idea of a poison being legally poured into a human body. I hate the idea of having to kill good cells to be able to destroy the cancer ones. The scan better show me some darned good results to make me accept its terrible side effects. Apologies to all those who swear by chemo but the intense research I have done on line has revealed many options that have proved to be successful. In R's case the decision was difficult as everyone, even my Tibetan doc, approved of chemo for Hodgkin's. But if I were ever to contract this disease I would stay away from all this poison and go for alternative therapy. And I would be as stubborn as Ma!

But I am playing the game by the rules for R. And it d***** well work or there will be hell to pay!

Thursday, 19 September 2013

CHEMO FIVE...AND THE BIG RED ICE BOX

Today is chemo five day and as always I find myself not sleeping and up well before dawn cracks over the city, even before the early bird chirps. This has been the case each and every time. One would have thought one would get used to it, but nada, not me! Actually what I would call chemo stress (CS) begins a day before. From the day we discovered the presence of Mr Hodgkin, confirmed and reconfirmed, chemo days have been the worst for R and every time I have tried to do my very best to try and alleviate issues. The first after chemo hours were terrible, as R had reacted to the steroid they gave him as part of the pre-med protocol.

We can now laugh about his time and space travel, but believe you me, it was scary to see him insisting we were in 1972 and he had had lunch with his pals at the Golf club particularly as he was aggressive, something R never is. We discovered the culprit and made sure it was eliminated from his pre-meds shots. I forgot one thing. On chemo 1 we got caught in the 'recliner' game. You see the day care has a certain amount of beds and the rest is what the hospital calls recliners, but I call back breakers. For almost 4 hours if not more, poor R and his bad back were plonked in a recliner which is a badly designed seating contraption that kills your back. We did manage a bed for the last 2 hours but the recliner had taken its toll. So we set out to find how to get a 'bed' and have been successful for the past 3 chemos and hope we make it today. It means getting there before anyone else and going through the tedious paperwork in time. Maybe that is why my body clock wakes me so early!

Then let us talk food. The food in the hospital is inedible. Period! One would have expected a hospital to have at least edible and healthy food but no. Their motto is save, save, save and charge, charge, charge! So be it breakfast - the worst bread - or lunch - strange looking slush and chewy rotis - you better stay away. The problem is that you are not allowed to bring food from home. You could buy food from the many commercial outlets they have, but they are all fast food joints. This beats me, as I would think fast food would be a no-no in a hospital. Money again.

So for the past 4 chemos R ate either the hospital food or the counter bought food and was sick. I presume eating organic for months now makes your body react to chemicals. So he has been nauseous and chemo days have been no eating days for R as he refuses any food when he comes back home. So this time I am smuggling organic peanut butter sandwiches made with organic bread and egg sandwiches made with organic eggs!

After chemo 3, R got a few blisters in spite of all my voodoo. I found out that making him such ice while the chemo was on could sort the problem so went to chemo 4 with ice and lo and behold it worked.

Post chemo 4 we saw his nails getting bluish. Search, search, search! Now they have something called cold gloves on the net but could not find any in India so am taking two bags of frozen peas in an ice box and will apply them on his hands while the 3 drugs that could have that side effect are forced into his system. Let us hope I get passed the security guy with my big red icebox!

ANOURADHA BAKSHI

Friday, 20 September 2013

CHEMO FIVE A PSYCHEDELIC TRIP

R is looking very dapper in his jeans and black T-shirt not to forget the trim silhouette as we set off for chemo 5. Could break hearts or so I would like to believe. Still has mine! Sadly that is not the way he looked when we left at 2 pm. The seven hours turned out to be a real psychedelic trip where the letters LSD (illegal) were replaced by ABVD (legal). Just to give you a picture ABVD are preceded by what is called pre-meds after the painful moment when the needle is placed in the port. However this morning the needle did not hurt as much as the last time and everyone was happy and hoped the trip would be a good one. We had arrived, R, Dharmendra[67] (who has been a rock) and self with our big red icebox stuffed with ice and two bags of frozen pears, my big bag with carefully concealed peanut butter sandwiches, the iPad and the book R was reading.

The pre-meds were given and we were waiting for the pharmacist who makes the deadly cocktail. R who had had his normal breakfast stated he was hungry and wolfed the first sandwich. I decided to come home as all seemed spot on and have a break and get him some lunch. Got a call informing me that the A had begun and the doctor was expected so rushed back with two egg paranthas hidden in my bag hoping that the smell would not attract the attention of the grim security guard. A was still on and R

---

[67] A Project Why colleague but more than a son to me

wanted sandwich number two! I was thrilled. It looked like we would have a happy trip.

The Doctor came and we had a nice chat and he found everything in order. A was over and it was time for B. I filled a glass with ice and R decided to watch and episode of his favourite 50s sitcom: The Honeymooners[68]. Dharmendra and I had some project matters to discuss and we did while keeping and eye on the drip. It must have been past 11 am. R stopped watching for a bit and wanted his lunch. So we gave him one parantha. Soon it was time for drug V before a short toilet break. We all resumed our positions, R with his movie, and Dharmendra and I with our discussion. Eyes of course were on the drip. Around 12.15 or so it was time for yet another change D to V. V is the dreaded one as it is the longest: almost two hours. But all seemed well as we tripped along. Parantha two was also consumed. We were hoping against hope that it would be a good trip. The episode ended and instead of putting on a new one, R put the iPad away and started looking different. No smile. That is when I remembered the peas that were meant to be put on his hand to keep the nails from turning blue.

I got them out and thought it would make smile if not laugh but he refused to put his hand at first and did after a lot of coaxing. That is when we realised that this was turning into a bad trip. The next 90 minutes were difficult. As V dripped into his veins, I could see his body language changing and his face contorting. Every question was answered in a brusque manner if at all. He refused the ice, the peas and even my poor jokes. I just watched him helpless, looking at the big bottle filled with the V and willing the drops to move faster. But it was a losing battle. Dharmendra and I watched helplessly. Our attempts at conversation with R were futile. Time took a Bergsonian perception and hung heavy on our heads. I asked Dharmendra to complete all the formalities so that we could leave as soon as V was over and head home. R started feeling nauseous so I gave him a medicine I was carrying in my bag. We managed to be out by 2 pm and blissfully there was little traffic and we were home in 20 minutes. R was miserable and just lay down. I lay quietly beside him, watching his disturbed

---

[68] American sitcom 1955

sleep. When I felt him he was hot. His temperature was 100.7. I called the doctor. He told me not to worry and to give him Paracetamol. I did. I just hope he feels better and has something to eat and a sound sleep.

Tomorrow is another day!

Sunday, 22 September 2013

MY NEW ALPHABET: ABVDBEACOPP

Chemo 5 is over but with it has come a series of questions that we may have to address at a given time. As a 'control freak' - that is what my elder one calls me - or an organised person - as I would like to call myself - I like being prepared for any eventuality, however bad. First of all let me bring you up to date. Chemo 5 was a an eye opener in more ways than one and also a glimpse of what awaits us. The stars have foretold a bad patch starting October and I have been scratching my brain trying to figure out what it could be. Well chemo 5 gave me a lead. Chemo 1 was bad because of the steroid in his pre meds, but 2,3 and 4 were not too bad. He came out of them after a good night's sleep. We had of course removed the steroid. Now chemo 5 has been strange. It has been more than 48 hours and R has not really come out of it yet. Poor appetite, lethargy and what is scaring me is his dark mood. I hope it is not another depression setting in. He has been telling everyone who called that this chemo has got the better of him. Not a good sign. Will call his therapist and see if he does not need some sessions.

But that is not all. As we are reaching midway if it is 12 and three quarter way if it is 8 chemos, I wanted to know from the doctor what we could expect. I like knowing my best-case scenario and worst-case scenario in all situations as a good control freak! A PET Scan is scheduled after chemo 6 and will reveal all. So if things are super better we stop at 6, if things are better but not as much as one would have wanted we go on to 12, and if things have not improved then we need to change protocols so from ABVD we move to BEACCOP. In other terms from a cocktail of 4 lethal drugs to one having 7! Phew! Now when you read in a medical review in the Lancet[69]: *Until now, the advantage shown for the BEACOPP regimen was improved disease control, with better progression-free survival (PFS) than is seen with ABDV. However, this came at the expense of more toxicity, including a suggestion that there may be an increased risk for secondary cancers,* your blood runs cold. The article is disturbing as it does not give a clear cut answer but then it is in sync with chemotherapy as a whole where people talk of remission and survival in months and days, and where 15 days of extra life devoid of any quality is a statistic to celebrate. In an answer to the authors of the above article, Dr Longo[70] in the Journal of Clinical Oncology states: *it is my understanding that escalated BEACOPP is sufficiently toxic that patients older than 60 years are considered too old to tolerate it.* Dr Longo ends his article by saying: *patients need to be fully informed of the various pathways to cure, their likelihood of success, and short- and long-term toxicity costs of each approach. A well-informed patient can participate fully in the decision about which path to choose.* Sadly that is not always the case.

To many it may seem premature to already think so much in advance. But I have my reasons. First of all I know that as soon as the results of the scan are out there will be immense pressure to take a decision as we are in the middle of a chemo protocol and would have to decide in a matter of days. I also know that the oncologist will be pushing us to accept a change of protocol based on facts and figures. But we are not talking of a patient amongst others, but of R. What makes it terrible for me is that he trusts me implicitly. I need to be worthy of his trust.

For the past two days, after his last chemo he has been feeling low and somehow the change of colour in his nails has been a watershed moment for him as he can see the toxicity of the chemo drugs. He has been looking at his fingers and toes over and over again and been feeling upset and down. Now the BEACOPP has far worst side effects than ABVD and I do not

---

[69] http://www.thelancet.com/journals/lanonc/article/
PIIS1470-2045(13)70341-3/abstract

[70] Valter Longo Professor in Gerontology, University of Southern California
http://fasten.tv/en/vortraege/longo

know if my brews and potions will keep him away from the side effects. I do not think he will be able to cope with those without sinking into depression.

Mama refused chemotherapy because she did not want the side effects or the short remission(s). She wanted to live life on her terms and though she suffered in the last month of her life, she enjoyed her last year and papa's pampering. Papa trusted me and I trusted the doctors who told me he would be up and about in a matter of weeks. He died in a matter of weeks robbed of his dignity.

I was seduced then, and was seduced in July 2013 when I accepted chemo because people I trusted told me it would work. They only told me one chapter of the story. I was not given a chance to try the alternative therapies that seem far more humane and stood to reason.

I do not like the R I have seen for the last 2 days! I do not want his life to be reduced to ghastly side effects, which he cannot tolerate. Anyway, if I am to believe what Dr Longo writes, then BEACOPP is not good for anyone above 60 and he is 64!

I do not want to be seduced again and take a decision that I may regret and that will make R suffer. If ABVD has not given the results that one hoped for, then I would like to stop chemo at no 8 and try alternative therapies full on. Most of all I would want to get out of this symphony of life in slabs of fifteen days from chemo to chemo. I would like to see his immunity go up and get out of the house and enjoy the time we have left. That time period is only known by the one upstairs. The only thing that would change is that R and I would live every day of the remainder of our lives as if it was the last day. What a ball it will be. And the only alphabet I want to use is God's Alphabet. The only way I want to see R is with a smile.

Sunday, 22 September 2013

TO BE TRUSTED IS A GREATER COMPLIMENT THAN BEING LOVED

To be trusted is a greater compliment than being loved wrote George MacDonald[71]. On October 20th 1974 R and I 'formalised' our love officially though our journey together had begun well before. We both knew that love had to be based on trust but in those days and even later the word trust was not put to test. It was understood, may have been relegated to some corner of ones mind waiting to be called upon. It is only yesterday that I felt the true tenor of this aspect of the relationship you share with someone.

It has been a difficult weekend as R took longer than usual to 'bounce' back and the (in) famous side effects of chemotherapy weighed upon both of us. Till date the happy potions and brews I concocted were spot on and we had kept side effects almost at bay. However this time it was different. I could sense R starting to feel fed up of this legal poisoning. We discussed options and tried to lighten the mood and chase the negative vibes that seemed to be more active than usual. Or was it that both of us were getting weary of this life in 15 days movements. I do not know. The famous PET scan is still 20 long days away. And that is when we may have to take decisions. We both know that! But my darling man has found the easy way

---

[71] George MacDonald (10 December 1824 – 18 September 1905) ; Scottish author, poet, and Christian minister

out. He simply said: *I trust you implicitly!* Voila! It was done. The ball was in my court and I had to find and be responsible for every decision henceforth. Easy peasy for R but a play in several acts and one protagonist for me.

To be trusted is a greater compliment than being loved. I feel humbled and scared. Never are such words more poignant than in times like the one I am going through. When me made a pledge, or rather many on that day almost 4 decades ago, we were young and in love and our world looked more like the one imagined by the Beatles in their song Lucy in the Sky with Diamonds[72] replete with marmalade skies. Nothing could mar our happiness and love. We were young and our dreams were fresh and immature. We could conquer the world if we wanted. And to make us believe this ludicrous chimera, everyone was on best behaviour; even those who later would try their utmost to hijack our love.

We had our turbulent times, our grey skies and bare trees. Spurred by others we even mouthed hurtful things to each other and banged many doors. But somewhere, the spark of love that had flared when we first met remained alight, even if at times it was a bare flicker. Lover conquers all it is said, and in our case it did. We had our share of elephants in the room and had to learn to live with them as best we could holding on to our love, even if at times it seemed impossible. But the Gods having tested us in their own inimitable way had mercy on us and the elephants vanished. Some mice are left but they are easy to deal with. But being together again came at a price. Today I have my man. Seems the Gods are testing me again. In the twilight of our love, I have been entrusted with his life and a host of difficult decisions the results of which are nothing short of frightening.

I wish I could be the girl in the snapshots of my wedding day, with the biggest smile stuck on my face. But that smile is only for young love. Mature and mellowed love is another thing altogether. The smile you give now bears the traces of every moment you have lived and may look jaded. Far from that, it is the smile of 40 years of loving and caring in spite of everything thrown at you. And when the one you smile at tells you he trusts you with his life, then you know that your love is of the kind that conquers all.

---

[72] Lucy in the sky with diamonds; Lennon Mc Cartney, Sgt Peppers Lonely Hearts Club Band, 1967

Monday, 23 September 2013

NOAH'S ROCK AND OUR BUCKET LIST

When all goes well, I may find myself sitting at what looks like the end of the world and gazing at the endless sky and calm seas. Just looking at a picture makes me travel, as I am probably the most enthusiastic armchair traveller. Life as a nomad in my childhood and teen years, and then in part of my married existence have taken away my desire to travel or even go out if not needed. And this time again the Gods had a plan as they gave the one who wanted to travel in space or at least be a pilot at age 10 after meeting Valentina Tereshkova, not just a fear but a terror of flying. A wicked ploy as one still has free tickets courtesy R's days in Air India. It does not end there. By making me a control freak who leads a life planned to the last second, travelling becomes anathema. Will you believe me if I told you I eat the same thing every day. I must one day share my schedule. It will astonish you. I guess I must have some sort of obsessive compulsive disorder so to my friends who beseech me to sleep longer, I need to say I just cannot. as, if I try even an extra 15 minutes makes me edgy!

A friend sent me a picture of Noah's rock. As I loose myself in the immensity of the sea under what could be called a *marmalade sky*, I am filled with a sense of peace and gratitude. I am sitting on Noah's rock and my thoughts begin to wander. I hold them for a second as I would like them to drift in the right direction as today I need a clear head with the ability to break out of the symphony in (C)ancer major and look at life beyond. The eureka moment was triggered by a conversation I had with a dear uncle who is playing the same symphony for almost a decade. When I shared R's mood over the week end which bordered on giving up, my uncle simply told me that what sees you through is the will to live to fulfil the unfinished tasks. I shared this with R and this morning we sat down and made our bucket list.

The one thing that is crucial and is on both our lists is making sure that S my younger one is settled and empowered before our final move. There are many options we need to discuss and we will now. I remember writing Dear Popples [73]when a child lost his home and went to boarding school at age 4. For me it was the right moment to share what I wanted to with him. I would like to quote a few lines from the first letter in the book: *As I sat down to write about you today, I sensed something had changed and that I needed to write to you and not about you. I realised that there were scads of things I wanted you to know but had not told you because there was no time, or because I thought there was still so much time; because you were too young to understand or simply because I was too tired to explain.* I feel the same today. Sending Popples to school was a heart wrenching experience. R's cancer is a heart and soul breaking one.

So R and I have to make our bucket lists. The common one is to settle S, make our wills wherein we protect the girls interests and make walking in our shoes easy for them. We may have demons to deal with and it is time we did it. I guess we both need to follow the Alcoholic Anonymous Steps 8 and 9 even if it is traumatic: *Make a list of all persons we had harmed, and became willing to make amends to them all and m*ake *direct amends to such people wherever possible, except when to do so would injure them or others.* This is the toughie.

R has only a family and some dear friends and colleagues. But for me it is a different game all together because I have another family, one I created myself and who have entrusted their dreams in me. It is easy to start an NGO and many do so because it is the in the thing to do, almost a page 3 sine-qua-non. I am not page 3 and do not aspire to that 'honour'. I created Project Why to fill the deep void I had sunk in after my parents' death. It took me 6 long years of emotional loss to find the way to live a full life again. Project Why was created to honour their memory and leave a trace

---

73   Dear Popples; Anouradha Bakshi, Undercover Productions; First edition (5 May 2008)

of our little ménage à trois that would disappear after me. I know that here again the Gods had a plan for me and that is why Project Why defies any definition and cannot be contained in a box!

Two Angels landed in my life and changed it forever. Manu[74] who showed me the way when I was lost, passed away gently having completed the reason he came to this planet. Utpal on the other hand is here to stay and has broken all the seemingly well-planned scenarios one crafted for him. Today he is part of our home as he is no body's child, a fate worse than an orphan as his mom just walked away. As he grows questions crop in his mind and we have weak answers if any. Today he is in a boarding school. But he will need mentors and a surrogate family, a network of friends and the skills to craft his future. Utpal always reminds me of the Little Prince[75] where he is the rose I am responsible for. So Utpal's morrows are high on my list.

But there is more on my bucket list and that is Project Why. Before I sing my finale, I want to build a small centre near the place where we run our women centre as it has a legal resettlement colony teeming with children. I need to sell the land we have and buy a smaller plot and build with the money left. Till now the money we raised was because of my writing and communicating skills. This is something I cannot pass on so we will need to make a corpus and trim the project to the size of the interest. Here I need a miracle. An Angel who would be willing to place a corpus that will not be ours, and leave the interest for us. But where do I find such an Angel? I know the trimmed project will not reach out to as many as we do now, but there are some staff who have give me their heart and soul and I need to leave them a sustainable project.

Then there is dear Popples II, The Project Why Story that needs to be told, as it is a portrait of a brave India no one is aware of. It is the lives of millions we just pass by but who battle every day to survive with dignity and dream big for their progeny. Project Why plays a tiny role in these dreams.

Maybe after all this is done, God will take my fear of flying away and free me of my prison like schedule and allow me to fly with my fondest friends and actually sit on that rock under a marmalade sky!

---

[74] Manu a beggar I met in 2000 and who was the reason for Project Why
[75] The Little Prince, Antoine de St Exupery, 1943, Chapter 21

Wednesday, 25 September 2013

THE OTHER SIDE OF 'SIDE EFFECTS'

You must have been wondering why such a long silence, as normally I find myself posting on this blog everyday and even twice a day! Before I tell you why, rest assured R is doing well though this chemo took a little longer to recover from. But then this is how it goes, from OK to worse, and we are not even midway if we go by what the doc said! So there were no terrible bad effects as my brews are still effective, but poison is poison and the body can reject only that much. What was different this time was a lingering nauseous feeling, a loss of appetite though he ate what we gave and lethargy. But he is back to normal (the chemo normal) and the blood results was as expected WBC tumbling from 19000 to 3800. The boosting shots will begin next Monday for 3 days and the 6th chemo will again kill 12000 of them in 3 days. One has got used to this.

This time it was I who reacted to a medicine given to me by my own trusted doctor. The story goes like this: I had been having a nagging knee/leg pain and asked for some magical cure as it was hampering my much needed 40 minutes of treadmill: my daily feel good dose. So he gave me a pill telling me that I may feel a little woolly the next morning but that it will settle down. The next morning I was not a little woolly but blown out as if I had had a bad acid trip. I slurred and banged into every wall, door or whatever came my way. Being me, I insisted on carrying on with my routine and came down to my den and sat at my computer but soon realised that I was not in a state of mind to write anything. I barely wrote two mails with great difficulty as my muscles seemed to be working on their own and not listening to my brain. I went back to bed feeling miserable. It could not have happened on a worse day, as I had to meet 2 donors at noon. I spoke to the Doc and he told me that the side effects should wear out by then. Not in the least. At noon I was just able to drag myself to the doctor. My BP was 56/79! I was asked to go back and drink electrolytes and rest. In the evening the BP was still 56/80. I slept and woke up this morning with a headache but feeling a tad better. The BP was 60/85 a shade better but not quite there. I hope that the side effects of this damn drug will wear off, as I am miserable not being able to follow my sacrosanct schedule.

At 2pm I will be taking R for his weekly visit to his oncologist. I hope I make it without swaying and wobbling and being a nuisance. As for my knees and legs, they better behave, as I am not even trying any new drug till R's chemo is over.

I DID NOT SEE THIS ONE COMING!

For the two months or so, since Mr Hodgkin's presence in our home was detected, the control freak in me has been trying to work out all possible scenarios, from the bad ones, to the good ones, and from the irritating ones to the funny ones! I have gone to the point of working out all steps if - God forbid- we had a medical emergency that needed hospitalisation or what colour eyebrow pencil to use were R to lose his bushy eyebrows. Along the way I dealt with the annoying side effects finding quick fix solutions and with each chemo the list of my arsenal has grown by leaps and bounds. We now go to the hospital for the chemo with a big red icebox filled with ice and bags of peas to deal with blisters and nails turning blue. I scouted the net to find all colour and hue of alternative remedies and established my line of supply. For those not available in India wonderful friends are just a mail away! I have sourced all organic food suppliers in Delhi and know where to get the best of each item needed. I felt in control or so I thought.

Two days ago a pill meant to relieve my knee ache due I guess to over stressing on my treadmill did not agree with me and the reaction was so severe that I was unable to walk, talk, think, write etc. for over 24 hours. And then to crown it all two large abscesses in my gums took care of the rest of me and I have been knocked out since. Frankly the control freak in me had taken my health for granted at least till the exit of Mr H. I did not see this one coming!

I would like to think of this mishap for want of a better word, as a message from up there to sort my house in order short term. The long term can wait and even be taken care of by others. But the now is only in my head and the first things that needs to be done is make sure that everything I jealously keep in my head - another control freak trait - is written in black and white. I remember Kamala, my mother and mentor, calling me one day in one of her lucid moments and asking me to sit down with paper and pencil and write all the things that needed to be done if she were to die as she felt papa would be broken and I lost. So she patiently told me where all phone numbers and addresses were and so on. It sounded grim at that moment and made me cross, but I did as was told. Another memory that comes to mind is one of the last entry in the final diary she wrote begging God to not take away her mind! He did. She died 8 months later. I found her diary many years later at a time when my life was at its nadir and I needed someone to show me the way. Her diary did. It was uncanny.

The other lesson I got from my other parent is that nothing happens without a reason so putting all the wisdom of those who gave me life; I too need to figure out what this mishap, which resulted in sleepless nights, actually means. The only thing I can think of is that I need to write down all the information about R's treatment on paper/screen: the contacts, the addresses, the phone numbers, the daily schedule, the brews and potions, the preventives and fixes, the nutrition requirements etc. I will do that later today. It also means that I need to organise my bucket list and begin ticking items ASAP be they family ones of extended family ones.

It means I need to live as if today was my last day and then set myself free to enjoy all the last days of my life to their fullest!

BUCKET LIST ITEM NO 1:
ALL I KNOW TILL NOW

In my last post I stated rather passionately that I would live each day as if it was my last! So let us walk the talk. So if today was the last day of my life, the most important thing that needs to be done is to share all the information I have in my head concerning R's day-to-day care and wellbeing. I am putting this in the 'public' domain as I know there are many across the world who are caring for dear ones with cancer and hope that the knowledge - a big word I agree - I have gained could be of use to them, should they want to follow my way.

To put things in context, this is my third if not fourth brush with cancer. My first one was when my Nani was diagnosed with liver cancer way back in 1957. My memories are that of a worried mom, a hurried trip to India - we were in Rabat - and a telegram on July 13th 1958 saying she had passed on. I was 6. Cancer was often talked about but to a growing teen it meant nothing. What mattered was getting passed papa with a short skirt and Twiggy eye lashes without being admonished. Somewhere along the way 2 lumps in ma's breast brought the beast lurking, but it kept at bay. It was in 1989 or so that we all knew Ma had cancer though the word was never whispered. She wanted it that way. She lived on bravely and died on her own terms. Papa somatised her cancer and was diagnosed on October 30th

1992 with cancer of the colon, had surgery on November 5th and left me on November 29th.

We moved to Paris and on a visit to a doctor for some silly ailment, I was told that I was high risk and that I had to have a yearly check up. Sorry! I was not at willing to live life from check up to check up. This was 1992. A chance meeting with a young woman with cancer open my world to alternative therapies and with the arrival of the Internet and Sir Google, I started my personal cancer research. Right from the outset I intuitively sensed that chemotherapy and radiotherapy were not for me. It was not the vanity of losing hair, but the vague feeling that it was poison. I knew simply that I would follow mama's footsteps with a caveat: pain management if the beast were to attack me. I must confess that I always thought I would be at the receiving end.

I began eating healthy, rainbow diets, giving up milk products though I occasionally binged on cheese, taking supplements and reading every book I could lay my hands on where people had beaten cancer with alternative medicine. I had a small fright almost a decade ago and I knew that if I opted for conventional medicine then I would be drawn into an infernal spiral. Thank God someone had mentioned a Tibetan Doctor. It was a eureka moment for me. When I met her, I was attracted by this spunky woman[76], who radiated a sense of wellbeing. I shared my history with her, my terrifying fright of having cancer. When she suggested a blood test, I burst into tears and told her I trusted her and would take all her medicines and did not want to know anything else. It has been 10 years and I religiously swallow her pills and powders and meet her at least once a month for what is to me a full body scan performed by simply taking your pulse. She specialises in cancer and has had many success stories.

My cancer never came, or if it did it remained in the brain of Dr D who must have cured it. I was happy that I had found the doctor I dreamt of! Then R got sick. He lost weight, appetite, had slight fever occasionally, and somewhat began to fade away. I must admit that my dread of the word C may have delayed diagnosis though I do believe that we took all the steps required. But please if you have a dear one who starts losing weight, has low fever and blood counts in free fall, think cancer. The way you deal with it is

---

[76]   Dr **Tsewang Dolkar Khangkar**; Dolkar House, D-10, Kalkaji, Delhi - 110019,

your decision, and only yours. Do not get seduced by what doctors tell you. My Pa was told he would be up and about in 15 days!

When R was diagnosed with Hodgkin's lymphoma, I rushed to Dr D hoping that she would tell me she had the cure. Instead she told me in her inimitable way that Hodgkin's Lymphoma, testicular cancer and one of the two leukaemia respond well to chemotherapy. I was stunned. I realised in that fleeting moment that the one thing I had always wanted to keep away from our lives had surreptitiously found a crack to slink in. Dr D also said that she would give her medication to boost immunity and ward off the bad side effects. So R has her medicine 4 times a day.

The next thing I learnt about cancer is the importance of nutrition. It is important to give up the things that cancer cells do like and feed the body with food they hate. The things to give up are sugar, white rice, white flour, white everything! All dairy products and all non-vegetarian food. Fish is acceptable as long as you try and find low mercury one. Though its is a huge environmental foot print, I buy his fish in a shop called The Taste[77], in Defence Colony and some of it comes from Chile! Organic vegetables are available and delivered to your home, so are other items like dals, red rice, spices, oils organic flour etc. I source mine from the different stores[78]

There are other options if you Google for them. But I have found these stores friendly and efficient. Altitude Store also has breads and farm eggs and organic chicken and lamb.

Of course if the patient has strong preferences, it is a bit of a juggling game as is the case with me. R does not like some vegetables like squashes and pumpkins so one has to be very creative. The idea is to give many different coloured fruits and vegetables every day.

---

[77] The Taste, #33, Defence Colony Market, New Delhi, Delhi 110024
     Phone:011 4656 8952

[78] I say organic A-53, Okhla Phase II, Okhla Industrial Area, Near Nathu
     Sweets, New Delhi, Delhi 110020011 Tel: 4108 7447
     Altitude Store Shop No-110, Mehar Chand Market, Lodhi Road, Near India
     Habitat Center, New Delhi, Delhi 110003 011 Tel:4905 0404
     Earth Organic E-588,Ground Floor, Greater Kailash II, Greater Kailash,
     New Delhi, Delhi 110048

Vegetable and fruit juices are essential and you can mix and match to your heart's content and hide all the things you know will be rejected: fresh turmeric, amla, cabbage, broccoli, beetroot, kale, radish etc. Ginger is a must.

Next come berries of all shades and hues. I again get my frozen ones from The Taste in Defence Colony. Cranberries and Blueberries are a must. I usually make a smoothie with silken tofu.

Seeds of all kind and specially linseed oil are very good so I put them in cereals and smoothies.

Another thing I give R twice a day is pure Ashwagandha Root Powder with honey. This is difficult to get as it is often mixed with other plants. The best place to get it in Delhi at Kottakkal Arya Vaidya Sala, Delhi[79] but you need to insist that you want pure root powder and not churnam. This works wonders with immunity levels and side effects of chemo.

Next is sour sop. A fruit that I must have eaten in large quantities when we were posted in Saigon in the early sixties. It is somewhere between a jackfruit and a durian! The best way is to get leaves and bark and boil them and then drink three glasses a day. I source mine from Alavi Herbs[80] in Hyderabad. They are efficient and send you the leaves once you have deposited the money in their bank.

Everyone is talking of the magic of Apricot Kernels also known as vitamin B17! Alavi herbs supply these too. You can of course learn more about these on the net before deciding to add them to your regimen. However if you want Vitamin B17 supplement you would have to order them from abroad.

Mushrooms[81] like shitake, maitake and reishi are known to help cancer patients. Some of the exotic ones are available at INA market, or some fancy

---

[79] Arya Vaidya Sala, Kottakkal, Ayurvedic Hospital & Research Centre, 18x, 19x Karkardooma Institutional Area, (Near Railway Reservation Centre), **Delhi - 110 092,**Telephone: +91 - 11-22106500 & +91 - 11-22376599.

[80] Alavi Herbs. 22-2-202/1, Dabeerpura, Behind Salar Jung Museum, Hyderabad-500024.
Mobile: 09959726547;09247377182

[81] http://www.cancerresearchuk.org/about-cancer/cancers-in-general/cancer-questions/mushrooms-in-cancer-treatment#shiitake

vegetable shops but you can also go for supplements that are available on line[82].

I also give R Salvestrol [83], which I did not find in India. I am blessed to have friends who order it and send it to me. You can imagine how much juggling it takes to handle all this. We are booked from 6 am to 9 pm!

This was the nutrition story.

Most of the bad side effects are kept at bay with all these brews and stews, but some may still appear. We had some blisters in the mouth. Now the antidote to that is to make the patient suck ice as long as the chemo cocktail is being poured into his system. It is not easy but coax your loved one but this works wonders. Nails turning blue are also a sign of the poison finding its way in all places. Cold gloves are available outside idea but two bags of frozen peas work as well. R was not very cooperative but I hope I can convince him. I also feed him home made food even though it is not allowed in the hospital that sells fast food! But the two times he had the hospital food he was sick so I am willing to break the law.

Another important part of my arsenal is to make the elephant in the room a mouse. I must admit there are times when it does loom large, but we have learnt to swat it by laughter and humour. R has an iPad full of all his favourite old funny sitcoms and he often watches them. We also talk about Zozo or Mr H as we call his cancer lightly. One of the side effects I could not help with was loss of hair and he has lost quite a lot on his body. I remind him how one of my sine-qua-non conditions was to marry a hairy man. So beware we have a cause for divorce!

Breathing is very important, as cancer cells hate oxygen. We are still fighting over this one. And by the way I forgot the trampoline. Believe it or not rebounding- jumping on a trampoline - is a fab way to boost your immune system. Try it!

What you need is to overload your life with positive thoughts and throw out all the negative ones. Just meet people who make you laugh and shun those who feed on your energies. Do not feel compelled to entertain any one you do not want around. People who care will understand.

---

[82]   http://www.healthkart.com/

[83]   http://www.salvestrol.ca/aboutsalvestrols.asp

So now I have written it all down. I may have forgotten some things and will write them down as soon as I remember. There maybe new things I add to my cornucopia as I go along. Will also make sure I share them.

Monday, 30 September 2013

THAT MAKES ME EXTRAORDINARY

After a very long time R sat at the piano and played some of his favourite tunes. It was magic as for too many months now the silence in the house was almost eerie, particularly at the times R played: practice in the morning and playing before dinner with a drink in his hand. For me this was the sign I was looking for. Remember the next two months are not great; that is what the stars foretell. But seeing R at his piano playing an Abba song was pure delight.

On the other side of the planet Agastya my grandson is learning to play the piano and shows us diligently his daily exercise that goes 1-2-3 as his finger taps the note 3 times and then the little hand is placed on the chest while he says 'rest'. But once the exercises over, Agastya becomes a composer and plays with abandon his hands flying on the keys as he sings his own composition. It is a rare treat. He likes Mozart and wants to see him play on You Tube. Now is poor mom is having to explain to him that You Tube did not exist when Mozart was alive.

So piano is a big part of our world. I kick myself for all the times when I got irritated when R would sit at any piano - in a hotel lobby, a mall, a friend's home - and play. I felt almost embarrassed and today in hindsight I feel sheepish. Piano is part of who R is! I learnt that the wrong way.

R's music is extraordinary!

Wednesday, 2 October 2013

CUT, BURNT, POISONED OR FLY HIGH

I have been researching alternative cancer therapies since 1993 when I was told that as both my parents had cancer, I was 'high risk'. I picked up innumerable books on cancer prevention and cure the natural way. With the arrival of the Internet, I scoured every site possible and altered my lifestyle and eating habits. I knew instinctively that chemo was not the right way to go. I guess I was influenced by my mother's aversion to chemo and her absolute refusal to any kind of medical care. And at that time I had no knowledge of natural options and could only give her all the love I could as she fought bravely till the end. For Pa the need of chemo did not arise as brutal surgery on a 81-year old man was enough to kill him.

Chemo entered our lives two months back when we accepted to go by people we trusted and fell for the charming doctor's seduction act! Hodgkin's is one of the cancers 100% curable blah - blah - blah. That is when my research on chemo began. It was first more a search for natural options to diminish the side effects and I think we have not done too badly. Fingers crossed! However there was a 'side effect' that I had not anticipated: innumerable accounts of persons who had beaten cancer the natural way [84] and refused chemotherapy. And not just that. What I came across was the harm that chemo does and the fact that no oncologist gives you the whole enchilada. If they did you would run miles away. But as small

---

[84]   http://www.chrisbeatcancer.com

changes happen - nails turning blue - you are told: it does happen with chemo! And of course you are also told that it will go away after chemo. Having subscribed to Chris's site I have accessed precious information on every aspect of cancer and was moved by Ann's story[85] who beat pancreatic cancer without chemo! There are many across the world who have done so. It is not easy as there are protocols to follow but the big difference is that everything you pour into yourself is good for you: a quart of carrot juice or large quantities of bitter apricot seeds.

These are not fads but have been tested over time[86]. Apricot seeds contain amagdylin that targets only cancer cells. There are many such natural remedies that one can use to treat cancer: soursop tea, ashwagandha root and many other plants that attack only cancer cells. This is a far cry from the cut, burn, poison approach of conventional medicine! You will find a lot of articles in serious looking journals praising chemo and totally suppressing any form of alternative therapy. Of course they will. Imagine if we all knew that apricot kernels, juices and other plants could cure cancer then what would happen to this billions of dollars worth cancer industry? The big Pharma industry scuttled the voice of natural therapy and it was easy when there was no Internet and all information had to be sought in time consuming and almost impossible ways. Today with the Internet people can share their stories and find out how practitioners of alternative cancer therapies and remedies and their messengers have been marginalised, harassed, imprisoned, and even killed[87]. That is how powerful the pro chemo lobby is.

A few days back I went to R's oncologist and asked him to brief me on the possible outcome(s) post the PET Scan due on 16/17th October. He tried to comfort me as he may have thought that I was worried and needed reassurance. Not at all. I needed the truth. So best case scenario: 8 chemos, midway scenario: 12 chemos and worst-case scenario change of protocol from ABVD to BEACOPP. The only thing he said was that the later was

---

[85] http://www.chrisbeatcancer.com/ann-heals-pancreatic-cancer-with-nutrition/

[86] http://www.naturalnews.com/027088_cancer_laetrile_cure.html

[87] http://www.thenaturalrecoveryplan.com/articles/The-Harassing-of-Natural-Health-Practitioners.html

far from aggressive. I wanted this input to be able to have the information needed to take the right decision. I again scouted the Internet and fell on a serious medical article in the Lancet[88] (you may have to register to read the full article, but it is free!) where it is clearly stated that: I*ts (BEACOPP) use is certainly restricted to patients younger than 60 years and to countries where sufficient clinical support is available. Besides acute toxicities, another issue is secondary malignancies and late cardiovascular effects.* So I know my answer should this be proposed: A big NO!!!

In a lighter vein a friend dropped by and though he is a serious professional, he is also an excellent alternative therapies specialist. He told us that one of the best treatment for cancer was cannabis! Not smoking it but eating its leaves. We had a good laugh but actually it is true and people are working on this. There are many articles [89]on the net that explain scientifically how it works. It also prevents cancers and many other ailments. That sounds good! Imagine if we went to a doctor who told us that we had 2 choices either accept to be cut, burnt and poisoned or to eat cannabis leaves. I know what I would choose!

---

[88]   http://www.thelancet.com/journals/lanonc/article/
PIIS1470-2045(13)70382-6/fulltext
BEACOPP escalated versus ABVD in advanced Hodgkin's lymphoma Marc André, André Bosly
[89]   http://www.collective-evolution.com/2013/01/03/
cannabis-is-key-to-good-health-when-we-eat-it-vs-smoking-it/

Thursday, 3 October 2013

HOW BEAUTIFULLY THEY COMPLEMENT EACH OTHER!

When I am not OK in my head and need to clear the cobwebs, I often find myself clearing up things: it could be the attic, old forgotten cabin trunks that must have travelled over the seas and across skies, or simply clearing book shelves in a vain attempt to organise them, I say vain because my books are always placed on shelves by 'heart' reasons and thus defy any logical sorting. As I was 'sorting' the bookshelves in my den, I came across my elder daughter's doctoral thesis[90] and found myself turning the pages. My eyes rested on the 'acknowledgment' page and the first credit was given to R and I, her parents. A rough translation - as her thesis is in French - would read as follows: *To my parents who do not realise how beautifully they complement each other!* When I first read this in 2003, it made me laugh as nothing could have been as further from the truth of the moment. In hindsight however, I realise that my first-born could see with her heart and beyond all the layers and unearth a reality that would take a long decade and a terrible blow to see how right she was/is.

In 1974 when we first met it was literally love at first sight. But then life took over, and the complementarity gave way to sporadic parting of

---

[90] Parul Bakhshi, PHD, Changement social et procédés identitaires : chez les femmes de New Delhi; Paris 5; 2003

ways often to please or fulfil the needs of others. The precious 'us' became sets of 'them' playing a futile game of one-upmanship. And as we dug our heels, complementarity seemed well and truly hijacked. The love at first sight gave way to all kinds of shades and hues of emotions as far from love as you would imagine.

But in hindsight the spark was there, alive, sometimes a little shaky, but refusing to be snuffed out no matter what. It manifested itself in more ways than one, some as furtive as a wink no one saw or a word only we understood. Sadly it was never centre stage.

The love that saw the light of day in February 1974 would reclaim its place with a vengeance 39 years later, but it would do so in a way one does not hope for one's bitterest enemy. I guess I owe one to Mr Hodgkin, as he is the one who played cupid in the life of this ageing couple. I only beseech him to move on quickly after having completed the task I guess the Gods assigned him with.

From the day we knew R had lymphoma, we both realised in our own way that it was the strength of our love that would get us out. R gave me the proof of his undying love for me: his complete trust and total surrender. He accepted every decision I took, every brew I asked him to swallow, even the bitterest ones. I on the other hand put my life on hold and devoted every single minute of my day to making his ordeal easier. The laughter that was lost somewhere along the way found its way back into our lives. All the words that lay unsaid in our mind and heart found their voice. Communication was reset. I hope we have enough time to say everything we need to, to each other and heal every wound and hurt. There is no time for recrimination or bickering. Only love and understanding.

They say every cloud has a silver lining. How true it is. Even the dark cancer cloud had a wonderful silver lining called love or should I say the final realisation of how we have and do complement each other.

Thank you Mr Hodgkin, but now please leave us after 8 chemos.

Saturday, 5 October 2013

A DAUGHTER LANDS UP

Now I am convinced. Sir Hodgkin has more good side effects than bad ones. The latest was a huge surprise that stunned R and I. yesterday afternoon, I was in my office writing something when Shamika came back from work. From the corner of my eye I saw she was dragging a suitcase and smiling like a Cheshire cat! I wondered what it was all about, got up to see who was there. It was CAT! (Sorry for the pun). I froze, as something was not quite right in what I was seeing. The lovely young lady that stood at my front door was supposed to be in Leeds. Space and time were out of sync. But no there she was, a huge smile on her face and then in my arms. She had come all the way to be with us, to be there when we needed her most.

Who is Cat? A volunteer who came way back in 2009 and walked in our hearts forever. More so in R's heart as his third daughter. She calls him Pops! Her landing lifted the mood of the house and our hearts sang. Was she the sign I had been praying for, the one that would tell me that all would be well, it was just a matter of time.

For the next 2 weeks she will be here holding my hand, a hand she has held virtually through every problem big or small I have had since the day I met her. God makes up in ample measure for everything he takes away from us. Cat is the proof of that.

Her Pops had a smile he could not get rid off. He was moved to tears and radiant with happiness. They could not stop holding hands and I felt an immense sense of gratitude I know I cannot ever repay.

Thank you Cat!

Now a quick update on Sir R. He recovered from chemo 6 much faster than last time. He is in a great mood and ready to go shopping for party shoes today as the ones he bought online turned out to be the funny never ending shoes that are in fashion but that he hates. They were returned. Today we go shoe shopping!

La vie est belle.

SHOPPING FOR SHOES

R has been wanting a pair of shoes for quite some time. A few days back he informed me that he had bought a pair of shoes on line! I was flabbergasted as my man is so finicky about footwear. He judges people by their shoes and women by their feet. Thank heavens we met in winter when he never got a glimpse of my feet before Cupid let out its bow or our love story would have stopped after a glance at my rather ungainly trotters! So when he told me to expect a delivery and to have the money ready I was ready for the worst. Mercifully the shop allows you to try the shoes before you decide to keep them.

The package arrived and we were all excited. By all I mean self and the young lad who works with us. We opened the box carefully and out came a shoe! I burst out laughing. It was a slip on as that is what was ordered but that is where R's perception and reality parted. The shoe was one of those never ending contraptions that are in fashion, with a boat like look and that go on well after your toes end and to crown it all they had synthetic soles. My man wears leather soles! When he put them on, Deepak, the lad who works for us immediately said: these are not for you. I was still laughing. Needless to say the man was disappointed. We all knew what had to be done. We repacked the shoes and gave them back to the waiting deliveryman. Anyway they were a size too big. My man has the tiniest feet you can imagine. But he would not give up and wanted to show me the pair he felt he had ordered and believed were not the ones in the box. After a long search we found them and to me they looked like the ones that had landed home. R called the store and was told that these were the smallest size they had. End of the story.

Since that day he has wanted to go buy a pair of shoes but being chemo week the shopping trip had to be postponed. I promised to take him to South Extension as I felt it was the place he may find what he wanted and as Saturday was the day we all got the lovely surprise of Cat's arrival it was 4 musketeers that went shopping: R, Cat, Shamika and I! No one listened to me so instead of going straight to the two shops where I thought he may find what he wanted, we meandered from shop to shop with R rejecting everything in sight and not finding his beloved slip-ons with rounded toes and leather soles. At one point he kept saying that he wanted Florsheim shoes. Now as they do not make women's shoes, I did not know where the store was located. I hung my hope on Clarks but even there he did not find what he wanted. I could see him disappointed like a child and I promised him to find the Florsheim store. There was a last shop left and I urged him to at least take a look. I preceded the posse and imagine my joy when I started descending the stairs to the men's section and saw F L O R S H E I M written in bold letters! The Gods were smiling.

It took another 30 minutes to find the right size, toe, fit and colour but finally he set his eyes on a pair that he liked. It was not the one the girls liked as they wanted him to add some style but in the end he won the battle and bough the shoes he wanted. He was smiling like a kid who just got his favourite candy. The shoes were packed and paid and we headed home.

It had been a lovely moment with no elephants around!

Wednesday, 9 October 2013

CODEX ALIMENTARIUS

Life is full of serendipities. I have always held that and been proved right. If I were not fighting a battle to cure R of cancer, a battle on many fronts, the incident I am about to share would have had scant importance in my life. But coming my way at this very time is definitely serendipitous! My intuitive and almost involuntary aversion to chemotherapy and my instinctive faith in natural remedies and alternative therapies have been vindicated over and over again by the daily research that has become sacrosanct as even the tiniest of things I can find to help R in anyway are precious. I read the Emperor of All Maladies to understand the 'story' of cancer and chemotherapy and was quite shocked to see how lobbies worked against any form of nature cure and made sure they were stifled and ridiculed. It was easy then as information was not easy to share. Today with the Internet everything is out in the open irrespective of these powerful lobbies. You just need patience and persistence and you discover a cornucopia of 'gems' nature has given us to heal every ailment under the sun. This is how I came across soursop, apricot seeds and even hemp! Not to forget jumping on a trampoline. We began talking of serendipity. The incident I refer to is a book given to R by one of his dearest friend. The book is the Healing Codes [91](It is R who read me an extract about Codex Alimentarius.

---

[91] Discovered in 2001 by Alex Loyd, PhD, ND. Every time you use a Healing Code, it activates a physical function built into the body that consistently and

Codex Alimentarius [92] sounds like a Latin greeting, is a chilling conspiracy spearheaded by the Pharma and other lobbies to kill the market of supplements by making them cost prohibitive. Rest assured it is very legal and very laudable! It promises safe food for everyone. The problem is that this will be decided by vested interests and lobbies. In reality the *Codex Alimentarius is a dark marriage between pharmaceutical and chemical industries and the WTO, conceived to exact complete and regimented control over all food products and nutrients worldwide.*"(Chantal Boccaccio)[93]. What it means is that we will lose our health freedom and our choices. *Codex*[94] *means legalisation of mandated toxicity and under-nutrition resulting in billions of deaths through cancer, the most profitable condition known to man.*

This is indeed very frightening and I for one will do as much research as I can, particularly as I am in the midst of it at this moment, fighting cancer! What is terrible is that few know about this, and before we realise it, these laws will come in place and we would not be aware of it. They are a complete affront to people's freedom to access clean, healthy food and beneficial nutrients and should be denounced. What it also means is that the lobbies are aware of the benefits of natural remedies and the humongous losses the Pharma industry would incur should such knowledge become available to everyone! People have been known to cure their cancers by eating large number apricot kernels! Apricot kernels have amygdalin, and this is known to kill only cancer cells.

Codex will advise their line of treatment: chemotherapy. It is like using a nuke to kill an ant. Funny that no blood test is advised - wonder if they are any, and if there are I am sure they must be very costly - post every chemo to assess how many cancer cells were destroyed. However, and I speak with

---

predictably removes the #1 cause of illness and disease from the body http://thehealingcodes.com

[92] http://members.iimetro.com.au/~hubbca/codex.htm, http://www.codexalimentarius.org

[93] http://www.thepeoplesvoice.org/TPV3/Voices.php/2011/06/08/codex-alimentarius-rated-rx; Chantal Boccacio; award-winning TV and screen writer

[94] http://www.consciousape.com/2011/05/20/the-codex-alimentarius-conspiracy-2011/

knowledge, a week after chemo a blood count is asked for. This shows how many of your healthy withe blood cells and platelets have been destroyed. For the past months I have been watching these terrifying figures week after week. This how it goes: a day before chemo your white cells could be 19000 and your platelets are 400000! A week after chemo they have stumbled down to 3800 and 100000. Now to prepare your body for the next nuking you are given a set of shots that make your immune system work overtime and bring the counts back to 19000 and 400000. Chemo again and tumbling again and the infernal ride goes on. In the mean time you do not know what is happening to your darned cancer cells, but what you know is that your immunity is at its nadir and you are open to every infection in the air.

And if that is not enough, in a recent post I had highlighted how you are never told the whole picture. A chemo protocol BEACOPP, that could be prescribed for R should the present one not have the wanted results should not be given to people above 60. And that is not all. It may get rid of Hodgkin but is known to increase chances of secondary cancers.

I know many the world over are fighting against these terrible realities. It is a true David versus Goliath battle. For me, at this juncture it is a fight for my husband's life and I am not going to be deprived of the freedom of making responsible choices even if my responsible choice is feeding him fresh hemp leaves and have him jump on a trampoline!

Thursday, 10 October 2013

R AND HIS GIRLS

R and his girls (S, C and M) played carom yesterday amidst much laughter and glee. I lay on the sofa opposite them and watched them in blissful silence. This was a special moment for me as it was after a long time that I saw the old boy in his elements. Sir Hodgkin had to slink away in the tiniest crevice he could find. This was fun time, good old days time. For some hours the tests, scans, chemos et al were all forgotten as it was all about blacks, and white and the red queen and of course winning. It was an absolute joy to watch these 4 children (the eldest being 64 and the youngest 18) have the time of their lives. Cat, R's special girl, had come all the way from Leeds to be with us for 2 weeks and what was incredible was that it was a surprise! M is a young volunteer from Germany who lives with us and has walked into our hearts. And Shamika is well Shamika! The fourth member of the pasha's harem was the ageing old wife who has been conjuring all the tricks possible to keep her man happy and good spirits. Yesterday was proof of that. I will give myself a pat in the back.

The rest I leave to the next post.

Thursday, 10 October 2013

REALITY BITES AND REALITY CHECK

Exactly 21 years ago, almost to the day, I had to make one of the most difficult decisions of my life. Papa, who looked like a man in the pink of health, though he was 81, was diagnosed with colon cancer. We had both barely recovered from mama's decision to refuse any sort of treatment for her cancer and accompanied her journey towards death the best we could. Those days there was no Internet or sufficient data on alternative therapies. So we evolved our own which was pampering her to the hilt and smothering her with our love, even when she was difficult and demanding. How can I forget the nights papa spent on a tiny stool holding her hand night after night and waking her up every hour before patting her to sleep again? You see she did not want to die in her sleep and he did what she decreed because he loved her! Her decision to refuse any treatment was difficult for those of us who loved her, but papa accepted it in spite of everything. Only I know what he went through.

18 months later, when he was diagnosed with cancer, he placed his trust in me. The ever and over optimistic surgeon told us he would be back on his feet in less than a month. Having seen mama go in pain, I got seduced by the doctor. Of course at that time the doctor's description of the procedure was not what actually happened. Though I had pleaded with him not to perform a colostomy and place a bag, as I knew my papa would not accept this stripping of his dignity, the doctor did not understand my side of the story. Papa walked into the nursing home smiling and with a spring in his

gait on November 1st and was handed back to me on the 15th mutilated and with a colostomy bag. It just took him 14 days to die. To see him go like this was heart wrenching as I had practically never seen him sick. I will never rid myself of the guilt of having robbed him of his dignity and given him such a humiliating death.

21 years later I find myself in the same place. This time it is R who has placed his undying trust in me to chart his medical journey. I did accept chemotherapy. I still wonder why. But many I trust told me to. The only difference between the 40 year old and the 61 year old is that I am armed with better knowledge and aware of the pitfalls I may encounter. True jargon is thrown at me with obsessive regularity and sometimes I am caught unawares, but it just takes me a few moments on the net to plan my counter attack. I so wish the medical fraternity was honest and laid out all the cards on the table before asking you for a decision. I am not saying that your oncologist should say: *well dear lady you can choose between toxic chemotherapy and a frozen lemon and hemp leaves*! What I would want to hear is all the possible side effects of the proposed protocol and not have them doled out when you are caught in the infernal spiral. I remember being told that 8 chemos might be sufficient and that would be decided after a scan post chemo 6. Yesterday the 8 chemo story was vehemently refuted and more letters thrown at me: this time A and B. If it were A then 8 was enough but as it is B then we need 12. But we knew it was B all the time so why did they tell us 8 at all. I get reminded of the Wolf in Little Red Riding Hood, who says: *To see you better my child*!

Now let me elucidate a little about the A and B story. 'A' symptoms mean that you should be able to detect your cancer without any symptom. Now unless it is visible or you have undergone a scan for some other reason and discovered the tumour, then it would be possible to detect it, but with no symptoms, or symptoms that resemble the ones of many other conditions, you are never likely to have just 'A' symptoms. 'B' symptoms in Hodgkin's are fever, loss of weight, chills etc. I must admit these are the ones that made us aware that something was wrong. When it all happened R wanted to lose weight and was on a diet!

The diagnosis was made after a CT Scan! But then we had to have a bone marrow biopsy, a surgical biopsy and a PET scan to confirm what we knew. The best-case scenario was stage 1B and the worst-case 2B. So please do not tell me today that 4 cycles (8 chemos) are for stage 'A' only. I did not dream that figure. It is just that someone had decided we need 6 cycles and everything will be said to concur with that.

I went to see my Tibetan Doctor yesterday to ask her opinion. I told her that they were doing a PET scan again before deciding how many chemos we still need. She laughed and told me that any investigation scan or tumour markers would show positive progress if done during chemo. The true picture would only emerge after 6 to 8 months post the last chemo. She told me that she would continue her treatment and then we will see the real picture in June 2014!

I tried to convey this to our doctor who shot it down because we had to follow a protocol. I also told him that so many PET scans cannot be good for any one but when you face a well rehearsed sales pitch, you have to concede defeat. To me the whole approach of chemotherapy is skewed. You are actually nuking an ant! And if that was not enough you give proof of that every 15 days. You need to have reports that show you how many healthy cells have been nuked so that you can artificially create more cells to nuke them again! It goes like 3000 WBCs boosted to 19 000 and then nuked to 3000 and boosted again to 18000. I find it difficult to believe that it can be good for the body. And throughout all the cycles that is all we know. How many good cells have died. No one tells you about the cancerous ones. Ah but there are tests but those are expensive and never prescribed. So you journey blindfolded till you are told OK, that is enough! Now chemo only destroys cells when they are dividing be it healthy one or cancerous ones. If you want to know how chemo actually works you could read Rebecca Sheehy's article: How Do Chemotherapy Drugs Kill Cancer Cells[95]. One only hopes that when the men in white decide to stop your chemos, most of the cancer cells have been destroyed and not too many healthy ones!.

Nature functions in a different way altogether. The natural cancer remedies attack only cancer cells. As an example let us take the apricot kernel

---

[95]   Rebecca Sheehy; University of Vermont
How Do Chemotherapy Drugs Kill Cancer Cells 2015
http://www.livestrong.com/article/123423-chemotherapy-drugs-kill-cancer-cells/

that kills cancer cells[96] Apricot kernels contain amagdylin. Amagdylin has cyanide that is locked in. Cancer cells contain an enzyme that other cells do not share, beta-glucosidase. This enzyme, virtually exclusive to cancer cells, is considered the "unlocking enzyme" for amagdylin molecules. It releases both the benzaldyhide and the cyanide, creating a toxic synergy that destroys the cancer cell. Sadly these studies have been suppressed. There are many natural products that work in similar ways one of them being hemp[97]! Cannabis for Cancer! What a great idea!

Talking of serendipity, I just got a mail from dear dear friends. It was God sent. They gently advised me to follow the doctor's protocol and then take over and make sure that by June 2014 all the tests will prove total cure! Bless them. I now see light at the end of the tunnel.

But one last thing before I end this rather lengthy post. I still would like to be told in details the short term and long term side effects of every drug that is poured in the veins of the one I love. The word protocol is too vague. During his first chemo, R was given a potent steroid in the pre medication and gosh he went on a real trip! He was time traveling and we were simply scared. Thank god that medication was removed from the protocol. Now we have been told that one of the medicines of his ABVD protocol namely 'B' or Bleomycin affects the lung and hence we need a lung function test to assess the situation and maybe change the protocol. Somehow, I would have liked to know that even if nothing would have changed.

Anyway I am a control freak and will remain one till my death. So I find comfort in knowledge and information. That is who I am and the old biddy will not change.

---

96 http://www.naturalnews.com/027088_cancer_laetrile_cure.html

97 http://www.trueactivist.com/there-is-no-mistaking-the-evidence-cannabis-cures-cancer/

THE ONLY TIME WE COULD EVER GENUINELY FEEL GUILTY

The only time we could ever genuinely feel guilty is if we take a decision against the doctors' advice and it doesn't work out. These are the words a very dear and loved friend wrote in answer to my previous post. I agree this post must have seemed to many as one written by a doubting Thomas, by one who refuses to believe anything until she is given proof! I guess it is part of my persona: a heady mix between a rebel, a control freak and a born Cartesian who also wants to see with heart. Quite a freak! Anyway cannot change in my old age.

I slept over these words and realised that my friend was right, even though I am still at war with the medical fraternity of our times. But as he says, should anything go wrong, my guilt would be unbearable. So this to tell you all that I have made my peace with the 12 chemos that the oncologist recommends. Actually it is a truce more than peace! I still iterate that it was the same doctor who had stated that we could stop at 8. I have said my bit. The last chemo is on 29 December 2013. 2014 will be my year.

However the elation that I thought I would feel when the results of the PET scan due on the 15th is now vastly tempered after what I was told by Doc D. As she rightly said all investigations done during chemo have to be an improvement on the one done before chemo began. Makes sense. The darned poison has to kill something. I have put my jubilation on hold till June 2014 where the truth will be revealed.

Voila. Thought I needed to share the fact that I have conceded one battle but will win the war.

Monday, 14 October 2013

JUST AN UPDATE

R has left the house for his PET scan and Lung Function test with his two favourite girls: Cat and Shamika. Yes you read it right without me! The control freak is sitting at home. Maybe a week back I would not have agreed to this arrangement, as the scan seemed all-important to me as I naively thought that it would show the real picture. But a little ferreting here and there put things in perspective. A midway scan, or for that matter a scan taken any time during chemo or immediately after has to show improvement. The question is how much as that may determine the remaining number but does not seem the case here as it seems everyone has fixated on the number 12! The real picture will be mid 2014 and that is when I will be stressed and anxious! I guess this scan is for commercial reasons more than anything else or would have some value if the patient was not showing any sign of progress. But R is looking well and come on he is even putting on weight, then why subject him to drink a radioactive cocktail ? It cannot be good for you. Maybe this midway scan is also to show the family that the treatment works. If you use a nuke it better work.

I am a little more concerned about the Lung Function Test as this may entail a change in the chemo protocol and would then necessitate more study to hunt out any short of long term side effects not revealed. But we will cross that bridge when we come to it. I just hope we can continue with the present protocol, as the devil known is better than....

Will know all this evening. Fingers crossed, prayers on the lip

Tuesday, 15 October 2013

THIS HAPPENS ONLY IN INDIA

Yesterday R and his favourite girls went to the super speciality hospital to get the much awaited - by others, not much by me - PET Scan and the needed Lung Test that we call the *phou phou* test as it involves blowing in a tube. I think it was an all time first for R as I do not remember him as the kind of dad who blew birthday balloons, that was the minions job, at best he would watch cigar in mouth and give instructions no one wanted, but most of the times he would be on the golf course barely making it in time for the birthday cake. Anyway the tests were done though it took forever and the poor man was not even allowed to read while waiting for the dreaded radioactive substance to be absorbed by his body. For God sake he was not having a brain scan and there I was hoping he would finish his book. Anyway the scans and tests were done and to the question: when do we get the results, the answer was day after tomorrow for the scan and the same evening for the *phou phou* one! I had scheduled the scan three days before the chemo because I wanted to show the results to people I trust, and there I was told I would get them the evening before chemo 7.

Now for the questions you may all be asking yourselves: why 3 days! Come on darlings this is India and today is a HOLIDAY! Yes one of the umpteen holidays that keep increasing to appease or woo one section of the society or the other. Vote banks you see! When I was a Government Servant, yes I was for less than a year as a Translator Announcer in the French division of All India Radio circa 1971; we never had holidays for

Rakhi or Karva Chauth or Chatth Puja. Come to think of it in those days no one knew what Chatth Puja was as it is very specific to eastern UP and Bihar and I had heard of it because my father told me his mom kept it. Today with the exponential increase in migrants from those areas it is a holiday and festivities are attended by top politicos! Woo and wow the vote bank. Anyway apologies for digressing. What I wanted to say that in our office where we needed to broadcast 365 days, we worked on those days and had compensatory offs. Now to me airports, hotels and of course hospitals should also work 365 days and 24 hours so a super speciality hospital that charges a bomb should be a city that never sleeps!

But that is not all. Today morning I set out bright and early to get R's *phou phou* report and hoping to try and find out if I could not get the scan report sometimes in the day tomorrow. Would you believe me if I told you that I could not reach the hospital. Wonder Why? Well today being Eid, all roads leading to the hospital were blocked as the hospital is situated next to a mosque and morning prayers were on. I found my way back empty handed of course, but imagine if someone had to reach the hospital for an emergency.

But then this happens only in India!

After I ended this post the driver came back empty handed though he reached the hospital once prayers were over. The reason: counter closed!!!

Wednesday, 16 October 2013

FOOD ON HIS MIND

My R is a gourmet and loves good food. He is not fussy but I can understand that he must be fed up of the 'diet' he is on for the past months now. He not only likes good food, but likes it served in style accompanied by the right bottle of wine served in crystal glasses and eaten at a leisurely pace. He has eaten at the best tables the world over and been to many multi-starred restaurants. Since the arrival of Mr Hodgkin in his life, all this has changed. As you know cancer can be beaten by eating the right kind of food. I give him an organic vegetarian diet - occasional fish and eggs - that includes certain products and excludes many. Milk is a big no- no and hence there is no cheese! A big sacrifice for one who loves good French cheese. Not to forget butter, how can one cook without butter. Eating organic also means eating seasonal vegetables and fruit and hence limits variety and thus become boring. Then there are the juices some quite foul: cabbage and broccoli, beetroot and carrot etc. Day after day after day. R does not complain but I have just realised that food is on his mind.

Would you believe me if I told you that I have caught him watching cook shows on TV, shows I usually watch and that is not all, he even asked for some crumbed aubergines he had seen in a show to be made for him. Snails have been on his mind, as he loves garlic-buttered snails. He has been urging Shamika and Cat to go have snails at the French restaurant. Does eating by proxy work?

His best friend, also a gourmet, is presently holidaying abroad and when they talk every day the main subject of conversation is food. His friend tells him which restaurant he has been to or is going to and R promptly Googgles for the menu and makes suggestion. I am amused but also a little concerned as to beat cancer all the way he will have to continue eating sensibly. Looks like cancer cells are also 'gourmets' and love all the things that taste yum. Will have to figure out some compromise when all is well.

For the moment I let him dream on as he quietly eats all that is given to him. God bless him!

Wednesday, 16 October 2013

CANCER BUDDIES

M, a young volunteer who is living with us at home for the past month came to our room yesterday evening and wanted to take a picture. I guess we were both not at our best, but then this is the way we look today. I call us: cancer buddies! Why? Because for the past months we have shared every moment of our life with a third unwanted guest: Sir Hodgkin. Our mission is to boot him out of our lives as soon as possible. Easier said than done, as he is a tenacious and difficult tenant who functions in his own ways. R is looking good after 6 chemos. I love the new fuzz on his head and have never seen so many black hair in a long time.!

Now let us get back to the Sir H! The best-case chemo scenario is that we get rid of 80% of the cancer cells. This stands to logic as chemo can only destroy cancer cells when they are dividing, or to use a medical term: during interphase or mitosis. Now to hope that there is a given moment when all cancers cells are in mitosis mode is absurd. There will always be some that cannot be destroyed. The downside of this approach is that it also destroys your immune system. Now how do the remaining cells get destroyed after chemo? The answer is: by your immune system. So the true picture can only appear when all traces of chemo have left your body and your immune system has recovered from the shock of having millions of healthy cells destroyed and has taken back its primary role: giving you immunity.

Chemo aside, I have been pumping R with all kind of remedies that aim at strengthening the immune system, but sadly whatever success I have is reversed by the next chemo. It is only after the last chemo that I will be able to boost his immune system and have it take care of the remaining cells. Right now the simple fact that I have been able to minimise the side effects and ensured that he has not lost any weight is more than I could have hoped for.

We are half way as we have been told that he needs 12 chemos. 6 more to go!

Thursday, 17 October 2013

HALF WAY THERE

Some good news. The scan results are finally with me! It seems that R has responded to the treatment and though I have not talked to his oncologist, it looks like the main lymphoma has shrunk at least 50% if not a little more. Will get the real picture later today. His lung function tests are also within normal limits so I guess the protocol will not be changed and better the devil you know!

The only little irritant is that this time, the WBCs have not shot up to the 15000+ after the booster shots and are only 6400. Normally we go from 3000 to 15000 after chemo. A little concerned about what will happen this time but let us see what the doc says.

Cat leaves today and we will all miss her.

Friday, 18 October 2013

CHEMO SEVEN

Not a great day. R is a mess after chemo. His temperature is high, he has chills, he is disconnected and lost. This is what chemo does and that is why I will always be weary of it. It all begins well but as the poison slowly drips into his veins his entire persona changes. You can feel the body screaming in silence but not being heard. The mind too functions the same way. As soon as R entered the chemo day care and before he even reached his bed, let alone had anything done, not even his BP checked he began telling me that he had a funny taste in his mouth, that he was feeling nauseous etc. It was psychosomatic but real. An innate and intuitive revulsion to what was to come. Anyway we had no choice and carried on with the procedure.

This is chemo 7. Once upon not so long ago the oncologist had said that we might stop at 8, though at our last meeting he retracted his words and insisted we needed 12! I did not meet him today but when he came to see R, he told him that the scan showed 95% results! This is again part of the seduction game and not reality. At best chemo can destroy 80% of the cancer cells the rest have to be destroyed by the patient's own immune system. Now the problem is that chemo also destroys the immune system so the quicker chemo ends, the quicker we can begin boosting the immune system. This was confirmed by both the family doc and my Tibetan doctor, people I trust implicitly

Yes I know I have stated in this blog the fact that I will go with the recommendations of the medical fraternity (sic) though I doubt their motives but seeing R's immune system fading is not easy. I just want it all to be over and then I will go all guns blazing to save his injured immune system and strengthen it to the maximum.

It breaks my heart to see him like this. I do not know how long I will hold.

Friday, 18 October 2013

LACE

Tomorrow we celebrate our 39th wedding anniversary!

It is said that the 39th wedding anniversary gift is lace. *It is an example of the beauty that comes from the intermingling and looping of thread. It demonstrates the artistry of the human spirit, and it is a timeless and classic illustration of winsomeness throughout time!*

This is so true. Every day you wake up as a new person as you have been enriched by the experiences of the day before as every today becomes a new yesterday with its new tomorrow. Marriage is much the same if we see it that way. A friend use to say I fall in love with my wife every day as she is a new person every morning. It is an *illustration of winsomeness through out time*!

40 is a milestone. 39 is the right time to look at the piece of lace you have woven together. No matter which way you look at it, it is perfect. True there have been times when a false move has created knots that seemed impossible to unravel yet you did, sometimes without realising it. There may have been some that made you shed tears of frustration before you got at them or even some where you were almost ready to cut the thread but you did not because something inside you compelled you to find a way, no matter how tortuous or confusing. You took a break, leaving the thread unbroken and then got back at untangling it once again. If there were some damage, only you could see it, it became invisible to others. The piece of lace remained beautiful because of a thread called love that endures all.

I realise today how much R has done for me and am grateful to God for having given me the opportunity to begin repaying him for being there for me even when I did not understand the extent of his silent love. Today I say with as much conviction as I can muster that if my parents laid the foundations of my life, R is the one who made me who I am. If he had not stood by me none of my so-called ambitions or silly dreams could have happened. I am not proud of not having seen things as they were, so blinded I was by my foolish aspirations. Not only did he not stand in my way, but also he reached out and helped me in his strong, silent, unobtrusive manner making sure I never fall.

We fell in love at first sight and today I find myself falling in love with him at every moment as I look at the ethereal beauty of the piece of lace we have woven together.

Sunday, 20 October 2013

JUST HOLD ON A LITTLE LONGER

Just hold on a little longer. You are just 3 feet away from Gold. I have been through the same when my 8 years old son went through 9 sessions of aggressive chemo. Just one thing more than the chemo and the immune system working in favour of him, it is what he and you think about the treatment., whether its doing good or bad works the most. Just believe that every single drop of chemo is working in his favour. you have the ability to change poison into medicine. These words sent by someone who has seen her child going through the nightmare of chemo felt like the words of a special Angel sent by God. I must admit I felt sheepish at all my recriminations and lamentations when I saw R under the weather. I guess the only excuse I have is love. The love I feel for this extraordinary man. But I would give it all up for the life of a little boy. Thank you for reminding me how deeply grateful I should be for every moment of my life. I pray this little boy recovers fully and gets all the happiness he deserves. Thank you M for this beautiful message and God bless your little one.

I know I have been dilatory about my faith in chemotherapy. But as this brave mother says one should have the ability to change poison into manna from the Gods. I find myself regretting my obsessive Cartesian mind that is probably the reason why I resent so much the fact that doctors are never 100% honest. Maybe they feel that sharing the truth in palatable doses makes it easier to digest. But this does not work for me. I need the truth, even if it is scary and dreadful. How I wish I were an uneducated woman who accepted the words of the men in white with total faith bordering on adoration. But I am not. I need to know and I need to be given the right to decide.

I am meeting the oncologist for a one-to-one! Let us see what happens. I will be honest to the core. Let us see how far he walks with me.

A SPRINKLING OF MAGICAL DUST

Yesterday was our 39th anniversary. R had still not recovered from Chemo 7 and spent the day sleeping or gazing at the idiot box. I was a bit at a loss not knowing what to do. I had been for my weekly session at the parlour and was hoping to take R shopping for shoes, as that is what he wanted for his anniversary but he was in no mood to go. Writing that normally fills many gaps in my life did not quite happen. I guess the sort of indolent mood set by R caught up with me to, and I found myself in lazy mode. Just lay down and tried to read but my thoughts were travelling on their own freewill. I tried to remember what I was doing at that time 39 years ago but somehow could not. So I let my memories flow and what ensued was a kaleidoscope of all the good moments R and I had together and that had been obliterated by the sprinkling of bad ones that had always taken centre stage when they occurred.

It was perhaps the first time ever that I had not been actively engaged in planning and executing the celebration. Since R has been diagnosed with cancer Shamika has taken over the running of the house. A true blessing. R, who is obsessed by food since he is on his diet, tried asking what we were having for dinner. Shamika kept a straight face and said something like: boiled potatoes! The house was unusually quiet for a party day, even if the party was just us! I had seen nothing party like in the fridge and when I asked Shamika what she had planned she told be to keep quiet. I did. The day passed, and still no movement in the kitchen. The control freak in me started fretting.

Come 7 pm we were asked to come down. R dragged himself out of his bed still muttering about the food. When we were all gathered, in comes Shamika with two plates of prawns and olives on sticks. I was taken aback and so proud of my little girl. But that was not all; there was smoked salmon, and lovely caramelised onion tarts. It was a real treat made even more special by the surprise arrival of R's best friend. But there was more, if the salmon was for me at it is one of my guilty pleasures she had a bigger treat for R: his all time favourite *Oeufs Mayo* or eggs with mayonnaise. To many this dish may seem the wrong one for a gourmet like R but it comes with a story. *Oeufs Mayo* for R carry the memory of him sitting in the café overlooking the Opera in Paris and savouring his oeufs mayo with a salad. The whole experience is special for him and like Proust's *madeleines*, the taste of these simple eggs bring back enchanting moments. I must admit though that in Paris the next dish is Foie Gras, a gourmet treat!

Shamika sprinkled her very own kind of magical dust and made this dull day a moment of celebration that I will remember all my life. Daughters are a very special gift from God. I have been blessed with two. Who wants sons!

Monday, 21 October 2013

EVEN DESCARTES WOULD GIVE UP

I give up! I guess in the given circumstances even my friend René (Descartes) would. The new medical bizmess[98] has evolved a kind of logic that would zap Aristotle! It is like trying to figure out Lobachevski's geometry with Euclidian precepts. Let me elucidate why. I went to see the Doctor today to try and work out the final number of chemos needed as I was a little puzzled by the inconsistency of having 6 more chemos when according to him the cancer was 90% gone. This game number has been nothing short of mind-boggling. The 8 becoming 12 even though we knew from the beginning that R had B symptoms did not convince me. I guess maybe the figure of 8 was part of the sales pitch and sugar coating. If this were the case I would have expected being told 60% cure! So what was this 90%? If think the sales pitch went a bit awry

Today I was given another spiel that made me put my hands up in surrender. I was told that though the oncologist felt it was 90%, the radiologist's opinion was that it was less, though I was not given a figure. The bottom line is that the hospital's protocol must be 12.

I capitulate but my reason is based on emotions. Should I insist we stop at 8 and God forbid something goes wrong than I would never be able to live with the guilt.

---

[98] word coined by my mentor DV

The reason I was hoping against hope that we could stop at 8 or 10 was that R is now finding it difficult and his spirit is dampening day by day. He does not say so as being a man he would never admit weakness. He has always maintained that he will fight it and get the better of it. But he is also humane and who would not be scared in his situation. I wish he externalised his feelings like I do by writing them down: bang on the piano, stomp the treadmill, or maybe find a new creative pursuit. But I do not see that happening.

It is again I who would have to take the lead and add to my arsenal. Maybe I should behave like a joker and make him laugh, find new comedy shows on You Tube, play indoor games with him. Stand on my head if I have to. Get friends he likes over; find new recipes, just anything to make the next two months fly by!

Monday, 21 October 2013

SERENDIPITY AND A PROUSTIAN CUP OF TEA

This battle has many protagonists but the main ones are R and I! And to ensure final victory it has been important to conjure two arsenals: one to keep R going and the other to keep me going. The later is simpler and I guess less critical though I wonder what would happen if I had a meltdown. My line up is simpler. I just write every emotion I feel, the good, the bad and the ugly before it can fester inside me. But the Muses have been kind and have also sent many serendipitous moments that set my involuntary memory very much in the way a simple cookie sets Marcel Proust's in his book: In Search of Lost Time[99]:

I must admit that when I was a student and even later, I often read Proust when sleep eluded me; it was the ideal soporific drug. The length and beauty of his prose lulled you to sleep. I must also admit that I was not a great fan. I guess you had to understand Proust's life and his final confinement in a cork-lined room where he wrote In Search of Lost Time. I guess memory was his greatest companion.

I guess I find myself in much the same situation today, as I am housebound, by choice, but nevertheless housebound. And though I am no great traveller or wanderer, the fact of having a choice is freedom. My

---

[99] In Search of Lost Time, Marcel Proust 1913

freedom seems to be the bouts of involuntary travel that have come my way and make me time travel.

My elder daughter who is at present on an assignment in Rabat sent me a picture of Moroccan delights. The picture took me back to when I was a little girl and lived in Rabat for more than three years. My all time favourite were the gazelle's horns! Just seeing the picture bought their taste in my mouth and all my senses were alive. The visits to the King's Palace were such treats and syrupy mint tea was served each time you went. Images that I had forgotten and would have never remembered if this picture had not landed on me came tumbling out. That is the magic of involuntary memory. Had someone asked me to remember Morocco, I am sure I would not have talked of these sweets. But now with the taste of the almond filled delight in mouth and the syrupy warmth of a glass of Moroccan tea filled with fresh mint leaves takes me to many places at the same time: the Palace of course, but also the club where we went swimming and more than the swim what attracted me was the yummy *cornes de gazelle* that we ate perched on a stool and dripping with water.

I AM OVER THE MOON PART1

I am over the moon (part1 because part 2 will be on the other blog). R's results are in, the ones I was dreading because we began chemo 7 with a WBC count of 6300 whereas normally the cells are boosted to 15000+ and then fall to 3000+! This time they are at 3800. This is great news and I am really excited. I wonder what worked this time. Maybe it is the fresh cannabis leaves we started a few days back! But that does not mean I am not cross with chemotherapy.

A dear soul who reads my blogs and thinks like me sent me a book called the Cancer Conspiracy[100]. I would urge people who believe blindly in chemotherapy to read it. The book does say that Hodgkin's is one of the cancers that responds to chemo but that does not mean that the terrible side effects are mitigated. The book also says that cancer patients who opt for alternative therapies have a four time longer healthy life span. I am confident that my brews and supplements are kicking in. Once the last chemo is over, I will pound and strafe him with everything that will cleanse him of the poison that has been injected into him and build his immunity so that his body, mind and spirit fight and destroy all remaining cancer cells.

So here is to apricot kernels, soursop tea, ashwagandha and the latest kid on the block: pot!

---

[100] The Cancer Conspiracy: Betrayal, Collusion and the Suppression of Alternative Cancer Treatments Paperback by Barry Lynes

Thursday, 24 October 2013

I'LL JUST BE THE THIRTEENTH CLOWN

"If there are twelve clowns in a ring, you can jump in the middle and start reciting Shakespeare, but to the audience, you'll just be the thirteenth clown," wrote Adam Walinsky[101]. Today I feel like the 13th clown. The other 12 are the ones who have been pounding me with all sorts of reasons to go for 12 chemos, be they emotional, medical, rational or even commercial. I can keep spouting all my reasons for stopping but to the world I will remain the 13th clown no one hears.

This morning we went to see Dr Dolkar my Tibetan Doc who let me down this time by stating loud and clear before chemo 1 that Hodgkin's responded well to chemo and we should go for it! Today when we asked her whether we should stop at 8 or go for 12, she laughed in her inimitable way and said: *Go for 12 if the doctor says so, I will make you some special anti poison medicine.* Voila! In these few words she managed to convey both sides of the coin: follow the protocol but yes it is poison. What she is more concerned about is the bone marrow as the cure lies there. If R's bone marrow recovers from the onslaught of the slow and continuous poisoning, and kicks in 100% then we are out of the woods.

---

[101] Adam Walinsky; 1958-1968. Lawyer. Attorney, Department of Justice (1963-64); legislative assistant and speechwriter to Sen. Robert F. Kennedy

I am reading a novel set during World War I and it has graphic descriptions of the effects of mustard gas on young soldiers. It is frightening and to think that mustard gas is the progenitor of chemotherapy and you are injecting it directly in the veins of a person, I leave it to you to decide what damage it does. Anyway 12 it is and then basta! I want my man back and so that I can rid him of all the poison and rebuild his immunity system so that it can take care of any remaining cancer cells for the rest of his life.

I for one know that my research on chemotherapy has convinced me that I would never allow it to enter my body should my genetic imprint take me that way. I will swallow a kilo of almond kernels a day if needed but will not allow anyone to poison me.

I agree to be the 13th clown and keep on reciting my Shakespeare, which in this case is my total aversion and non-acceptance of chemotherapy even if no one hears me. I wish there was Google and information technology when both my parents were diagnosed with cancers and theirs were cancers that are not the ones that respond well to chemo. They had lungs and colon cancers. The only redeeming factor is that in both cases we did not go the chemo way: mom refused treatment (she listened to her intuition) and pa died just after surgery! I am so glad I did not subject them to chemo. In R's case he had one of the 3 cancers that supposedly respond well! There was no logical argument my Cartesian mind could come up with and no one can pitch apricot kernels and hemp against the fancy sounding chemo drugs and the drama around it. I capitulated, keeping my cards up my sleeve, as I know chemo cycles have an end.

However I will continue to share whatever I can find on chemo and expose to the best of my ability the conspiracy that keeps this form of treatment alive and kicking with the help of big bucks and vested interests. I am not saying do not go for chemo. What I want to convey is that you should be fully aware of the treatment and its consequences, short and long term, and of alternatives and make an informed choice.

So to be continued....

Thursday, 24 October 2013

THE GREAT CANCER BIZMESS

It is breast cancer awareness month! Across the globe 'events' and mammoth advertising campaigns are on. A dear friend who thinks like me sent me a link[102] to an article in French! For those of you who can read French it is a must read. For the others I would still request you to go to the page and click on the links given, which are mostly in English! The article questions the relevance of mammography. A study[103] that appeared in the New England Journal of Medicine concludes with this statement: *Our study raises serious questions about the value of screening mammography. It clarifies that the benefit of mortality reduction is probably smaller, and **the harm of over diagnosis** probably larger, than has been previously recognized. And although no one can say with certainty which women have cancers that are over-diagnosed, there is certainty about what happens to them: they undergo surgery, radiation therapy, hormonal therapy for 5 years or more, chemotherapy, or (usually) a combination of these treatments for abnormalities that otherwise would not have*

---

102   http://blogs.rue89.nouvelobs.com/node/227625/2013/10/24/
      cancer-du-sein-aux-etats-unis-le-ruban-rose-fait-polemique-231462

103   Effect of Three Decades of Screening Mammography on Breast-Cancer
      Incidence
      Archie Bleyer, M.D., and H. Gilbert Welch, M.D., M.P.H.
      N Engl J Med 2012; 367:1998-2005

caused illness. I draw your attention to the highlighted words: the harm of over diagnosis.

The obsessive 'marketing' of screening mammography must have had some very sad consequences. Imagine having to poison yourself for something that nature and your body would have taken care of is criminal in my lexicon. More so if it is given to someone who has been to use the politically correct word: Over diagnosed.

Same is the case with prostate cancer where the only test marketed is the PSA. This again has been misused by the cancer industry and subjected painful, expensive and life threatening treatments to patients who never needed it. This became so bad that Richard Ablin the person who discovered the PSA test had to listen to his conscience and write a book[104] called: The Great Prostate Hoax: How Big Medicine Hijacked the PSA Test and Caused a Public Health Disaster. The book cover states: *Every year, more than a million men undergo painful needle biopsies for prostate cancer, and upward of 100,000 have radical prostatectomies, resulting in incontinence and impotence. But the shocking fact is that most of these men would never have died from this common form of cancer, which frequently grows so slowly that it never even leaves the prostate.*

Need I say more!

But let us get back to the awareness week. You do not have to be a rocket scientist to see that all the products that have got pink washed are those that are known to cause cancers! A tongue in cheek article[105] writes: *Breast Cancer®, the America's Sweetheart of deadly, disfiguring diseases that it is, inspires a deluge of pink junk for sale every October. Some of that pink junk, in addition to being ugly, cloying, and infantilizing, contains chemicals that have been linked to boobs full of tumours.* What do you say to that!

I will not go into a long apology of my feelings and beliefs!

I am now a self -appointed rabid researcher on cancer healing!

---

[104] The Great Prostate Hoax: How Big Medicine Hijacked the PSA Test and Caused a Public Health Disaster. Richar Ablin, Ronald Piana 2014

[105] Fun Breast Cancer® Awareness™ Products That Can Cause Breast Cancer®, Erin Gloria Ryan, http://jezebel.com/fun-breast-cancer-awareness-products-that-can-cause-b-1445639237

Thursday, 24 October 2013

TWO LITTLE WORDS: THANK YOU

Over the past three months when R was diagnosed with cancer, I decided to start this blog to be able to cope with the stress, fears and all the emotions you feel when a loved one is diagnosed with the big C! My initial reaction felt strange to me. Where were the tears, the recriminations, the anger! Why was I not reacting the way people often do. There are even support groups to help loved ones deal with such news. Yet I felt a sense of calm and a determination to win what I called my last battle.

Yet I needed some place to share the flood of emotions that would and could choke me. So I decided to bare my soul and write everything that happened. And this has been the best coping strategy I could come up with.

Today I am overwhelmed with the support and love I have got from people I know well, but also from people I have only met virtually.

Today I feel the need to express my gratitude for each one of you who has taken time off their busy schedules not only to read my meandering thoughts but also the leave a little note. I will not give out names but little clues and hope you recognise yourselves! So here goes. I need to say Thank you to: the beloved uncle[106] who never fails to comment on every post in spite of all the challenges he faces; my friend from sunny Spain who never fails to leave a message of encouragement just as N, who remains anonymous; the white haired gentleman who makes it a point to read my posts and

---

[106] Sadly he lost his battle with the big C in 2015

drops in when in town, my two wonderful rediscovered friends who wait for my morning email - by morning I mean 4.30 am - and should I forget to email them a worried message comes on my phone; the one I remember every time I see a crooked picture hanging on my wall; the one that made sure my toes are warm in winter, the one I have never met but who sent me books to read and the one I have met who sent me books to help me cope. And of course all the ones who take time to 'like' the FB posts! How can I forget the mother whose child is battling with cancer and who still found time to tell me to hold on! The one who sends me chocolates and the one who.. the list is endless!

I have received so many virtual hugs that I feel humbled, blessed and confident that I will win this battle.

Saturday, 26 October 2013

THE SUNDAY BEFORE CHEMO DAY

Sunday before chemo day! Normally a quiet and good day. Sunday after chemo day is usually bad so let us enjoy it as much as possible. R has decided the lunch menu: oily, sinful but organic poorie and aloos! (Fried bread and potato curry) For me it is the normal visit to the beauty parlour for my weekly and only self-indulgence. However this time there is an almost life changing or rather look changing decision: do I or do I not shave my nut. The bets are on and the views multiple. Perhaps I will go mid way and keep a fuzz on. Or maybe as my daughter says chicken out. All revealed by 11 am. Oops I forgot. Before the parlour I have to give R his first or three White Cell Boosting shot. That is what actually sets the chemo mood in motion.

After the oily lunch I will leave R to his idiot box and hopefully books and take a trip to Utpal's school to give him his new skates and a big hug. He is not coming home for Diwali. He will spend it with his new friends in his brand new school. I hope we meet some of them and I am sure I will have a good time as I jump of my whirling world for a few stolen moments.

So an exciting day.... more later!

Monday, 28 October 2013

BREAKING NEWS

Breaking News! R played 9 holes of golf yesterday with his best friend and no cart! This is the most wonderful news I have got in months. Yes, yes I know the course is closed on Mondays but the B course is opened and for me it was the best day for him to go, as there would be fewer people and thus less risk of infection. But the best news is that he played well (his friend said he beat him but I do not know if that is true) and came back happy and not tired. My mind goes back to the days when he use to come back from his game in a bad mood muttering that he would give up the game. Those were the days when we did not know what was wrong with him and he was tired and without energy. And then once chemo began he stayed indoors. I think we were both a bit frightened of possible infections.

But we put our fears on hold and took the big leap. It was the best decision ever. R came back a different man. The fact that he hit a straight ball and did not go in the rough (so I was told) meant he had regained some of his strength.

Wednesday, 30 October 2013

A MATTER OF CHOICE

Some of you may think that I have made my peace with chemo as I have capitulated and accepted the 6 cycles 12 chemos for R. Far from it. When I accepted the protocol I had an intuitive aversion for chemo and did not have enough knowledge of the long-term side effects. As many of us I knew about hair loss, nausea, loss of appetite, fatigue etc. But I was totally unaware of the destruction occurring inside the body. All I was told was that Hodgkin's responded well to chemo and was even cured. I wonder what I would have done if had been told Hodgkin's lymphoma does get cured with chemo but *survivors of Hodgkin lymphoma have a higher risk of developing a secondary cancer, especially acute myeloid leukaemia, non–Hodgkin lymphoma, lung cancer, or breast cancer.*[107]

This is the problem with medicine and doctors today. They tell you half the truth and fill you in if you see a new side effect or if you come to know of something on your own. *Oh yes that happens* too is the pet answer. It is ok for the immediate side effects but no one tells you about the long term ones. You may get to know about them in an indirect manner. You may be asked to get a test on the way, and when you pester to be told why the answer is: *Bleomycin can affect your lungs and so on.* By then you or your

---

[107] http://www.cancer.net/cancer-types/lymphoma-hodgkin/
late-effects-treatment

loved one is in the middle of the treatment and your choice option has been already usurped.

I have watched helplessly R having his seven chemos. It gets worse with each one. During those fateful 4 to 6 hours one can actually feel the poison that is dripping into his heart via the port placed on his jugular and then seeping through his body. No matter how upbeat he is at the beginning it always ends with a tired, agitated and shocked being, one I can barely recognise. I guess the body reacts in its own way to all the poisoning it has been subjected with. The body then turns into a killing field where good and bad cells are destroyed mercilessly. I presume, the body that is a magnificent machine working at its own pace is suddenly jolted into become a killing field. It now takes R more than 3 days to somewhat recover. And the body is not given time to regroup its forces before the next assault. A series of injections compels it to go in frenzied mode to build good cells before they are again destroyed. And this goes on in cycles of 15 days. This is chemo for you.

I am writing this blog and there will be others to help you make an informed choice before you embark on chemo journey. I can only speak of the ABVD protocol, the one known to work best for Hodgkin's or what is known as the first line of treatment. Oncologists would tell you ABVD is a great progress on previous protocols, which were far more toxic. The problem is that toxicity remains no matter which way you look at it!

(I would like to say that all information in this blog is from serious medical journals and websites. This is not based on alternative therapy die hard or sensational websites)

What is ABVD? It is a combination of four drugs dripped into your system over a period of 4 to 5 hours. They are: Adriamycin, Bleomycin, Vinblastine and Dacarbazine.

Adriamycin was discovered in 1950 with clinical trials in the sixties and is a compound made from soil-based microbes. By 1967 it was known that the compound could produce fatal heart toxicity. Adriamycin is also known as Doxorubicin. You would be amused or rather bemused to know that Adriamycin gets its name from the Adriatic Sea and the *rubi* in its other name signifies ruby colour. The heart toxicity is higher in older people. This would be enough to make me think twice or a zillion times before accepting it to be dripped in a loved one. An article[108] lists the side effects both for the layman and the health care professionals. If you or a loved one is likely to go for chemo, I urge you to read this as even the scientific mumbo jumbo is partly understandable. For ex when it is written: *Doxorubicin-induced heart failure can be present one month to one year or more after termination of therapy.* So now one has to live with this constant fear and keep a look out for the signs and I guess do regular investigations however costly, painful or humiliating. The article lists the other side effects too, but this one is a big one. In plain words it would read like: you will be cured of your lymphoma but may die of a heart attack.

Bleomycin is the next guy on the list. From the heart we move to the lungs. Here again we were told about this about half way through the chemos when the Oncologist wanted a lung function test and I badgered him to learn more. Mercifully the lung function test was within norms but that was at chemo 6. Wonder what things would look like when 6 more chemos are done. Here again the lung side effect can come after the statement: you are clear of Hodgkin's. An article in the health Care Blog[109] written in simple terms and says it all. So post chemo and even the possibility of hearing the words: Hodgkin is gone, a heart and lung watch has to be in place.

So with 2 out of 4 we have to keep watch on two main organs: the heart and the lungs. Of course let us not forget all the short-term effects on digestive tract, the skin, the hair, the nails etc.

Next is Vinblastine[110]! Over and above the usual mouth sores, low platelets, low white cells, anaemia, pains etc. that seems to be there for all chemo drugs, this one seems to be a little less toxic than the others. It can affect your hearing though and turn your nails blue! However there is a caveat: it has to go directly into the vein as if it leaks into muscle and/or tissue it can cause severe damage! The mentioned article states:" Deaths have occurred when vinblastine was injected into the spine".

Dacarbazine is R's bête noire! He somehow finds this drug the toughest and as luck would have it, it takes the longest to inject: 90 minutes! It lowers

---

[108]   http://www.drugs.com/sfx/adriamycin-side-effects.html
[109]   http://www.drugs.com/sfx/adriamycin-side-effects.html
[110]   http://www.medicinenet.com/vinblastine-injection/article.htm

your blood and platelet counts and makes you sensitive to sunlight and could damage your liver.

One of the major side effects of treatment of Hodgkin's lymphoma is the development of a secondary cancer. That is the scary[111] one. You celebrate the cure of one and start worrying about the possibility of another. In men it is lung and leukaemia! So I guess not too many cigars for R! His Doctor has allowed him one a week. Maybe I will ask him to stop once chemos are over. This is what I mean when I say you are given information in small palatable doses. I would like the whole enchilada!

One of the worst if not worst side effects of chemotherapy is its assault on the immune system. Let us not forget that it is this very system that will ultimately ensure total cure. Again serendipity at work as I was just handed a book about the Healing Codes and opened the page that said: *The immune system is capable of healing just about anything if it is not suppressed by stress.* I am still to read the book and find out whether it is in sync with me but I too agree that ONLY OUR IMMUNE SYSTEM can heal any disease of the mind and the body we may have.

Conventional cancer therapies be they radio or chemo weaken and depress your immune system[112]. That is a known fact. For the past 3 months now I have been a silent and helpless witness to this fact. The blood work that is done on R every week shows the WBCs falling at a frightening rate: from 19000 (boosted by Grafeel injections) to 3000 two days after an ABVD session. This yoyo game is repeated with obsessive regularity. I wonder how our body and brain perceive it. It must be nothing short of shock and confusion.

---

[111] Second cancers and late toxicities after treatment of aggressive non-Hodgkin lymphoma with the ACVBP regimen: a GELA cohort study on 2837 patients Marc André, Nicolas Mounier, Xavier Leleu, Anne Sonet, Pauline Brice, Michel Henry-Amar, Hervé Tilly, Bertrand Coiffier, André Bosly, Pierre Morel, Corinne Haioun, Philippe Gaulard, Felix Reyes, Christian Gisselbrecht, and the Groupe d'Etude des Lymphomes de l'Adulte (GELA) http://www.bloodjournal.org/content/103/4/1222.full?sso-checked=true

[112] http://www.everydayhealth.com/cancer/chemotherapy-and-your-immune-system.aspx

I am a little weary of the alacrity with which doctors add chemo sessions. It is as if 8 or 12 do not make a difference. But when you read about the effects any chemo drug has on your immune system, you feel that doctors should be more concerned about adding even one cycle. A study revealed that oncologists would not take chemo[113] themselves or recommend it to their loves ones. If this is the case, then it is nothing short of scary. Some may think that this statement is made to promote alternative cures. Again I leave it to your judgement. I read a book on chemotherapy where the author suggested that only cancer survivors should be oncologists or that every oncologist should administer him/herself with a chemo cycle before treating a patient. This is far fetched but not that silly. Your vision changes when you experience something first hand.

Chemo or no chemo what matters is the immune system. It is difficult to accept a therapy that destroys your immune system. An article in a health website[114] that outlines ways of strengthening your immune system states: *Intuition that tells you (more like SHOUTS at you) that you need to build up your immune system to combat the cancer and to restore your overall health. Once you understand that you need effective treatment to deal with a threat as serious as cancer, and you go ahead with your treatment, you still need to listen to your intuition. It does make sense that your immune system needs to be nurtured.* It suggests exercise, nutrition, stress reduction etc.

I have a series of strategies to try and protect R's immune system to the best of my ability. My Tibetan doctor's words resound in my head 24/7. She has always maintained that she is only concerned about keeping the bone marrow intact and healthy. Keeping the immune system kicking!

Just read an interesting article[115] about ageing. By the way I am not the one who is scared of ageing and have never: dyed my hair, applied anti ageing gloop or fallen for the ad campaigns promising you an 18 year old forever. What caught my eye is the opening para: *A few weeks ago, a group of researchers including maverick American physician Dean Ornish*

---

[113] http://www.conspiracyplanet.com/channel.cfm?channelid=63&contentid=4846&page=2

[114] http://www.healthcentral.com/breast-cancer/r/breast-cancer/article/boosting-immune-system-4229?ic=506048

[115] http://www.openthemagazine.com/article/living/the-battle-against-ageing-0

and Nobel laureate Elizabeth Blackburn published a study that caught a lot of eyeballs. In the study, which appeared in Lancet Oncology[116], a prestigious medical journal, Ornish's team compared two sets of prostate cancer patients. Both had undergone dramatically different treatments for five years—one received conventional therapy while the other made drastic lifestyle changes, exercising, meditating, attending support-group sessions and eating a diet of whole foods. At the end of the study period, Ornish found that while the blood immune cells of patients in the conventional therapy group had aged as all normal human cells do, the clock had seemingly turned back in the cells of the group that had made lifestyle changes. The article is about a new agent called telomeres but is all in trial stage. They do have a supplement called TA 65. By the way it is available in India but at a cost I cannot afford[117]! But Dr Ornish makes a point that we should keep in mind. He has developed the Ornish method, which is *a mix of several interventions, such as switching to plant-based foods, meditation and regular exercise. The most unique feature of the programme, though, is its acknowledgement that loneliness and social isolation can cause illness and premature death more than poor diet or smoking ever can. Therefore, the Ornish Spectrum requires a person following it to seek love and intimacy. It may sound like a hopelessly vague task, but the programme recommends several ways to achieve this, such as improving communication skills, meditating, group therapy, psychotherapy and even learning how to confess and forgive.*

It brings all back to mind over matter and to the fact that stress is the worst culprit. I know exactly how and when R's cancer cells began their frenzied dance. I kick myself for not having pushed him enough though God knows how much I tried. Could I have done more? I do not think so as he was blinded by emotions he believed in and had to witness their destruction with no coping strategy. The harm was done. Now one has to undo it all.

I am counting days till the 27 December, which will be the 12th chemo. 2014 will be my year when I go all guns blazing to get his immune system back in place and ready to fight every assault. Something will be easy but getting R to do yogic breathing and meditate is a tough one. Have been

---

[116] http://www.thelancet.com/journals/lanonc/article/
      PIIS1470-2045%2813%2970366-8/fulltext
[117] http://www.biovea.com/in/results.aspx?KW=TA+65

trying for long but not much success. Maybe acupuncture. I still do not know. Have been scouring the net for suggestions to boost immune system Guavas and oranges, carrots and papaya, almonds and green tea! Much of this he is having already. I am also looking for supplements and have found astragalus[118] and hope it all works and gets his bone marrow to produce all the good cells needed to take care of the few left over cancer cells.

I titled this post a matter of choice. I know most people will be weary of trying out alternative therapies as the first line of defence should they or their loved ones be diagnosed with cancer. What I insist upon, is knowing all the side effects and also being aware of all the support regimen that one can build. For me it has been a constant research to try and keep one step ahead. The reason I share all this is that maybe it could help someone and make their last battle that much easier.

---

[118] http://www.naturalnews.com/035924_astragalus_cancer_prevention.html

THE DAY BEFORE TOMORROW

It is the day before tomorrow, tomorrow being Chemo 8. It is always a difficult day as one hopes and prays that all will go as planned. I mean not only the chemo per se but the efficiency of the hospital and the unnecessary delays that make R edgy. Imagine sitting on your bed by 8.15 and then waiting to things to begin. The mood takes a big dip. One wants it all over and there we are waiting for the nurse to get her act together, the doctor to sign the protocol, the pharmacist to mix the deadly cocktails to be ingested and the whole damn thing to start. The best-case scenario for the gun shot has been 9.30 the worst 10.30! After that is waiting time as one watches the drops falling and tries to convince one's self that the poison is actually manna from the Gods! Not an easy task for me as I have read too much. Maybe being a neophyte or an illiterate makes this easier.

Have been thinking of how to make the waiting for this Godot easier. Maybe I will try to find some fun card game that we can play while waiting or a joke book. Don my clown nose and do some tricks. I do not think I really need a clown nose, as my new hairdo will amuse the whole chemo care centre:) I will also try and conjure something more palatable than the sandwiches so that the waiting time can be used in feeding him as after the drip begins, the appetite goes AWOL sometimes for days. Of course the iPad is replete with funny movies and that does help him pass some time. I watch him while I pretend to read and am thrilled and even moved when he laughs with his headphones on.

By the time the trial is over R is lethargic, the Bleomycin induced fever begins to creep in and the nauseous feeling kicks in. Actually the last time he started feeling nauseous as soon as he entered the centre. The ride back home is always horrid. And tomorrow with Dhanteras[119] it will be worse. I just hope the whole thing ends early. Once home, R will take to his bed and as the fever rises and the confusion sets in, I will sit beside him and soothe him to the best of my ability. I will keep watch on the fever and pray that it comes down and that the morning after tomorrow is a good one.

Maybe I should rename myself as chemo girl! Feel like one!

---

[119]   Hindu Festival where people shop!

Thursday, 31 October 2013

CHEMO 8 DAY

It is chemo 8 day! As always Morpheus went AWOL. The night was long. Chemo days are not my favourite. Anyway one has to bear 5 more. Hope this one goes well. Yesterday I finally got the hairdresser to comply and hence 2 baldies will march into the hospital today. Hope it bring some smiles on faces. Anyway I like the new look and more than that it makes me feel closer to R. Quirky? I always was.

Have 'armed' myself with lots of chocolates, as that is the only thing he likes eating. I know sugar is not the best things as cancer cells love it but all is allowed today. Have also got 2 card games in case he feels up to it. I also pray things move fast and we are home soon.

Wishes and prayers needed.

Thursday, 31 October 2013

I AM LIVID AND SHOCKED

I am livid, incensed, furious!. I am still trembling with rage. As you know we went for chemo 8 this morning. As always in spite of our pleadings it all began late. Finally the nurse arrived with her trolley, inserted the needle in the port making poor R wince as always. Actually he starts wincing before the needle touching him. The pre-med bottle was also placed on the trolley so I decided to have a look and to my absolute horror saw that it included dexamethasone, a medicine R had reacted to violently That is what had made him take off on a time travel at chemo 1. It was then decided that he would not be given this the next time as is clearly stated in his file.

I got up to take a walk and glanced at the bottle with its hand written label and to my UTTER HORROR found that Dexona 8mg was included. This in spite of the fact that the junior doctor had come to see him and I had reminded her of this. I immediately reported it to the nurse station and the doctor on duty. There was a bit of confusion and the bottle was removed. I also waited to inform the senior oncologist and though he tried to go into damage control mode, I guess he needed to protect his team, I told him categorically that there had been a mistake and I had seen it with my own eyes. Thank God this was before they began the drip.

I am now sure that Dexona was given to him in the last chemo. Actually nothing had started by the time I left and Shamika took over and she would

THERE IS ONLY ROOM FOR HOPE 277

not have read the label, but R's extreme reaction to chemo 7 and his state of mind and confusion were due to the wrong medication.

What makes me beside myself and seething in anger is that this is a SUPER SPECIALITY hospital and one would expect things to be spot on. It is a serious matter as most of the patients have an implicit trust in the people in white and submit to their 'protocols' blindly. Imagine if a wrong medication results in serious consequences or even death. In India one cannot even sue them.

The commercialisation of medicine has made health caretakers into moneymaking hounds. Who can one trust? One pays hefty amounts in the hope of getting cured, not to die because systems fail. When you are handling medication as lethal as chemotherapy drugs you must have multiple checks. What I have seen in the past months is a happy-go-lucky who cares attitude that one does not expect of what is now known as SUPER SPECIALITY hospitals.

It now puts into doubt everything that I have been sold with glib and smooth spoken assurances. It is time to take things in my hand. Thank God I am a control freak!

NIGHT AND MORNING AFTER

4 am or so. R is still sleeping. The Gods were kind: he had a good night no fever this time. I pray he wakes up with a smile or at least a quirky repartee to my silly morning greet. It would mean the world to me.

I for one had a sleepless night. A disturbed one to say the last. When it was kosher time to creep out of bed I did and took out all the old chemo discharge files. To my absolute horror and if I am to go by what is written my poor man had been given the Dexona each and every time in spite of the: **no Dexona to be given**. It is only in yesterday's file that I saw it had not been given.

I kicked myself but then I remembered an SMS I had sent to the Doctor on August 9th telling him that I felt that he had been given Dexona and he answered with a: Oh no! And then silence!

I feel terrible having trusted the doc and his team blindly and subjected R to unnecessary side effects. Great for one whose Holy Grail has been to ensure no or minimal side effects. Deserve a kick in my ****.

When I took on my first job at the Belgian Embassy as Social Secretary to the Ambassador - a priced job in the 70s - I once made a mistake and waited to be admonished. It never happened. My immediate boss took the wrath of our mercurial Excellency. When I asked him later why he had not scolded me he simply said: I lead the team: share the success and am responsible for the failures! It is a lesson I never forgot and tried to apply and teach to others. As my good old Doc P said when I shared my ire yesterday: It is the fault of the captain of the ship.

What this horrid incident has done is made me loose faith in the whole treatment. Time for a second opinion!

Friday, 1 November 2013

SOME GOOD NEWS

Got an early Diwali gift! Though a bittersweet one. R woke up from chemo 8 with a smile and feeling good, just a bit tired by the chemo and the lack of diet and my special brews for a day, not to forget the cannabis shot! This is super news. At 5.30 am he even had a long chat with Agastya and is now lying in bed watching TV. He had his morning juice and even decided what he wanted for lunch!

For all past chemos it took him at least 2 if not 3 days to emerge back from his poison shots. He says he is not hungry, feeling like hell etc. etc. We did not even have fever yesterday. Just a slight body ache that a crocin and a good night's sleep took care of.

Bittersweet because it is now confirmed that the darned hospital was giving him the Dexona shot at every chemo notwithstanding the instruction boldly written on page one of his file. I am angry at myself for not having checked before. I should have, as I knew that my support arsenal should have taken care of side effects.

Moral of the story: do no trust any hospital, doctor etc. Do your research and take informed decisions. Scream if you have to. In today's day and age we are not patients and doctors are not healers. We are consumers and they are service providers where we have the right to demand explanations.

Friday, 1 November 2013

THE ANATOMY OF A MESS

I was horrified this morning when I realised that all R's chemo discharge files from 2 to 7 had a glaring discrepancy between pages 1 where it is clearly written that no Dexona is to be given to the patient and page 4 where it is stated in the list of premedication that it has been given. I noticed this on August 19 as R was acting strange and I checked the file and sent an SMS the oncologist. He assured me that it was a mistake and would be rectified. In hindsight I am feeling awful not to have checked. I thought that as all this was a printed format it was a simple typing slip up of the nurse not deleting the Dexona from the protocol list. I now remember Dharmendra telling me on the phone that the '4' pre-meds had been given and not reacting to the number four. Somehow the glitter and glam aspect of these super speciality centres lulled me into a false sense of complacency and made me believe that at least in such places, such mistakes could not occur. How wrong I was!

Now that my anger has cooled down a little, I will try and dissect the issue. It is a fact that I have always felt that this chemo day care centre is poorly organised and have been dying to give suggestions as one of my forte is organisation, but held back as I thought that it was not in my place to do so and did not want to rock the boat for R. But now I feel compelled to at least write this blog to give you an idea of how it runs and how things can go wrong.

Before I do so, I would like to share how we handled conference documents in Summits where I headed the multi lingual Technical Secretariat. We had pre conference documents, in conference amendments and the final document. In conferences of this level even a coma can change everything and create diplomatic incidents. If a mistake should occur then you face the wrath of the likes of Indira Gandhi or the Foreign Secretary and also get ridiculed in sessions. When a document would reach us after being vetted by the conference secretary it would go to a pool of translators and then to a reviser. It would then be sent to the typing pool and then be proof read. It was then be duplicated and came tome before being sent to the conference hall! I can say that in my career as Conference organiser I never let a mistake pass. Even if the delegates were screaming for the translations we never broke our system. That was the reason for our success rate.

The chemo centre runs much like the rest of India in a sort of crises management mode. Patients arrive by 8 am and after useless paperwork that has to be done each and every time - wonder why they cannot enter all the information on their computers and hand you a print out to sign - you enter the day care. The staff is also in the process of checking in. First mistake. Staff should be in place and at their stations an hour earlier. Then your vitals are checked and then you are left unattended. When you ask the junior nurse you are told that the junior doctor has to OK the medication. Then you wait some more and the junior doctor arrives and asks you if all is well and then disappears. You ask the nurse again why they cannot at least place the needle in the port. You are told that it can only start after the doc's OK. By that time you have waited an hour. You then go to the desk where the junior doctor sits and ask her what is happening. The answer is that she is waiting for an OK from Senior Doc whom she has messaged. When that arrives then the show begins. The feeling you get is that no one knows anything and is waiting for Godot.

Now let me enlighten you a little. Most of the patients are the same on a given day. The cycle is a fortnightly one. You are told in your discharge papers to get your CBC counts down and inform the hospital a day before the chemo. I SMS these to the oncologist. The likely hood of anyone having a problem is according to me less than 2% as I have seen the same faces getting their chemos again and again. So if the system worked the medication protocol should be worked out, signed and countersigned the night before. If this was the case, your chemo could start by 8.30am and not 10 am, as is the best-case scenario.

But that is not so. Sending information earlier is of no use. It is all done in the morning in a state close to panic, as everyone is anxious to start the show.

Let us go on. Once all papers are signed and your pre medication given, you have to wait as the pharmacist has either not arrived or is in the process of making the cocktails for each patient. Again it is done under stress and the likelihood of an error is there.

In R's case, no one bothered to read page 1. I guess they should skip to page 4 where the normal pre-meds protocol is written as the correction was never made and the 4 medicines are put in a saline drip. I was at the right place at the right moment and saw the bottle with the 4 names scribbled on it. Had I not seen it, R would have had another bad experience. And yet with a little organisation things could work well. Actually in a hospital of this reputation it should be clockwork orange. The system followed is haphazard with no proper direction or delegation. I am sure that if everyone was given a fixed responsibility and a final check was done by the doctor on duty with the patient file and the medication bottle, all would be well.

There is more. As I wrote in an earlier blog, it took us an hour to get a simple discharge slip. After the proverbial Indian crisis management we faced the proverbial bureaucratic system of a series of no objections. The person giving the slip is on the same floor than the chemo care centre. Yet we were told that the paper had to go to several floors whether virtually or manually, as was the case yesterday. Come on, you want to run like an international outfit but cannot get rid of the Indian small shop attitude.

All this would be acceptable in a small mufassil town or at a big overcrowded state run hospital but when you enter the portals of a five star hotel like lobby, replete with fast food outlets and bookshops you expect basic efficiency and responsibility.

The cherry on the cake is that in the chemo centre every patient has to have an attendant keeping a hawk eye watch on the drip and the patient. This is a government hospital rule not befitting a medical palace that is replete with suits of all kind who are masters at collecting dues or trained to seduce you into handing out more than you have.

I still do not know how I will take this further. At present I need to keep things going as R still has 4 more chemos. Time will tell but I know I will not keep shut.

I still feel the guilt of having subjected R to unnecessary hurt. As Voltaire[120] said:" *Every man is guilty of all the good he did not do.*" I am too.

DIWALI IS THE DARKEST NIGHT OF THE DARKEST PERIOD, YET IT IS A CELEBRATION OF LIGHT!

Diwali is the darkest night of the darkest period, yet it is a celebration of light! Diwali is heralded as the triumph of good over evil. This is a definition of Diwali I found and liked. Let today be the darkest night of my battle and a celebration of all the light that awaits me. The last year had been difficult but so empowering and blessed. This Diwali I implore the Gods of all the Pantheons in the universe to grant the dreams of all those who have stood by me and made my difficult journey a breeze. When I light one of the diyas painted by Shamika and her special children this evening as the sun sets, I would like it to convey my undying gratitude to all the beautiful souls that have lit the dark road I had to embark upon at every step. One often forgets to express our gratitude to those closest to us. Love if often taken for granted. My first thought goes to Shamika who has silently and without fuss taken on the running of the house and made it possible for me to care for R. I am so proud to be her mom. Next comes R whose trust has been so complete that it is sometimes scary! And how can I forget the house staff Geeta, Deepak and Savita[121] who have done everything I asked for with a smile and without reacting to the most inane demand.

My thoughts and blessings will also go to Mamaji, Rani and Dharmendra who have kept Project Why thriving and to all the staff of Project Why who made it possible. But they could not have done it without all those who have trusted me for years and have made sure we have all the funds needed to carry on. I shall not name them. I know they will understand.

But above all I want to express my gratitude and love to all the people known and unknown who have stood by me and proved that people who see with their hearts exist in ample measure. Every little word that is written on my virtual canvass is proof of that and makes me stronger and more determined in my resolve to rid R of his cancer and make Project Why a sustainable and worthy effort.

Then there are the ones who wait for my morning mails and are there 24/7!

Last but not the least are my two little chaps who bring a smile on my tired face. My little Agastya who comes on Skype and makes me laugh and cry at the same time and his parents of course. My elder child who has always been my voice of reason and her dashing man who is a rock. And last but not the least Popples who settled down in his new school like a dream and made sure I need not worry.

This Diwali I want to celebrate life and love. For an only child who lived a nomadic life, I feel grounded and surrounded by so much love. I am blessed and overwhelmed.

Happy Diwali!

Monday, 4 November 2013

THE CHEMO BIZMESS

This morning I received a link to 2 stories that sends chills down my spine. The first one tells how If you have a child diagnosed with cancer, the government can force you to subject your child to chemotherapy and radiation treatments. And if you don't comply, Child Protective Services can take your child away. The other is about an Amish girl who had to be taken out of the US to avoid experimental chemotherapy. This story gives you an account of the ugly side of chemotherapy and experimental trials and the big bucks! It also tells you how the State takes away the right of parents to chose the treatment they would want to and believe in. The story also gives you an honest account on the cancer bizmess, which is a whopping 550 billion business. No wonder they do not want to give up their chemical poisons

The bottom line is that chemo kills! Chemo is still in experimental stages. It has been so since the mustard gas discovery over half a century ago. You will be flabbergasted to know that over[122] 39 clinical trials on children are going on presently and sometimes against the will of parents courtesy some skewed laws that are made to help big businesses and their supporters. There also 12 000 other clinical trials on the anvil.

---

[122] http://www.cancer.gov/clinicaltrials/search/results?protocolsearc hid=12089412

But the most important link I found was to the film entitled Cancer - The Forbidden Cures[123]. This film is an eye opener and is worth watching at least the first 12 minutes. It sent chills down my spine and validated much of my visceral aversion to chemo as well as my mother's stubborn and child like aversion to chemotherapy and other 'legal' cancer cures as well as the well-planned and horrific chemo bizmess.

I watched the film many times to make sure I was seeing and hearing right! To put it in a nutshell this is how the business of medicine and therefore cancer goes. I will try and put it in a tongue in cheek way to make it palatable. Imagine someone has been unwell for some time, like in the case of R, and one is worried and wants to find out what is the cause of the ailment. Even if you are weary of conventional medicine and your good Doctor has not been able to fix it you are forced to enter a dark tunnel: tests, more tests, investigations, more investigations and more as nothing comes out. It is an infernal machine in which you get caught in spite of yourself, particularly if the patient is a loved one. And then one day a diagnosis is given but it has to be refined so more tests, more investigations, some pervasive, some dangerous. But the tunnel is long and you have no way out but moving forward. You are now at the mercy of the disease, in our case cancer. As you have chosen the dark tunnel you are now in the hands of the conventional holy trinity: surgery, radiation and chemotherapy. Should you dare suggest alternative medicine you are rapped on the knuckles or seduced. The way out of the long tunnel is to accept everything you are told, pay the money (in the US ~ 50000 $) and let out with a 5-year remission chance if you are lucky! But there is a catch you have submit yourself to regular investigations.

The problem is that this holy trinity does not cure you. It actually increases your risks of secondary cancers, another tunnel and more money in the bottomless pockets. You are never told that radiotherapy and chemotherapy are carcinogens and some remain toxic even after they are incinerated! And that is what has been poured into your veins. That you maybe affected in zillion of ways is never revealed to you before you begin.

How did all this happen?

---

[123] https://youtu.be/km2cqQNFtEs

The film gives a detailed account about how allopathy got the upper hand though when it all began there were two schools of medicines: allopathy and empirical medicine. One was brutal and the other in tune with the body, one used chemical weapons, the other one nature, in one case you died of the cure in the other of the disease. The bottom line is only the body can cure itself but we have forgotten that. From healing allopathy made medicine a business and what a business.

It goes like this. Big money entered the hallowed portal of healing. They hijacked the teaching universities and dictated what would be taught and what would be taught was what could make money. Every thing had to feed the big Pharma industry. With surgery having become a viable option, hospitals were needed and then radiation was discovered and chemotherapy drugs. Drugs could be patented and the only way money could be made was by prescribing them with alacrity and impunity. Health providers were seduced with gifts and goodies and in 2004 the Pharma industry was estimated at half a trillion dollars! In the 90s the big Pharma took over teaching, licensing, drug testing and finally drug approval. If you got better or cured how would they earn so all they aimed at is what they called remission! Empirical medicine was renamed quackery. And anyway who would spend money on anything coming from nature, as you cannot patent nature! The movie above relates how alternative medicines was crushed and riled.

Tuesday, 5 November 2013

TOO MANY HATS

I have always worn many hats. I guess we women are destined to do so and do it with aplomb! Maybe that is why God has made our brains more evenly balanced between left and right brain processing! But jokes apart, it is a fact that we are made to wear several hats as we saunter along the journey called life! And somehow many of us, including me I must confess, wear them quite happily and secretly dream of being a superwoman. Kamala my mom, God bless her soul, was a very practical and even astute woman and had a very different take on what a woman should do. When I got married and began donning hats at the speed of light, she warned me and told me to remember that one day I will grow old, my knees will pain and my back will break, and people around me will still expect me to juggle my hats with the dexterity of a 20 year old! Of course I did not listen, as I did want to be superwoman. I was wife, and mother and daughter and workingwoman and friend and cook and hostess and shoulder to cry on and punching bag and more. Each persona has its set of variations that came with the demands of the day. I looked at them as adornments to add to each hat: flowers, feathers, stars. Sometimes there were thorns that needed you to give more attention to one hat: sitting by your sick child the whole night and then making it to work after carefully making up so no one would see. It was exhausting and still is.

With time some hats were worn less often, and some even set-aside for a while and new ones donned. The best part is that many of them were put on one's head willingly: that of mother-in-law, grandmother, Utpal's Maam'ji and Project Why's Anou Ma'am. And somehow I enjoyed them all but never let go off the main hat: me! I always made it a point to take that alone time that kept me going. Being an only child with a nomadic life, it was easy to do so as you have to master the art of creating games to beat your loneliness. Solitude was never a problem. I had my books, my invisible friends that were part of my life and whom I talked to and there were times I talked to myself in the mirror and even sang and danced. As I grew older the games changed a little. Books took a large place in my life and even today I read while in my auto rickshaw! I have also discovered a new stress buster that worked wonders. I play my iPod very loud while walking on the treadmill and as it has songs that I have liked from my teens and even before to now I time travel while exercising. When I get off the treadmill I have a spring in my gait and a smile on my face. And a few years back I fulfilled a long cherished dream and published my first book. Writing is now my biggest catharsis.

On the 4th of July 2014 I was forced to don a hat I never wanted. R was diagnosed with cancer and I had to become his cancer buddy. It is a hat that weighs heavy on my head, like Baudelaire's *heavy lid of low sky* so beautifully evoked in his poem Spleen. This hat is too heavy to juggle and all other hats have shrunk under its weight. I struggle to keep them in place and ensure they are not damaged. But what frightens me most is the fear of losing myself as should that happen then I would not be able to bear the weight of this new dark lid.

Tuesday, 5 November 2013

FEAR FACTOR

One element of the 15-day chemo cycle we have been following for the past months is a visit to the Doctor on day 6 or 7. That is when R's immunity is at its nadir and he is most prone to infections. Logically it is a time when he should be kept away for sources of infection and hospitals are the biggest sources of all types of infections. We did follow the 'protocol' a few times but then I realised that R's presence was not needed as all the questions were answered by me. Moreover R was fine and there was nothing to report. The Doctor simply asks something as inane as *how are you* and R answers he is *OK*. I then fill him in on silly details that are not of any consequence and ask him some questions to which I get evasive replies. With R sitting in the room, I cannot ask the questions I need to. So on the next 'appointment' day I went alone as honestly nodding your head and mouthing OK is no match to the risk of infection R is put through when waiting in a hospital OPD. And wait we must sometimes for more than an hour. From the moment I entered I realised that the Doc was not pleased or comfortable with R's absence. For me it was the ideal situation as I had his attention and could ask disturbing questions and also press for answers. I got some and had to be satisfied with vague ones in some cases. When he wrote the 'prescription' for the next chemo he did not fail to write in bold letters PATIENT NOT BROUGHT. I was still clueless about his being so vexed.

The next time R was fine again but remembering his dismay at R's absence I SMSd him asking him whether I should bring R though there was nothing to report. He answered with a curt: bring him. We made another pointless trip, which was a waste of time.

It is only after seeing the film[124] mentioned in my last post, that I understood the reason for the need of R's presence. It is all part of the fear that is installed and peddled seductively or even brutally in the hallowed institutions of modern medicine. A fear that can only feed on our total sense of helplessness that forces us to kneel at the altar of allopathy. This fear psychosis is based on the ability of the peddler to make you believe that he and only he can help you and that your only option in the instance of cancer is drugs. A carefully crafted and enacted drama is played in front of your eyes, and the eyes of the loved ones accompanying you. All other options are carefully hidden or should you suggest one, immediately derided. By the time you leave, your are seduced or frightened to death.

So the presence of R during any meeting with the doctor is crucial to keep the power equation in favour of the doctor. My power is reduced in great measure and many of the questions I would need to ask are left unsaid.

I must say that my seduction was minimal as I stated from the day go that I would continue alternative therapies and nutrition regardless of the chemo. I had enough knowledge to stand my ground and I have stood it till now.

But for the past months I have also been researching in details all the elements that are carefully kept hidden, or doled out in tiny measures so as not to rock the boat. The terrible side effects, the long and short term ones. I was taken aback at the fact that statistics change when R asks a question alone or in my presence. The 1/5000 easily becomes 1/100000! I have ample examples of this. To cut it short it makes me sick and sad.

The fear of the disease is so well peddled that it has a led to an entirely new branch of medicine called preventive medicine, and here I do not mean the one that suggests drinking clean water, washing your hands, eating well, exercising etc. but the one that instils fear of having cancer in the far future. This has brought into existence new expensive paraphernalia of tests and unnecessary if not fraudulent and amoral treatment. I remember having been told by a doctor in 1992 that I was a high cancer risk as both my parents had succumbed to the disease and that I should have yearly check ups. I told

---

[124] The Forbidden Cures; https://youtu.be/km2cqQNFtEs

him to go to hell as I refused to live a life in fear. This had been an intuitive decision, as I knew zilch about the big C at that time.

There are two tests that are done with alacrity and impunity and have now been exposed.

Every woman is told to have a mammogram every year after 40. It has now been proved that mammograms can cause cancer[125]! It is not an effective tool to detect cancer, as 70 to 80 per cent of all positive mammograms do not, upon biopsy, show any presence of cancer. And even with the latest machines that emit fewer rads, each mammogram increases the risk of cancer by 1%. Not to forget that mammograms are expensive and cause unnecessary angst and worry. Remember the fear factor!

The other one is the PSA test that is supposed to detect prostate cancer. Would you surprised if I told you that the man who discovered PSA, Dr Ablin has written a book [126]called the The Great Prostate Hoax: How Big Medicine Hijacked the PSA Test and Caused a Public Health Disaster! A man with high levels of PSA does not necessarily have cancer. And the reverse is also true. Men with low levels may have prostate cancer. The screenings have adverse effects: financial, psychological and unnecessary biopsies. A prostate biopsy is something that most men dread… And with good reason.

Need I say more!

[125] Dawn Prate, Mammograms cause breast cancer (and other cancer facts you probably never knew) http://www.naturalnews.com/010886_breast_cancer_mammograms.html#ixzz3WWUXczLg

[126] The Great Prostate Hoax: How Big Medicine Hijacked the Psa Test and Caused a Public Health Disaster, Richard J Ablin, Ronald Piana 2014

Wednesday, 6 November 2013

MY CHEMO CYCLE

In medical parlance, chemotherapy is given in cycles. In our case every second Friday. For them a 'cycle' means the day on which chemo is given. My picture is a tad different. My cycle never stops from day 1 to 14 and I have just realised that I have chemo on my mind almost 24/7. There is a side effect in chemotherapy called chemo brain[127] chemo fog or Post-chemotherapy cognitive impairment. I just heard of it a few days back and now understand why R is unable to concentrate. Chemo fog entails loss of memory, concentration, remembering names, problems multi tasking etc. One of the chemical drugs that bring this is a steroid the very Dexona R reacted too so badly too in the first chemo and that was given to him SEVEN times thanks to the super efficiency of a super speciality hospital! I owe him apologies for having kept badgering him to read or do Sudoku! Poor chap.

But let us get back to my chemo cycle and let us begin it just like the medics do on day one. Day one is chemo day, you get up early, pack your goodies: edible food, ice, chocolates, iPad, a book (ha-ha) and set off for a day of battle. Yes it is battle day from start to finish: you battle to get a quick admission and a bed - the alternative is what they call a recliner and I call a torture chair -. That is battle one. Then you move to battle two where you

---

[127] http://www.cancer.org/treatment/treatmentsandsideeffects/physicalsideeffects/chemotherapyeffects/chemo-brain

ANOURADHA BAKSHI

battle to get the chemo started and from now on to ensure that the right drug is poured in the veins of your loved one. Then as every patient has to have an attendant - shocking in a expensive super speciality hospital, this sounds more like a state run one - you keep looking at the drip and scoot when you think it is finishing for a nurse to arrive. And then you battle to get your release. Coming home means dealing with R who has reacted differently to every chemo so you have no reference point and have to deal with a new situation and find a solution.

Day 2 and 3 are days when R is really down and you just watch him and try to make things better, coax him into eating and just feel helpless and angry.

Day 4 and 5 are better days when R revives a little and you can pretend that all is well.

Day 6 is blood test day and you wait with bated breath for the results hoping they will not be too low. Once you have them you SMS the doctor.

Day 7 was when you had to see the doctor, but I have done away with this as it was just part of a drama that I did find unnecessary but rather counter productive.

Day 8 and 9 are again quiet but then day 10, 11 and 12 are when I have to give him his booster injections.

Day 13 is blood test and waiting for the results and getting confirmation from the doctor that he is OK for chemo.

Day 14 is chemo again.

This has been my life in 14-day cycles!

Saturday, 9 November 2013

IN THE FACE ATTITUDE

This morning I got a phone call asking why there was no new blog! I guess it was a bit of no news is good news on the R front. It feels good to see him like this but I will not tempt Clotho, Lachesis and Atropos, the famous Fates who hold the thread of our destiny. I also guess that my virtual absence was also due to the fact that I tried out a raw diet recommended by a friend that kept me yawning all the way to bedtime! Maybe that is the remedy for my sleepless nights.

But this morning I got a mail from my friend and mentor who wrote that I was filled with *so much positive energy and in the face attitude* in this battle I wage. Got me thinking. Actually he is quite right and maybe this is one if not the biggest side effect of chemo/cancer! When I first allowed myself to let the word cancer spring in my brain - must have been a little before we got the confirmation - I quickly pushed it back in the dark closet it had slithered in after my pa's demise. The C word frightened me and made my blood run cold; it was associated to the death of loved ones, and had to be relegated to dark oblivion.

It must have been in June or so that the first thought about R's ailment being the dreaded crab came to my mind but I just pushed it back with undue haste. But the seed was planted and I knew no matter how little I watered it or put in the sun, it would germinate. It did on July 4th. It must have been part of the big picture that it was I who got the news. That gave me some time to decide how I would take it and in the short ride between the Doc's office and my home I knew I would break the walls of that closet and face the sod head on. I presume that is the *in the face attitude* that my friend speaks about.

In the light of this perception I realise that perhaps this is the very first time that I have taken a challenge with so much determination. In the past there were always others to help and support me, but this battle is mine alone. It has been very empowering and must be part of a larger image. I met a man in the Tibetan doctor's waiting room yesterday. His wife had cancer and he was running from pillar to post just like me, the only difference was that his wife was not cooperative and all the poor man's efforts landed in the dustbin. I have been blessed by the fact that R is the most cooperative patient in the world and swallows everything I come up with. And with the help of everyone who has stood by me I know we will get his immunity back and kicking.

Sunday, 10 November 2013

DOWNTIME

Many of you have asked me how I manage to keep going without losing it. So I thought I would share my coping strategies today. First and foremost 'losing it' is not an option I have. At least not till I get a real ALL CLEAR for R that would be not before June 2014. So without quite realising it, I have almost surreptitiously crafted a schedule for myself that fits in the few free slots I have in the day. I call it my downtime or alone time! First and foremost I make it a point to wake up very early, sometimes at 3.30am and tiptoe down to my little office and write. At that time no one is awake and the world is mine. From total silence with an occasional dog barking, I can hear the first birdcalls. It is pure magic and I feel alive. I am ready to take on the day.

The other things I have found myself doing quite regularly is a bit of retail therapy. Often it is simply visual retail therapy: browse in my favourite bookshop, have a look at the new collections at Fabindia or simply walk past the shop windows. Sometimes I indulge but just a little.

Reading is of course the all time favourite and the frequent trips to diverse organic products outlets allow me to devour books. As many of you know I have mastered the art of reading in a moving auto rickshaw. Sometimes I do not even realise we have reached the destination so engrossed I am in my book. It is also good for my nerves and my annoying backseat driving.

Every Tuesday I have a date. Don't go imagining things! It is with a girl friend and we have a cuppa and chat sense or nonsense depending on our moods.

And since a few weeks I have a new weekly treat: going to see Utpal at his school and watch him bloom from minute to minute. It is a huge gulp of fresh air, an unbeatable feelgood shot, a moment when I truly jump of the spinning world and catch my breath. It works wonders.

So all these bits of downtime make me strong and ready to fight to the end!

Monday, 11 November 2013

THE SECOND OPINION

For quite some time many have been pushing me to get a second opinion. As far as I was concerned a second opinion from any Doctor part of the medical bizmess seemed a waste of time as I knew that it would be a case of you scratch my back I scratch yours, but any way once again it was people I care for and who have stood by me who asked me to get the second opinion. I guess I too hoped against hope that the second opinion may stop the chemos at 8! How gullible can I be, even after my recent close encounters with the commercial medicine ilk. Anyway I finally got an appointment with a supposedly eminent oncologist of another five star super speciality hospital. This one is located at the other end of the city. This meant braving the evening traffic. We did and reached yet another hallowed portal. Found our way to the right place and settled down to wait. Blissfully the wait was not too long. I had taken all the papers and put them in chronological order to allow the Doctor to have easy access to the case history. I was prepared to answer all questions and maybe ask some of my own. To my mind basic bedside manners and even the minimal second opinion protocol would at least entail the Doctor looking at the papers, even perfunctorily, to at least make the person who has come seeking a second opinion feel reassured.

You seek a second opinion when in despair and often for a loved one. Even if you ultimately will agree and second the treatment prescribed by a colleague, at least play the game by some basic ethical rules. That was not at all the case. The Doctor did not look at any papers. He did not even ask me why I wanted a second opinion I was hoping he would compare the 2 scans one before chemo and one after chemo 6 and then pretend to think, look at a few papers and finally give his opinion. My second opinion lasted precisely 3 minutes or 3.30 at best. No report was looked at. I gave a very brief case history and that was it. He said we were on the right track and he would be cured after chemo 12. Of course one more PET scan would be needed to as he put it 'record' the situation.

We were dismissed but I wanted a few more answers. What about secondary cancers. Well they could happen in 20 years was what I was told. I then could not resist telling him that at best chemotherapy would cure 80% of the cancer, the balance 20 had to be taken care by the patient's immune system. The young doctor who was sitting there looked at me and smiled. I then asked for the fee and was told a sum that I handed over.

I did not know whether to laugh or cry or be angry. I only knew two things: one that I would never seek a second opinion unless it is from a Doctor in a Government hospital, and two I just need to grit my teeth and go through the remaining 4 chemos and then bid farewell forever to this line of treatment. Every dog has his day; mine will come after the 27th December 2013!

136 000 TIMES

For the past month now, two priests have been chanting the Maha Mrityunjaya Mantra for R. Tomorrow the puja will finish and the priests would have chanted it 136 000 times. The literal translation would be the Death Conquering Mantra and is from the Yajur Veda (3-60). It is known to be an extremely powerful mantra. *This mantra is said to have the power to remove all sufferings, ward off all evils, remove diseases and bestow the aspirant with health and energy. And it is said that when this mantra is it chanted with great devotion and serious contemplation it is said that the knowledge of this birth and death cycle is revealed to the aspirant. And thus it helps in overcoming the fear of death.*

One may wonder how a Cartesian like me would get such a ritual done. But as I have said many times in this battle I will leave no stone unturned, and no known remedy untested. And though I am Cartesian I am also the one who has been brought up on the big picture theory by a father who too was Cartesian by nature. He turned to spirituality in the later half of his life and embraced pure bhakti. If I recall correctly, it was during his posting as President of the UN Commission in Saigon that he turned to God. Maybe he sensed what lay ahead and was frustrated by how little he could do is spite of his best intentions. I guess it is at moments of crises that we remember a greater presence. When his elder brother got seriously ill and we all feared for him, Papa got a Maha Mrityunjaya Puja for him. My uncle outlived my father by 10 years!

When R got ill I had a small version of the Puja done. At that time we were helplessly groping in the dark not knowing what was ailing him. When the beast was exposed and turned out to be the one I dreaded, I decided it was time to unleash the big canon. I must admit that things have gone well and R has showed remarkable progress in the last few months. He is looking much better and barring the few post chemo days, is almost back to his old self. I do not know if it is the prayers or the cannabis! For me it is everything put together as part of the Big Picture.

Thursday, 14 November 2013

ONE SIZE FIT ALL

R is looking far better than he was a few months ago. Tomorrow we will be going for chemo 9! Then just 3 left and hopefully the word chemo will be removed from our lexicon forever.

I wish medicine were not a series of protocols that had to be followed to the T! I wish treatment were tailored to the patient, keeping in mind his needs, his progress and above all his wishes. If God made each one of us different then how can one size fit all? The new commercial medicine approach reads more like a mathematical equation than a prescription for healing. Hodgkin's Stage II B = 6 cycles ABVD + 3 PET scans! There is no fine-tuning. There is no room for listening to the patient. One thing modern medicine forgets is that true healing comes from within the person and if the patient gives up, then no mathematical equation can work.

Those of us, who have experienced the healing approach of the good old family Doctor, cannot but regret the total extinction of this breed. I still remember good old Doctor Agarwal who was our family doctor in my grandparents' house in Meerut way back in the early sixties when I was a kid. I can still recall his portly presence as he entered the house when called to tend to one of the family. A house servant carried his big black bag. Before going to see the patient of the day, he would sit in the lounge and chat with the elders, have a cup of tea and some snacks. In the course of conversation he would be enlightened about the ailment by someone or the other and ask a few questions. He knew the each member of the family and their idiosyncrasies: the hypochondriac aunt, the stoic uncle, the shy sister in law and so on. He was as much a psychotherapist as he was a doctor and knew exactly what to say to each one to make them feel better. If it was one of us kids who was sick, another was sent to find out if he had opened his bag, taken out his metal syringe box and asked for it to be boiled. Those were still days when the same needle was used over and over again! If that was the case, then we knew we would have an injection and were terrified. If not we waited patiently for him to finish his chat and come to us. He examined us and then prescribed some pills or potions. And that was it. Everyone was happy: the parent of the sick child was reassured, the child happy as there had been no painful shot and wonders of wonders the potions worked each and every time.

Today there are very few doctors who heal the person and not a part of the body. There is no bonhomie and comfort. There is no laughter or mindless chitchat. The equations have changed. What we have today is a power game tilted in favour of the doctor. You just have to listen and obey. Should you break the protocol, then you could be in for a dressing down.

Friday, 15 November 2013

NUMBER NINE

Today was chemo number 9. Of all the chemos we have gone through, this was the strangest. I do not know why it reminded me of the Beatles song Revolution no 9[128]! I read the lyrics again and no matter how spaced out they may seem, they somehow fitted the mood I was in all day. Of all the explanations given to this experimental piece of music the one I like best is: the one that defines it as a sensory attack on the citadel of the intellect: a revolution in the head aimed at each listener. When you read the lyrics they make no sense but push you to find a meaning within the nonsense. Chemo 9 was just that.

It all began much too efficiently. The admission was spot on, the pre chemo act like a dream. It almost felt like this time we may be home early. Though R as usual felt queasy the moment he entered the chemo day care, he was smiling. The pre meds were given without the DEXONA and all seemed too perfect. I took a break as Shamika had come and came home. I called her and she told me that they had just begun the chemo but that R was extremely agitated. I rushed back and found him restless something that had not happened before. The chemo was a nightmare. He barely lay down, ate nothing as he said he was nauseous even after having been given an anti emetic. I felt very uncomfortable and helpless. My heart wanted to

---

[128] Revolution no 9 Lennon Mc Cartney with George Harrison and Yoko Ono 1968 white Album

pull out all the needles and poisonous potions and go home to never return but reason took the upper head. The one who always sees with her heart had to look at things with her brain.

I was as restless as him. I felt wretched. I knew why he was feeling this way. He was just fed up, his body was saturated and screaming for relief, a relief I could not conjure even with my best intention. I located the Doctor and we had a tête a tête. It was once again the usual dialogue of the deaf each of us defending our points of view: I wanted him to treat the person; he was treating the ailment. I wanted him to hear the cries of a tortured body; he stuck to protocols and numbers. Having come so far I knew I had to capitulate. The only condition I could put was that we finish before the last day of 2013: chemos, PET scans and removal of the port. Now I need to put on yet another mask and convince R that this is the best for him. It is a tall order for me and will need me to put up an act worthy of an Oscar! For the man I love, I am sure I will find the script, the set and the props to do so.

I guess it is my *"revolution in the head"*, albeit an unsolicited one.

Friday, 15 November 2013

MY MOTHER'S DAUGHTER

Yesterday R's oncologist could not resist asking me why I was so much against chemotherapy. This was during our heart to heart where we found ourselves talking as usual at cross-purposes. His question took me by surprise. How could I explain to him that for me it was a visceral reaction? I simply told him that the very idea of having to kill the good with the bad did not sit well with me. I realised later that my answer would have sounded very hollow. So be it. Even if God descended and asked me to change my opinion, I would and could not.

Later at night when sleep eluded me, I again thought of my strained relationship with chemotherapy and wondered where it came from. My thoughts wandered back to Kamala, my mother. Her apparently illogical and childlike reaction to cancer was probably the reason, if reason there is. At that time both Papa and I were so steeped in our love for this incredible woman that we followed her wishes blindly. Neither of us ever asked ourselves why a woman who had withstood every blow that came her way with courage and clarity had suddenly become an unreasonable and obstinate brat. We only wanted her to be happy and thus played by her rules. Last night, I tried to make sense of that fateful year that began in July 1989 when she was diagnosed with lung cancer and July 1990 when she breathed her last. And suddenly I saw it all: mama had scripted her swansong.

Knowing that she could not beat us and have her way if she remained the pillar of strength she had been all her life, she knew she had to become someone different. A brief fainting spell, whether real or willed allowed her to recast herself into a little girl who has lost her recent memory. This allowed the poised and rational lady to throw tantrums and make ludicrous demands. She could run out of an MRI scan and not be derided; she could refuse any form of treatment without having to give a logical reason; she did not have to win battles, as there would be none. But what was it that she was so petrified of: chemotherapy of course. It was not the fear of losing her hair as though, she was a little vain, she would not have insulted her intelligence by proffering such lame excuse. Her fear was visceral and intuitive. She needed a battlefield that was to her advantage and she found one. We played the game by her rules and she won her last battle with her dignity intact.

Mama knew she did not have the arguments she needed to convince her Cartesian husband and daughter. She was right. In 1989 there was very little information about alternative therapies and options. The information revolution had not taken place. Internet did not exist. Where would she have found the arguments to convince us?

Even today, with all the information I have, I was unable to stop chemotherapy from entering my life. It is a very powerful opponent with astute proponents who are masters at seduction. The best I could do was provide additional support. I was even unable to answer why I was so much against chemotherapy with conviction. Such is the power of modern medicine.

The best I could do yesterday was tell the doctor that should I fall prey to the big C, I would prove to him that options that worked existed. That is the only turf where I know I can and will have my way! I am my mother's daughter.

Sunday, 17 November 2013

I FOUND AN ISLAND IN YOUR ARMS COUNTRY IN YOUR EYES..

As I have written time and again, there have been a series on serendipities in my life in the past months as I wage the most crucial battle of my life. This morning as I stomped on my treadmill, and I use the verb stomp as that is exactly what I do, with music blaring in my ears, a phrase from the Doors famous song Break on Through[129] caught my attention. It is the one that talks of islands and countries found in another's eyes. It somehow summed up my relationship with R and also prompted me to take some time and expand on the words in the light of my life. Before I started to write this post, I browsed my Facebook page and wonders of wonders serendipity was at work again. This time in the form of two links. The first one was a link to a video clip that urges you to love life to its fullest even when faced with the fact that everything you love will eventually come to an end

The last stroke of serendipity this morning was another link, this one about a nurse revealing the 5 top regrets people make on their deathbed[130]. Two of them really struck me: *I wish I'd had the courage to live a life true to myself, not the life others expected of me* and *I wish I'd had the courage to express*

---

[129] The Doors, Break on Through, Jim Morrison 1967

[130] The Top Five Regrets of the Dying; A life Transformed by the Dearly Departing; Bronnie Ware 2012

my feelings. Maybe it is a boon to have read this today as it gives me time to redress the situation, even if time is short.

All this is a lot of processing at one time. But let us just say the ball has been set rolling. If we take it from the top, by this I mean the way the serendipities occurred this morning it would translate like this. Jim Morrison's words made me understand what R means to me: the one who gave me security and opened the whole world for me. I just did not see this till now. Time I did. The video clip brought to light the fact that it is in our hands to make the transient permanent in our own ways and not accept to go gently and lastly even if there is little time left, there is still enough to make that bucket list that remained in our head and have the courage of being who one is and expressing all repressed feelings.

It is a tall order I know. But somehow it began surreptitiously when I decided to start this blog on the very day Cancer entered my life again. Serendipity again?

Monday, 18 November 2013

ROLE REVERSAL

Most of my earlier blogs have been grim or serious. Today I would like to share the lighter side effects of Mr Hodgkin's stay with us. It all amounts to many role reversals that are quite amusing. Even since I embarked on mission R, I gave up a hat I had donned for years. I mean my chef's hat! Cooking use to be my favourite hobby. Here again I was following my father's footsteps. Papa was a mean cook. While reading law at the Middle temple, he found time to cross the Channel many times and pursue his passion for cooking. With his law degree he also acquired a Cordon Bleu ribbon. He became neither a lawyer nor a Chef but a diplomat with a passion for cooking. Cooking was his one and only hobby. He always told me that that it was better than any other hobby as you created and got appreciated almost on the spot. Throughout the first 4 decades of my life I have been fortunate to taste his food a myriad of times. He was a man who could spring up a starred dish with whatever he found in the fridge. The more stressed he was, the more delicacies he churned. Some of my favourites were his fried rice, his crispy sweet and sour fish, or his small potatoes cooked two styles in the same frying pan. They are my Proustian madeleines. Many know Anou the cook. But you will be surprised if I told you that I began cooking late in life, when I was almost 30. Stressful family issues brought out the cook in me and just like Papa the more upset I was the more complicated the dish I produced. I remember many times when I use to cook with tears rolling down my face.

Cooking was my best stress buster. The array of cookbooks that adorn the shelves of my large kitchen, it used to be my mother's bedroom and mine before my marriage where R and I had some good times, are ample proof of that. When R was diagnosed with cancer, I should have been cooking like a Fury so stressed I was/am. But strangely the exact opposite happened. I did not feel like cooking at all. In fact I now shun the kitchen and my books are gathering dust. I guess I had to put my life on hold and cooking was an integral part of who I was. I am eternally grateful to my first born who sensed that this would happen and organised things while she was here. The house is now being run efficiently by my younger one ably supported by the house staff. It is godsent, as I truly do not feel like cooking! My day is spent looking after R and dispensing all his pills and brews. Strangely I even do not feel like cooking for him. My Chef's hat lies in wait for better days.

As I wrote at the beginning of this post, there have been amusing role reversals post cancer. R spends a lot of time watching the box, particularly on days when he is feeling tired and I often find him watching cook shows. And believe it or not, he even remembers some recipes and asks for them to be made. He has not yet entered the kitchen and donned a hat. Maybe that too will happen. Our household will be looking very different in 2014.

As R does not move out much he has been watching our maid clean the room. R has always been punctilious about cleanliness and had the irritating habit of finding the one speck of dust that had escaped the eye of the person dusting the house. Last week he finally decreed that carpets could not be cleaned with a broom as we have been doing but that I needed to get a vacuum cleaner! I wonder what other surprise awaits me in the next six weeks.

Tuesday, 19 November 2013

THE DREADED MELTDOWN

For the past months I have been dreading a meltdown. I know it is lurking somewhere and just needs that one little word or act that would be the trigger. Whether it would be a short emotional outburst or a mental collapse is any body's guess. It almost happened yesterday when R came up with a preposterous idea engendered by a misplaced sense of duty. My eyes started welling but I knew that if I allowed one tear to fall it would be the end. Crisis management was needed. I left the room and strangely got reminded of the Rolling Stones song: 19th Nervous Breakdown! I still had a long way to go! The crisis was averted and the tears quietly crawled back to the space I had carefully crafted for them the day I heard the news! There will be a day when I will allow them to flow freely. Mingled with abundant tears of joy. I am sure you have guessed when that would be.

Actually in the given context I do not know who is rearranging whose mind. I just know that I have to keep my head cool. But yesterday showed me how close I was to that dreaded breakdown and how crucial it was for me to evolve new coping strategies to ensure that I never reach the point I reached yesterday. Till now I had believed that my rants and raves on this blog were catharsis enough and provided the emotional release I so need. But the past 17 months have taken a huge toll on me and the wear and tear on nerves is phenomenal. First it was 12 months of seeing R fade away in front of my eyes and I running like a chicken without a head, from pillar to post, leaving no stone unturned and yet not being able to find the monster gnawing happily at my loved one. Then getting the one news I did not want and struggling with a situation I was not happy with; agreeing to live in 14 day cycles and abiding by its stringent rules. Imagining the havoc being played in R's body with cells dying and generating in the most unnatural way imaginable and remaining mute and helpless.

I realise I am just a word, an action, a look, a gesture away from collapse and know that this cannot happen. Should I write more and bare it all even if it hurts someone? Should I stomp harder and longer on the treadmill? I know that the only thing that can work is seeing the lighter side of things and God knows how much I have tried to! But I am not a humorous and witty person. I have always been a serious one, even as a child. I guess it is the price you pay for being an only child, born to older parents and destined to a nomadic life.

Maybe I should play some brain games on the computer. Will give it a try.

Thursday, 21 November 2013

OPEN THE EYES OF MY HEART

I have over the past months now often counted the blessings or happy side effects of the temporary presence of Mr Hodgkin's in my life. There have been many and I am deeply grateful. But nothing could have prepared me for the sublime experience I experienced yesterday when I clicked on a link prompted by the title: blind autistic boy sings[131]! The angelic voice and simple lyrics resonated deep in my soul, as am I not the one who has always urged people to look with their hearts! It is only when I heard this young Angel who cannot see, beseeching the Lord to open the eyes of his heart that words I had used too oft took on a new meaning altogether. It was magic.

For the first time the words 'seeing with your heart' revealed their true meaning. That little boy sang not from his heart alone, but from deep within his soul and guts. It did not matter what colour or hue or shape or size his Lord was. He was his, he was yours he was mine. What mattered is how each one of us interpreted the words and whom we wanted to see. Till now seeing with your heart had a very mundane and limited meaning in my lexicon. I use the phrase to urge people to help those in need and to say things as they are, as it is not the right time and place for sugar quoting, to help Project Why. How trite and even selfish. Makes me feel so small.

---

131   https://youtu.be/wPTMA7HIIyk

The power of the voice of this little blind and challenged boy changed it all. When you open the eyes of your heart you should be prepared to see that omnipotent, omnipresent and omniscient force called by different names. The question is how do we see Him. The answer is simple: in all the places and things you never bother to look at and see: the tree growing in front of your house, the lone butterfly sitting on a flower for a fleeting instant, the funny shaped cloud in the sky or the star that shines brighter than the other. You see Him in the caress of the gentle wind that blows or the first drop of rain that falls on the parched earth. But that is not all. You see him in the eyes of the little child begging on the street, or the old woman who sleeps under the bridge. You see him when you gather the courage to look into the eyes of those you wish to avoid, reach out to the one that needs you or share your last loaf of bread with the one hungrier than you.

The Lord will only open the eyes of your heart when you are ready to truly see with your heart.

Friday, 22 November 2013

GAMES PEOPLE PLAY

On July 4th my life changed in the space of a second. A simple word on an investigation report was all that was needed to catapult me into a world yet unknown but feared. For an instant I was thrown off a cliff without a parachute or a bungee jumping cord. I had to create my own before I hit the ground or in my case reach home with the terrible news. Just like in a free fall I had seconds to decide how I would break the news to the family.

On that day the whole family was there: R, my girls, my son-in-law and my grandchild. My mind travelled at the speed of light if not faster. A multitude of images and thoughts zigzagged madly and needed to be processed and put in order and above all I knew unequivocally that I was the one chosen to set the rules of the game we had suddenly been destined to play. It accrued to me to make the right decision and I was scared as it concerned the life of my loved one. As I entered the house I found my way to the dining room where the family was seated around the table. By then I knew that the only way was honesty and straightforwardness! So I told them the reality without 'maybes' and 'perhaps': R had cancer! Now let us get on with it. The stage was set and the game was on! Parachutes and jumping cords would be fashioned along the way.

It has been a cliffhanger in more ways then one. A roller coaster ride! At every bend something new awaits you and you need to face it come what may. There are no rules, no explanations, no guidebooks and above all no going back. You just learn at every step of the journey and work out your coping strategies. It has been a real learning experience. The one constant has been to adjust to life in fifteen days cycles with bad days and good days. One has learnt to bear the bad days and enjoy the good ones in the best way possible.

Today we have completed 9 cycles and have 3 more to go. Habit is second nature it is said, and I must admit that we have become inured to these cycles or should I say lulled into a false sense of security. Even I, who resisted like mad and kicked and screamed in the early days, have laid down arms in spite of myself. The battlefield was not even, I conceded temporary defeat.

Now it is just a matter of *let us get on with it* and numbers dance in my head: 3 more chemos, 12 bad days, 15 good days, 1 PET scan and then game over!

Sunday, 24 November 2013

SLEEPLESS IN DELHI

I have been having sleepless nights after sleepless nights for the last fortnight or so. Come to think of it all seems on course and choices made willing or unwillingly. The second opinion was a watershed in our chemo journey. On the face of it, it did not yield any reassuring counsel. It simply reinforced the fact that no matter what, 12 was the chosen number. I simply took it as a message from the empyrean and decided to just get on with it. Yet I found myself sleepless and somewhat disturbed till it occurred to me that this was the time exactly 21 years ago when Papa was battling cancer. November has never been a happy month since that fateful November of 2002.

It was on November 5th that Papa was subjected to a brutal seven hours surgery that robbed him of his dignity in the name of probable cure. He would come home a few days and leave me on the 29th of this month. November is a month I now dread. But at the same time it is a month when I cannot but remember Papa and his struggle and ask myself the question: where did I go wrong. To mama's absolute and very vocal refusal of any kind of treatment, Papa's quiet and tame acceptance came as a relief, or so I thought at that time. Conventional medicine was the only option available. My knowledge of Cancer was close to nil and the Internet did not exist, so all existing alternative options remained undisclosed. One simply had to trust the men in white. When Papa walked into the nursing home he was a healthy 81-year-old when he came out 10 days later he was a mutilated man. For the surgeon the operation had been successful. But Papa never recovered. Seeing him lying helpless led me to pray for his deliverance and the Gods were merciful enough to hear my plea. I was left to live on with the guilt of having suggested the conventional approach. Mercifully he was spared the radio and chemotherapy. In my defence: I did not know better.

I wonder why God has put me in the same place 21 years later. I hope it is to somewhat rid me of the guilt I carry and redeem myself. As I lie awake in the dead of night waiting for the clock to show a reasonable time for getting out of bed, I find myself wondering whether I have done all that is in my power to ensure R's recovery. I ask myself is there is something more I could do to make it easier on him. I can imagine how frustrating it is for him to be housebound and unable to lead the active and fun loving life he so enjoys. My heart goes out to him as he meekly drinks his soursop tea in lieu of his 12-year-old large malt whisky or eats his organic vegetables whilst dreaming snails and foie gras! I just dream of the table laden with all his favourite dishes that I will conjure for him once he is well again. I wonder how many sleepless night will reach me to that coveted morning.

Sunday, 24 November 2013

COMING OUT OF MY CLOSET

Serendipity has been by big mate during this last, oops sorry biggest battle I have been waging for months. As I browsed my FB page this morning my eye fell on a link[132] that said: Coming out of your closet I do not know why I clicked on it and listened to Ash Beckham's video. What caught my attention was the sub title: *A 4-Year-Old Girl Asked A Lesbian If She's A Boy. She Responded The Awesomest Way Possible.* After listening to this incredible life lesson I realised how many closets I had had, and some I still have and how we hide in our dark closets with a grenade in our hand. She says: *At some point in our lives, we all live in closets and they may feel safe, or at least safer than what lies on the other side of that door. But I'm here to tell you, no matter what your walls are made of, a closet is no place for a person to live.*

The words were prophetic. They explained the feeling of extreme disquietude bordering on fear that I have been experiencing and have not been able to comprehend and voice. Just a she says I was in a dark closet and needed to break out no matter how hard. I crawled into this closet on the day I knew about R's cancer and hid in it too frightened to scream my fear. I put up a show for the world, but night after night I was back in the closet. And too make matters worse, I came across pages and pages of medical jargon such as remission and secondary cancers, and one statistic

---

[132] http://tedxtalks.ted.com/video/Coming-Out-of-Your-Closet-Ash-B

that screamed at me at every page: the 5 year survival rate. My closet is the gnawing terror of losing the one I love most. Here I have said it loud and clear. I am scared of losing the one I love just as I lost my most loved ones 2 decades ago.

THE OTHER COUNTS AND THE NEXT 66 DAYS

For the past five months my life has been controlled and steered by counts, I mean blood counts. R's! Before chemo, 6 days after chemo, 2 days before chemo and so on. The figures are staggering to say the least as they fall or increase at bewildering speed from 3 000 to 19 000 in a day, or from 14 000 to 2 800 in 2 days or from 145 to 400 and so on, depending on whether they are WBCs or platelets. One almost lives from blood test to blood test, heaving sighs of relief if all is well, or getting a bout of nerves if they are too low. In the early days it was a real stress but slowly one became accustomed, as habit is indeed second nature. It is said[133] that it takes 66 days to form a habit. The Canadian Magician Doug Henning once said: *'The hard must become habit. The habit must become easy. The easy must become beautiful.'* With chemo I agree on the first two.

For the past few days I have been feeling low. I finally made a trip of the doctor this morning and lo and behold found another set of counts to be address. My BP had fallen to 60/80. Well I do normally have a low BP but when it dips this low it is always due to stress and worry. My good Doc P unravelled the puzzle for me. According to him and I cannot but agree, with

---

[133] It takes 66 days to form a habit; Jonathan Rowson 2010; http://www.rsablogs. org.uk/2010/education/takes-66-days-form-habit/

chemo coming to an end in a month and one day to be exact, the comfort zone we had sunk into in spite of ourselves as chemo has been going on for more than 66 days is soon coming to an end. The elephant in the room is WHAT NEXT. Entering chemo zone was a first and kept me on my toes in more ways than one. But what comes after December 27th is unknown and even scary. The carefully crafted programme that kept me going 24/7 for the past months comes to an end and now it is time to get back to the drawing board and work out a new one to fill what now looks like a huge void. No wonder the counts were low.

I had a long chat with my dear Doc. Many things were said, some left unsaid. The elephant in the room was the question: will he be cured? But we did not address it directly. The conversation was about what was needed to be done after the last chemo and for the next 6 months when we would perhaps get the news we were waiting for.

I have a month to work out the next 6 months. We know that only R's immune system can bring the miracle we need. For the past 5 months his body has spun out of control under the assault of toxins of all kind and hue. His immune system must be in shock and will take time to get rid of the toxins. Then it will slowly get back in control and hopefully do the needful.

I guess it will take another 66 days post 27/12 to find a new comfort zone. Just hope the BP behaves.

Tuesday, 26 November 2013

NO ONE TOLD ME THAT GETTING ON WITH LIFE AFTER CANCER WOULD BE SO HARD

In my last post I shared my apprehensions about the new elephant that has taken possession of my brain, albeit momentarily, and is creating havoc in my body demanding to be acknowledged, heard and then sent to a tiny corner. Everyone in my nuclear family and extended family of friends and well wishers are looking forward to the 27 December 2013, the day of R's last chemo. The mood is almost euphoric as they countdown to 0. I had initially shared the elation but for some days now, I have found it difficult to do so as when I think about it, I realise that much of the glee is once again based on the seduction approach of the chemo sellers. It was the oncologist who first said that all be well after the required numbers of chemos!

December 27th is exactly a month away and what looms large in my mind is WHAT NEXT! One does not have to be a rocket scientist to believe that some miracle will happen on the morning of the 28th and R will wake up as fit as he was two years ago. The 28th morning will be the usual day 1 after chemo when R is really low. The difference is that though the counts will fall as usual, this time there may not be the booster injections. The PET scan will at best give an 80% all clear. 20% will still have to be taken care of by his completely blown immune system. The past 6 months could be summed up as a bad 'trip' for the immune system as it has been subjected to completely mind blowing drugs. These have taken their toll as just a look at R's blue nails is proof enough of the fact that the immune system has a lot of work to do before it rids the body and all its organs of the toxins that have been pumped into it with alacrity and even impunity. The fight is on!

As I wrote in my previous blog, we have been lulled into a (dis)comfort zone of life in 15 days cycles. A study reveals that it takes 66 days to form a habit. We have lived this way for over 150 days. Now we will have to unlearn this and get accustomed to another rhythm and if we begin in earnest on the 28th then I have less than a month to work it out.

Step one was to simply Google 'Life after chemotherapy'. What you get is nothing short of scary. The first article[134] I clicked on was: *No one told me that getting on with life after cancer would be so hard*. The article is written by a doctor and the part that caught my eye was: *But when treatment is over? Well, life gets back to normal. Right? Hmm … not so fast. It's just not that easy. That's what we forget to tell patients. Getting back to normal, getting on with life is harder than everyone expects.* Yes Dear Doctors you forget to tell too much to poor unsuspecting and trusting patients who hang on to very word you say as if it was God's Gospel.

Getting back to a normal life before chemotherapy has wrecked your body and soul is no mean task. Maybe one has to find the new normal, not just for R, but for all of us. I know the new normal will be again life in cycles. I guess this time the cycles will be longer: from one test to the other. But cycles there will be with their share of angst and fear and also hope. But life will never be the same again.

So what do we need to fear? A question that has to be addressed so that we can all conjure our coping strategies. I am reminded of the time when shortly after my father's death I had some health issue and needed to see a doctor in Paris. When he heard I had lost both my parents to cancer, he immediately told me that I needed to have a yearly cancer check up. I was 40 then. I told him I had no intention to live the remainder of my life in fear and yearly cycles. That was then and that was me. But today I find myself thrown into a similar situation but the difference is that it is not me.

---

[134] Merry Jennifer Marckham MD; No one told me that getting on with life after cancer would be so hard

I like to be prepared. Remember, I am a control freak. I like to know the worse case scenarios so that I can have coping mechanisms ready. Hence it was time for some more digging. The one thing that sprung like *a leitmotiv* in almost all the articles was fatigue and memory and concentration changes. Come to think of it the memory thing has already kicked in as R finds it difficult to concentrate for a given period of time. Fatigue it is said takes a long time to get rid of especially when blood counts are low as is the case with R. What is suggested is exercise, lots of fluids, meditation, relaxation and so on. I have been trying to get R on this track but with not much success.

Then comes memory and attention problems or what is known as chemo brain or chemo fog. Here again I have been trying to push R to read or play brain games but gave in as chemo was on. Come 2014 there will be a lot of reading and Sudoku!

Next is Neuropathy or changes in the nervous system: tingling, burning, loss of sensation and so on. These can be alleviated with medication and can take time to go. Will have to do more research on this one.

All these are small side effects. But there are the larger ones. The ABVD protocol delayed side effects are scary: pulmonary toxicity, cardiac toxicity and secondary malignancies.

I will deal with these in a later blog. I need a break and some fresh air. Retail therapy??

•

Wednesday, 27 November 2013

THE WORST CASE SCENARIO

In my last post, I mentioned the delayed side effects that may occur post chemotherapy ABVD protocol. One has to be aware of these even if they are rare. I have had my walk in the sun and am ready to address these, however difficult it may seem. But better the devil you know. So here goes.

This protocol can cause pulmonary toxicity. The culprit here is Bleomycin. This toxicity develops months to years after completing chemotherapy, and usually manifests as cough and shortness of breath. The statistics are 18%. What is disturbing is that a study[135] done in 2004 questioned whether Bleomycin is necessary at all! However, at this point it remains a standard part of ABVD. Wonder why?

Adriamycin can cause heart toxicity but the occurrence is rare if the cumulative dose is less than 300 mg/m2 during the 6 cycles. 6 cycles means 12 chemos and R has been receiving 25mg/m2, which is 300 mg/m2. Just the limit. Worrying!

The last of the big ones is secondary malignancies: lung or acute myeloid leukaemia. Studies confirm that the risks after ABVD protocol are less than

---

[135] How Important Is Bleomycin in the Adriamycin + Bleomycin + Vinblastine + Dacarbazine Regimen?
George P. Canellos David Duggan Jeffrey Johnsonand Donna Niedzwiecki
http://jco.ascopubs.org/content/22/8/1532

with other protocols. A study concludes[136]that *the administration of six ABVD cycles to patients with stage I and II Hodgkin's lymphoma is a safe therapeutic alternative that might reduce the risk of late and potentially lethal toxicity.* Amen to that. One thing is certain: there will be no further chemotherapy or radiotherapy in our case.

It is definitely reassuring to know that the regimen we have followed is the least toxic. But what still disturbs me in all these studies are words like: relapse, survival, remission etc. I just want one word: cure!

But can beggars be choosers. No. So one will have to be careful and plan the coming days keeping all possibilities in mind, even if the incidences are minimal.

I will now look for support alternative systems.

To be continued.

PS: Why are we not told all these things before one decides!

---

[136] Treatment of stage I and II Hodgkin's lymphoma with ABVD chemotherapy: results after 7 years of a prospective study; A. Rueda Domínguez,ˉ, A. Márquez, J. Gumá, M. Llanos, J. Herrero, M. A. de las Nieves, J. Miramón and E. Alba; Annals of Oncology; http://annonc.oxfordjournals.org/content/15/12/1798. full

Thursday, 28 November 2013

A SMALL SETBACK

It was too good to be true. The last 9 chemos went well and we all slunk into our comfort zones expecting the last three to be the same. But the Gods had other plans. R next chemo, chemo 10, is due tomorrow and he has developed a slight fever. There seem to be no other signs of infection: cough, nose running, pain etc. The fever is hovering around 100. The discharge slip simply advises paracetamol in case of fever. Different websites however urge you to contact the doctor should the fever be above 100.4. I have sent a message to his oncologist and have been asked to call him up at 6pm. Believe you me these two hours are going to seem like an eternity. I do hope it is nothing serious and we can be on schedule for our chemo tomorrow. I so want the chemo protocol and scans and removal of the port to be in 2013 so that we can usher the New Year chemo free! But this entails our remaining on schedule. Prayers needed.

Thursday, 28 November 2013

NO ONE ELSE CAN FIT

While rummaging in a drawer I found what I think is my favourite picture with my father. It was taken in Ankara in 1968. I was 16 and all dressed up in mama's turquoise blue sari. The picture was shot just before a cocktail at home. I can feel the warmth and magic of that precious moment 46 years after the event and 21 years after he left me. He died on November 29th 1992.

However much I tried, I have never been able to fill the huge gap he left in my heart and soul. Papa, or Tatu as I called him was more than a father to me. I guess it sounds clichéd but he was my friend philosopher and guide. But more than that he was my 'copain' French for pal, my brother on the two festivals dedicated to brothers and sisters and was the one person I ran to whenever I was hurting be it the small scratch on my knee, or the big fight with my life partner. Often he did not even have to say anything. Words were not necessary between us. I think the most poignant example of all was when Ma died and I looked at him expecting him to break down. He just opened his arms and hugged me tight. I truly felt the loss of my mother the day he died. He had filled the space she left gaping with his love.

Tatu and I were partners in 'crime. We both loved food and shared many meals à deux be it in fancy Parisian restaurants or at the pakora stall of INA market. His way of making up for his mercurial temper that always resulted in a mercurial slamming of the door by yours truly was to whip up a delicious treat and sheepishly knock at my door. All was forgiven as the first morsel entered my mouth. Today the tempestuous child does not bang any doors as no one will knock at it plate in hand.

That I miss him is obvious. I miss him every day and more so when I am in a dilemma or facing a problem. Today when I am fighting the biggest battle of my life, I long for his arms and his healing touch. When I was too old, or rather he was too old to have me sit on his knee, I use to sit on the floor beside him and place my head on his lap and in an instant all problems were solved. I miss the early morning cup of tea we shared when the whole house was still asleep. That was our time and we made and remade the world to our hearts' content. Maybe this is why I still wake up early and creep down the stairs to the very place where his favourite armchair was kept and maybe that is why I remodelled the house to enclose that space and make it mine.

I so long for his warm embrace, for his wise counsel, for his soothing coos that made every hurt vanish and every cloud pass. Each time I have to take a decision regarding R, I send a silent prayer seeking his guidance and I feel his presence each and every time. I do not want anyone to fill the gap he left in my heart. It keeps him alive in my heart.

I miss you Tatu.

Friday, 29 November 2013

NUMBER 10

When I was an absolute neophyte and could just about spell the word chemotherapy and comprehend acronyms like ABVD, I was told by the oncologist, that the last chemos would be the worst ones. The greenhorn in me could not quite fathom that, as I would have thought that the first ones would be tougher and things would get easier as *better the devil you know*, as it is said! Well not quite true with the beast called chemo as it is not your regular neighbourhood devil, but a lurking hydra headed monster that grows a new head each time you get rid of one. The problem is that your poor tired body does not have time to rid itself of all the poison it has received before it is assaulted again and again and again. Our euphoria of getting almost to the end, 2 to go as of today, took a big dampening. It almost feels like the last two heads of our monster will be the toughest to slay and we will need Hercules's craft to do so, I guess.

Chemo 10 started on time. Surprise, surprise! We naively hoped it would end on time and all would be well. R seemed surprisingly calm and we again were gullible enough to believe that it all would be well. How could we suspect that Hydra was crafting a wily head! The fourth drip was almost finished when R started shivering and his teeth were clattering. He said he was cold and felt feverish. The nurses took the fever but it was normal. The shivering did not stop so I SMSd the oncologist who prescribed an Avil injection. By then the fever was 100. The oncologist asked me to inform him when it went above 100.5. The drive back home was never ending and the silence oppressive. By the time we reached home R felt nauseous and sat on the tub next to the pot refusing to move. Saying anything to him was countered by an aggressive word or movement. Where was my R! Slowly we moved him to his bed and he commandeered us to put his electric blanket on, switch the heater on, and give him a quilt, a woollen cap and socks. He then fell into a disturbed sleep. When I took his temperature again it was 103.2. I was scared or should I say terrified. A quick message to the doctor to be told to remove all the heating implements and report back after an hour. 102.6. Another message! A pill to be given. Temperature to be checked. 101.2. I breathed a sigh of relief and decided I needed to come down and write. It was critical I do so.

I now hope and pray that the night will be peaceful and that the fever would have gone in the morning. But my mind is on overdrive. How do I handle chemos 11 and 12? It seems that my support therapy needs fine tuning as the poison is accumulating by the minute. Big guns are needed. More research to be done. The weeks to come will be busy.

I have to get the better of 11 and 12!

Sunday, 1 December 2013

AWOL

I have been AWOL for the past two days. Many of you would, I think, have expected an update after my last blog, as it was full on angst and despair. Yes that was when I talked of a hydra headed monster and his 12 heads, 10 of which I have slain, of a fever that touched 103.3. You can imagine in what state I was! My mind on overdrive wondering whether the infection one at been able to keep at bay for 5 months had broken through the carefully erected defences. My fingers busy on the electronic keypad of my phone sending frantic messages to all the doctors I knew. The fever refusing to break. And then finally, one convinced a grumpy R (the only time I have seen him grumpy is on chemo day) to switch off the electric blanket, turn off the heater, take off his woollen cap and his sweater and remove the quilt, and the temperature fell to 102. Still worrying. But then the oncologist prescribed a medicine that did the trick. Would you believe if I told you that R even asked for the fan to be turned on? I did, for a few minutes, as there was no scope for argument. But then the fever broke and he slept well while I kept vigil.

The next morning, R was as well as he is on day 2. And I decided to give myself a break and go AWOL. I needed to, as too many questions crowded my tired brain and I felt absolutely incapable of dealing with them unless I took some time off.

What did I do? Nothing much. Visited my favourite bookshop and browsed to my heart's content, did some window shopping and even bought a trinket and then tucked myself in bed with a book, but was asleep even before I could read a page. That was yesterday.

Today I took more time off. Got my nails done, yes the ones bitten down to the quick! And then went to see Utpal and gorge myself on the oxygen laden air whilst watching him skate to his heart's content. No better feelgood shot!

Am back now. I think my mind is quieter and I can see the way. So more on that later.

Monday, 2 December 2013

THE NEW NORMAL

December 27th 2013 will be upon us sooner than one thinks. Time flies, as you get older. So chemo 11 and 12 will happen in no time and with it the adrenaline rush that kept me going will peter out unless I find another mission to keep me going. I know that without a zealous mission the meltdown may just happen. So time to figure out what next. To think that things will resolve themselves once chemo 12 is over is naive and absurd. On December 27th R will begin recovering from his chemo and his counts will drop dramatically. This time there will be no booster shots, or so I think. This time his shattered body will have to pick up its pieces and try and build itself, slowly and patiently, hoping that no cracks remain.

He will have to pick himself up and carry on, no matter what. It will be no easy task, with no defined time line. The totally misplaced idea that life will be normal again, just as it once was is a chimera. I guess we all held on to it to steer us through the difficult times when chemotherapy was on, but now it is time to face the reality that awaits us and break it gently to R. Life will never be normal, as we knew it. We will have to build a new normal.

So what will this new normal look like? For one, for months to come, R will have to be kept away from any source of infection which sadly translates into limited mobility: no beers in crowded club pubs, no parties, no meals in crowded restaurants and so on. Doctors never tell you that life will be different after cancer treatment. On the contrary they fool you by telling you that all will be well. How can I forget the surgeon who told me that papa would be good as new after his surgery for colon cancer? He did not survive, but if he had, I shudder to think how he would carried on a normal life with his colostomy pouch.

In R's case, his oncologist continues to 'fool' us, by making it sound like all will be well after the 12th chemo. And somehow we have been lulled into believing it. But that is not the case. Chemotherapy keeps you from jumping into life again. It is not as if you got off the spinning wheel of life for a few months and can jump on again and hope all will be the same. In the US you now have cancer rehabs that helps survivors overcome the new normal. We do not have these programmes here so I will have to conjure one for R.

It is believed that cancer survivors can face myriad ailments: pain, fatigue, weakness, immobility, cognitive impairment, sleep difficulties, sexual dysfunction, anxiety and depression. That is a whole lot to deal with. I guess one has to wait and see what happens and address each situation as it occurs in the best way possible.

Cancer treatment is not kind to the body and taking care of the body is what will be first and foremost on the agenda. The body has gone through hell and will now have to be molly coddled for all times to come. The new normal has to combine good diet with exercise on a daily basis. The weight has to be kept stable and thus physical activity is essential even if one is tired. The new normal is not easy and takes courage and determination.

The immunity has to be built slowly. Blood counts will have to be done on a regular basis. The progress may be slow and frustrating, but one will have to keep the faith all the way. Not easy.

Tuesday, 3 December 2013

CHEMO COCOON

It sounds like almost an aberration but seems like chemotherapy has been almost cocoon like for both R and I, and I guess others in the family and friends network. For the past 5 months we have been living in the 'false' comfort of chemo cycles. You see chemo has a timeline with an end in sight: i.e. the last chemo. Not so long back this last chemo looked far away, like a light at the end of a long tunnel and as we all trudged along willingly or unwillingly, there was a feeling that we were doing something right even if it had too many downsides. Cancer cells were being attacked and killed. Never mind the healthy cells that had to be slaughtered at the holy alter of conventional medicine. We all thought that the butterfly would break out once this nightmare was over. But that is not to be.

As the last chemo day approaches I am conscious of the fact that cocoon season is not over and I must be careful to ensure that the cocoon matures fully before it morphs into a beautiful butterfly. That means that the body has to rest and recuperate before it can fly.

So December 27th is not the end of the tunnel but the beginning of a new one. It could be a wider one with more light, but tunnel it has to be till the cocooning time is over. Till now the word chemo was almost like a magic wand that called us to order any and every time the thought of digressing a little from the tight and unforgiving schedule. The idea of having a chemo delayed because of an infection was so scary that it took care of any want or even need. There was something strangely comforting about the chemo schedule.

R and I lost ourselves into the chemo routine and had some very emotional and touching moments. We never felt closer. At times, particularly on chemo day or the day after, R was so vulnerable that he almost felt like a little child that needed to be tended to and comforted. I spent many nights touching his brow to make sure that the dreaded fever had not raised its ugly face. As he slept next to me, I felt responsible for his well being and helpless when I could do nothing to make things easier. Then there were the days when he felt better and my heart swelled with love and pride. As we mentally checked each chemo off the calendar, a sense of elation filled us both and we talked about the end of the road.

But soon the chemo cocoon will be over. It will have to be replaced by another regimen that will have to be given a comforting name. This new normal that we have to work out together has to be able to assuage all the unsaid fears that will soon assail us if we are not watchful and prepared.

Tuesday, 3 December 2013

TO LIVE IS TO BE SLOWLY BORN

It is strange but the trials and tribulations of the passed 18 months have certainly brought to life a 'stranger' unknown to me. But more than that it revived a relationship that began almost 4 decades ago. The stranger I refer to is me, and the relationship is of course the one with R. True we are older and a bit faded, but the past months have seen us closer than we ever were. We are slowly being reborn every day we live, in spite or rather because of the unwanted and unsolicited stranger that has crept between us. However I have made sure that no space exists between R and I, and hence Sir Hodgkin's has to deal with the both of us. For the past 6 months I have shared every moment of his troubling presence in a way I could not have imagined. That is the new me, or the stranger I refer to. I must admit I did not know I was capable of this and feel blessed.

For better or worse, in sickness and health, vows we hear so often have really come alive in this experience we today share. And ultimately it is moments of crisis and adversity that put your love and commitment to test. I saw this in my father when Mama battled cancer and did not want any treatment. He stood by her wishes and tended to her as you would to a child, respecting all her demands and idiosyncrasies, the most poignant one being her insistence on not going to sleep unless he sat by her and woke her up every 45 minutes. You see she did not want to die in her sleep. Today I truly understand him and hope I too can stand by R all the way.

Wednesday, 4 December 2013

PIECES OF THE PAST

To say that I have not been thinking of death in the past months would be a perfect lie. From the instant I came to know about the nature of R's ailment, death that was till then a philosophical idea so beautifully described by Oriana Fallaci when she writes: *life is a death sentence*, suddenly became a reality. The oft repeated words - if you are born than you have to die - assumed a new meaning altogether. Death that seemed so faraway became that much nearer. Mine more than anyone else's. Please do not take this as an essay in morbidity bur rather as a reflection on days gone by, a reminder of the items that still sit unchecked on the umpteen bucket lists one has made, a contemplation on one's existence and walk down memory lane.

Yesterday as I sat alone, sipping a cup of tea in the rather formal drawing room we rarely use, my eyes wandered on the cornucopia of objects that fill every corner of this rather large space and a sense of nostalgia engulfed me. Each object had a story to tell, a story that would die with me if I did not find the time to put in down in words. But then, I asked myself, who would be interested in the tales I wove as I know that to my kids, these rather encumbering and aged objects are clutter that they would have to get rid off as in today's world space is limited and costly and no one has rooms just to keep memories alive. Today's kids are practical and they should be. But I cannot get rid of these treasures, as they are the repositories of my passage on earth. The reality is that they will find their end in some garage sale or maybe in some auction house. So be it.

However I would like to take that walk down memory lane and relive some of the forgotten moments of my life. Most of these objects were bought by my parents who travelled the world not for investment purposes but because they liked them. So you may have a very expensive object sitting next to a trinket, both imbibed with the same passion and both treasured in the same manner.

There is a Louis XV chair but the tapestry was woven by my mother. She embroidered this in Vietnam in the sixties when my father had a difficult posting that kept him away in dangerous situations. Mama calmed her nerves by concentrating on her petit point reminding me of Penelope.

Behind it sits an Amphora. It is from Halicarnassus, now Bodrum in Turkey and was embedded in the seabed till it was discovered. Papa had to seek special permission to take it out of Turkey and it was his price possession. One day our Dalmatian was chasing a mouse and the amphora fell and broke. Papa was heartbroken and had tears in his eyes. It was my uncle who with extreme patience repaired it and though there are still some visible cracks, to me it remains papa's most prized possession even if thanks to Furiya our dog, it may be of no value today.

There are vases from China and crystals from Prague, lacquered objects from Vietnam and porcelains from Dresden. The innocuous looking cupboards are filled with priceless dinner sets Meissen, and Rosenthal some dating before the war. I still remember the *piece de resistance* of my mother's dinners, which was a boned whole fish, stuffed with innumerable things and served on the larger than life fish platter that barely fits in its present abode. The dainty *demi tasses* filled with strong coffee witnessed many dinners, some where royalty mingled with the diplomats, writers and ordinary people amidst laughter and cigar smoke, not to forget the colourful Sobranie cigarettes that mama loved and smoked occasionally making sure the colour matched her stunning saris.

So many memories, all tucked away in a ageing and tired brain but still having the ability to bring a much needed smile and a sense of well being I have no words to describe.

ANOURADHA BAKSHI

Thursday, 5 December 2013

THE FIGHT IS ON

Perhaps my writing has been a bit nostalgic and a tad defeatist lately. Some of you may even be feeling I am giving up. NO WAY! I am as charged up as ever though it is true that the past months have made me review and rethink about life in a new light, hence there are moments when one feels a little blue. I guess these are also much needed breaks when the adrenaline is pumping, breaks that remind you of essential things that get swept under the carpet when you are on a mission as I am.

Then of course there is the overwhelming reality of chemo ending that entails conjuring new schedules and timetables. Batteries need to be recharged and a walk down memory lane does just that.

There is also the need to step off the spinning wheel and take a moment to look back at the months gone by and bow one's head in gratitude for all the blessings that have gone unacknowledged. I remember how frightened I was of all the terrifying side effects imputed to chemotherapy. The past months with 10 chemos went almost side effect free. What a blessing it has been. R who I thought would lose weight actually gained some, much to his chagrin as he had visions of remaining a size 0. What a blessing again. I do not want to dissect why this happened, whether it was brew x or brew z, the important thing is that someone guided me in the right direction and for that I am truly grateful and humbled.

I thought it would be a lonely battle, but far from that, I have never felt so loved and supported by people known and unknown who have reached out to me at every step. I again feel blessed and humbled.

The fight is on. It would be foolish to underestimate the adversary.

Friday, 6 December 2013

Friday, 6 December 2013

HAVE A NICE LIFE

When a cancer patient asked her oncologist: *when do I see you next*, the answer was: *You don't. Have a nice life!* How easy it is for doctors to make such statements without actually thinking. I have heard so many that nothing surprises me anymore. Doctors of our times seem to have forgotten that they are dealing with individuals, each with their own fears, their unformulated questions, even their idiosyncrasies and they see the men in white as saviours and messengers of hope. But to a doctor a patient is just a series of medical abnormalities, jargon, statistics, acronyms and numbers. You have Hodgkin's lymphoma, stage 2B, your protocol is ABVD, 6 cycles of 2, 3 PET scans and have a nice life. Next please! But that is not quite as it goes.

Even if one is not a control freak like me, I guess every patient realises how shattered his body is after the toxic assault it has been subjected to. Every one wants to know how long it will take for the body to eliminate the toxins. How long will it take for the blood counts to begin their slow ascent to normalcy? How long will it take for the chemo fog to lift, for the fatigue to go, for the energy levels to rise? How long will it take to get back to normal if normal there is?

There will be elephants in the room both for R and for those who love him, elephants that one will be too scared to address, but that nevertheless have to be acknowledged if one is hoping for a semblance of normalcy. The fear of debilitating long term side effects, the fear of the darned hydra headed monster growing another head, the fear of the immune system never getting back to its good old self. *Have a nice life* assumes an entirely new meaning.

No matter how optimist or fatalist one is, the fears are real. Just like the fear that got the better of me when I read the words: ? lymphoma. It is human to feel frightened and only if you fear the fear will you be able to conquer it. I remembered Nelson Mandela[137]'s words this morning and realised how true they were: *I learned that courage was not the absence of fear, but the triumph over it. The brave man is not he who does not feel afraid, but he who conquers that fear.* It is only if you experience fear that you find the strength to conquer it.

I have resolved to acknowledge my fears and voice them loud and clear as I know I will conquer them. And if no one gives me the answers, I will find them and accept them even if they are not quite what one expected. The first step is to list down all the questions that are clogging my mind.

The first is of course: will everything go back to what is was like before. The answer is a big NO. There was a life before cancer and there will be a different one after cancer: BC and AC! Will the life after cancer be worse and again the answer is a big NO as it is in our hands to craft the new normal and as I had read somewhere it will take 66 days for this new normal to become a habit and hence 'normal'. So that is not too bad.

You may ask why I say with such confidence that our AC will be better. The answer is that in many ways it is already better than it was. I am not talking about the treatment and its acolytes. What I am alluding to is the quality of our emotional and personal life, the new found closeness, the myriad of well wishers and their love. I can say without an iota of doubt that life is happier and merrier. There is so much laughter, so much more time is spent together doing things we never did before: hilarious carom games, animated scrabble sessions where people with different mother tongues scratch their brain finding English words. There are also intimate moments when we revive memories of days gone by or share stories we never revealed. Skype calls with the grandson who laughs at nana and nanou's new hairdo. And let me tell you that this is and will be an integral part of our new normal. And how can I forget the gentle daily banter over the medicines

---

[137] Nelson Mandela, Long Walk to Freedom; 1995; Little Brown & Co

that I proffer all along the day from the moment we get up to the instant we go to sleep. Not to talk of the brews and potions. That too will be part of the new normal. It looks good does it not?

But there will things to remember and keep in mind. The new normal will have its shades of grey. R's ravaged body will take its time to heal and we will all need to remember this and learn to live at his pace. He cannot jump back into old routines straight away. So life will have to be a gentle stroll with breaks whenever needed. We will all need to learn to listen to R's body. Something I have already learnt to do. Every sniffle, sneeze or twitch earlier ignored now has me jumping out of my skin. I will need to continue to do so, with perhaps a little more tact.

I know that in the best case scenario, there will be still be a certain percentage of cancer cells that need to be destroyed and only R's immune system can conjure that miracle. Hence the big priority will undoubtedly be getting his immune system back on track. I know there are many ways and will do some intensive research and share my findings. As his immune system springs back to normal, his fatigue will go and his risk of infection diminish. But here again there is no fix time line. Every body is unique and thus it's healing is unique too! So many of the questions that disturb me today find their answer in one simple statement: boost the immune system to its earlier glory.

Food and supplements will help strengthen the immune system, but if you remember one of my early blogs where I talked of jumping on a trampoline or rebounding as a way to boost immunity, life AC will have to include a lot of physical exercise. Walking, stretching and yoga. I tried my best to include as much of these as possible in the last months but chemo played spoil sport. No excuse now particularly if R wants to resume golf as in the BC days as fast as possible.

Let us not forget that mental stress is by far the most potent carcinogen. This is my strong belief. So the mind has to be pampered and stilled, with meditation, relaxation and happy thoughts. That is one thing I am going to ensure no matter what, even if I make more enemies along the way.

Now to the question about how long it takes to flush the toxins out of the system, a conventional figure is at least 6 months. The challenge is to cleanse the system. I do not see R embracing a stringent yogic regimen, so we will have to take it slow and easy. And we are talking of one helluva lot of toxins. *In addition to eliminating chemical toxins and heavy metals from the body, says the New Hope Medical Centre[138] in Arizona, cancer patients need further detoxification support in order to remove the toxic load that comes from the death of cancer cells.* Water is the best way to detoxify your body so I will make sure R drinks his 8 glasses a day and *exercise gets the heart pumping, which circulates blood, moving toxins out of the body. It also encourages perspiration, which decreases toxins, and makes you thirsty, so you'll drink more water.* No excuses my darling. Then of course a lot of green juices but will talk of the diet and nutrition plan later.

So I have my plate full and even overflowing. The one thing I want to say hear LOUD and CLEAR: We are going to have a nice life!

---

[138]   http://www.newhopemedicalcenter.com

Saturday, 7 December 2013

THE BALANCING ACT

As I have often said, the men in white never tell you of all the side effects that may occur during and after chemotherapy. Here is a new one we discovered lately: loss of balance. For the past week or so I have seen R losing balance when he gets up or does something like slipping into his shoes, or reaching up for a shirt in his cupboard. Today I finally asked him whether he felt a loss of balance and his answer was affirmative. A quick search on the net[139] confirmed that chemotherapy affects the nerves and one of the possible outcomes is loss of balance. Others mentioned are : tingling, tired muscles, numbness in hand and feet, clumsiness, stiff neck, loss of hearing etc. Wow! Did not see this one coming. The scary sentence was : *These symptoms usually improve when the chemotherapy dose is lowered or treatment is stopped; however, in some cases, the damage is permanent.* So urgent damage control is needed.

A perusal of the possible causes[140] was quick to identify the culprit: Vinblastine - the V of the ABVD protocol. One of the remedial action suggested is *Physical therapy, to improve physical strength, balance, coordination,*

---

[139] http://www.cancer.net/navigating-cancer-care/how-cancer-treated/
      chemotherapy/side-effects-chemotherapy
[140] http://www.cancer.net/navigating-cancer-care/side-effects/
      nervous-system-side-effects

and mobility. So poor darling will have yoga on the menu and a lot of balancing on one leg eyes opened and eyes closed. Breathing and acupressure also help.

Must now look for other options.

Tuesday, 10 December 2013

WILL YOU BE MY GIRL FRIEND

One of Hodgkin's best side effect is undoubtedly reconnecting with R, a delightful consequence of the forced seclusion we both have been subjected to, he because of his low immunity and I because of my determination bordering on obsession to see him well and kick Hodgkin's out of our lives. I think this is the first time in almost four decades that we have spent so much time alone together. For this I am eternally grateful to Sir H! These stolen moments have been replete with slowly ambling down memory lane and reliving sweet and bittersweet moments as well as more difficult ones. It has given us time to complete what was left unsaid, to ask forgiveness for the hurtful words that were never really meant.

I must admit that this would never have happened without the help of Sir H as I cannot imagine what else could have made us stop and give ourselves the much needed space we never had. Never have we talked so much, laughed so much or just held each other in silence that said more than any word could. Never have we watched so much TV together, be it cricket or golf or cook programmes. Just sharing that time in perfect togetherness is worth the most precious thing on earth.

Imagine my surprise and elation when he turned to me yesterday and said: *Will you be my girlfriend*! I did not take me a second to say a big YES, just as I had when he asked me to marry me in a cinema hall in February 1974! Then he asked me to have lunch at Fujiya, a restaurant close to where he lived in those days. I would have loved to say yes again but the memory

THERE IS ONLY ROOM FOR HOPE   355

of the oily Chinese food served in that place stopped me. The oily American chopsuey which was our favourite then with the over fried egg swimming on top was not something I could have him eat now. But how could I stop the memories that came gushing. I cannot remember the number of times we ate that oily food that tasted like manna from the Gods as it was laced with our love. We will definitely go one day and share a plate of the oily fare. But for today we need to take a rain check.

Sadly those were still days when photographs had to be taken with camera and rolls of films and I realise that I do not have any of our courting days but believe me R was a dashing young man.

Wednesday, 11 December 2013

FIRST DATE

As I was asked by R a few days back if I would *be his girlfriend*, I thought it would be amusing to share with you our first date! It was truly picaresque.

For those who are of my vintage and lived in Delhi, you would remember where the Cottage Industries was located and its famous eatery Bankura that was located outside with wrought iron chairs and big pedestal fans. You had a choice of mutton, chicken or vegetable lunch. The mutton had two options: stew and cutlet. My favourite was the oily stew served with potatoes and boiled veggies and two slices of bread, all stuffed on a plate so that by the time you got it the bread had already soaked much of the sauce. It was yummy. So date no 1 was a lunch date and the venue Bankura. I had worn one of mama's saris, a yellow with red border if I remember well, high heels and though it was late February had not bothered to take anything warm. We were young and vain. I had thought that the date would be lunch and the proverbial Saturday afternoon English movie.

We settled down at a table and I was already to order my mutton stew delight when I realised that R was a little fidgety. Imagine my surprise when he said he would not eat anything. I wondered what was wrong! It took him a few minutes to tell me that he had to play a hockey match in Dhaula Kuan at 3pm and had to go home to change! He asked me if I would come along. I said yes without batting an eyelid! I could not have imagined what awaited me. Of course there was no mutton stew.

R had a scooter so sari, heels and I perched on it and we drove to his abode, a barsati on Malcha Marg. I followed him all the way up sari and heels notwithstanding and was impressed by how neat his room was. He opened his cupboard and changed behind it. I again did not bat an eyelid. It was down the stairs on the pillion of the scooter and more zipping.

We reached the army hockey ground wherever that was and suddenly I found myself seated on a bench and R muttered something and disappeared to join his team. I knew no one. I had no clue about what a hockey match was. And having not worn my glasses could barely make out R on the ground.

Mama and me had a deal. I had to tell her what time I would be back and not be a minute later unless I had called and informed her. I could see time flying and had no way of getting to a phone. Remember there were no mobiles then. When the match was over, I begged R to hurry up as my deadline was approaching. By that time, the weather had changed and it was getting chilly. We made another stop at his house so that he could lend me a sweater and get something warm for himself.

When we reached close to my house, I saw mama pacing the road. I hopped of the scooter, barely introducing R and hurried home ready for a dressing down. Mercifully it was not too bad. The rest his history.

That was our first date! A date to remember!

Of course we had had nothing to eat, but who needs food when one is in love!

NUMBERS NINE. EIGHT.. AND WORRIES

Over the last months I have been concerned about R's low haemoglobin. When we found out that he had Hodgkin's lymphoma his haemoglobin was 7.2. After we began chemotherapy it climbed up to 9 and has been hovering between 9.2 and 9.8. This week it is again 9.2! It has never gone beyond the 9 range.

Chemotherapy can damages the body's ability to make RBCs, so body tissues do not get enough oxygen, a condition called anaemia. Nearly all chemotherapy agents suppress the bone marrow that, in turn, causes a reduction in the number of blood cells and thus becomes the cause of chronic anaemia. I hope this is the reason for R's low counts. I wait with bated breath for the blood counts post the last chemo session and cannot begin to imagine how it will all go. At present when R hit his nadir usually a week after his chemo, a set of injections were given to boost all the counts. The results are spectacular: from 3000 his WBC shoot up to 16000 in the span of 3 days. But what will happen after the last chemo.

Yesterday's results were scary has the haemoglobin went below 9. It was 8.9 and this time the WBC did not climb above 4900 in spite of the booster shots. The oncologist of course said : no cause for worry! For them the patient is just numbers and protocols.

I read[141] that the *blood counts will return to normal within three to four weeks, after the body's feedback system has told the stem cells in the bone marrow to increase production and begin making new cells,* and hope that this is what will happen to R. The next sentence in the same article made my blood run cold: *If chemotherapy is given at the time that the stem cells in the bone marrow are increasing their production this could cause permanent bone marrow damage.* I was never told that and hope that the doctors knew what they were doing. It is nothing short of terrifying.

The big question is how long will it take for R's immune system to regain its lost abilities. The answers are confusing as most of the survivor blogs I have read give different numbers: from 6 months to 5 years and more. Some even say that it is never quite the same so I rephrase my question to how long will it take for R's immunity to get to its new normal. And the answer is: no one knows!

According to the WHO haemoglobin counts between 8 and 9 mean moderate anaemia. This where we are today. But there are two more chemos that have to be gone through. I am at my wit's end as it seems that all my support therapies and coping strategies are not working as well as they did. I will try and see if there is something else that I can do protect R's bone marrow that has become the most precious thing in my life.

A quick search on the Internet reveals that shark liver oil helps the bone marrow. Then there is a supplement called astralagus[142] that boosts the immune system. Studies have proved this fact. So this goes on the menu too. I guess I have a lot of research to do to be ready to face the post chemo days!

---

[141] http://chemocare.com/chemotherapy/what-is-chemotherapy/what-is-nadir.aspx#.VSNt7LpCP8t

[142] Astragalus is also called huang qi or milk vetch. It comes from a type of bean or legume.

Friday, 13 December 2013

FROM HAPPY TO GRUMPY

Chemo 11 is over. It was not as bad as I expected. I guess compared to chemo 10 when R had high fever and terrible shivers, this one went on rather well. But of course he did not eat! He slept some and watched his Three's Company, a favourite TV show of his on his iPad. But as always he turned grumpy at the end of it as always. I do not know why I was reminded of Snow White's dwarfs!

R has always been the Happy one. For the past 4 decades I have rarely seen him in a bad mood, crotchety or churlish. If my memory is to be trusted I can only recall one incident where I saw his temper and I must say that I was the one responsible for his outburst. Anyone would have hit the roof. I can be infuriating at times. Those who know me well must be smiling!

Anyway for the past 6 months and for 11 times to be exact, R has turned from Happy to Grumpy in the span of a few hours during his chemos. To be honest, his Grumpy avatar is quite endearing though I wish he did not have to suffer the way he does. This lasts for the entire evening of chemo day till he sleeps. When he awakes he is back to his Happy self, though tired and miserable. Two days later he is his good old self and remains so for the next 10 days!

I will have to see one more Grumpy R on December 27th and then I will make sure that he remains Happy forever.

Saturday, 14 December 2013

WHEN THE ONE YOU LOVE IS HURTING

When the one you love is hurting you fell utterly, totally, consummately helpless. Since yesterday, after chemo 11, R has been listless and completely zapped. For the first time since we started this darned therapy he admitted feeling confused. Chemo fog! My heart shattered seeing him like this. I did not know what to do, how to make it better, how to provide some relief. The toxins that have by now found their way in the tiniest crevices of his body and now mind are playing up and taunting me. At this moment it seems they have won the battle as R is refusing all the brews and cocktails that I proffer.

I just sit or lie next to him powerless, watching him drift in and out of a disturbed sleep, listen to his mumbles trying to make sense of them but failing miserably. The TV may be on but I register nothing, I may have a book open at a given page but am incapable of reading a word, even if its the hottest thriller of the season. I too am lost in a fog of my own strangely also caused by the hated chemo though not a drop could have strayed my way. This is another brand of chemo fog, the one that is caused by your total uselessness in this moment.

The toxins will have to be flushed out slowly. The equation is skewed, as the body is unable to eliminate all the toxins in the short 14 days between chemos, so there is a logjam that grows with quantum leaps leaving the body exhausted and knocked out. The total loss of appetite and the nagging nausea does not help much.

Each chemo has been more and more difficult for both of us. The euphoria of initial days has died down and given way to a sense of acceptance of the inevitable. Both of us are lost in an uncanny trance that will continue till the last chemo. Only then will we be able to take our first steps towards a new normal that will be ours to determine.

I only know that this new normal will be more perfect than anything we can imagine!

Sunday, 15 December 2013

OF PINHOLE CAMERAS, FIBROUS ROOTS, QUADRILATERALS AND ASHOKA THE GREAT

The last chemo has been nerve wrecking for all of us. It is as if a pall of giving up has descended on all of us. The next 10 days seem eternal and time as heavy as Baudelaire's lid. Mercifully my little bundle of sunshine and endless energy a.k.a Utpal has landed for his winter break: one whole month. For me it is good augur as Popples has always brought me luck and joy. This time it has come in the form of three whole pages of homework! From English to Hindi via Sanskrit and of course maths, science and all the other subjects a class VI child had to learn. We both hate homework, but cannot do anything about it. Normally we fight and make up and do the tasks amidst tears and laughter. But this time homework has come as a relief as it will help me fill up the 240 hours left before chemo 12.

I am not cheating as in many places in the homework sheets we find the phrase: *you may take the help of elders whenever needed*! This time the phrase will be turned on its head as it is the elder who needs the help. So in between all other chores that have now become habitual, I am Od'ing on home work. This will entail hours of net search for subjects I learnt more than half a century ago; it will mean making charts, and maps and drawings. It will mean downloading pictures, getting them printed and then making files. How blissfully therapeutic!

God his kind and merciful! This time he appeared in the form of homework! Never thought I would welcome this!

Sunday, 15 December 2013

LISTEN TO ME PLEASE

We far too often underestimate and undervalue our brain. I have realised in the course of my existence, how powerful the mind is in more ways then one. Our mind is the best healer we have at our beck and call and yet we rarely use it preferring to rush to our pill box and pop one not giving a thought to the harm it may do to our brain. Have you ever taken a moment to admire the working of our brain? I never did for long but now find myself taking that nano second to acknowledge it's functioning. A word can trigger uncountable memories, so can a sound or a fragrance. But that is not all. Sometimes just lying down and letting your mind wander works far better than an analgesic.

I have also realised that medicine or therapies of any kind only work when your mind wills them too! If your are not in a positive frame of mind then no matter how good the medicine, it will not have the desired effect. On the contrary, it could work just the other way.

The mind/brain sends you messages that often go unheard. And then when we push them to a corner and ignore them comes the depression, the dreaded stroke, the heart attack! I have tried to keep R's morale as high as I could but since his last chemo I feel a pall of gloom descending on him. His initial will to fight Zozo seems to be dwindling. I was really terrified when he told me yesterday that he may not live long as the dreaded crab had entered his body. He has forebodings about the next chemo that are almost visceral.

I know it is his brain talking, sending a message that it is saturated with toxins and cannot take any more. But who will listen. The doctors are blinded by their protocols and they treat every individual in the same way. But God made us unique, Dear Sirs, and gave us humans the capacity to think and make choices. But we too have fallen into the trap and forgotten to listen to our instinct and intuition. We listen to others but not to ourselves.

Why can we not stop at chemo 11? What is so sacred about chemo 12 when the body is screaming ENOUGH! But the darned protocol says 12. I wonder if it is about money, or targets or insurances, or simply hubris as it does not seem to be about the poor patient and his abused body. Let us not forget that however successful the protocol, it can at best deal with 80% of the cancerous cells and that it is this very body that will be called upon to take care of the remaining 20.

I wish I could take that chemo 12 in my veins. It would complete the protocols and all other agendas and also make me go through what my poor love has gone through 11 times. I guess that I too, like all ageing human bodies have some cancerous cells dividing at that precise moment that would be destroyed, never mind the healthy ones that will die along the way. The protocol will have been followed.

Tuesday, 17 December 2013

WE ARE THE MASTERS OF OUR FATE, WE ARE THE CAPTAINS OF OUR SOUL[143]

With 2013 we will bid farewell to the now known and venture into new territories yet unknown. I am not naive enough to think that come chemo 12, R will be cured and life will once again be what it was in June 2012. I so wish this could be true but it has been many moons since I believed in Father Xmas. Life will never be what it was before June 2012 and never be what it has been till date. Come January and he will have to live what is at best called a new normal. For perhaps the first time in our lives R and I will be truly masters of our fate and captain of our souls[144]. Not everyone is given this second chance in life, a chance that comes when you are faced with an adversity you never wanted. But there it is and you have to face it. You could buckle in and give up. On the other hand you could dig deep within yourself for strength, resilience and fortitude you never imagined you have and make the adversity into good times. That is what the both of us sought to do.

I remember how after hearing the news of having lymphoma, R's first reaction was : I will beat the b******! This was even before the treatment

---

[143] Invictus William Ernest Henley 1892

[144] Invictus; William Ernest Henley; 1888

course was set. I decided to call the lymphoma ZOZO, hoping to lower the status of Sir Hodgkin and make light of him. It was almost as if we were on a high, and we had reason to as it had taken us 13 months to find the cause of R's waning away. I think that in those moments we had not registered what it all meant and what lay ahead. Then reality struck in the guise of a feared bone marrow biopsy and then a surgical biopsy and finally the dreaded chemotherapy. R had decided to go and get one of the 3 cancers that respond well to chemo. This was confirmed by the two people I trust most in matters of health: my Tibetan doctor and Doc P! So chemo it was and we decided to confront it head on. The doctor had said 8 or 12 and we all hoped it would be 8. The chemos were hard but we still hoped for 8 but when the oncologist decided on 12, I must admit we were disappointed. But we soldiered on.

In the meantime I tried to find all I could about protocols and side effects, and the information I got was again not what I hoped for. I then realised how little the men in white reveal and how you are given information piece by piece and often have to worm it out cunningly. That is when you realise that the real battle lies ahead, after chemo time when your resilience is put to test.

To say that one has not thought of the worse case scenario would be a lie. Both R and I have talked of death and several times. Sometimes it has been light hearted with my saying that I would be a merry widow; at others it has been serious, each one comforting the other and easing out fears. Some may think it morbid to talk of death, but I feel that if we are to come out winners then all elephants in the room have to be exposed and addressed. Then they are out of the way.

That is when you realise that the time you have is not perdurable and this makes the second chance a reality. It is up to you to live life to its fullest or waste it in unnecessary pursuits. It is up to us to make the best of what we have and celebrate life with joy. This can only happen if we do not let any elephant in our space and share every thought however difficult it may seem. Sharing always makes things easier. I wish I had known this 40 years ago!

So come 2014 and we embark on a new journey with hope in our hearts and a song on our lips. We are masters of our fate and captains of our soul.

Wednesday, 18 December 2013

BREAKING NEWS

It is over! The chemo I mean! NO CHEMO 12! You heard me right no chemo on December 27th. Wonder how this happened? Well all within rules. Went to see R's oncologist and we had a long chat about R and he felt that there was no need for chemo 12. Just one PET scan and then follow up.

I jumped out of my chair and gave him the biggest hug. I had to pinch myself and restrain myself from shouting or jumping. The doctor felt that R's spirit and positive approach were far more important than one extra chemo that would not make much of a difference.

I really had to pinch myself all the way back home. R's expression when I told him the news was a one in a life time experience and mind blowing. I think the both of us are still processing the news. But had to share it with all of you who have stood by me at every minute of this battle.

But all this comes with a rider. We are now going to have to walk on broken glass as for the next 8 weeks or more he will have to be kept in a cocoon as his immunity is at its nadir and he is open to all sort of infections. His immune system will now have to take over and will need all the help to do so.

But before I start planning the next chapter of our lives, I am taking a day off to quietly celebrate this small victory. Tomorrow we get ready for the next chapter.

ANOURADHA BAKSHI

Thursday, 19 December 2013

THE NEW NORMAL

When R's oncologist told me that we could skip chemo 12 - this after I had pleaded that he had reached saturation point both physically and emotionally and actually told me in a touching moment that brought tears to my eyes that the best Xmas present would be no chemo 12 - I felt elated, as if the clouds that had weighed on my head were suddenly lifted. All I could think of was that we did not have to live another chemo cycle, ever! My feet barely touched the ground as I flew out of the hospital and its sterile corridors where even the painting seem to frown at you and prayed for a quick drive home to share the news with R. It was a joyful homecoming when every one screamed and laughed.

I cannot exactly remember when, but suddenly I froze and realised that though it was indeed a joyful moment, it was just a fleeting moment. The enormity of what lay ahead hit me like the proverbial ton of bricks: the battle had just begun. Gone was the however despicable crutch called chemo, which had surreptitiously lulled us into a false sense of safety. As long as chemo was on, we were lured by the reassurance that something was killing the cancer cells. The regimen that we all followed made us forget the harsh reality that R's immunity was under attack and his body getting saturated with poison by the minute. The booster shots that conjured fabulous blood counts made us forget that too easily. There would be no more shots to encourage us. Suddenly I felt totally alone and terrified. Life would never go back to what it was. Cancer, unlike other ailments, never leaves you.

The fear of recurrence is real. It is up to you to address it and accept it with equanimity or let it spoil every moment of the days to come. Our new normal had first and foremost to deal with this fear. Whatever course of treatment we chose to follow, there would be tests and reviews with the angst they carry. What I could do is find out every thing that would help in ensuring that the crab would not crawl back and establish a new regimen that would guarantee success.

What goes in must come out says the old adage. So all the poison and dead cell residues would have to be flushed out and then his immune system would have to be practically resuscitated. There are many articles that talk about life after cancer[145] or life after chemotherapy! All talk about the new normal, and the fact that it takes long to reach this new normal! It is up to me to find the new normal pronto! All articles also mention the fact that there is no celebratory moment after treatment ends and that is something that both the patient and the family find difficult to accept. There is undoubtedly a feeling of nostalgia for days gone by.

Let us not forget that there are long-term side effects after treatment: fatigue as counts are very low, depression and even anxiety. The biggest scare is that of infection and thus one has to keep very careful till one sees the counts taking an upward trend. This can be frustrating as one has the false 'all is well' feeling as treatment is over. I just go his blood counts and they are the lowest ever. This time there are no booster shots on the menu. I have just stopped him from going for a game of golf with his best friend as I am petrified of him catching a cold. So you see the new normal is not an easy ride.

I will spend the next hours or days finding out more and working out a schedule that helps us survive the difficult months ahead.. Hope you will follow the second part of this journey and give me the support you so generously gave as I need it more than ever.

145

Thursday, 19 December 2013

A TASTE OF DAYS TO COME

I was just starting to process the news of the cancellation of chemo 12, as I knew that the spontaneous elation we felt was to be short lived, and had just begun to plan days to come by visiting the Tibetan doctor when R's blood counts results landed on me. They had never been so low! I was hoping for the usual comforting and ever optimistic : *don't worry* from Doctor D but she looked at the figures and said nothing for a while, her brows frowning. She then looked up and stated: *the WBC counts are alarming.* They read 1.5. I have never see Doctor D react this way in the long years I have been visiting her. I jumped out of my skin and started babbling incoherently, totally unlike me! She told me to keep R away from people and any source of infection and get the counts done again after a week. Normally we gave R booster shots pre chemo, but this time his oncologist had said to wait and watch.

I was in panic mode. Doctor Paul, my reassuring GP, is away till Monday! I did not know what to do. I SMSd Doctor V several times. No answer. Normally he does respond asap. I waited for some time and then tried again. I cannot begin to tell you the state I was in. One was at the start line again and had no precedent to go on. I realised that this was a situation I would find myself in the days to come. The famous new normal was to be far more challenging than I had imagined. I realised I had to build a second defence line with alternate doctors that I could call should none of the front line was available. I was wondering how to go about it when my phone buzzed and I got a reply from Doctor V. I was to give R the booster shots and then get another count done a week later. The PET scan was also to be postponed. What a relief.

This incident gave me a glimpse of the days to come. Till R's counts are not 'normal' I guess there will be many such challenges. What I need to do now is find out all I can about ways to boost the bone marrow as healing and keeping cancer at bay depends on its functioning properly.

Friday, 20 December 2013

TIMEOUT

It has been stressful times since I don't remember when. I have been functioning on an adrenaline high and I guess will continue to do so till I truly believe that R is cured and Mr Hodgkin thrown out of lives for good. There is no time line, but I guess it will be when all R's counts are well above the minimum limits. No matter what, I cannot forget that his haemoglobin still hovers around a tiny 9. We have not touched double digits for almost 2 years. So there is still a long way to go and I cannot afford to let the adrenaline fall. Till now everyday has brought a new challenge keeping me on my toes.

But we all need a little break and I had a hilarious moment when I visited the Punk shop with Utpal, who wanted some strange looking handcuff, and Emily. I could not resist picking up the outrageous wigs and trying one on. Emily was there to capture the moment for posterity:)

There were many wigs in all colour and hues and I remembered the man who had worn a tutu[146] to make his wife laugh during her chemo sessions and to raise awareness for cancer. I should have worn one of these and gone to the chemo day care. I guess it would have cause a riot, or perhaps, this being India, would have got security to throw me out of the premises. We

---

[146] Bob Carey, The Tutu Project; http://thetutuproject.com

lack humour at the best of times, and hospitals are meant to be serious bordering on grim.

On another note however, this is the closest I will ever get to be the long-haired girl of R's dreams. You see he always wanted to marry a Rapunzel!

Monday, 23 December 2013

DON'T ASK!

I met good old Doc P yesterday. I had gone to plan the medical side of the new normal for R. After we had done so, he looked at me and asked me how I was. My almost reactive answer was: don't ask! Doc P knows me almost better than I know myself. He decided to take some time in spite of his overflowing waiting room and talk. Remember it was in this very space that I got confirmation of R's cancer in July. On that fateful day it was in this space that my eyes welled with tears that remain unshed because I willed them to. In the short time when silence spoke more than words, I felt my eyes moisten again and had to draw on all my strength to keep the tears from falling yesterday. I still cannot afford the luxury of a good cry, I know it will break me and as long as R is not out of the woods, tears will have to remain somewhere within me.

Doc P put on his counsellor's cap and spent some time saying the right things: that I had gone through a lot and had done a great job; that he knew I was on edge and that I had to be strong. I told him that I would remain strong and not let R down.

This brief interlude when I let my guard down, albeit for a brief instant made me realise how fragile I had become. It was just a trigger away from breaking down and that trigger could be anything: a word, an gesture, an act, a call, an email or a mere whisper. The only thing I knew was that it would not be about R. That was secure and steady as it was my life's mission. But my reality is larger than R's lymphoma. I have a home and a family and a larger family that all have depended on me for far too long and have not truly got used to my being AWOL.

So I gathered the troops yesterday and shared with them my state of mind and vulnerability and begged them to ensure that no trigger would come my way. My stress levels are high but it is a catch 22 situation as if I allow the adrenaline to drop, then I will not be able to fulfil my mission.

I am sure that those who love me will understand and that my ship will sail on calm waters.

Tuesday, 24 December 2013

I WOULD AGAIN LIKE TO BELIEVE IN SANTA TODAY

There was a time when I believed like many children in Santa Claus. I was recalling some memories yesterday with friends and remembered the one Xmas - must have been in 1961 or so in Rabat - when I was convinced that Santa existed. That was the year I decided to put the existence of Santa to test in my own childish way. That year I refused to write my letter to Santa with my parents who then normally took the missive away, presumably to post it to Santa. That year, in spite of my parents' entreaties, I wrote my letter secretly, put it in an envelope and addressed it to Santa and put it in the post box next to my home. I eagerly waited for Xmas morning and surprise found everything I had asked for. Santa has passed the test with flying colours. You must be wondering how that happened. The answer is that I had used and Embassy of India envelope and some kind person at the post office had redirected my letter to the Embassy where it had found its way to Papa's table!

It would take me a couple of years to realise that Santa did not really exist.

Today I would again like to believe in Santa. My letter to him would read something like this.

Dear Santa,

    This letter is not from a child but from an old woman who desperately needs to believe in someone who would make her wishes come true. Today I ask you not for toys or games. Neither do I want gold, frankincense, or myrrh. What I seek today is for you to give me back my husband's health and rid him forever of the ailment that is ravaging is body. Today I want you to give me a sign that all will be well sooner than later. This is all I need.

    You only fill the stockings of children who have been good for a whole year. I promise I have done everything I possibly could to deserve the gift I seek.

    Please do not forget me!

Anou

Wednesday, 25 December 2013

WE HAVE COME A LONG WAY

In the past months, I have often wondered how long it will take for R to be well again. Seeing him every minute of every day made it impossible for me to assess the progress, and my benchmark were the innumerable tests that he had to undergo an their see saw results.

It is said, and quite rightly so, that one often does not see things around us unless there is a reason. Our room is filled with pictures of the family, but I rarely find myself looking at them, and as I have not been the one who dusts the room for as long as I can remember, the pictures sit there, their presence a comfort though one rarely looks at them closely.

This morning, I happened to look at the pictures behind me and was shocked to find one of R and Agastya taken in July, when R was just diagnosed of Hodgkin's lymphoma. I was horrified to see how terribly ill he looked..

I just could not believe my eyes! Next to this picture, sat another one taken a month or so ago.

What a long way we have come. It was heart-warming to see the difference. This is the first time I actually realised that notwithstanding the counts and results, he was definitely better. And this is the first time I saw a glimmer of light at the end of the long dark tunnel I am in.

Is this Santa's miracle?

Friday, 27 December 2013

ONE MOMENT AT A TIME

Life reveals its story one moment at a time. Never have these words been more relevant than now. We are through with the chemo and now the mission is to strengthen R's depleted immune system. What will still remain for the times to come are regular blood counts. The counts last week were scary and in spite of booster shots the results I have just got are not great. His TLC is still way below the minimum acceptable of 4000. His are 2360. That means that in spite of the shots that normally pump the white cells up dramatically - there was a time when they went from 3000 to 16000 - this time they only went up from 1500 to 2360 a tiny 736! His bone marrow is terribly suppressed. That is not the best news. In fact it is a red flag to remind us that we have a long way to go. So we have to let life reveal its story one moment at a time. Step 1 is to get the immune system kicking again.

Booster shots cannot be given forever. The way to go is nutrition and exercise. I have tried to give R a balanced diet all through his chemotherapy and it seems to have worked as he did not lose weight but now it seems that one will have to fine tune the diet.

I have been scouring the net for more information. The one food that seems to have a bad rating in every article is SUGAR[147]! Now I know it is going to be a very uphill task to get R to eliminate sugar from his diet. Though I am sweetening his smoothies and other 'sweet treats' with

---

[147] http://drsircus.com/medicine/cancer/sugar-cancer-growth-research

alternative options, R still craves for sugar. Chocolates, biscuits, cakes and sweets. How do I convince him that sugar will have to be a no-no for some time at least. We all know that even if his 11 chemos worked fabulously they could have only killed 80% cancer cells. 20% still remain and we absolutely do not want to give them what they love most: SUGAR. But that is what R loves most too: cheesecakes and chocolate brownies. I will have to find a substitute

What is recommended is much of what he has been eating. The only thing I guess I will have to do is increase the protein intake. His diet is mostly vegetarian though I give him eggs and fish occasionally and of course all plant based proteins. But it does not seem to have been enough so will need to add more protein rich foods. Funnily it is said that green peas are rich in protein and that is a win-win situation, as he loves green peas. The other possibilities are quinoa, chia seeds, nuts and nuts butter, beans etc. So new menus will have to be worked out.

The uncharted territory or new normal is undoubtedly going to unfold one moment at a time. It is definitely going to be a mixed bag with good and bad moments, fear and elation. A new roller coaster ride for R and I.

Saturday, 28 December 2013

THE OXYGEN YOU NEED

I finally garnered the courage to write to my astrologer friend who has always been accurate about my future. I had delayed writing to him before as I was apprehensive about what he would say, as he never sugar coats his predictions. But as we usher a New Year I needed to know what awaited us even if it was not what I hoped to hear. This is what he wrote: *Looked at R's chart. He has crossed the danger zone but unfortunately there will be after effects until June '14 since Shani antar (Saturn period) is still on. A negative feeling of being useless will also have to be handled until then. You seem to be cleaning up things and from April 2014 you have a more constructive time with new people and stimulation giving you the oxygen you need. So on the whole it looks like both of you are moving forward after that terrible patch. I do wish you all the best and the strength to reconstruct.*

I read and reread these lines. At times they looked frightening but at others they do seem positive. June 2014 is not so far away' a mere 180 days or so and if we tread carefully then I am sure we can avoid the pitfalls or at least minimise them. I am not so naive as to believe that with chemos over everything will be back to what it was in 2012. His blood counts and the way they are behaving are ample proof that his bone marrow had taken a big blow. But as Doc P said this morning, the body is a miraculous machine and once it realises that there are no more underhand attacks it will spring back to its good old self, however let us not forget the R's miraculous machine is in its seventh decade so the going may be slow. We need to be patient, a virtue I sort of lack.

Now let us come to the feeling of being useless. Well it is just a matter of knowing and pre-empting it. I will have to delve deep into my bag of tricks and conjure new things that will make R feel useful. Why not revive a crazy dream of mine of learning to play the drums and then form a duo as R plays every instrument. I know I am fantasising but what the heck am I not the one who always tells my Project Why kids to dream huge as only if you dream big are you dreams fulfilled. I discovered that you can buy a set of old drums on line for not much. I can just imagine the din in the house but with it the giggling sessions that I am sure will wipe the negative feelings at least for some time. But jokes aside, let me think of new activities for R.

Now let us come to the predictions about yours truly. My friend has hit the nail on the head. The last months have been filled with love and compassion but I must admit that I have been deprived of the oxygen one needs to thrive. True writing had helped me remain sane but I look forward to the day when I will accept that we have reached the point when I can resume life as it was. Maybe the drums will also help oxygenate me.

So the next six months look challenging. Let us get on with life!

Monday, 30 December 2013

WISELY, LIKE GOOD CHILDREN

The doorbell rang. It was a parcel for me. A surprise as I was not expecting anything. Normally the parcels I receive these days are various supplements for R and things like soursop leaves and hemp seeds! As I had not placed any order, this parcel with German stamps was something out of the blue. I was excited and opened it and out came tumbling loads of chocolate bars and boxes of chocolate truffles. And above all they all had the word ORGANIC written on them! They were a Xmas treat from a wonderful and generous person whom I consider my child. She knew how much R and I love chocolate. In the packet was a lovely letter. There was also a note saying that she had read my post on how bad sugar was for R and left it to me to decide what to do. I was tempted to hide the packet from R but then I simply gave in. How could I keep this wonderful gift from R and then they were organic, so I guess that made them kosher.

But that is not all. These chocolates were not simply some bars taken off a shelf and sent off. Each one of them was laced with love and overflowing with good wishes and they could not in any way harm R. They had been lovingly packed one evening and were accompanied by a letter that was filled with all that is beautiful and good. These were not sugar-laden titbits. They were an expression of love and goodwill.

I rushed upstairs with the letter and a packet of truffles, sorry organic chocolate truffles, and stuffed one in R's mouth. The surprise and delight in his eyes was worth the world and more. He looked like a little boy getting his favourite treat. It was a precious moment.

We will eat the chocolates wisely like good children. I think we both deserve this.

Bless you Claudia!

Friday, 3 January 2014

OVER THE MOON

I needed a sign to give me the boost I so need to keep the adrenaline pumping. For the past months life had moved from chemo to chemo in rhythmic and almost lulling movements of 15 days. It was to go on till December 27th, but then chemo 12 was cancelled and suddenly time took on another pattern. We were a bit lost and I was frightened of the future. Let us not forget that the last two blood counts in spite of booster shots were scary to say the least. I felt that I had let my guard down and missed something. I felt almost guilty. I was convinced that all the support brews and pills would have protected the immune system, but seemed like it had not quite happened the way I had hoped. I went into damage control and pumped R with extra protein and other stuff. Then came blood test day and the wait for the results. I was anxious and paced like a lion in a cage.

By 6pm I had bitten my nails to the quick. That is when I got the SMS informing me that the results had been uploaded. I was scared but could not wait and downloaded and printed the results out and WOW there was the sign I was so desperate for. **FOR THE FIRST TIME IN MORE THAN 18 MONTHS R'S HAEMOGLOBIN HAD CROSSED TWO DIGITS: IT WAS 10.21.** There was my sign. Somehow I knew that it would be all uphill from now on. True we were not completely out of the woods but it looked like the immune system was working. His White blood cells were 4200 and platelets 350 000. The adrenaline rush was comforting and welcomed. It was time to take the challenge head on.

ANOURADHA BAKSHI

So tomorrow is PET Scan and I am sure it will be good news. Then we will schedule the removal of the chemo port as having it there is a reminder of cancer and I do not want ANY such reminders. Then we will go full on with the alternative therapies and I hope that June 2014 will bring the miracle I seek.

Tuesday, 7 January 2014

THE PET I HATE

I hate this pet! Let me quickly reassure my animal loving friends that the pet in question is not a fluffy or furry soul but the Positron Emission Tomography better known as PET scan. This is part of what is called nuclear medicine and uses a radioactive tracer that is introduced in the body. No matter what anyone may tell you the fact is that it involves exposure to ionizing radiation. *The total dose of radiation is significant, usually around 5–7 mSv. However, in modern practice, a combined PET/CT scan is almost always performed, and for PET/CT scanning, the radiation exposure may be substantial.* Not very reassuring as again no matter what anyone says radioactive substances do not leave you easily. I remember being told when we were in Prague and the Chernobyl disaster took place that we had all been exposed to the acid rain that fell on the city the next day. Remember this was communist Prague and there had been a complete black out of the news. Those were days before the net and cell phones. I only came to know about it when Mama rung up from Delhi! It was a French Doctor who had come to measure radioactivity levels and told me that one should not forget to mention this fact where we faced with a health issue in times to come. I did mention it to R's oncologist and he sort of acquiesced.

Till date R has had 2 PETs! The first one gave us a better understanding of his cancer, the second which was after 4 cycles showed improvement one being the reduction of the size of the largest node by about half. If you remember the saga there was a time when we were told that 4 cycles, 8 chemos would be sufficient. However though the oncologist said we were 95% through, he insisted on another 2 cycles of 4 more chemos and we caved in. However R's physical and mental state after chemo 11 compelled me to 'negotiate' with the doctor and make him admit that the last one would not make a difference. However he insisted that we have a PET scan immediately. Both my other Docs were apprehensive and thought that we should wait 3 to 6 months to get a real picture. However negotiations are all about give and take and I had to capitulate and accept the PET!

R's low blood counts delayed the procedure by a week and we had the scan last Saturday and the results yesterday. I do not know anything about scan plates etc. but my knowledge of English is tolerable. This is what was written in the conclusion: *as compared to previous scan dated 15-1-14 the scan findings are largely unchanged. No new lesion noted.* Puzzling is it not? When I sent this to the oncologist and asked him if it was good news, he answered: *Yes!*

Donning my common sense hat I feel a little disconcerted. If there has been no apparent change, then it is not wrong to think that chemos 9, 10 and 11 had no real effect on the cancer but increased the toxicity in the body for no real reason and suppressed his bone marrow unnecessarily thus reducing the effectiveness of the body's natural immune defences. I could not but kick myself for not having heard the silent cries of R's body and my gut feeling. Actually it was a catch 22 situation and there is no point of crying over spilt milk. One lesson learnt is that next time, though I hope there will be no next time, one will listen to one's gut feeling.

Yesterday my heart skipped a beat and I almost choked when R candidly asked me whether his cancer had gone. How could I tell him that for the medical fraternity any cancer patient was in remission for 5 long years with a Damocles sword hung on his head? All I could say was that we were done with the modern medicine line of treatment and that I had always told him that in the best case scenario chemo could only deal with 80% of the problem, the remaining 20% was to be taken care by his own immune system. I know modern medicine does not believe in total cure. However there is a cornucopia of treasures that nature has given us that can heal and cure cancer if one is willing to play the game.

Thursday, 9 January 2014

LET US CELEBRATE

Today we need a small celebration. I wish I could write to all those who have stood by me in the past few months and made today dawn. But I cannot, so this post is meant for each one of you without I would have given up long ago.

We are just back from the oncologist and according to him R is in metabolic CR (cancer remission). He now wants a scan in 6 months. Metabolic remission means that the PET is not showing any cancerous activities. *It is just short of saying complete remission because doctors wont actually say that until about 5 years or so of clear PET and/or CT scans.*

So yes, let us rejoice as this is the best news we could get from conventional men in white. Will ponder about other matters when tomorrow dawns.

Tonight R gets a peg and cigar and I give myself a pat on the back!

Thursday, 9 January 2014

REMISSION - THE NEW KID ON THE BLOCK

We live in a world of specialists. I mean medical specialists. The human body is no longer treated as an individual whole, with its idiosyncrasies and quirks and its unique way of perceiving, reacting to and feeling things. This aspect of medicine died with the demise of the good old family GP who knew you better than you knew yourself. He would treat the person, not the disease and would modify and fine tune his treatment in accordance with the person he was healing. In modern medicine you are dissected into infinitesimal pieces and each piece has a specific specialist who will only treat what he is specialised in. Let me elucidate.

Yesterday we went to see R's oncologist with the results of his latest scan. I was very apprehensive as I was terrified that the said specialist would utter something that would alter reality. My prayers went unheard as when R asked if he was 'cancer free', the doctor in question said yes! My heart skipped a beat. Everyone knows that no cancer is cured with a few cycles of chemotherapy! If that were the case there all cancer patients would be cured.

You would be justified in thinking that R, like any educated human being, would be aware of the course cancer takes, with remission and five years protocols. I guess at one level he is. But at another he is just a scared human being who is yearning to hear the words: *you are cured*. Two days ago he asked me the same question: am I cancer free and it took all the skills of a diplomat's daughter to give a well sugar coated answer that would assuage his fears within the spectrum of reality. So you can imagine how angry I was when the doctor answered a convenient YES!

I knew how wrong he was. True R is better and doing the best possible but he is in no way cancer free. My Tibetan doctor did not even want to see the latest scan done shortly after his last chemo as she said it was nothing short of useless. The scan after 6 months will reveal the true picture and that is what we are all working towards.

True there are no more FDG avid cells at the moment but only God can tell us whether they will or will not reappear. The doctor was referring to the present moment in its shortest definition. His next 'diagnosis' would be post the June scan and there is no guarantee in their books that the Yes will remain a Yes! I was also surprised when the oncologist said nothing about the enlarged liver. When I mentioned it he simply said that this was for our family doc to deal with. Specialists, remember specialists.

You simply need to type the words *remission in Hodgkin's lymphoma* on Google search and you will get the answers you seek and nowhere do you find the kind of YES I heard yesterday! In one article[148] I read the following words: *Remission means that your lymphoma has been either eliminated or reduced. When the tumour is completely gone, doctors call it "complete remission." When the tumour has been largely reduced but it still remains, it is called a "partial remission." Even if your disease stands eliminated after treatment is over, it is still not called a cure. Lymphomas have a chance of recurring, and the doctor will often wait for a few years before he is confident that your disease will not return. Only after that can he tell you that you are cured.* The questions are endless[149] and the answers vary. The reality is that one has to remain on guard for all times to come as *in a minority of people with Hodgkin's the disease relapses after treatment; this is most likely to happen within the first two years of remission.* One has to be ready for all eventualities. That is what wisdom suggests.

For conventional medicine, if the disease relapses we get more of the same: chemotherapy, stem cell transplant etc. They have no real cure as their approach does not target the possible causes. But blissfully we are also

---

[148] http://lymphoma.about.com/od/livingwithlymphoma/p/remission.htm

[149] http://www.healthtalk.org/peoples-experiences/cancer/lymphoma/recovery-remission-and-follow

using a host of alternative therapies and nutrition. These aim at making the body strong enough to fight any recurrence. When my Tibetan doctor read through the PET report she was concerned about the enlarged liver and the non avid nodes in the lung. She immediately fine tuned the medication to deal with these issues. But her main concern has been the bone marrow and the immune system as if these kick in then most of the other issues are taken care of.

Keeping all the above in mind, the new kid on the block - remission - is another challenge that will need me to be on my toes. So no question of the adrenaline dropping. The first thing is to gently explain to my darling man the true meaning of the doctor's YES!

Saturday, 11 January 2014

BYE-BYE HOSPITAL

Yesterday, that is January 11, 2014 at 6.45pm we bid farewell to the hospital I hope for a long long time. For over 7 months we had had to visit the hospital for consultations, biopsy, chemo port placing, X-rays, lung function tests, PET scans and 11 chemos! We had to deal with incompetence, incomprehension, pain, attack on all our senses and much more.

Yesterday was the chemo port removal, a surgical procedure done in the OPD. It was long and quite messy but oh darling this being India, I was able to stretch across the bed and hold R's hand through the procedure. It was comforting for the both of us but come to think about it, quite scary if one thinks of infections et al.

The doctor was very gentle and I kept saying silly things to make the mood as light as possible. But it was intense as it took 20 minutes and more than 15 odd stitches. I also decided to ask for the port for keeps. Come to think of it, this is something that I could possess that had actually touched R's heart!

Now the hitch was about how to give me the port as it was actually quite a mess. The Doc had a brilliant idea and it was given to me in a surgical glove. Quite a unique fashion statement is it not!

It was suddenly worth a few laughs and a unique photo op.

Had to share this with all those who have lived this journey with me.

Saturday, 11 January 2014

THIS IS ALL I NEED

Many friends and well wishers are convinced that it is time I took a break! R has been hounding me about where I would like to go when all this is over. From cruises to holidays in exotic lands, the options he offered were endless and yet all the poor man got from me is a litany of noes! It is not that I do not appreciate his concern but quite honestly there is not a place in the world I want to go to. My elder daughter is wanting me to take a break and go to a spa. I have invites from the world over to take a break. But though I am overwhelmed by the generosity and concern of all those who care for me, the answer remains a whispered no! Wise counsel I guess, in normal circumstances and for 'normal' beings. But not quite for me.

When I look back at my adult life, I realise that the occasions I have taken time off alone are close to nil. It is not because of lack of opportunities or resources, it is simply because I feel the best when I am in my home, surrounded by the myriad of things that make me comfortable: my books, my music, the pictures on the wall, my cosy work room and the tiny corner I tuck myself in to write. The list is endless. It took me a lifetime to set the stage the way I liked it.

As an only child I learnt to create an imaginary world replete with imaginary friends where I could take off for any place in the universe simply by picking a book from the shelf and finding a tiny space to devour it in. I could in the flash a moment become a Navajo girl fighting for her tribe, one of the famous Five or Secret Seven, or any heroine of the novels I read. Space and Time were in my control and I liked that. It gave me a strange power that was mine alone. And somehow nothing could compare to my way of traveling. Maybe that is why I dislike any travel that takes me away from my little nook. I have travelled more than my share as my parents dragged me to every possible destination from the time I was a child to when I turned into a moody and rebellious adolescent. By the time papa retired I had had my fill of archaeological sites, ruins, wonders of the world and more.

Then came marriage and domestication. It suited me as the children were a good excuse to not having to go places. The idea of packing was always disturbing. I guess this feeling had its roots in the nomadic life I led as a child when every three years or so I was told that we were moving to a new place. Then came the stern instruction from mama that I was to sort out my toys and books and give most away. That was heart wrenching. Leaving friends that had been so painstakingly nurtured was a nightmare, as one had to deal with the fact that one did not 'look' like others. What awaited was unknown, scary, terrifying as I traced my finger across a globe from Rabat to Saigon, or Saigon to Algiers and then Ankara: a new school, the need to make new friends. Packing was nothing short of daunting. And somehow, even today, the idea of having to pack for a holiday is still terrifying.

So when about 2 decades ago, I could without guilt dig in my roots, I did with alacrity and impunity comparing myself to a banyan tree. I was done with suitcases and overnight bags and for the past 2 decades have not ventured very far away from home. I have my favourite haunts when I need to get out and air the old biddy but they are in a radius of 5 km from home.

But I have evolved my ways of taking off. My early morning daily tryst with my computer when all around me is silent, the book I read in the three wheeler each time I need to venture out, my book on my night table that lulls me to sleep and above all my writing.

How do I tell those I love that this is all I need.

Sunday, 12 January 2014

WON'T DO YOU OR THEM ANY GOOD

Giving all of yourself up to take care of another won't do you or them any good wrote a someone very dear and who loves me very much! So because the words came from such a person, I did not brush them away as I would have, but pondered over them. The first question that came to my mind was whether I really did give all of myself up for others. True this is the impression I may have created over the last months as I became R's cancer buddy, but is this the way I seem to others? Time for a bit of soul searching and time travelling. The question I need to ask myself honestly is when am I at my happiest, at my most productive and at my best, whatever that may mean. The answer is not difficult. It is when I feel useful and wanted. And though I love solitude, that solitude has to come as a counterpoint to a situation where I am not alone. Let us forget all these convoluted explanations. The simple fact is that to feel alive I need to be doing things for others. Devoid of that ability I am no one. Nothing!

I need to give all of myself. I need to take care of others to be me. It is only when I do so that I - to use a coffee ad line - come alive! I have to have my adrenaline pumping to be able to give my best. I thrive on crises situation, need to take decisions. This makes me feel wanted, if you know what I mean. This applies to my personal as well as my work life.

And it is in these moments that I know who I am and why I am.

If I reach out to someone then it is a commitment that has to go all the way. I am prepared for the worst if that is to be as any other option cannot be acceptable. The pain, if any, is part of the deal. I simply take cared of along the way!

Tuesday, 14 January 2014

LET US TAKE IT FROM THE TOP

BoneMarrow-BoneMarrow-BoneMarrow-BoneMarrow is the new mantra I need to chant if I want to see R cured. I was aware of this but maybe did not take it as seriously as I should have. A call from a friend whose dear one lost the battle to Hodgkin's reminded me of this when she told me that they had not quite taken the steps needed to strengthen the bone marrow. And let us not forget that from Day 1 itself my Tibetan Doctor has been repeating that all she is interested in is to ensure that R's bone marrow remains healthy.

I could have kicked the oncologist you know where, when he told R that he was cancer free. Oh how wish doctors used their brains before uttering half-truths! We all knew that chemo had done its bit and how can one forget that people like my two trusted healers told me that a scan taken right after chemo can only be good and did not reveal the true picture. The true picture will emerge after at least 6 months if and only if we take care of the bone marrow.

Before I rush into conjuring another cornucopia of cures, I think it is time I sat back and understood what lymphoma actually is. Quite frankly I never had the chance to understand the disease as things went a little out of my control freak hands when after 13 months of R fading away, a name had finally been put on what ailed him. Then I got caught in a spate of things beyond my control - scans, biopsies, bone marrow aspiration, chemos and more of the same. My task was to ensure minimum side effects to the chemo and keep R's morale up. Long term had to give way to short term. And I ran an obstacle race just keeping a few tiny steps ahead of the dreaded treatment.

We are now off any conventional treatment after the almost incautious and thoughtless remark of the oncologist that could be summed up as: *you are cancer free, see you in six months!* Was I to go by that, then we should life like king size and hope for the best. That is the way with specialists! They are only concerned with their tiny window of specialisation and its protocols. The rest is of no importance. They would enter the dance again if, God forbid, cancer was to reappear and would spew another set of lethal protocols.

I do not work like that. Time I took over again.

So what is lymphoma and why does it destroy the bone marrow. Come to think of it, if I look at R's blood results over the last six months, it looks like the culprit in the bone marrow issue are the (in)famous 4: Adriamycin, Bleomycin, Vinblastine and Dacarbazine a.k.a ABVD. But we are over with that and I have been handed back my man with loads of side effects that need to be addressed and taken care off.

To be able to do that it is important to know what lymphoma is. Dictionary definition: *cancer of the lymph nodes.* So step one is to understand what lymph nodes are. One definition[150] is: *Lymph is clear or white fluid that travels through vessels moves within tissues and work to keep all the parts of the body clean. After passing through the channels of the lymphatic system they drain into the lymph nodes.*

The lymph nodes act as filters along the lymphatic system. These nodes trap germs like bacteria, viruses, toxins as well as cancer cells and ensure that these are removed from the body. The lymph nodes hold the lymphocytes, a type of white blood cell. These act as fighters against foreign invasion by bacteria, viruses, cancer cells or toxins. The lymphocytes also help control the immune response. These lymphocytes originate from stem cells in the bone marrow. And thus *lymphoma is a type of cancer that begins in immune system cells called lymphocytes. Like other cancers, lymphoma occurs when lymphocytes are in a state of uncontrolled cell growth and multiplication.*

There are two primary cancers of the lymph nodes: Hodgkin and Non Hodgkin's lymphoma. R has the former. There are differences between the

---

[150] http://www.news-medical.net/health/What-are-lymph-nodes.aspx

two. Hodgkin's *tends to arise from what is called the Epstein-Barr virus and contain Reed–Sternberg Cells, which are necessary for diagnosis. The malignant cells that form usually remain localized in one lymph node or a surrounding chain.* Is that good or bad news. I do not know. It is said that *Hodgkin's Disease is one of the most curable cancers with a 'cure' rate (5 years or more cancer free) between 60 and 90%.* That is if we go by conventional medicine. This is not acceptable to me. Between 60 and 90% and 5 years are statistics I refuse to go by. I seek total cure till infinity.

I had always felt a small sense of guilt at the length of time it took to diagnose R's cancer. I must confess that having had both my parents taken away from me by this dreaded disease, I did not want R to be diagnosed with the same. But reading an article today has brought me a small measure of comfort as it states quite clearly that *the symptoms of this form of lymphoma are so nearly like those of some other diseases that it is necessary for a physician to arrange for the removal and microscopic examination of one of the enlarged lymph nodes for diagnosis.* And one must not forget that R's lymphoma was hidden in the abdomen and not visible at all. I guess we did our best. An Epstein Barr virus test done in July 2013 was negative, and this virus is one of the main cause of Hodgkin's. Wonder how we could have done it better.

Now let us come to the causes. This seems to be nebulous territory. One article[151] states that *the exact cause of Hodgkin disease is not known. However, scientists have found that the disease is linked with a few conditions, such as infection with the Epstein-Barr virus. Some researchers think that this may lead to DNA changes in B lymphocytes, leading to the development of the Reed–Sternberg cell and Hodgkin disease. Scientists do not yet know what sets off these processes. An abnormal reaction to the Epstein-Barr virus or to other infections may be the trigger in some cases.* In R's case the Epstein-Barr Virus was negative 3 weeks before we got our final diagnosis.

So let us look for other causes. Like all cancers it is a genetic mutation that causes cells to multiply abnormally. A list of possible triggers is given in an article[152] I read but none apply to R: he never had a medical condition that suppressed his immune system, nor was he exposed to the Epstein-Barr

---

[151]   http://www.cancer.org/cancer/hodgkindisease/detailedguide/
        hodgkin-disease-what-causes
[152]   http://www.nhs.uk/Conditions/Hodgkins-lymphoma/Pages/Causes.aspx

virus nor did he have any chemo or radiation therapy as his is a primary and not a secondary lymphoma. I perused article after article and could not find any probable cause. It seems like always that the medical fraternity is clueless about the cause issue. I even found an article[153] that listed causes like: *Fewer siblings, early birth order, single-family homes, and fewer playmates are associated with an increased risk of developing Hodgkin lymphoma -- possibly due to a lack of exposure to bacterial and viral infections at an early age.* I guess living in India gives you sufficient exposure to bacterial and viral infections. If you try and interpret this in another way it may sound like having multiple infections may protect you from cancer. Sounds far fetched to me.

This leads us to something I have always believed in and that is that cancer is an emotional shock. In an interesting article Dr Keith Nemec[154] states that *the two mental /emotional causes of cancer are acute high stress traumatic shocks and chronic long-term negative stress called distress. Traumatic shocks, which are totally unexpected, cause a mind, brain and body reaction that can trigger the formation of cancer. The first mental/emotional cause of cancer is chronic distress or negative stress that causes the hormone cortisol to go out of balance and weaken the immune system. This opens the door to cancer growth.* I need not go any further. This is the reason for R's cancer. I will not say more.

So I now sort of know what lymphoma is and have sort of figured out why it happened to R. In hindsight I could not have done much to prevent it. Now that we have given a shot to conventional therapy and got our first remission, I need to try and figure out what we need to do ensure that it does not come back and mission 1 would be to deal with stress and emotional traumas and mission 2 with his bone marrow and immune system.

Lots on my plate. Let us get on with it!

---

[153]   http://www.webmd.com/cancer/
understanding-hodgkins-disease-basic-information

[154]   Dr. Keith Nemec is a holistic doctor who has been treating patients for the last 30 years.
http://www.naturalnews.com/035503_cancer_causes_mental_emotional.html

Tuesday, 14 January 2014

UNDERSTANDING R'S LYMPHOMA

I have been a little anxious about what awaits us all for the months to come. Six months seems a long time to wait for what we may call the 'real picture': when we actually know whether we have won our battle or not. I met my friendly neighbourhood doctor yesterday who had put my health on hold many many months ago. The adrenaline fix I was under seemed to be keeping my mind-body-soul going if not kicking. Now that the chemo saga was over and that conventional medicine has given its interim verdict: remission, the next six months looked rather empty as all one had to do is wait, a wait quite akin to that of Vladimir and Estragon in Beckett's play Waiting for Godot! So my good old Doc feared a massive adrenaline drop that could lead to other problems and even depression. I guess he is right from his point of view, but that is not quite the way it is.

I am an adrenaline junkie and do not function unless in a state of stress. The few moments in my life when I have been on an adrenaline low have been dark times. I need a mission to survive. A true zealot! Now that we are over with conventional therapies and have to live with the fear of the morrow, I have set my heart to ensure that there is no return of Mr H or any of his acolytes. There was a reason why he landed upon us and the one way to ensure that he does not come back is to remove that reason. Along the way, unfortunately, we will have to repair the damage made by the nasty 4 (ABVD).

I searched for the supposed causes for lymphoma and realised that in our case the cause was emotional and not physical. The only physical damage is the one the disease made before it was unearthed from the dark corner it was hiding in and the damage done by the treatment that seems to be akin to using a bomb to kill a fly. But as long as we can remove the main cause that brought about the problem we are home safe.

I know what the problem is but sadly again it is something that I cannot be of great help in as only R can quieten his demons and find the closure he so desperately needs. I can only try and nudge him as diplomatically and gently as possible. I will certainly give it my very best. However I can create all the most enabling environment and tackle all the physical issues that need to be addressed.

So to begin I need to ferret some more and find out what lymphoma does to one's body. First and foremost it affects the drainage of the lymphatic system and the dysfunction of the lymphocytes affect the body's immune system and defence against infections. In hindsight this has been the case as R's blood counts were in free fall from August 2012. R's lymphoma is located in the abdominal cavity. They are the abdominal retroperitoneal and pelvic lymph nodes and receive drainage from the upper gastrointestinal tract and the abdominal organs. So any blockage or dysfunction would create digestive tract issues, even the ones we would like to avoid, at least when we are not alone. But the big culprit in this case is chemo as let us not forget it is a progeny of mustard gas[155]I am inured and as I am neither a pregnant woman nor a nursing mother I am safe! On the lighter side someone invented a special anti flatulence underwear[156]! Believe it or not it has has a pocket on the rear that has a replaceable activated charcoal packet, which the subject farts through ! But we have not come to that! However the man was a little concerned about the magnitude of this problem. I can reassure him now.

In my quest towards understanding what Hodgkin's disease really is, I came across an interesting article by Dr Otis Brawley[157]. It gives quite a

---

[155] https://mikehamel.wordpress.com/2008/08/28/chemo-farts/

[156] http://www.mensfitness.com/training/lowdown-flatulence

[157] Dr Otis Brawley, Chief Medical Officer, American Cancer Society; http://edition.cnn.com/2011/HEALTH/expert.q.a/11/08/hodgkins.disease.brawley/

balanced description of the ailment and ends with these words of caution: *Patients with HL do have some immune suppression because of the disease and have a higher risk of getting certain infections. Patients who are successfully treated for HL continue to have this immune suppression and long term have a higher risk of leukaemia and some other cancers because of their therapy.* So there is no way to keep the guards down.

It is all about the immune system, is it not!

LET US BOOST THE IMMUNE SYSTEM - STEP 1 STRESS

The first step in my new mission that aims at ensuring that Mr H does not come visiting again is to take all steps possible to boost R's immune system. Let us first acknowledge with respect that our body is nothing short of miraculous and that our immune system is an amazing internal healing system that was designed to keep us healthy and strong from a physical, mental and spiritual perspective. As I wrote in an earlier post the most probable cause for R's lymphoma has been negative stress, also known as chronic stress. This is not the healthy stress that keeps us on our toes and gets our adrenaline pumping for the right reasons and is often more like a situation reaction process and thus short lived. The stress that leads to severe illness is the one that puts us in a fight or flight mode over an extended period of time. It is one, which often affects our deepest emotions and nurtures to negative thoughts that become the main cause of physiological stress at the cellular level and lead to our immune system weakening and eventually breaking down. Thus one has to deal with these problems at a deep level and often one cannot do it alone. Actually it is our belief that we are able to address such issues by ourselves which leads to breakdowns. I must admit that this is R's case. For far too long he tried to deal with deep emotional issues on his own and we are witness to the consequences. We are blessed to have come out of the initial problem but if we do not address the root cause, we will land ourselves in trouble sooner than we realise.

It is proven fact[158] that stress affects the immune system. *When we're stressed, the immune system's ability to fight off antigens is reduced. That is why we are more susceptible to infections. The stress hormone corticosteroid can suppress the effectiveness of the immune system (e.g. lowers the number of lymphocytes).* When the stress is chronic as is the case with R then the consequences can be terrible.

A scholarly article[159] in the Lancet Oncology, entitled Stress, depression, the immune system, and cancer studies this in depth: *Here, we overview the evidence that various cellular and molecular immunological factors are compromised in chronic stress and depression and discuss the clinical implications of these factors in the initiation and progression of cancer.* It goes to say that *Cancer is a heterogeneous group of diseases with multiple causes, and immunological involvement varies across different cancers. Cancers induced by chemical carcinogens might be less affected by psychological, behavioural, and immunological factors than are those associated with a DNA tumour virus, retrovirus insertion near a cellular oncogene, or other viruses such as Epstein Barr virus, which is immunogenic. Suppression of cellular immunity is associated with a higher incidence of some types of tumours, particularly Epstein Barr virus-associated lympho proliferative diseases in organ-transplanted patients, and Kaposi's sarcoma and Epstein Barr virus-associated B-cell lymphoma.*

So here we have it, the pattern that R's case followed: the unsolvable stress leading to depression that led to suppression of the immune system and then the B cell lymphoma! I have been crying this till I went hoarse but few believed me. But now I feel strong enough to assert my ideas, however idiosyncratic they may seem to doubting Cassandras'.

Hence if we want R to heal and be cured we need to address first and foremost the cause of his chronic stress which sadly is still very much there. I will not reveal the details as they are too personal but have to work out a

---

[158] Saul McLeod; Stress, Illness and the Immune System 2010; http://www.simplypsychology.org/stress-immune.html

[159] Stress, depression, the immune system, and cancer Edna Maria Vissoci Reich Sandra OdebrechVargas Nunes, Helena Kaminami Morimoto, Lancet Oncology Volume 5, No 10 pages 617-625

coping mechanism that will remove the toxic stress. In this case, it may just have to be a one way street.

The usual remedies suggested for dealing with stress are yoga, meditation, acupressure, music, biofeedback, relaxation and even just standing still. The net is replete with articles on the subject. One needs to find coping mechanisms and make mild life style changes.

In R's case I think he should begin each day with Reinhold Niebuhr's Serenity Prayer:

God grant me the serenity
to accept the things I cannot change;
courage to change the things I can;
and wisdom to know the difference

Thursday, 16 January 2014

BOOSTING THE IMMUNE SYSTEM -STEP 2 SUGAR

The battle to boost R's immune system is on! In my last post I talked about chronic stress and how it was the main cause of R's cancer. Today I take on sugar, a tricky one when the man loves sugar in all its avatars not to forget the Scottish one. I have been badgering about how sugar feeds cancer but though he makes all the appropriate sounds and gestures, I do not think the gravity of the situations registers in his brain. The proof: his perennial question after every meal *and what's for dessert*!

Convincing him that sugar has to be given up is going to be my biggest challenge. I need to arm myself with as much knowledge as I can and hope that my constant nagging will bear fruit. In this case I do not mind being called the nagging wife! So let us begin.

Eating or drinking too much sugar curbs immune system cells that attack bacteria. As if that was not enough CANCER CELLS FEED ON SUGAR!

There are innumerable articles that prove this fact. Nobel Prize winner Otto Warburg made many startling discoveries[160] about cancer. According to him cancer metabolises through a process of fermentation and fermentation requires sugar. Voila!

---

160 http://www.mnwelldir.org/docs/nutrition/sugar.htm

It is interesting to note that the way laetrile[161] or the component found in apricot kernels acts is because cancer loves sugar. *Here is how it works: cancer loves sugar. The sugar in the apricot pits surrounds a phytochemical called: nitriloside. The cancer draws in the sugar, eats it, and releases the nitriloside. Now cancer cells contain great quantities of beta-glucosidase, an enzyme. When beta-glucosidase meets with nitriloside, they create hydrogen cyanide and benzaldehyde. Both are poisons. Since they've been released at the cancer site, they kill the cancer.* Interesting!

And there is more a new MRI study shows that cancer thrives on sugar. *After sensitising an MRI scanner to look specifically for glucose in the body, it was revealed that cancer tumours, which feed off sugar, light up brightly as they contain high amounts of sugar.* Maybe in the future MRI would not have to use radioactive materials but inject sugar.

There is no doubt, cancer feeds on sugar. It is now considered as toxic as alcohol and tobacco. It is believed that *sugar and cancer are locked in a death grip, yet oncologists often fail to do what's necessary to stop their patients from feeding their cancers with sweets. In research published June 26, 2012 in the journal Molecular Systems Biology, Graeber and his colleagues demonstrate that glucose starvation—that is, depriving cancer cells of glucose—activates a metabolic and signalling amplification loop that leads to cancer cell death as a result of the toxic accumulation of reactive oxygen species.*

I think I have sufficient data to prove my point. Now I need to make it palatable and acceptable to someone who loves sugar and yearns for it. It is not mean task. Wish me luck.

---

[161] http://www.mnwelldir.org/docs/cancer1/altthrpy2.htm#Laetrile

Friday, 17 January 2014

AFTER STRESS AND SUGAR
HERE COMES THE SUN

Vitamin D3 is essential to our immune system. The best source is the sun! However we seem to shun the sun, or affront it after sloshing all kind of sunscreens. Vitamin D deficiency is much more common than we imagine. You will be surprised to know that *Vitamin D3 is a repair and maintenance steroid responsible for the regulation of over 3,000 genes. It is also a potent antibiotic that is intimately involved with a vast amount of disorders and diseases. This makes it a vital component of a healthy immune system and is best obtained from the sun, with supplementation being an alternative option[162].*

There are many articles to substantiate this. In a major breakthrough discovered, that *Vitamin D is crucial to activating our immune defences and that without sufficient intake of the vitamin, the killer cells of the immune system -- T cells -- will not be able to react to and fight off serious infections in the body. For T cells to detect and kill foreign pathogens such as clumps of bacteria or viruses, the cells must first be 'triggered' into action and 'transform' from inactive and harmless immune cells into killer cells that are primed to seek out and destroy all traces of a foreign pathogen. The researchers found that the T cells rely on vitamin*

---

[162] 10 Ways to boost your immune system; Kara Bauer; 2013; http://www.healthcentral.com/diet exercise/c/299905/158484/ten-immune/

THERE IS ONLY ROOM FOR HOPE

D in order to activate and they would remain dormant, 'naïve' to the possibility of threat if vitamin D is lacking in the blood.

So a very simple and inexpensive way of recharging your body's defence system is sitting in the sun. This applies for everyone, not only cancer survivors! So do spend sometime in the sun without SUNSCREEN! You can get up to 90% of your requirements from exposure to sunlight.

As I said there are innumerable articles on how Vitamin D influences our immune system. Some studies *explore the health impact of suboptimal circulating levels of vitamin D, with association studies linking vitamin D 'insufficiency' to several chronic health problems including autoimmune and cardiovascular disease, hypertension and common cancers.*[163]

Vitamin D plays a key role in boosting the immune system. So the question arises about how to boost your immune system with vitamin D. Well sunshine of course and we in India are lucky to have plenty of it. One should try and get 20 to 30 minutes of exposure per day. You can also take a supplement or still better eat foods rich in vitamin D. The best sources are: cod liver oil, salmon, eggs, mushrooms and shrimps in moderation.

R does like sitting in the sun in winter. I guess once he resumes golf than he will have plenty of sunlight. Will have to figure how to manage the 30 minutes in the hot summer.

---

[163] Martin Hewison; An update on Vitamin D and human immunity; Clin Endocrinol. 2012;76(3):315-325.
http://www.medscape.com/viewarticle/758650

Friday, 17 January 2014

WHAT'S NEXT ON THE MENU

After stress, sugar and sunshine what's next on the immune boosting menu[164]? Just that a menu! Or should I say nutrition. The diet recommended to boost immunity is an alkaline diet. A diet rich in plant foods that includes lots of vegetables, greens, fruits, raw seeds and nuts, fermented foods, beans and whole grains is essential to a healthy way of life. Ideally, you'll also want to eat a high percentage of raw foods, 50-75%.

R's diet includes almost all the foods mentioned in the chart above barring those not easily available in India. It also includes lots of raw seed and nuts and whole grains. The problem I envisage is to try and get him to eat more raw foods. I began an alternate day raw food diet on the advise of a friend who had terrific results and had gone all raw food and I must say I felt great on the days I ate only raw food and seeds. I stopped a while back when it became very cold and the sight of a salad at lunch and a gazpacho at dinner was quite unbearable, but will resume as soon as it gets a tad warmer. I will also have to convince R to try it out at least twice a week or so or have one raw meal a day. I am sure it will be possible. Raw foods provide live phytonutrients, enzymes, vitamins and minerals that are eliminated substantially when foods are cooked. They nourish and enhance the growth of healthy cells and keep your entire body working at optimal levels.

---

[164] http://www.healthcentral.com/diet-exercise/c/299905/158484/ten-immune

As far as fats are concerned only good fats are recommended: avocado, olive oil, coconut oil, nuts and seeds. Here we are spot on! Just have to convince R of staying on this diet. Not easy as he dreams of raclette and achar meat!

While we are talking nutrition I think we should also talk of the importance of antioxidants as they play a big role in boosting the immune system and many are found in foods. *Antioxidants include Vitamin C, Vitamin E, beta-carotene, bioflavonoids, selenium, lipoic acid, and many others. They are essential for fighting or neutralising free radicals caused by oxidation, which occurs as a result of environmental and dietary toxins. Free radicals are incomplete electrons that are looking to steel electrons from other molecules, thus creating a chain reaction (molecules steeling from molecules) and ultimately damaging cells and DNA.*

Some of the best foods include green leafy vegetables, other vegetables (such as peppers, broccoli, eggplant, cabbage and carrots), berries (including goji berries), nuts and beans. Here too we are spot on barring eggplant a vegetable R dislikes, but accepts in the form of baba ghanoush.

Sunday, 19 January 2014
THE WAY THE COOKIE CRUMBLES

Apologies for this post being about yours truly but I guess some of you out there do care about how I am doing and I must admit, albeit sheepishly, that I am in need of some TLC. For quite some time now I have been wondering if, when and how my adrenaline crash would happen. I had thought that it would be emotional and mental. Seems I was wrong. My mind is still travelling at the speed of light and rearing to give that one way ticket to the moon to Mr Hodgkin. There is no doubt on that. My battle to get R's immune system back on the track is spot on. No change there. But it is my darned body that has decided not to cooperate. First there was stress colic that was so bad that it needed an injection to calm down. Now my back has decided to play up. Excruciating pain that again needed a shot yesterday but is back this morning with a vengeance!

Those who know me, are aware of the fact that I can stand any attack at the emotional level but am a wimp when it comes to physical pain. Moreover courtesy my back I am unable to sit for long hence cannot indulge in my favourite stress buster: writing! But that is not all. With this back issue it is has been bye-bye to my fix of happy hormones as no treadmill! Grrrr! This is infuriating. The back, according to good old Doc P is not a backbone issue, but a muscular one. As painkillers and anti-inflammatory pills have not worked I guess it will have to be physiotherapy. What a pother! It is time consuming and irritating. Anyway has to be done.

Sunday, 19 January 2014

ALL THE NUMBERS

Children speak in the voice of God and a often carry God's messages to you. That is what I firmly believe. Sometimes when you are going through a bad patch and when all seems dark, an innocuous remark by a child brings that much needed ray of light. My grandson who will be 5 tomorrow always manages to save me from myself. A few days back he came on Skype and decided to teach his Nanou and Nani a new game. It goes like this: I love you 75 says he to which you reply I love you 135 and the games go with numbers high and low till he says: I love you all the numbers! Of course only he is allowed to say the punch line as he has to win. We laughed our hearts out and have been playing the game ever since. But the message I got was that as long as that little Angel loves me all the numbers we are safe! And I child love you all the numbers and all the letters in all the alphabets of the world.

Sunday, 19 January 2014

I AM FALLING APART

R's last results came in. His haemoglobin is now 11 and all the other results are good. You cannot imagine how happy I am. It has been a long battle as for over a year R's haemoglobin had not touched 2 digits. At one point it dipped to 7 and we had to transfuse him! So you can imagine my elation when I saw the number 11! And that too without any booster shot. I can never forget the day when he came to me after taking is weight that had dropped to 68 kilos and told me: I am falling apart. My heart skipped many beats as I swore to myself that I will do everything I can and more to put my *Humpty Dumpy back together again*!

It has been along battle with many ups and downs. But today I know he is back together again and will remain so! True we are not out of the woods and cannot let down our guards but somehow I know that we will reach the end of the tunnel sooner than later.

Monday, 20 January 2014

SUNSHINE TO SUPPLEMENTS

One needs more than a healthy diet to boost an immune system that has been practically annihilated by aggressive chemotherapy. I am talking of supplements in its broadest sense: vitamins, minerals, herbs and what is know as superfoods. From the instant I knew that R had cancer, I began my hunt for such supplements across the board. There are many options that you get whilst surfing the net. Some of those one commonly comes across are: reishi, shitake and maitake mushroom, cacao, bee pollen, maca, spirulina, goji berries, coconut oil, garlic, echinacea, ginseng, turmeric, gingko biloba, cat's claw, elderberry and astragalus. Some are already on R's menu.

In addition to these I have also included some less conventional options that seem to be working well. Some strengthen the immune system, others target remaining cancer cells. I have talked about them in previous blogs but will run through them again giving links that confirm their benefits. Let us keep in mind that my search has always been for cancer preventive options and immunity boosters.

Soursop or graviola tea was one of the first supplements I added to R's diet plan. Soursop tea[165] helps in preventing and fighting cancer. It is also known to strengthen the immune system. Three cups of soursop tea are sufficient. Soursop has many benefits and is now available in India. I have

---

[165]   https://sites.google.com/site/cancercuredeasilywithsopursop/services

ANOURADHA BAKSHI

been giving R soursop leaves and bark tea for over 8 months now and have been taking a glass myself. I have not seen any adverse side effects, quite the contrary as R had very few side effects during his chemotherapy and I believe that soursop tea did have its role to play. It is for you to decide whether you want to give it a try. R and I are living and kicking after 8 months of soursop.

Apricot seeds are the other supplement that has been part of R's diet for the past 8 months. Whereas he has about 15 seeds a day I have 6. They are meant to kill cancer cells without touching healthy cells. Apricot seeds are also called B17 or Laetrile. This is the recommended dosage: *The usual recommendation for prevention is around 5 to 7 over the course of a day. For actual cancer cases use 2 to 3 times that. Some say one kernel for every 10 lbs. of body weight. For maintenance after a cure, go back to 5 to 7 per day.* Again I believe one should give it to try.

Mushrooms are big component of my treatment approach. I have been able to find fresh shitake mushrooms but reishi and maitake not being available fresh, I have added a mushroom supplement to his diet. It is known that these mushrooms can fight cancer[166] Ganoderma or Reishi has many benefits: *It enhances and helps regulate the immune and endocrine system, prevent tumours, improving the circulation and eliminating harmful free radicals.* It is available on line in India.

Cannabis is somehow a strange option to add on my list. It was suggested my a very dear friend. The benefits of cannabis leaves[167] for curing cancer are now a known fact. To those who associate cannabis to psychotropic drugs, let it be known that raw cannabis is *actually loaded with a non-psychoactive, antioxidant, anti-inflammatory, and anti-cancer nutrient compound known as cannabidiol (CBD) that is proving to be a miracle "superfood" capable of preventing and reversing a host of chronic illnesses.* I have not gone into cannabis juicing as yet as I lack resources, but on the advise of my friend, R and I have 6 to 7 cannabis leaves crushed with some sugar and some cardamom seeds. I will try and grow more on my terrace!

---

166   http://www.naturalnews.com/027308_mushrooms_cancer_medicinal.html

167   http://www.trueactivist.com/there-is-no-mistaking-the-evidence-cannabis-cures-cancer/

Hemp seeds and oil are also supper foods. They are available in India on line. And what's more is that they can be turned into great recipes. Hemp seed and oil pesto is out of this world. In India they have been used to make chutneys for ages. Hemp seed oil is reputed to be the most unsaturated oil derived from the plant kingdom. *Hemp seed oil has been dubbed "Nature's most perfectly balanced oil", due to the fact that it contains the perfectly balanced 3:1 ratio of Omega 6 (linolei/LA) to Omega 3 (alpha–linolenic/LNA) essential fatty acids, determined to be the optimum requirement for long-term healthy human nutrition. Hemp oil cures cancer as the essential and non-essential amino acids are present in abundance in the oil and thus when hemp oil is regularly used by cancer patients, there are chances of cure.* Hemp seeds are gift from nature. They are a complete protein. *This is one of the most potent foods available, supporting optimal health and well being, for life. Raw hemp provides a broad spectrum of health benefits, including: weight loss, increased and sustained energy, rapid recovery from disease or injury, lowered cholesterol and blood pressure, reduced inflammation, improvement in circulation and immune system as well as natural blood sugar control[168].* Need I say more.

It is my search for vegan proteins that brought hemp seeds my way. I also brought quinoa and chia seeds. They are now available in India but slightly expensive. Quinoa[169] has a very high protein content and many other nutrients. Chia seeds are also a real superfood. They are packed in protein and have many more nutrients. Both these are excellent to boost the immune system.

These are some of the supplements I have been using. They seem to have worked!

---

[168] http://hemphealthytoday.blogspot.in/2011/11/hemp-food-nutrition.html

[169] http://www.mindbodygreen.com/0-4994/7-Benefits-of-Quinoa-The-Supergrain-of-the-Future.html

Monday, 20 January 2014

HAPPY BIRTHDAY AGASTYA

On January 21 2009 a little Angel landed in my life. From that day one I acquired a new cap: I became Nani[170]. My life changed forever as no matter where the little wanderer was, he always remained in a very special corner of my heart. You see God makes a space in your heart and leaves it empty till you become a Nani. The magic of this tiny space that lies vacant for decades, fills up on the blessed day you become a granny and then seems to take all the space in your heart.

My darling Agastya turns 5 today. He is a big boy or so he says. My love for him grows by the second and much to the horror of his parents, he has me around his little finger and just has to look at me with his huge melting eyes and Nani runs to the toy shop and buys all the remote cars, even the screeching ones knowing I will be greeted with angry stares.

My little chap has enabled me to live through these very difficult days as whenever I get a little sad or scared I just have to look at the umpteen pictures of him around me and a huge smile breaks on my face.

I wish him a life full of happiness and laughter and hope that when he grows up he remembers that his Nani loved him unconditionally.

Happy Birthday Agastya Noor Francesco Trani

---

[170]   maternal grandmother

Tuesday, 21 January 2014

SO LET US TALK HAPPINESS

Today I am taking some time off from the immunity, cancer beating and waiting for June scene. Today I want to talk of happiness. This is because I stumbled upon an article[171] that claims to give you 10 simple things that will make you happier, and they also claim that these things are backed by science. The reason for this aside is due to the fact that someone I love dearly and who is an image of myself albeit 2 decades younger is going through a difficult time, as just like me he cannot reconcile the person he is to the way the world turns. I have had my share of this existential crisis and have only learnt to deal with it when I was faced with my biggest challenge: R's cancer.

So let us talk happiness as it is only by being happy within the world we live in that can make us productive and grounded. I am going to quote from the article whilst I give it my twist. It will be more like 10 simple things you can do to make you happier when you are an adrenaline pushed, perfectionist and honest to a fault kind of being.

Exercise more is the first suggestion. It is suggested that 7 minutes could be sufficient. I agree totally as the last 7 days have been exercise free for me because of a back condition and I never realised how happier I felt after trudging on the treadmill for 40 minutes at 6km an hour. The happy hormones released were sufficient for the day. The article states: *Exercise*

---

171   https://blog.bufferapp.com/10-scientifically-proven-ways-to-make-yourself-happier

has such a *profound effect on our happiness and well-being that it's actually been proven to be an effective strategy for overcoming depression* and I second that wholly. Exercise *can help you to relax and, increase your brain power.* The article gives scientific proof of that. I would just like to add from my personal experience that you have to sort of switch off from the world and my way of doing that is by listening to a medley of songs I liked from age 10 onwards played randomly and which take me on an incredible time travel spin bringing smiles of my face as I sing along. In the span of 40 minutes I veer from becoming a child, to a teenager, to a woman and back to being a child. It is exhilarating. Try it. I guess the added time travel bit with music blaring so loud in my years that it shuts present is a plus point.

Sleep more. That has never been a problem with R. I am the one who sleeps erratically and all tensed up. Once upon seeing my toes all stretched R thought I was pretending to sleep but when he tried to wake me up, he realised I was sound asleep, though my sleep is so light that any movement or noise has me jumping up. Sleep it is said in the article, is *important to our happiness.* It goes on to say that *negative stimuli get processed by the amygdala; positive or neutral memories gets processed by the hippocampus. Sleep deprivation hits the hippocampus harder than the amygdala. The result is that sleep-deprived people fail to recall pleasant memories, yet recall gloomy memories just fine.* Now to the question how much we should sleep. Eight ours is a myth. An article[172] on the subject states that *"people who sleep between 6.5 hr. and 7.5 hr. a night, live the longest, are happier and most productive"* What's even more interesting here is that sleeping longer than that might actually be worse for your health mentioning that: *"Sleeping 8.5 hr. might really be a little worse than sleeping 5 hr."*

A little aside for the sleep deprived person. *Whether we are sleep deprived or not, we lose focus at times. And that is precisely where the sleep deprived person lands in a trap. The person bragging that they only slept 4 hours and still do great work, well, they are actually right with what they are saying. The only issue is that, they have no brainpower to steer them back to focus once they lose attention. Even worse so, sleep-deprived people don't notice their decrease in performance.*

---

[172] https://blog.bufferapp.com/how-much-sleep-do-we-really-need-to-work-productively

Napping is an excellent habit. 20 minutes is all you need. And if you have a sleep problem, develop a sleep ritual. First you need an activity that disengages you from the every day work: it could be a late evening walk, playing with your kid though the kid often sleeps before you, listening to your favourite music with earphones, reading fiction or poetry; what is most important is to go to bed straight after this ritual. And have a clear ritual for you wake up time too. No matter what time I sleep, I get up at the same time and after a wash say my prayers, come down to my office and after lighting a lamp in the outside alter I sit at my computer and put on my mantra tape and spend time with myself.

The next simple thing to do to gain happiness is according to the same article: is move closer to your work as a short commute is better than a big house. This does not apply to those I know but the logic given is the following: *Our commute to the office can have a surprisingly powerful impact on our happiness. The fact that we tend to do this twice a day, five days a week, makes it unsurprising that its effect would build up over time and make us less and less happy.* I leave to you to decide upon this one.

Another ingredient in the happiness recipe is to spend time with friends and family – don't regret it on your deathbed. There is a lot of good sense in this. I have come to realise this after R's illness.

Next comes the one I can swear by. Help others – 100 hours a year is the magical number. My life changed in 2000 when I met Manu and decided to do something for him. Since I have never felt happier. The trick is to dirty your hands and not just write a cheque. It makes you happier to help others and can change your life for the better in more ways than you can imagine.

Smile is the next thing on the agenda! Smiling is a science[173]. *Smiling stimulates our brain's reward mechanisms in a way that even chocolate, a well-regarded pleasure-inducer, cannot match. Smiling can change our brain, through the powerful feedback loop we discussed above. And your brain keeps track of your smiles, kind of like a smile scorecard. It knows how often you've smiled and which overall emotional state you are in therefore.* So create your smile bank and make huge deposits in it. Smile whenever you can, even on the street to an unknown person and see the magic.

---

[173] https://blog.bufferapp.com/the-science-of-smiling-a-guide-to-humans-most-powerful-gesture

The next suggestion is a strange one but one that I can again vouch for as I am the greatest armchair traveller in the Universe. Plan a trip – but don't take one! Have you never experienced the fact that planning for something that brings happiness is the best part of the exercise. *As opposed to actually taking a holiday, it seems that planning a vacation or just a break from work can improve our happiness. The highest spike in happiness comes during the planning stage of a vacation as employees enjoyed the sense of anticipation. One study found that people who just thought about watching their favourite movie actually raised their endorphin levels by 27 per cent!* So plan an event and whenever you need a boost in happiness think about it. No wonder I the eternal planner am so happy!

Now comes the tricky one: Meditate. I have tried forever and find myself planning things whilst supposedly meditating. *Meditation literally clears your mind and calms you down, it's been often proven to be the single most effective way to live a happier life.* Must give it yet another go. Meditation does wonders to you: it reduces anxiety, helps you to focus better, makes you more creative, more compassionate and so on. Must make R do it and try it myself too, It may prevent the meltdown lurking round the corner.

And last of all, practice gratitude. I have made my motto: busy being grateful and it has helped. I am grateful for everything the good or the bad. My father was a real bhakti yogi. His prayer went something like that: I am grateful for all You have given me, the good and the bad. I know that you will steer me out of all the challenges that you have sent my way. I will simply continue being grateful and praising you. Now it is for you to keep the faith of one who has surrendered everything to you. And it worked. I have been a witness to that. The article puts like this : *There are lots of ways to practice gratitude, from keeping a journal of things you're grateful for, sharing three good things that happen each day with a friend or your partner, and going out of your way to show gratitude when others help you.*

The article ends with this statement: Getting older will make yourself happier. I am getting there!

Tuesday, 21 January 2014

NOW ITS TIME TO MOVE

Let us take one more step on our immunity building journey. And here the word step is appropriate as one of the good immune boosters is undoubtedly exercise! Moderate exercise is good for the immune system. It stimulates the immune system by increasing oxygen flow and blood circulation throughout the body. It also slows the release of stress hormones, flushes out bacteria from the lungs, eliminates cancer-causing cells through urine and sweat, and circulates white blood cells at a faster rate. Wow!

But it is important not to overdo it. So what are best forms of exercise one should adopt?

For someone with lymphoma, rebounding or jumping on a trampoline is priceless. Rebounding [174]kick starts the lymphatic system. *Lymph vessels are like blood vessels except they are full of clear lymphatic fluid that carries white blood cells (B cell and T cell lymphocytes) throughout your body so they can attack invaders and infected cells. We have about three times more lymphatic fluid than blood, but here's the catch, there's no pump!* So the more we move the body the better we are. Jumping on a trampoline *creates an increased G-force resistance (gravitational load) and positively stresses every cell in your body. As a result, it strengthens your entire musculoskeletal system: your bones, muscles, connective tissue, and even organs. And it promotes lymphatic circulation by stimulating the millions of one-way valves in your lymphatic system.* One should rebound at

---

[174] http://www.chrisbeatcancer.com/rebounding/

ANOURADHA BAKSHI

least 2 to 3 times a day for 5 to 10 minutes and see the wonders that will follow.

Walking every day for 20 to 30 minutes is a great way of improving your immunity. Regular Golf is also a great immunity booster as you also get your sunbath! But no stopping at the 19th hole. I hope R can resume his week end golf soon. I also hope it warms up soon as R's excuse for not getting on the treadmill is that it is too cold.

The toughie is yoga. In spite of having a wonderful yoga teacher who comes every week day, R's excuses are now getting ludicrous. He does not realise how much yoga can help him particularly in boosting the immune system and strengthening his heart and lung capacity that have both been affected by chemotherapy. *Yoga detoxifies and oxygenates your system, balances the hormones you need for a strong immune system, reduces stress and fatigue, two precursors to lowered immunity and triggers acupressure points said to help evict viruses and bacteria from your body.* There are many poses that help and Sanjeev the yoga teacher is the best person to guide him through this. Some of the recommended poses are: bow pose, shoulder stand, down dog, full cobra etc.

However pranayama or yogic breathing is a wonder cure for boosting immunity. I must now try all the tricks in my bag to get R on course.

Wednesday, 22 January 2014

FLY R FLY

Some of you, of my vintage at least, would remember the Silver Convention and their hit song Fly Robin Fly[175] up up to the sky! I remembered this tune when I sent R off this morning to Kolkata where he has a business meeting. He will be back tomorrow late night. This is a big step after the almost decadent life we have been compelled to live courtesy Sir Hodgkin, but also because it was appealing with the cold winds blowing and the delicious comfort of our electric blankets purchased this year and that turned the bed into a real cocoon. At first it was a bit awkward and one felt sort of guilty lying in bed, I mean me as R was truly unwell, but with time it became a habit. 66 days is all it takes for something to become a habit! This bed became virtually home.

The Robin had to fly, I mean R! So this morning at 5am he left the house and I just received a call that he has landed safely. I am so relieved. The last 2 days were tense as I was planning to figure out how I would pack his medicines and supplements and more than that what he would eat. I spend hours briefing him, kudos to him for not having given me a whack.

I guess the control freak has to give in a little as R has to live a normal life, but I am still scared. The last results were better but two tumour markers were still somewhat above the acceptable minimum. I will have to

---

[175] Fly, Robin Fly; Silver Convention; 1975 Album: Save me

find some coping strategy that allows me to keep a hawk like eye without R feeling watched.

But I am thrilled he has gone for a night to attend to his business. I am sure he will be back empowered and energised.

Friday, 24 January 2014

THE NO NOES

In the last few blogs I have spoken at length about the things to do to boost the immune system from rebounding to supplements to sunshine and nutrition. Today I will address the no-noes and these are Alcohol, Smoking and Drugs. Drugs are no issue with R and has never been. But the other two are big problems.

When we got married I was the 'boozer'. R only drank shandies with more club lemonade than beer. But things changed over the years and now his idea of a good life is 2 large whiskies, preferably Single Malt, a day. But it is said that *alcohol consumption not only blocks nutrient absorption, but also reduces white blood cells in the bloodstream impacting the amount of oxygen that flows throughout the body. [2] It also impairs the function of lymphocytes, which produce antibodies to fight off invaders, making you more vulnerable to viruses and bacteria*[176]. Oops that is not great news. Doctor P suggested he drinks on special occasions, the Tibetan doctor felt he could have one small drink a week. Now Doctor Anou has still to decide and that is what I am trying to do. After chemo the *liver will be working overtime to clear the chemo toxins* so it is no point loading it with extra toxins. Alcohol can interfere with

---

[176] Kara Bauer; Ten Ways to Boots your Immune system; 2013; http://www. healthcentral.com/diet-exercise/c/299905/158485/ten-immune/

the liver's ability to do its job and the patient can suffer. *Alcohol[177] does affect the immune system as it produces an overall nutritional deficiency, depriving the body of valuable immune- boosting nutrients. Alcohol, like sugar, consumed in excess can reduce the ability of white cells to kill germs. High doses of alcohol suppress the ability of the white blood cells to multiply, inhibit the action of killer white cells on cancer cells, and lessen the ability of macrophages to produce tumour necrosis factors.* So even if you do not have a declared cancer, we still have some cancer cells that the immune system takes care off. Alcohol comes in the way!

Most articles on the subject consider moderate drinking safe in healthy people. However Doc Anou truly feels that as things stand now, it would be irresponsible to get back to the daily sundowners. We all know that no matter how well all therapies have worked better than expected there is some chance alcohol would make any residual cancer grow again and spread. That to my mind this is sufficient to accept the occasional drink option.

Let us look at smoking now. In R's case it is the cigar. Smoking also makes it more difficult to destroy viruses, bacteria and cancer cells by effecting the antibodies. The chemicals introduced by smoking leads to oxygen depletion, lung damage, susceptibility to illness, and impaired heart rate function and blood pressure. Smoking cessation lowers the risk of cancer recurring or of new cancers developing. Now we know that R was given Bleomycin, which is known to affect the lungs. I found this comment [178]interesting: *If you are receiving Bleomycin as part of the treatment of lymphoma, smoking is especially dangerous. Bleomycin by itself has the potential to cause lung damage, and this can be worsened by smoking. Ultimately, this may impact how well you are able to carry out regular exercise or activities and could lead to lung cancer.* So here again I would say the occasional cigar. Though there are studies[179] that highlight the bad effects of cigar smoking and even say that smoking these maybe worse than cigarettes. Cigars and pipes differ

---

[177] http://www.askdrsears.com/topics/feeding-eating/family-nutrition/
foods-to-boost-immunity/4-habits-weaken-immune-system;

[178] http://lymphoma.about.com/od/livingwithleukemia/f/Should-I-Quit-
Smoking.htm

[179] http://www.webmd.com/smoking-cessation/
effects-of-smoking-pipes-and-cigars

in design from cigarettes, which are made from tobacco wrapped in thin paper. *Cigars are wrapped in tobacco leaves, and unlike cigarettes, they don't typically have filters. In pipes, the tobacco sits in a bowl at the end, and a stem connects the bowl to the mouthpiece.*

Need I say more!

Saturday, 25 January 2014

LET US NOT WASTE A SINGLE MINUTE

Cancer is limited. Actually it is all about how we loo at it. If there are many things cancer does, there as many that it cannot do. Cancer cannot diminish love, hope or confidence! It cannot take away your memories or stop you from dreaming and most of all, it cannot kill your spirit.

If there is one thing cancer has taught us, and I mean R and I, as it affected both of us deeply, is that it can only take away from us what we allow it to. And even if it does take away a little something it is nothing in comparison to what it gives us: it gives the ability and propensity to savour every thing we once took for granted and urges us to look at life as the greatest gift that God has given us. I understand today why Kamala my mother refused any pain killer stating stubbornly that she wanted to live life till and remain aware till her last breath, in spite of the pain and suffering. Cancer also gives us the opportunity to be grateful for everything bestowed upon us, even what may seem unfair or unjust. I understand today the unwavering faith of my father, the many 'leave it to guru Maharaj[180]' that use to make me so angry specially coming from a man who was Cartesian in all other matters. The last 'leave it to Guru Maharaj' led to his passing as his life had come in the way of my freedom.

It would be foolish for us not to understand the lesson that God has sent us in the form of an uncontrolled division of R's abnormal cells. This is a

---

[180] Ramakrishna Parmahans

one in a life time chance and we need to grab it with both hands. I do not know what R's view is. Unlike me he is a private person and rarely opens his heart. I would so like him to start writing, even if it is for himself. It is such a cathartic experience!

What R and I need today is to create the physical, mental and spiritual balance that is a necessity for good health. We need to cultivate balance and harmony in every way possible. One of the first things I plan to begin tomorrow itself is breathing and meditation. Maybe if we do it together we will not slink away with silly excuses.

It is said that walking barefoot on the grass - and we have a small patch - does wonders to one's immune system. Grounding is a way to receive negative electrons from the earth and balance out the body's biological rhythms in order to self-regulate and heal itself. When the body has an excessive positive charge, inflammation and physiological dysfunction arise. The benefits of grounding[181] have been extolled by many. There are scientific facts that prove this. *Earthing research shows associations between lack of grounding and autonomic nervous system imbalances; immune system irregularities; chronic pain and stiffness; endocrine disorders including thyroid, cortisol and glucose regulation problems; sleep irregularities; low zeta potential on the surface of red blood cells (the electrical charge that influences blood viscosity); and respiratory conditions.* That should convince all of us to take those darned shoes off and walk on the bare ground. And if this does not convince you then it has been proved that *physical contact with the Earth—or lack thereof—affects inflammation, a causal influence in most common diseases. Inflammation has been linked to rheumatoid arthritis, diabetes, asthma, multiple sclerosis, lupus, autism, atherosclerosis, Alzheimer's, bowel disorders, osteoporosis and cancer.*

Grounding is not difficult. *In its most basic form, Earthing is as simple as doing what people have done for eons: walk, run, or sit outside barefoot. Anyone can do it. Conductive surfaces include sand, dirt, gravel, grass and concrete. Wet surfaces are more conductive than dry.* So I guess we will put this on our life menu.

---

[181] http://www.holisticprimarycare.net/topics/topics-o-z/
psyche-some-a-spirit/1198-earthing-restoring-health-from-the-ground-up

But the most mind boggling discovery I have made in my research on how to boost the immune system is that gratitude[182] helps boost the immune system. It said that gratitude has 31 benefits[183]. Let us stop complaining and be grateful for everything that has come our way.

A whole new life awaits R and I for as long as God wills it. Let us not waste a single minute!

---

[182] http://www.livescience.com/25901-how-gratitude-improves-happiness.html

[183] http://happierhuman.com/benefits-of-gratitude/

Saturday, 25 January 2014

I KNOW HE IS BETTER

R is much better. Actually in more ways than one he is back to his good old self! I never in my wildest dream thought that I would miss the 'ill' R but in some ways I do. Wonder why? When he was unwell and in his on own words 'felt that his system was falling apart' he was as compliant as the most angelic child. He never grumbled, ate what you gave him, did not make any demands, came to whichever doc I took him too even the Ayurvedic one who limited his diet to rice and squashes! He swallowed pills and powders and brews, bore his chemo with remarkable courage. I knew he just wanted to be well again. And thank God he did. Forget remissions and similar medical jargon. I know he is well as he is back to his favourite game: bantering with me. Oh he still has his brews and pills but not without a bit of jesting. Though he will eat what I give, his first answer to 'what do you want for lunch/dinner' has to be raclette, achar meat or any of the things he loves but cannot still have. Cigars and Scottish water are also reasons to quip, all in great spirit but I who would have taken everything he threw at me till a few weeks back find myself reacting and feeling a little vexed.

But I know R, I know he is grateful and appreciative of all I have done and I know that all his jesting and quipping has another meaning altogether. But then am I not also prisoner of the faults and idiosyncrasies of an only child.

Must find a way out as we still have a long way to go. Maybe one raclette this winter would be a way out!

THE POSITIVE TETRIS EFFECT

This post is extremely important for us to ensure that the big C does not reappear in R's life. I am convinced that it is an overload of negative thoughts and energies that opened the door to Sir Hodgkin and thus the only way to keep him out for the years we have left on our planet is to rewire R's brain for positivity. This is no easy task and has required some research on my part. Here are the fruits of that research.

It is said that we need to rewire our brain for positivity and happiness. The power of the negative seems stronger than that of the positive and there is a reason to that. *So why is it, that our brains have a such a negativity bias? The reason is quite simple: They're actually wired to pay more attention to negative experiences. It's a self-protective characteristic. We are scanning for threats from when we used to be hunter and gatherers. But such vigilance for negative information can cause a narrowing, downward spiral and a negative feedback loop that doesn't reflect reality.*[184] If you just press on your pause button - not an easy task for hyper people like me - and reflect on your thoughts, you will, if you are honest to yourself realise how much time you spend on negative thoughts as compared to positive ones. I often tell the Project Why kids how we remember for long the ONE time our mother put too much salt in the food and forget the hundreds of time she did not.

---

[184] http://lifehacker.com/5982005/rewire-your-brain-for-positivity-and-happiness-using-the-tetris-effect

Now we all know that negativity in any form is bad for us in every which way possible. We know that negative emotions can eat away at our productivity, creativity, decision-making skills and health. *What is amazing is that we have the ability to break out of that negative feedback loop and we can actually rewire our brains to think positively. Understanding how the brain can refashion its own connections is the key to unlocking the durable power of positive thinking.*

Fortunately we can rewire our brain. It is called the Tetris effect. Anyone who has played the game knows *the game's surreal ability to spill into real life. After you shut off the game, you still see those Tetris blocks falling in your mind's eye. A recent study found that playing Tetris can grow your brain and make it more efficient.*

Since R started feeling sick, I realised that he was losing his concentration be it his ability to play the piano or his propensity in reading books. I am not a brain game fan but have found myself playing them sometimes as I was told it was a way of exercising the brain and keeping it from rusting. I also found how one got better and better at a particular game if one played regularly or how quickly one's scores dropped if one had not played for a while. I suggested this to R but he was not at all willing. It was a time when we did not know of his cancer.

Tetris affects the brain's plasticity, or the brain's ability to change structurally. Every time you reactivate a circuit, synaptic efficiency increases, and connections become more durable and easier to reactivate. So to sum up, whenever you do specific tasks over and over again, they take up less of your brain power over time. And that's pretty amazing, as this will be the basis for a huge opportunity to change our behaviour for the better.

The question that arises then is how to fight or negative bias? *We can harness the brain's plasticity by training our brain to make positive patterns more automatic.* We need to practise looking for, and being aware of the good and positive things in our life and thus *we fight off the brain's natural tendency to scan for and spot the negatives. Naturally we bring ourselves into better balance.* We can retrain the brain to scan for the good things in life!

Yes, so something as trivial as the game of Tetris can have a scientifically measurable effect on people's brains and invade their dreams. If that's the case, the impact of practising and retaining a more positive thinking pattern, especially on our well being and happiness, can be even more powerful.

The question you may ask is how does one go about it. It is like learning a new language and so though at the beginning. We need to build a habit. I as once said it takes 66 days!

So let us get started:

1. Scan your brain for three daily positives. Every evening think of 3 good things that happened to you and ponder over them and record them. It could be anything: a call from a old friend, the sound of rain, a nice meal: try and celebrate every small moment of joy.

2. Give a shout out to someone daily. Take the positive you are now noticing and let one person know, your partner, a member of your family. You can send an e mail to someone who cares. I do this daily with my blog:)

3. Do something nice. Acts of kindness bounce back on you. I am a veteran in this and have said it from day 1 more than 13 years ago. I get more than I give. If you pause to do something nice for someone you get out of your negativity loop and it is the best way to make yourself happier. Say something nice to someone, buy them something or just smile and say thank you to those around you.

4. Mind your mind. Pay attention to the present moment without judgement. Open your mind beyond your negativity. Mindfulness meditation has also been shown to affect the brain's plasticity, increasing grey matter in the hippocampus, an area of the brain important for learning, memory, and emotion, and reducing grey matter in the amygdala, an area of the brain associated with stress and anxiety.

The best teacher is undoubtedly Thich Nhat Hahn, the Zen Buddhist monk. I had given R a book of his but at that time I did not know how much it could help him and though R read it, I do not think he implemented the approach.

To be mindful, this is what the master suggests:

1. Do one thing at a time. Single-task, don't multi-task. When you're pouring water, just pour water. When you're eating, just eat. That means that if I am pouring water I should do it with full

concentration. Let us remember the Zen proverb: Zen proverb: "When walking, walk. When eating, eat." Again an toughie for me

2. Do it slowly and deliberately. You can do one task at a time, but also rush that task. Instead, take your time, and move slowly. Make your actions deliberate, not rushed and random. It takes practise, but it helps you focus on the task.

3. Do less. If you do less, you can do those things more slowly, more completely and with more concentration. Not easy for me.

4. Spend at least 5 minutes each day doing nothing. Just sit in silence. Become aware of your thoughts. Focus on your breathing. Notice the world around you.

5. Stop worrying about the future – focus on the present. Become more aware of your thinking — are you constantly worrying about the future? Learn to recognise when you're doing this, and then practice bringing yourself back to the present.

6. Keep practising. When you get frustrated, just take a deep breath. When you ask yourself, "What should I do now, Self?", the answer is "keep practicing"

When I look back at the past 5 years or so, I can now pinpoint when R's descent to hell started. From that moment most of his time was spent talking about the hurt he had been subjected to and he entered a negativity loop that he has still not broken out of. And what is worse is that keeping the topic on the front burner turned on high, more and more negativity was unearthed, even things unknown and forgotten. He has to get out of the loop otherwise no matter what we do, what course of treatment we take, what nutrition programme we follow, it will all come to nought.

Wednesday, 29 January 2014

MUSINGS

It has been a while since I have not updated this blog though before I go into my rants and raves, let me assure you that R is doing well. He even went for a one night business trip and wonders of wonders did not forget to have his medicines or mix them up as he did in the past. I still remember the day when he called me up and said that he had had his morning medicines at night! It is hard to do this as I give him neatly marked packets and instructions and when possible call him or SMS him when it is pill time. This time he was spot on. But it was only one night out. He has to go for 5 nights out end of next month and I am wrecking my brain to work out the way in which I will need to pack his medication. I am also worried about his food as there is no way I can get him organic food in Calcutta, I rang up the hotel where he stayed last and asked them if they had 'organic' food and pat came the reply: *yes Ma'am we have 'oriental' food*. So must give him instructions about what to eat and what not to eat within the choices available at Golf Clubs and hotels. This I guess is also part of the *new normal* I have been talking about for some time now. Will get to that soon.

R has been complaining about losing his college day weight. It had reached 67 kilos at its nadir and though he felt kicked about fitting in my jeans, he looked like death warmed up. He is now back to his normal weight hovering around 75 kilos and this morning Doc Paul told me that putting on weight was one of the most positive things that could happen.

As I said we are getting used to our new normal. For the next 5 months or so there are no earth shattering medical tests, just a few routine blood counts. The next one is on Feb 10th. So the new normal is actually trying to put into practice all the research I have done. Some things are easy: nutrition, supplements etc. Others more difficult. Whereas R has begun mild exercise today - Hurrah - as till date he kept complaining of the cold, the yoga, breathing, grounding, meditating and reversing the negative loop are appearing to be quite a challenge. So my day is spent nagging and my partner in crime in this is Agastya my grandson who never forgets to ask his Nanou if he has jumped on the trampoline the required number of times, and either makes him jump there and then while keeping a watchful eye, or makes and angry face and gets off Skype. This works. Actually I think I may just ask his help for the yoga, meditation etc.

I too am trying to find my new normal and have to do so without help as it is all in my head. The days seem empty. I need to kick myself and get back to writing my second book that is half way through. I also need to start thinking of the future of Project Why. Above all I must start ignoring the elephant in my head: the June scan and its results.

I will get there. I have to. When and how remains to be seen.

Sunday, 2 February 2014

ON A WINDING PATH THAN ON A STRAIGHT ONE

In the past decade and more I have been blessed in more ways than one. One of the extraordinary thing that happened in my life is the abundance of Angels that have appeared from nowhere to help me when everything looked dark and despairing. And as Terri Guillemets[185] said: *You'll meet more Angels on a winding path than on a straight one.* I chose the winding path the day I chose to close my eyes and see with my heart.

Last July the world, as I knew it crashed. I too could have crashed with it had not an Angel taken my hand and shown me the way. I had less than 3 minutes to conjure a life that would replace the one that I was so comfortably ensconced in. 3 minutes, the time it took to go from my doctor's office to my home and climb the stairs to the room where my whole family waited for the verdict. I do not know which Angel guided me then as I announced in a almost cheery way that R had cancer. The mood I wanted to set was one of hope and optimism and certainly not place a humongous elephant in the room, especially after having lost two battles to the beast. In hindsight, I think that the Angels that helped me must have looked like the two people who gave me the gift of life.

---

[185] http://happierhuman.com/benefits-of-gratitude/

R has just left for a game of golf with his best friend and to anyone who has not seen him for the past 2 years he looks just like he did when he was in the pink of health, barring maybe his Yul Brynner mane! Seeing him scoot off filled me with joy but also made me realise how easy the dreaded roller coaster ride had been and most of all how many Angels had come to help me through this difficult time. It struck like a bolt out of the blue that I could not have done this alone. It was time to look back and bow my head in gratitude to every Angel who worked behind the scenes to make this day happen. I realise I began this journey just like the Little Prince who went bewildered from planet to planet, each more puzzling than the other but found the answers to every question that came my way.

So who are these Angels? I would like to be able to name each and everyone but will not do so to maintain good form, but nevertheless I will share the wonderful ways in which they touched my soul. I still do not know which Angel made me begin this blog. Without the possibility of pouring out my heart to the world, I would have crashed before taking off.

A screen, a keyboard, a mouse and the world-wide-web that breaks all barriers of time and space were my life saviours. I do not know how to thank the two persons who till that moment had remained remote and even somewhat inaccessible but opened their heart to me unconditionally and bore with the dawn mails that I shot out every single day even though they are night people and sometimes must have just laid there head on their pillows when my mail reached them. They never failed to answer immediately and calm my fears or share my joy. They have been with me at every step of this journey. There is also a little girl who lives in a faraway land where it is night when my day dawns. We have an on going battle of whose hugs will reach first and she wins hands down. And that is not all. She has also been plying me with unexpected goodies that come as a surprise and lift my mood in a quantum leap. Then there is a wonderful uncle who has stood by me every inch of the way, a warrior facing the same enemy. His love and counsel have been precious.

My family of course has stood by me like a rock. My grandson is my partner in arms to get R his Nanou do all that is required be it jump on the trampoline or eat his food. Thanks to Skype he is able to make his angry frown and scare his grandpa when needed.

However I could not have waged this battle if my other family had not stood by me at every step. I mean the Project Why family which encompasses my staff of course, but also all those who have believed in my dreams and made it possible. When I went AWOL and put my professional life on hold, they held the safety net that ensured that nothing went wrong. Every supporter of Project Why walked the extra mile to keep things as they were and rid me of the guilt I could have felt or of the necessity of having to make choices.

As some of you may know, over the years my role in Project Why got curtailed, as that is what I wanted, and was limited to raising the missing numbers. Last year a very special Angel, whom I first met as a young school girl and who is now a spirited and beautiful young lady, heard my silent prayer and managed to send us a bag of gold that allayed all my worries and kept Project Why alive and kicking. Without her I do not know what we would have done.

And then there were the innumerable people who commented on my posts, sent prayers and positive energies and advice and never made me feel alone. One such person is someone I grew up with way back in the sixties in Saigon, where our lullabies where the sound of guns and bombs. To have reconnected with her was nothing short of a miracle.

I also feel grateful to the ones who sent me books and even medicine to strengthen my determination in walking the winding path and fighting the men in white. That reinforced my will to try all shades of alternative therapies and come out a winner.

I was touched beyond words by the heart warming comments by people I did not even know. Yet each one of them was an intrinsic part of this journey that was once frightening but ultimately turned out to be the biggest boon in disguise for someone who grew up as an only child with her imaginary friends. Today that little girl is an ageing woman whose life is abundant in friends who care.

To all of you I say thank you and to use my grandson's expression: I love you all the numbers!

Tuesday, 4 February 2014

UPDATE IN ORDER

I found a picture of my man playing the piano. Looks like some friend's place where my man could not resist playing the piano, tuned or not! Actually he has always stopped and played whenever he has come across a piano: in hotel lobbies and once even in the deserted atrium of a mall! I know I am guilty of having tried and stopped him and even of getting riled at times when he played at home in the evening, but one of the most heart wrenching things that occurred in the last months was the deafening silence that reigned in the house as the piano remained shut. Some feeble attempts had turned to disaster and my man decided to stop playing. The chemo brain had shut the music.

But for some days now, R is playing again and it is wonderful to hear the happy medley of Beatles songs and classical pieces. It is one of the most wonderful return to normalcy. That is not all, he has been playing golf at least once a week, went to watch his best pal play with Tiger Woods yesterday, been to Calcutta for 1 night and 2 days and is slowly returning to normal work life. Of course he is still on a stringent diet and all the juices and brews I concoct. They do get a little disrupted when he is out, but no harm done!

He is back on the treadmill though we still have to work the yoga, meditation and positive thinking bit. His blood counts seem to be going up slowly. The next test is in a week. My doctor told me that he should avoid crowded spaces and be careful of what he eats as we do not need any infection or viruses coming our way. June is now the month when we will truly know where we stand.

Sunday, 9 February 2014

LET US CELEBRATE EACH DAY

The next red-letter day in my big battle is June 2014 when R's next scan is scheduled. Then, if we are to go by existing protocols, and if God willing all goes well, I presume the men in white will decree another date, possibly six months hence and the drama will go on till July 2018 when according to existing protocols again you can be finally declared cancer free! Wow. July 2018 seems so far away. R will be 69 years old and I 66! Is this when we are meant to have the big celebration then?

This is far too long and I do not think I can live with a Damocles sword hanging precariously on my head and an elephant in my room. I am not strong enough for that and do not see why we need to waste so much precious time to abide by senseless protocols. I have decided to celebrate every day from now on as a precious gift and damn the rest. I know it would be foolish to not keep in mind what has happened. But let us simply take it as warning signal telling us to slow down, to alter our lifestyle and make changes that are sensible. That we shall do though I guess that R has now earned the right to a few raclette evenings and sundowners, not to forget his Romeo and Juliet no 2!

I must admit that I am a little scared of letting go completely as I have had my most loved ones taken from me by the monster in various garbs, and I would prefer erring on the side of caution. Let us not forget the control freak side of me:) I guess I will have to work on that one however tough it is. I guess a few more prayers will do the trick.

ANOURADHA BAKSHI

Tomorrow R goes to Calcutta again for one night and then on the 22nd for one whole week. I am happy he is doing so, though I shudder to imagine what he will be eating and drinking. But I also know that the trip will build his confidence and make him realise he is back to normal.

I would like to believe that a great part in his recovery is due to all the brews and potions I conjured and the rather stringent diet he followed. That is why I feel a little concerned as travelling for an extended period means that many of his add-ons cannot travel along and that his diet will go for a six. I cannot send him with leaves to be boiled or crushed and given at specific times.

I feel a bit like a mother who is unwilling to realise that her child has grown and is ready to fly and that my role now is to sit in the wings and only intervene if the need arises. Looks like the new normal is more difficult for me than I thought. R, one the other hand, is like a fish in water, as if the last two years had not happened. God bless him and let us celebrate every day.

Monday, 17 February 2014

AN AWARD FOR MY MAN

In a few hours my incredible man will be receiving an award for the best tourism brochure - do not know the exact nomenclature - by no one less than the President of India! Wow! The brochure is of course about the love of his life, not me, but Golf! This is all part of the National Tourism Awards. The venue none other than Vigyan Bhavan my home away from home in the 70s and 80s when I donned the cap of conference administrator and interpreter. I cannot remember the number of hours and the days and nights I spent in those hallowed corridors. It all seems like life coming full circle.

The said brochure is for his company PASH India, a company that saw the light of the day in the very house I am writing in. I remember when it all began, how we brainstormed and decided upon a name, a logo and how I sat for hours with my newly acquired and rather shaky web designing knowledge and built its first website. If anyone ever saw the way it was coded, they would have a hearty laugh. Blissfully the only place where you still find that version is probably on my computer hard disk! And good that it remains there as at best it would be up for the award of the worst designed website. But in those early days we were all on cloud nine and come to think about it tacky or not, the website lived up to expectation. I also remember the first tournaments organised and the laughs and heart misses as we soldiered on. There was one in which the Project Why children made the goody bags and the brochure folders.

Today PASH India[186] is an uber professional organisation going great guns. And today is also the vindication of all the work put by so many people over the years. It is also a big feather in the cap of my man who doggedly worked away to make this happen. Even when he was extremely ill, he never stopped working. The only small change I made was move his office to his bedroom - mercifully we have a large one - and barring chemo and chemo + 1 day, he sat at his desk with 2 computers and made sure everything was spot on.

I am so thrilled that his passion and tenacity will be celebrated today and for those who have been part of his battle, it is undoubtedly the best and well deserved recognition of all the trials and tribulations of the past years.

I am a very proud gal today!

---

[186] http://www.pashindia.com

Wednesday, 19 February 2014

OFF WITH HER HEAD

Off with her head said the Queen of hearts to Alice! Today I feel like Alice in more ways than one. I need to pen my emotions or else they will gnaw at my soul and may leave indelible scars, scars I do not accept, as I did not wrong. But scars there will be in the hearts of those I love while I stand helpless. Could it have been otherwise, I do not know. Hindsight is always twenty-twenty but sadly not in my case. Were I given a second chance I could not have done things otherwise. And in the words of Sophocles in Oedipus Rex: *I have no desire to suffer twice, in reality and then in retrospect.*[187]

Mine was a real Cornelian dilemma[188] an inner conflict forcing me to make a choice. However in my case there was no real choice as mother I was. The consequences were mine to bear however difficult, painful or ugly. Today was the final blow: off with her head said the Queen and I as Alice did obey!

---

187 Sophocles. Oedipus Rex, Athenian Tragedy ; 429BC
188 http://en.wikipedia.org/wiki/Cornelian_dilemma

Tuesday, 25 February 2014

SMILE, OPEN YOUR EYES, LOVE AND GO ON

In my last blog I wrote about Cornelian dilemmas and the choices you have to make in life. I also recently wrote about Hubris, extreme pride and arrogance and its opposite Sophrosyne, or the virtue of healthy-mindedness and from there, self-control or moderation. All these are sort of coming together in my mind as I write this rather painful blog.

R lost his father a week ago and today his mother breathed her last. He is in Calcutta organising his pet project: the SAARC Golf tournament, something he created more than a decade ago. I was so thrilled that his return to his professional new normal was this tournament and prayed to all the Gods of all the Pantheons that it would go well. I was thinking of the humdrum glitches that occur in such events. I could never have imagined that such tragedy would strike. It was traumatic enough for him to perform the last rites of his father just a week back, and now he has to bid a final adieu to his mother. I know he is a strong person but how can I forget that cancer cells have invaded his body, and no matter how brave a front one puts up, the emotional shock of losing both parents in a week is nothing short of devastating. I feel terrified and helpless.

It is difficult for me to write about a relationship I was never truly privy to. R is a man of few words and is never comfortable talking about himself. I do not know how much time he spent with his parents as a child as he was sent to boarding school at a very early age. I do not know whether he sat on his mother's lap and heard a bedtime story or how many times she soothed his grazed knee. I know very little of him as a child but I am sure that there are some very tender memories that will help him at this difficult time.

I started talking about hubris and Sophrosyne and there was a method in my apparent madness. We all at some time or another get swayed by hubris and think we are masters of our lives. We make decisions and choices that we foolishly think are ours. It is not so.

I cannot but remember my father's words. He always use to tell me that not a leave moves without His will and foolish and hubristic me wondered who that Him was! But today as I write these words I am compelled to accept the wisdom of my father. Nothing that happened in the past years, good or bad, was fortuitous. It was all part of the life path that we hide in our closed fist when we enter this world. Do not think I am fatalist though I may be sounding so. I spent the better part of my life as a Cartesian and had my Cassandra moments and my Pollyanna ones. As a true Doubting Thomas I put every experience to test and had my share of ups and downs. But there is one lesson that I was compelled to reject and that was the one that says that hindsight makes you wiser. Hindsight is a chimera. There is no way things could have happened otherwise. You have to take responsibility and move on.

When R is back home tonight, I will try and soothe him as best I can. I will listen should he want to talk or just share his private silence and respect it. I will conceal my fear for his health and try and stand by him in his hour of sorrow.

It is not hubris we should embrace, but Sophrosyne at least in our twilight years.

Tuesday, 25 February 2014

GIVE SORROW WORDS

When I set up to 'define' my R's 'new normal' post chemo, I never dreamt that I would need to factor in the grief of the loss of both his parents in one week. Today I find myself lost and alone in my battle with R's cancer. One must admit he made a remarkable recovery and to many he looks as fit as he was before the crab struck. Even I sometimes tend to 'forget' how ill he was and above all that he is nowhere near cured. Let us not forget that modern medicine needs 5 years to declare you cancer free and even then the risk of having a secondary one looms large. Come to think of it the Damocles sword hangs on your head till your last breath.

Till now my main concern was to take care of R's diet, nutrition and give him all the alternative supplements needed. My only challenge was to coax him towards meditation, yoga and exercise. But today an insidious and surreptitious adversary stands in my way, one that is more dangerous than any as it is somewhat invisible and in my opinion, a cause for cancer cells to begin their toxic march.

For the first time the control freak is rattled. How do I help R through is grieving? Grief gnaws at your very being and does so furtively and the processing of it is personal. I have my ways of dealing with pain and loss and that is to write.

But much I would like R to adopt this way, I do not think it will be possible. Maybe coax him into talking so that he can get out all the negative and destructive feelings in him. I could also urge him to make it a point to highlight 3 positive things that have happened each day. Let us not forget Shakespeare's words in Macbeth: *"Give sorrow words; the grief that does not speak knits up the o-er wrought heart and bids it break."*[189]

---

[189] Shakespeare, Macbeth, Act IV, Scene III; 1611

Friday, 28 February 2014

IT IS IN THE JOB DESCRIPTION

John Green[190] wrote: *But mothers lie. It's in the job description!* Strange quote when almost all others glorify and extol them in all ways imaginable. But yes mothers do lie sometimes, even if their heart is choking from a love they cannot express for reasons that remain unsaid. I cannot begin to imagine the agony they must be going through when they are compelled to keep a lid on their love for a larger good, or a duty they cannot shun.

Sometimes it is a case of Sophie's choice[191], the need to choose one among many, or to shun one among others. For those around these are always sound reasons, reasons that can even bring them kudos and applause. No one sees the unshed tears or hears the unspoken words.

There are times when it is a clash of two mothers, both facing terrible dilemmas and being unable to reconcile them. Each has no option but to walk their Calvary. In such cases the final judgement only comes when one faces one's maker.

But mothers are made of another mettle and always have the last word as they leave a cryptic proof of their love before they leave. It is for us to discover and decipher it.

---

[190] John Michael Green; American author of young adult fiction,
[191]

Mine was a diary that survived innumerable spring cleanings and only appeared when I was on the verge of breaking down more than 14 years after Mama left.

I pray everyone discovers theirs as it sets aside once for all, all the lies that needed to be told, all the silences that needed to be broken and provides the final healing that is so desperately sought.

Friday, 28 February 2014

LET US LOSE THE DRAMA

R is back from Calcutta, after having successfully organised the XIth SAARC Golf Tournament, a baby he conceived 11 years ago! This time he also had to fly back for a day to cremate his mother and then fly again to close the tournament. This meant getting up at unearthly hours, eating rubbish and not sticking to his strict regimen. The great thing is that he took it all in his stride and to those who do not know about his cancer, he looked just as he did, albeit a little less hair and maybe a few less kilos. Yes, R is looking good and feeling good too and that is a great relief. But to me it comes with a caveat: the 5-year cooling period.

This morning he told me that he wanted to spend the day shopping with his Pakistani pals. Shopping and R! I fell off the proverbial chair. The man has never gone shopping, certainly not with me and certainly not for la-di-da sunglasses and saris. At first I had vision of crowded markets, lurking viruses and infections and my initial reaction was a big NO. The shopping spree also meant lunch at the club with vision of oily cutlets and day-old salads. But then I remembered an article I read recently entitles *10 Ways to Cure Cancer Without Taking A Single Pill*[192]. I was thrilled to see that we were doing most of what is suggested: the turmeric, the cannabis,

---

[192] http://naturalhealthwarriors.com/10-ways-to-cure-cancer-without-taking-a-single-pill/

the juices, the soursop and had others on our to do list: meditation, yoga, grounding and maybe one needs add gardening.

But there are two points that caught my attention and that I think we need to concentrate on now. The most important is: Let go of your prognosis! It is so true. We need to let go of all the Damocles swords: the 3 months and 5 years, the July PET scan and so on. As the article rightly says: *Doctors should be banned to do so.* I would add we should be banned to do and simply listen to our body, to the drop in weight, the fever, the loss of energy. Should they not happen, the 3 months and 5 years can go to hell.

The one I liked the best though was: Lose the drama! Stop talking about the cancer as if you talk about it, you keep it alive. *Like the main character in a soap opera, the soap opera can only survive while the character is alive.* So we need to concentrate on how well the body is doing and BASTA!

The one red flag the article those give though is: Preserve Energy! And that is crucial. Do not please others and give your time and energy away. Learn to say NO and conserve your energy to do only things that make you happy.

So finally we have our new normal. Do what makes you happy, eat and continue your alternative therapies and listen to your body.

Sunday, 2 March 2014

R THE NEW SHOPPER ON THE BLOCK

Believe it or not R, the man who never shops spent a WHOLE day shopping with his friends from Pakistan. When I say the whole day, I mean the whole day! And as the | day went on and I called with obsessive regularity to ask if he had: drunk water, eaten something etc. the answer was no as the shopping was still on.

The spree began with me meeting the trio at GK market to introduce them to my opticians, as the first item on the list was shades for the son. The model they wanted was not available. Then one of the friends told me he needed a rubber for a pressure cooker so off we went to my general store and got what was needed. By that time I had had my fill as I knew this would be a long and protracted shopping spree as they had to buy clothes and much more. The programme was still to finish all the purchasing and have a lazy lunch at the Gymkhana club. I sent them to Lajpat Nagar hoping they would find all they needed. It must have been 11.30 am. I was tickled pink at the idea of R is Lajpat Nagar, a market he had NEVER set foot in.

I began my calls. At 1pm they were still at LN looking for lehangas and suit pieces. Idem at 2 am. Lunch was nowhere in sight. Then courtesy another call I discovered they were in Connaught Place as one of the guests said he had to go there! More shopping for pants and the elusive eyeglasses. No lunch, water or anything else. I was livid but at the same time amused. At 5 or so I was told R had eaten some papri chaat - street food!! - and my heart missed a beat. I almost screamed at him and told him that he could have looked for bananas instead but too late. I started praying as never before for the chaat to be digested without any consequences that we may regret. At 7pm I was told that they were heading back to GK market to finally purchase the sunshades from my shop! The shopping stalwarts returned home at 8pm. I must confess my welcome was not tender.

R has not eaten or drunk any water for over 10 hours. Gone was the regimen that makes him swallow something or the other every time the clock strikes the hour. But it was not over. I had to give in to the Saturday shot of Scottish water and cigar.

Though I was angry to say the least as I would have packed his medicines, some water and some sustenance had I known how long it would take, seeing R happy and above all seeing that he could survive such a day was in many ways proof that he is better and that was balm to my heart. Though I do not advise too many such days, this experience is ample proof that he can resume his golf days and more, with temperance of course. I have also found a new shopping partner... and that is precious!

Sunday, 2 March 2014

SANSKARAS - LOST IN TRANSLATION

Sanskaras is one of the most difficult word to translate correctly. On Wikipedia it is said to be t*he imprints left on the subconscious mind by experience in this or previous lives, which then colour all of life, one's nature, responses, states of mind.* This is how I chose to define it in Dear Popples: *The closest would be values, but samskara is more than mere values. It is something we hold sacred in our traditions, almost an atavistic genetic imprint, and yet in today's day and age, it seems to skip many and find root in some. To me samskaras are what makes you intuitively do the right thing at the right moment and is visible in simple gestures.*[193]*)*

The reason why I feel the need of talking of Sanskaras today is that never before have I felt the importance of these inbred values that you often accept automatically without questioning them however Cartesian you may be. That is because more often than not they do not clash with your reality. They are simply the way you function. But there are times, when they clash in a way that shake your very core. For many years my samskaras compelled me unequivocally to stand with my child whose only support I could be, even if that entailed alienating the whole world. I did and bore in Hamlet's words: *The slings and arrows of outrageous fortune.*[194] I had no choice. But

---

[193]   Dear Popples, Anouradha Bakshi, Undercover Productions; First edition (5 May 2008) page 184

[194]   Shakespeare, Hamlet, Act III, Scene I. 1603

today my samskaras take on an new meaning as I need to include those of a partner with whom I shared wows forty years ago where I pledged to participate with my husband in all his noble and divine acts. This pledge is not to be taken lightly. Any religious ritual will not be complete without me by his side in heart and soul.

In a few days we will be doing all the rituals enabling his parent's soul to fulfil their onward journey in the best way possible. I will ensure that I accompany my husband in this solemn ceremony with my heart and soul, just as I did for my own parents over two decades ago. This is what my Sanskaras tell me to do.

Tuesday, 4 March 2014

SOULFUL EVENING

R got some CDs of his favourite Pakistani singer Pathanay Khan[195] last week. The songs are soulful and stirring. I must confess that they are not my cup of tea, but watching R enjoy them is pure joy! After a long long time I saw my man lost in his own world and in total bliss. How far we have come from those terrible days when it was a battle royal to get him to come and sit in the drawing room with us.

The last few days have set the tone of our new normal. Surprisingly it has been quite encouraging and somewhat unexpected. A set of circumstances, some happy and some not so, compelled my man to step out of the house and even attend functions with large crowds, travel to and fro to Calcutta not two but 4 times and give up his strict regimen for far longer than I would have wanted. He came out a winner, even after a whole day traipsing crowded markets without any sustenance!

He looks as good as new, and I have to pinch myself have to remember the cancer cells that still roam his body. The next blood test is weeks away and will tell us the true picture.

Last week an uncle dropped by and shared what had happened to him some time back. He had been 'diagnosed' with a liver cancer by top hospitals in India and was declared serious. He called a pal in Paris who asked him to come over and meet a specialist he knew. The said specialist saw all his

---

[195] Pathanay Khan was a great Seraiki folk singer from Pakistan. 1926-2000

papers and asked him 2 questions: are you losing weight and do you have temperature. When my uncle said he did not, the doctor told him to forget the whole matter and go and have a feast at the best restaurant in Paris. He also added that, had he been operated upon as the doctors in India had advised, it could have been fatal. My uncle has had other ailments since but no liver cancer.

In hindsight I guess that R's weight loss and fever were the red flags we did not see. But there is nothing we can do now so why cry on spilled milk. However we must remember this and keep watch on fever and weight loss. And of course keep up all the magic potions that keep cancer cells in control.

Saturday, 8 March 2014

COLORADO OR CALCUTTA – THE WORLD ACCORDING TO MY GRANDSON

My grandson Agastya is quite a character. And it is not the old granny rambling. He has a unique worldview and a very singular ways of expressing things. He loves you the *whole world and the United States* and is now off to Calcutta! Stop. I think all this needs a instruction booklet. His grandpa went to Calcutta twice last month and he is off to Colorado today. However he says his going to Calcutta just like grandpa. Reading between the lines you may think the following:

He has confused the two that somehow sound alike

He wants to go where grandpa went

He has a sixth sense and knew that grandpa was off to Calcutta again.

Yes that is the case. A few hours after this conversation courtesy Skype, R got a call asking him to come to Calcutta! And he is off on Tuesday while Mr Agastya will be in Colorado

Now this is the world according to Agastya where Delhi is India and the world does not contain the United States and where Calcutta and Colorado are one!

God bless him for making the sun shine on the darkest day!

Friday, 14 March 2014

I AM OVER THE MOON

I am over the moon! Ecstatic, euphoric, thrilled, overjoyed, elated, delighted, on cloud nine! Tomorrow R is back on the greens and will play 18 holes with his four ball after over a year. It may not seem a big deal to some, but for me it is nothing short of a miracle and an answer to my prayers. When he told me the news I was taken aback and I must admit a little scared. Stupid questions crowded my mind: will he be OK? Should he play 18 holes? Will it to be too much? What about his medicines and brews? Infections? Viruses? It went on and on till I gave myself the hardest virtual kick where it hurt most. Hey woman, what are you thinking, is this not what you wanted most?

And yes indeed it was. R back to his home away from home, to his four ball, where he should be! Wow what an incredible happening. This is what I had been hoping every minute of every day since the terrible day when he just could not play anymore as he had no energy left. The terrible day when he told me he was falling apart. How far we have travelled in these past months.

Tomorrow, March 16th 2014 is a day to celebrate and celebrate it I will!

Wednesday, 19 March 2014

ENOTIKOITOI

Whilst reading A Strange Kind of Paradise[196]by Sam Miller, I came across a description of Ancient India as a semi-legendary land at the edge of the known world full of riches, marvels and monsters and strange beings one of them being Enotikoitoi (or ear sleepers) whose ears were so big and pendulous that they could curl them around their bodies and use them as sleeping bags. Legendary or not, I was immediately drawn to these ear sleepers. I tried and Googled for an image, but it seems this wonderful creature has escaped the imagination of illustrators. I wish I had some artistic talent as I would have loved to draw an Enotikoitoi! Actually I could imagine myself as one. Just like the snail or the tortoise that can retreat into its carapace, imagine being able to curl your ears around your body and shut the world whenever you wanted to take a break, and jump off the spinning wheel.

The more I imagine what a Enotikoitoi would look like, the more I see myself as one, metaphorically of course. Over the years I have mutated from a fun loving, rather rebellious young girl, who had mastered the art of breaking rules to a sort of happy recluse. Of course it has taken time and many slings and arrows of life to reach this rather beatific and seraphic state of mind but I can say with a certain amount of confidence that I am not only happy but feel somewhat blessed.

---

[196] http://indianexpress.com/article/cities/delhi/journey-to-the-east/

The past months have been difficult to say the least as I battled to get R back on his feet, and am still very much in the fray and will remain so till the battle is won. I however realise that I would not have been able to wage this war had I not become this happy isolate. It is probably this ability to curl my ears and shut the world when needed that enabled me to carry on without breaking.

I have often wondered why I had not felt the need to shed even a lone tear when faced with such a terrible challenge. I realise today that it is who I have become over time. Call it wisdom or foolishness the choice is yours. I simply feel that everything that happens, happens for a reason and carries within itself the way out, if you are willing to seek it.

When life overwhelms me, and believe me it does, then it is time to enfold the allegorical ears and shut yourself for the time it takes to spring back to life.

I am often asked why I do not wish to travel. The answer is simple: who needs to travel when you can simply tuck yourself in your ears like a true Enotikoitoi!

Wednesday, 26 March 2014

I'VE LOOKED AT LIFE FROM BOTH SIDES NOW

The past days and even weeks have been strange in more ways than one. Rest assured they have been filled with quietude and felicity, almost as if life itself decides to give me the breather I so needed. The constant worry about R's health seems to have taken a break off its own volition. Odd but true, I have not thought about Mr Hodgkin's at all and certainly not about the possibility of him coming back into our lives. Life has resumed a new normal where the only things that are different to times before Hodgkin days is the food on the table and the juices and brews that have become second nature. One does not even think of them as cancer preventive or curative. Actually we both gulp the brews with alacrity.

We do quibble about the weekly peg of Scottish water and the Cuban cloud but I give in most of the times. It almost seems as if we have unwittingly and surreptitiously accepted to live life to its fullest and leave the rest to the man upstairs. I must confess that there are times when I silently question the decision but I keep mum as I watch R happy and healthy.

Serendipity has always been my friend and once again it was spot on as three bits of news came my way last week. One was a video clip sent by a dear relative. Dr Peter Glidden states with confidence that chemotherapy is a waste of money and does not work in 97% of the cases. The video is worth a watch. He has written a book entitled The MD Emperor Has No

Clothes,[197]which I am trying to get a copy off. Serendipity often works at several levels. A dear friend wrote to me about a book entitled the China Story,[198] which I have just ordered. It's the largest comprehensive study of human nutrition ever conducted. It was launched via a partnership between Cornell University, Oxford University, and the Chinese Academy of Preventative Medicine. The ground breaking results from the study (and other influential nutrition research) recommend the best diet for long-term health. *Eat plants for health* is the book's mantra. It states that *it's not just cancer and heart disease that respond to a whole foods, plant-based diet. It may also help protect you from diabetes, obesity, autoimmune diseases, bone, kidney, eye, and brain diseases.* Need I say more! Vegan is my mantra now and for dinner today I have made a super salad of quinoa, beans, chia seeds, hemp seeds, peppers and olive oil laced with apple cider vinegar.

Part III in the serendipity saga is yet another book my daughter told me about Forks over Knives [199]that advocates a low-fat whole-food, plant-based diet as a means of combating a number of diseases. Eat your way to health. They even have a cookbook that I am dying to get my hands on

All these serendipitous occurrences have been the sign I was waiting for. We have done what was needed so that there would be no regrets as was the case with mama when she refused all treatment for her cancer. But now we want to live free and happy and with no elephant in the room or Damocles sword on one's head. We will become vegan -we almost are- and live each day to it's fullest.

It is time we began discovering life the right way.

---

[197] http://itsrainmakingtime.com/dr-peter-glidden-exploring-holistic-medicine/
[198] http://wellandgood.com/2011/09/23/
      china-study-cheat-sheet-10-things-you-need-to-know/
[199] http://www.forksoverknives.com

Sunday, 30 March 2014

THAT EVER HAD A FACE OR A MOTHER

Avoid eating anything that ever had a face or a mother (Forks over Knives)[200]. You may be wondering why I chose this quote to begin today's blog post. As I wrote in an earlier blog, I have recently been flooded with information on alternative therapies and nutrition as not only prevention, but also cure for cancers of all kind. I have also received information on the quasi uselessness and even futility of chemotherapy and other conventional 'cures' for cancer. In one instance it has been said that chemotherapy is ineffectual in 97% of cancer cases.

My 'association' with cancer happened circa 1958, when my grandmother was diagnosed with liver cancer. All I remember is that my parents then posted in Morocco use to send my Nani medicine to relieve her pain. I was told that she was in terrible pain and that there were no medicines available to her in India. Palliative care was still not known and strong painkillers deemed illegal. It is only in 2014 that that the Narcotic Drugs and Psychotropic Substances Act has been finally amended and will enable millions of Indians suffering chronic pain get better access to pain medicines. Amen to that! But in1958 my poor Nani had to suffer her pain helplessly.

Cancer came again into my life in 1989 when mama fell ill and though we were not supposed to mention the C word, we knew she had lung cancer that had metastasised all over her body. She refused treatment and her coping

---

[200] http://www.forksoverknives.com

THERE IS ONLY ROOM FOR HOPE   475

strategies were her betel leaf with tobacco, her moans and howls that use to terrify papa and I, but that she insisted made her feel better and her daily routine replete with pampering as an array of beauticians and hairdressers were summoned by my father to keep his beloved in good spirits. Added to that were lunches at restaurants and evenings at the theatre. All this worked spot on till a month before her death. Her last 30 days were terrible but she lived them on her terms and died fully aware, as she had always wanted to. Life was meant to be lived to the fullest, pain or no pain.

Come 1992 and Papa has colon cancer. Not willing to put me through the dilemma of having to make a decision, he accepts with alacrity the brutal allopathic treatment suggested. The colostomy goes against every grain of this spiritual man and he breathes his last 25 days after his surgery.

Today cancer is again in my life. This time it has chosen another loved one. The shock I got when I heard the news made me falter a little and accept conventional therapy as I was promised miracles. However this time was a tad different as, not many know this, I had started researching alternative therapies after papa's demise as I had been told that I was a probable candidate and thus would have to be 'tested' every year. The idea of anyone prodding inside me was abhorrent so I decided to look for alternatives. This is how I landed at the doorstep of my Tibetan doctor and burst into tears when she suggested an ultrasound. She being a healer and not a butcher understood me and has never asked for a test in the past ten years. I see her regularly, she takes my pulse, prescribes her pills and I swallow them diligently. I never ask her what is wrong with me. The poof of the pudding is in its eating and I have not been ill. In the meantime, and more so after the arrival of the Internet I have searched for information and modified my diet and life style.

What I came across quite some time ago is the rainbow diet which means eating things that have different colours. I began doing this quite some time ago. Then I stumbled upon an article that stated that one should not eat anything white - salt, milk, white sugar, white flour and white rice. I introduced that in my life as best I could. Of course there were many cheat days as in those times no one had cancer. Come July 2013 and R's cancer and my mastering the art of Googling and sharing brought a whole new perspective and the more I researched the more I found out how inefficient modern medicine was and how a whole range of options has been surreptitiously concealed by the devious agendas of the medical and pharmaceutical fraternity making us believe that the brutal trio of cutting, poisoning and burning - surgery, radiation and chemotherapy - was the only available option.

Today I almost regret having subjected R to 11 lethal chemo sessions. Had I managed to learn all I did in the last 10 months in a day, I would never have done so.

As I mentioned in the opening paragraph of this blog, in the recent days I have been privy to lot of sound and reliable information about alternatives that work. First and foremost the best way to keep cancer at bay, in control and even cure it is to go VEGAN! One needs to eat plants, grains, and legumes, eliminate dairy, avoid processed foods etc. This is what Forks over Knives[201] urges us to do.

The China Study[202] backed by the most extensive study of nutrition ever conducted and bolstered by dozens of additional studies and cases — gave us a simple but powerful answer: The key to good health is nutrition. By adopting a diet based on whole, plant-based food you can reduce your risk of degenerative diseases like heart disease, cancer, and diabetes. In this study we are urged to give up dairy

I also found out about a new book entitled The MD Emperor Has No Clothes. In this book Dr Peter Glidden reconciles the ancient methods of holistic medicine with the urgent health needs of our modern world, offers a key to the very survival

It is not difficult to become Vegan. I urge you to avoid eating anything that ever had a face or a mother!

---

[201] Forks over Knives; Researchers explore the possibility that people changing their diets from animal-based to plant-based can help eliminate or control diseases like cancer and diabetes; http://www.forksoverknives.com

[202] The China Study; T Colin Campbell, Thomas M Campbell, 2005

Tuesday, 1 April 2014

ANOU FROM 8 TO 8

Gosh I feel a little like the protagonist of Cleo from 5 to 7.[203] In this beautiful and sensitive film of the sixties Cleo the 'heroine' of the film waits for the results of a critical medical test. Yesterday after a long hiatus of more than 66 days (remember 66 days is what it takes to create a habit), we got R's tests done. I had forgotten the process and I must admit got used to a new normal where the elephant in the room had somehow vanished. It was a shock to have him hog the place again!

The blood counts were done and 'normally' should have been uploaded on the site of the very efficient lab by 5pm. Between 5 and 8 pm I must have checked the site umpteen times. Type in the lab number they give you, type in your surname that is the password, type in the verification code that changes every time and click on GO! Normally a PDF file appears and you download it. This time all I got was: *Sorry for the inconvenience, your report is not available at the moment.* This carried on till 9 pm.

You may have guessed right, sleep was not forthcoming and the night somewhat disturbed. The what ifs were unending and the questions alarming. When things do not happen as expected, we humans have a tendency to think the worst.

Come morning and a few futile attempts again. Finally I have just sent someone to the lab to get the results and the waiting is killing me.

---

[203] Cleo from 5 to 7; Agnes Varda 1962

I have said many a times during this journey that things happen for the best. So let me try and seek the silver lining to this unexpected cloud. The past months have seen R getting better and better and resuming his activities albeit gently: one week end golf game instead of two, occasional visits to his office; three trips to Calcutta and an upcoming three day trip to Manipur this Sunday. He is putting on weight and even feels he needs to lose some. He is following a strict and wise regimen that gets disturbed occasionally. Life seems normal.

I guess the silver lining of this inordinate delay in getting the blood counts is a gentle reminder that we are living a 'new' normal lest we forget it. And the 'new' in this case is not to forget that there are cancerous cells in his body that need to be kept in check. It also means that I must keep on my toes scouring the Internet and all other source of information for new things to help keep the cancer cells at bay. For us normal has mutated to the a *new normal;* no matter what and above all one has to keep all sources of negativity and emotional stress far-far away. That is of the essence as that is what makes the body go haywire and out of control.

I just heard the gate. The results are in and they are good. The haemoglobin that had once dipped to 7 is now at 12.30.

I am thrilled beyond words! And I guess R has earned the right to an extra shot of Scottish water and a cigar.

YOU SAY ITS YOUR BIRTHDAY

Birthdays are special no matter which way you celebrate them or even if you don't as they mark the time you have spent in this world and take you one year closer to the day you take your final bow. When I look back over the past six decades of my life, I see how birthdays play a role you only realise in your twilight days and how they are actually milestones in the journey called life. Though I have a vague memory of my second birthday in Peking, yes it was Peking then, the first real memory would be of my 4th birthday. In those early years birthdays were actually special days for your parents, or at least that was the case with me the only child. In 1956 we were in Paris and my mother had got it in her head to get me ringlets, not an easy task for one with ramrod straight hair! So the day began with a long session at the hairdresser's and then one had to stop by the professional photographer's, as there were no digital cameras then! The yearly flouncy frock had already been bought and would be the going out party dress for the whole year. This was my parents' rule: one nice dress on your birthday and toys at Xmas. Of course the day would end with a party for my school friends. This birthday pattern lasted till I my early teens. Only the city changed: Peking, Paris, Rabat, Tunis, Saigon and Algiers! Oops I forgot the cake. Mama use to order the most fabulous cakes imaginable, with multiple tiers and whirling objects. There were games and treasure hunts and lots of fun. In those days the time between one birthday and the other seemed endless.

Then one grew up and it was the sixties. Rebellious times had arrived. The frocks were the first to be discarded. What I wore or how I did my hair was my decision: we had mini skirts and then frayed jeans to the horror of my doting parents who I guess did not want their child to grow. There were bangs that hid the eyes and then one fine day the hair was shorn to a pixie as Twiggy had appeared. The games were replaced by music and dancing.. Birthdays were still celebration time and growing up time as one awaited the ones that were real milestones with undue haste: 16, 18 and 21! In those days if one believes in Bergson's theory of time, it moved at a snail's pace if not slower.

Then time changed its perceptible duration and slowed down. More important birthday's became part of one's life' as husband and children entered your space and eagerness is replaced by habit, and you celebrate your birthday with the family till the day comes when your kids celebrate and organise your birthday. You reach your 30 and 40s and then wait for the big one the 50th. But that too passes and you realise that the 365 days that looked like eternity when you were a kid or a teenager now fly faster than light till the day you realise that time is short and there are still many things on your bucket list. The birthday become a scary reminder of the indubitable reality that the final hurrah of your life can happen any moment as friends start passing on and you try to rush madly, list in hand hoping to tick the boxes along the way but your body has aged even if your mind is still that of a spring chicken.

62 and counting is where I am at, and in my case it is not only the loose ends of my family that I have to tie but also those of the family I acquired when I decided to talk a walk along the other side: my Project Why family that depends on me 100%. Scary!

I needed a shot in the arm so on this birthday I visited all my centres and was greeted with so much love and presents that had been made by the children. There was no way I could let them down and the body had to be revived so I have just signed for Pilates classes and made a birthday resolution: exercise come what may and eat healthy by turning vegan with a caveat: some cheat days!

The little girl with the ringlets is now an old biddy whose time is short and who has to set her house in order before the last birthday!

Tuesday, 8 April 2014

OVERHAULING THE OLD BIDDY

A picture was taken as a lark on my 62nd! Gosh I almost look Botoxed and caked with make up and believe me I do none of the above. Let us blame it on the light, angle and other technical glitches. But the picture did its trick as I shrieked when I saw it and wondered what had gone wrong. It is true that over the past ALMOST 2 years now I had surrendered myself 100% to the choking embrace of Sir Hodgkin and rarely even looked at myself in the mirror or bothered about what I wore as long as it kept me warm/cool whatever. My exercise regimen was cathartic and varied with the intensity of my angst. I could spend an hour on the treadmill stomping my worries away or could simply find a million and one excuses not to set foot on it. And even for the past weeks when things have got better, I was not in the mood to start looking at myself and doing the needful. When my lovely yoga teacher came, I found myriads of excuses and often landed up treating myself to an acupressure session and some stretching at best and because I could not send the poor boy off. And each time I did it was with a promise that I would begin earnest tomorrow, a tomorrow that never dawned.

True there have been changes often triggered by new information gathered for R the latest being turning vegan, at least as far as one can. However the said picture was an eye opener and brought to light the fact that extreme measures had to be taken. The quasi-lymphatic state I had allowed to sink myself into as I shared R's lymphoma had to be bid farewell too now.

ANOURADHA BAKSHI

So I signed up for Pilates classes and I am off to my second one now. Back from round 2 and survived it just by the skin of my teeth! Today was workout with the Swiss ball and I just managed to keep my balance. I only realised today how bad my balance it. I guess this is a true sign of ageing so more balance work for me in the coming days.

It is not vanity that is urging me to overhaul the body believe me. Far from that. This rather is emergency repair to avoid falls and other avoidable mishaps as with what I have learnt in the past months, there is one helluva of a lot you can do to avoid many if not most of the ailments that lurk in the corner. We do not need to have our ribcage sawn and our heart exposed – takes out all the romantic aura associated to this organ – to get some artery fixed. According to many doctors it is not the arteries that are the problem. If you have 90 minutes to 'spare' to learn more and hopefully make the needed change then I urge you to watch Forks over Knives[204] It may change your life but may also spare your children as you age gracefully and in good health and remain the support you have always been. We do not need toxic chemicals pumped into us with alacrity and impunity through one size fits all protocols made to keep you sick and your doctor rich. You do not need to swallow innumerable pills that your poor body has then to eliminate by making your liver and kidneys work overtime.

But there is one thing you HAVE to do and that is to make a commitment to yourself and ask yourself whether you are worth it. If the question is yes then you are a winner all the way. Is it tough? Well nothing comes easy my darlings but let me remind you that habits are made in 66 days and that is all the time you need your willpower to stand by you. I guess one can do that at our age.

We have started, R and I, a plant based diet, nothing with a face to a mother, and are quite happy and feeling good. Actually we were almost vegan though there was the occasional egg or piece of fish the first having a mother and the other a face. To me it is giving up two of my all time favourites: cheese and eggs but when I look at the equation, there is no option.

·

Joining classes means I have to go through the whole regimen, as I cannot manipulate the teacher as I did in my one-on-one classes. Actually after two classes I am feeling good and tomorrow is treadmill day.

Now I will only take a picture of self when I feel I look like a human being!

Sunday, 13 April 2014

BECAUSE YOU DESERVE PEACE

Forgive others. Not because they deserve forgiveness, but because you deserve peace wrote Jonathan Lockwood Huie[205]. Had I heard these words in early days, when life still seems full of promises and innumerable morrows, when a tinge of hubris is part of every individual and you feel you can conquer all, I would have brushed them aside with the easy contempt of youth or the misplaced confidence of an adult. But these words have reached me in my twilight years when bucket lists are being hastily completed as one looks back upon the years gone by with certain sadness and wonders if one did go wrong. But time moves only in one direction and the past cannot be reversed. In your twilight years all you can do is tie up loose ends and above all avoid further hurt.

I grew up with abundant love and practically no hurt. I was smothered in almost stifling love by parents who wanted to shield me from all that was bad and tried their best to do so. I know that my papa would have plucked the moon from the sky and brought it into my space had I so desired and were it possible. But life is not a bed of roses and the thorns start appearing sooner than one thinks. Some are easily removed and barely leave a scar, others fester for far longer than you would want and leave ugly scars that even time does not heal.

---

[205] John Lockwood Huie, Inspirational Author, http://www.jlhuie.com

Then one fine morning when things seem almost unbearable and unending, you suddenly realise that it is you who holds the key to your release, as all you actually seek is peace, even if it means to forgive those who have hurt your most. Forgive them in your heart and walk on without looking back and above all ever allowing them to enter your space.

To some it may seem cowardly as if one was running away from reality. Not at all. It is simply not allowing something that had taken all the breathing space in your life to cast even the smallest shadow on your twilight years when you have finally earned the right to peace.

Monday, 14 April 2014

ARMCHAIR LIVING

Many of my friends and well-wishers and most of all the husband have been almost hounding me to take a holiday. Friends have suggested exotic locations where some have swanky homes, the husband has suggested umpteen options including cruises and diners in starred restaurants, the family wants me to come and 'rest' in my father's birth island - Mauritius - where we even have a home next to the sea and where you can lull yourself to sleep to the sound of the waves, my grandson wants me to come to St Louis, I have homes waiting in France, Germany, the US, New Zealand and many other countries. I am overwhelmed by the love and generosity of every one and even feel it is somewhat undeserved. True the last months have been tough and trying, but I was simply doing what anyone would for the one you love. I do not deserve any kudos at all and I feel terrible not accepting all these wonderful biddings. But to tell you the truth I am beatifically content within the four walls of my crumbling home. And in this blog I will try and explain how hard I have worked to find my holy grail.

I know that many find traveling a way of escaping the day-to-day grind and recharging sagging batteries. Some need to take a break after a gruelling time such as the one I experienced. But not me. Even as a child whose parents were over the top enthusiastic explorers and lived in many exciting countries, I hated having to accompany them particularly once I had discovered the magical world of books. Perhaps if there had been iPods or the likes of them in those days, I may have relented a bit, but having to leave my room and the imaginary world only an only child can conjure, my books, my music in a word my life was nothing short of traumatic. I realise today that perhaps it was an instinctive coping strategy for a little girl who had much older parents with overflowing social calendars and a smothering love for their only progeny, which resulted in very limited forays into the outside world. Hence the need to create mine. It was my comfort zone.

Rebel I did. More than anyone else and there was a time when I left my lone wolf life to try and imbibe as much as I could with or without the consent of my parents. I went wilder and wilder as I sought more and more. In hindsight now understand that I was seeking the comfort I enjoyed in my world on the outside and that could not be because in my space I could time travel, be anything I wanted and enjoy experiences that could not happen in the real world.

After the rebel came the wife, the mother etc. each with their responsibilities and commitments that had to be fulfilled as best one could. Then the blow of losing my parents and the despair that ensued as what had made my imaginary world possible was above all their caring presence. I was lost, completely lost. Only kids with nomadic lives do not have life long school friends or family ties. They just have the parents that they have to follow across the seas. When parents pass on, the boat rocks and loses its moorings till you create them again. The day I lost my father, a year after my mother the first thing that came to my mind was the fact that I would never bang a door again as there would be no one to hear my cry and knock at it murmuring words of love.

Part of the huge hole that was dug in an instant in my heart after papa went took a long time to fill. Where do you find the kind of love parents give you, a love that asks nothing in return? You have to look hard and think outside the box. It took years of depression to find my way to what would become Project Why. It was the love of these children that filled the immense sense of loss I carried like a stone around my neck in the form of a stiff collar I wore for years.

I thought Project Why had filled up the life of this only old kid forever and that I had come home. But not quite as I would soon realise. R's illness forced me to remain indoors and at home for a long time and what should have been a difficult if not painful experience was strangely joyful.

Surreptitiously I found life coming full circle. I had crawled back to my cave and claimed my lone wolf status again; the one where I was fully happy.

I call it my armchair living and I love it. I tuck myself in my tiny office and write to my hearts content. I lose myself in not one but several books at the same time. I travel to whatever land I want and can fly through time and space at my pace with abandon. The thought of having to tuck my life in a suitcase to go and see some exotic land is anathema to me. Actually it is impossible.

But how do I explain this to those who love me.

Saturday, 19 April 2014

RUNNING IS FOR YOURSELF

I cannot remember when I started writing but what I do know is that it was very early in life: poems that no one read, innumerable diaries that began in earnest and then stopped of their own accord. What I know is that writing was a always a form of catharsis and always came when things were not, let us say, on track. Letters too were part of my fire fighting arsenal, some written to real people, and some to the array of imaginary friends only children often conjure. Putting things on paper always made me feel better.

Some years back when things were so bad that even my imagined creativity had taken a blow, I began writing quotes from books and songs I liked and pasting them in a scrapbook. A strange pastime for an adult but nevertheless critical to me as putting pen on a sheet of paper beat all anti-depressants in the world. Whereas all my early 'writings' got lost along the journey of my life, two scrapbooks still remain on my shelf and I sometimes leaf through them and like figuring out why I chose that particular line from a book or a song. Sometimes, and that is somewhat uncanny, I remember having written something relevant to the present and then go looking for the quote. This what happened recently.

However before I get to the quote, I need to explain the situation. As I had written in my last blog, I have been hounded by all those who love me and have shared the past year with me in thoughts and love to take a break and do something for myself. Travelling is what most suggested but as I always say I am an armchair freak and cannot think of putting my life

490   ANOURADHA BAKSHI

in a suitcase. However I guess there is someone up there who makes things right or is it just synchronicity, I recently viewed the stunning video of an 80 year old contestant of a reality show who danced the most acrobatic salsa ever, a dance form she learnt in her twilight days and felt motivated to do something totally out of the box. I decided to train for a 5K run! As soon as the thought entered my mind, I recalled in a flash having pasted a quote in one of my scrapbooks about running though I could not for the life of me remember what it was. I rushed to my workspace and found the dusty book and located the quote: *Running is singular. Running is for yourself. The number on the back is yours. The only one they look at is you. No matter what your family does you can run. No matter where they set roots you can run!* I forget whom the quote is by. Must try and find out.

What is funny though is that when I wrote down this quote I was the laziest couch potato in the world having never liked any form of sporting activity. I wonder what attracted me enough to these words to have taken the pain to write them down. Maybe it was some intuitive power at work. In those days I did not even own a pair of sneakers.

Today when I read these words I realise how running is probably what fits best in my reclusive and anchoritic world. *Running is singular*! That is what endears me. Of course the running I do will be on my treadmill, but with my iPod and its songs that pan across decades I will be travelling too.

The shoes are bought. The Internet has been scoured keeping age, knees etc. in mind and I have zeroed on a Couch to 5K programme whose app has been duly downloaded on my phone. So tomorrow I hit the road. The programme is a nine-week one. Let me see if I can make it!

ONLY THE MOUNTAIN AND I

All the birds have flown up and gone;
A lonely cloud floats leisurely by.
We never tire of looking at each other –
Only the mountain and I.
Li Po[206]

R always dreamt of owning a piece of land on the mountains. He wanted his own top the world. He wanted his eyes to indulge unabashedly on the infinite immensity of the eternal snow. He got is dream and now possesses a tiny parcel of the roof of the world. He drove to see it yesterday and came back tired but gratified. My man has a poetic side few know of.

---

[206] Li Bai (705 – 762), also known as Li Po, a Chinese poet

Tuesday, 22 April 2014

HOME IS THE PLACE YOU COME FOR SAFETY

Danger lies outside; home is the place you come for safety. This quote is mine, if quote it is. Home for me began with just two other humans: Ram and Kamala, my parents. Home was were they lived as the 'where' changed more often than I would have liked. And with each 'home' came new people: the staff at home, the friends at school but R and K remained as constant as the North Star. So no matter what the hurt as hurts also change as you grow and assume new personas, home and therefore safety was where my parents were. Prague, Peking, Paris, Rabat, Saigon, Algiers, Ankara and finally Delhi where they built a home that belonged to us. Nomadic days were over; we had come home to safety. And when Kamala left, Ram took on both the roles and I knew I could run to him and feel safe. Then he too left and call it Fate for want of a better word, I had to close my home and move to Paris. But this time Paris was never home as 'they' were not with me so I had many trips back to the empty house I still call home. I think it was when I was in Paris in the throes of an everlasting mourning period that I decided that once we were back in India, I would set roots and never move again.

Today I feel the need to write these words because the pressure on me to 'take' a holiday is mounting and becoming past bearing. My explanations seem weak and tenuous. The fear of flying excuse does not hold ground anymore. And frankly there are times when even I ask myself why I have this terrifying phobia of leaving home. It was time that I analysed the situation and hence this post.

It is many a times that an off the cuff remark triggers a ripple effect in your mind and that is what happened when I was once again trying to slide out of the very warm invitation to visit Paris from two charming friends. I do not know why but I found myself saying: *I cannot put why whole life in a suitcase again*! And that was it, not the fear of flying or any shallow excuse, my fear was to have to leave home and never find it again!

Earlier it was easy to fly off the coop for a while as home was lovingly kept warm by Pa and Ma, but now leaving it, even for a short time, could bring about its annihilation. Home is no more the building in any part of the planet. It is the empty shell that has taken me years to make home again, in spite of the fact that my parents are no more there to hug me and make everything all right.

Coming back from Paris for good was traumatic to say the least. The house felt empty and desolate. For a while I would not allow anyone to move a thing even an inch, as I wanted to keep everything, as it was when 'they' were there. I wandered in the house lost and disconsolate trying to make them come alive by some miracle. I can never thank my best friend who one day told me to stop making the house into a museum in the memory of my parents but to make it mine. Thank God better sense prevailed, - it rarely does - and I took her advise and remodelled the house in a radical way: to give you and example Ma's bedroom become the kitchen and I carved out my hobbit hole out of the drawing room assigning myself the space Papa use to spend most time in. Things were better, but it was still not home. Home needed some permanence, some continued presence and surreptitiously and insidiously the fact that it could only remain home if I never left it till my last breath emerged. So here you are this is why any offer, however loving, generous and heartfelt cannot be accepted, as the price to pay may be fatal.

You are right in wondering what was the suitcase all about as it seems I have explained it all. Not quite because it is the suitcase that made it home. The suitcase I talk about is an imaginary one. It is actually the sum of everything that has been part of my life from April 4th 1952 and is scattered all over the house: from the ugly ceramic cat I created when I was 4, to the painting of an eminent artist; from the pictures that trace my life from babyhood to grand motherhood; from Papa's beautifully bound law books dating from the XVIII century onwards that are carefully dusted to the book I bought yesterday! Little objects and bigger ones, each choking with memories that only live in my head but that are revived each time my eyes settle on one or the other. You may say and rightly say why all the fuss, you will come back and still find everything there. You are wrong. You see I cannot be me without each and every of these things and cannot pack them in a suitcase.

I hope my loved ones would read these lines and understand what I mean.

Saturday, 26 April 2014

TO ME, YOU WILL BE UNIQUE IN ALLTHE WORLD.

In my last post, I tried to the best of my ability to pen down what the house I live in - C 15 Enclave - means to me: this is the most beautiful place on the planet. True the paint is peeling off and there are cracks in the walls but these are all battle scars my house bears proudly as it has survived these battles with dignity and courage and never crumbled. Every year Mother Nature is as bountiful as ever and the plants and flowers hide the ungainly scars better than the best face job! Come to think of it, it is these very bits of crumbling plaster and peeling paint that make this brick and mortar structure into a living home replete with stories and memories.

Breaking this house, even if it makes financial sense, would be as traumatic as the moment a child aged 4, 7, 12 etc. was told to sort her toys and books as one was moving to the other end of the world. The agony of deciding which doll would have to be sacrificed was heart wrenching. In my own way I had to mourn a lost child far too early in life. Dolls became books and clothes and the beat went on. True along the way, just like the Little Prince I too met my share of weirdoes but also saw the world and met people who I may not be in touch with, but who have remained in my heart. Thank God for memories!

When I had to face the daunting task of making an empty shell home again after its true progenitors left, it was these very memories that helped me turn it into a safe haven again. Memories and the lessons learnt along the way, the biggest one being to see with your heart. So I set out the task scouring reminiscences of days gone by carefully and patiently, so that nothing is forgotten forever. Some stories were happy, others poignant and yet others infuriating, but with the passing of time a certain mellowness enters your life and you learn to view things in a softer light. And then you also have the wisdom gathered along your life that colours the way you see things.

It is strange how objects I had barely looked at, and even some I had never liked, suddenly became real and talked to me. Each in its own place in my house and its own story to tell and each story is a stroll down memory lane. But it is not only the objects or the pieces of furniture that are precious. These could be packed away in boxes and carried to a new place. What about the walls and the doors and the floor the ones who have been a mute witness to the story of my life. Each one whispers words of comfort when I need it and gives the strength of their half a century tenacity. Some are walls that heard me cry or watched me bang my head against them. They shared my happiness, my frustration, my pain and my hurts. Can I ever watch them be broken down. No, never! Just like me, this house has a story to tell: mine! I can never pack it in a box, however large, and walk away

Monday, 28 April 2014

SHE LOVES YOU YEAH-YEAH-YEAH

Found a picture of my man circa 1966. The picture was taken in his school during a performance of the school rock group aptly named the Logarythms and a self confessed clone of the Beatles. He was George. The band was a huge success, so I am told, with the boys but also with the girls of their sister school. Those were the good old jam session days, remember? At that point in time, I must have been in Algiers all of 14. Had I been in the sister school I guess I would have been one of the hysterical fan followers. In those days in India, I guess boys were a rare treat and one had to lap up every occasion. But I was thousands of miles away. The only thing we had in common, my man and I, was our love for the Beatles. 66 was Rubber Soul, I presume their repertoire included songs from Please, Please Me, With the Beatles, A Hard Day's Night and so on.

Of all the Beatles, my favourite, and this is no joke, was George Harrison. I had all their records and listened to them on my turntable day in and day out. Later I would move on to the Doors but 1966 Beatles it was.

R is a born musician. Even this morning he was practising his flute and now that his guitar has new strings, he plays both piano and guitar when in the mood. These are stolen moments and blessed ones.

He wanted to be a musician and would have if he had been born today when parents are more understanding and open. But in those days every parent wanted his son to be a doctor or an engineer. R wanted neither so the middle path was an MBA.

I wish R had lived his dream, as he would have made a mean musician and who knows become famous. I can see the little boy's dream even today in his eyes when he is in the mood and picks up his guitar. But had he lived his dream, I guess we would have never met. He would have had to go to the UK or the US and I needed to sink my roots. And anyway in those days no boy from a 'good' family became a musician. I wonder what my parents would have said if I had brought a rock star home!

But the dream never left and R is and will always be a musician at heart. God bless him!

Thursday, 1 May 2014

THE CHINA STUDY

I have just finished reading the China Study[207] hailed as *The Most Comprehensive Study of Nutrition Ever Conducted*. It is not an easy read but I read it like you would a thriller as I felt the book held the key to living my twilight years on my two feet, something that is the one dream I have for myself. The question was: what was I willing to do to fulfil my dream or should I say how much was I willing too give up!

Over the past years, being what they call a high cancer risk as both parents succumbed to the crab, I have been trying to find alternatives as just like my mom, cutting, burning and poisoning - surgery, radio therapy and chemotherapy - were, are and will be a big NO NO! I found myself changing my eating habits but not drastically as I would have quite a few cheat or indulging days. In July 2013, when R got diagnosed with Hodgkin's Lymphoma, I went ballistic in my research - God bless Aunty Google as I do not know how I would have done it otherwise - and saw myself adding strange brews into our day to day eating. But there were still some elements that we found hard to give up though I knew that we would when the penny dropped.

---

[207] The China Study; T. Colin Campbell, Jacob Gould Schurman Professor Emeritus of Nutritional Biochemistry at Cornell University, Thomas M Campbell II

ANOURADHA BAKSHI

And the proverbial penny dropped when I finished, or rather began to read the China Study. Nutrition was the only way out and nutrition in this case meant going Vegan all the way. When I closed the book I knew I would never touch any dairy product in my life again. Yes you heard right. Even my favourite French cheeses. Bye-bye Camembert, Brie, Roquefort etc. etc. Bye butter on the bread, which was my comfort food till now! Bye bye eggs. Bye bye smoked salmon my péché mignon that still graced the table on special occasions.

As you read the China Study you realise how nutrition is not only the best preventive medicine you can ever get but can also reverse health problems as severe as cancer, diabetes, heart attacks, strokes and many of the auto immune diseases. You also learn why the secret was never revealed and may never be revealed to you. Just imagine what would happen if milk was declared toxic! The reality however is that cow's milk is not good for you or for your children. Animal proteins trigger what is called disease of abundance and which are the ones I have mentioned above.

Before getting a knee or any other joint replacement, please read the China Study. You will be surprised to learn that the good old glass of milk we women are often urged to drink to prevent osteoporosis is actually the culprit that sets it off. And please do not fall for the drama enacted when you reach a hospital with a loved one that has symptoms of a heart attack. The surgery that is almost forced on you is not the solution at all. The book explains what heart tracks are and how to deal with them. You guessed right: nutrition.

The book is treasure trove of information about how to live a healthy and full life without much ado. Ok it means giving up some of the things you like or are being forced on you as panaceas for all ills. The bottom line is that ANIMAL BASED PROTEIN INCLUDING CASEIN WHICH IS THE PROTEIN IN MILK is bad for you and is the causes of our poor health.

Yes it sounds a bit like a fairy tale, but trust me it is worth reading and hopefully getting seduced. Come on we fall for the honey traps that are laid by men in white and accept to be poisoned and burned and mutilated, so why not give the other end a chance. It definitely will not kill you!

I am off to my scrumptious vegan meal.

Tuesday, 6 May 2014

TRAVELLING A STYLE

Traveling A style. Funny name for a blog so let me elucidate quickly. A style means Agastya style and Anou style and they are poles apart. The idea for this blog came from a story I read him entitled Busy Busy Grand Ant[208]. The story is about a grand- ant that has travelled the word. But she has travelled in her own unique way: by crawling on an Atlas! I have been reading this story to Agastya for quite some time but it is only today that I realised how appropriate it was to me! This is just up my street. No bags to be packed just crawl on the map in a manner of speech.

Agastya has been a wanderer from the time he came into this world. He has travelled to many countries and places and is quite a pro at it. Since his babyhood he had his bag and suitcase and as soon as he could walk he dragged his little bag whilst carrying his tiny backpack. His travel companion is Lapinou a little rabbit he got when he was a few days old and has never left since. As a baby he slept most of the journey and now watches his favourite movies on his mother's iPad that he handles like a pro. His mom always carried his favourite food. Today he told us that he was all set to come to India in 21 sleepies. Sleepies are his ways of counting days. Decoded it means that he will be with us after 21 nights. He is coming via Paris where he will meet his grandparents and maybe via Ischia in Italy where is grandaunt lives. Agastya has no problem in packing suitcases and

---

[208] Busy Busy Grand Ant, Sandhya Rao, Tulika Books

getting on the move. Be it a car, a plane or a boat, he is game for everything. That is one A style.

The other A style is quite different. It involves no packing of suitcase, no taking planes, bus, boat or train but just sitting comfortably and crawling across an imaginary map. Plane and other modes of transport are replaced by memories, daydreaming, books, music or just silence. For those who have not experienced this travel mode, it is worth a try. You get off the spinning world in the batting of an eyelid and reach known and unknown places. I would suggest you do this alone as you may look quite silly sitting in your chair with a beatific smile that would be difficult to explain. And there is more. This A style allows you to break the barriers of time and space, something the other A style does not permit.

I would never trade my A style for another!

Thursday, 8 May 2014

I ALMOST LOST IT

4 am. The time I normally get up as I like catching the morning hours to write, think and savour the silence broken by the call of the early birds. It is my alone time, my ME time and I realised only today it is also the time when all guards are down and the mask that I wear for the world to see is not yet clamped on my face. In others words it is the only time I am vulnerable and totally unshielded. The story goes like this.

4 am today. I get up and get out of bed as silently as possible as the husband sleeps late courtesy the IPL. But this morning I had barely got up that R told me he had not slept at all as he seemed to have not digested last night's Vietnamese rolls with peanut sauce. I knew the culprit was the peanut sauce that he had devoured rather than savoured. In normal times, that is BC (before cancer) I would not have paid much attention and maybe handed him a Digene or rather chided him for his gluttony. But we are in the midst of our new normal, which has no benchmarks and is uncharted terrain. A simple cough or sniffle gets me on the edge and worried. Only this normally happens after my morning routine when all guards are up and I am in charge. Today I was caught unawares.

I immediately suggested some medication that I knew would make him better in a jiffy but he, who normally accepts my suggestions, blatantly refused and I found myself raising my voice and getting into a fight, something we have not had for ages now. My eyes started smarting and I rushed into the bathroom before things went out off hand and words were said that one would regret later.

The outcome was that I sneaked downstairs to my office and tried to calm down and follow my routine but my mind was disturbed. I had to analyse the situation and ensure it never happen again. Was I overreacting or was it simply my concern and my fear of the beast lurking. Had R sunk into a comfort zone as things are going better than one would have prayed for and hence needs to be reminded that he is still not out of the woods and that every sneeze had to be taken seriously. Were the Gods getting jealous as I had spent a long time yesterday evening boasting about how well R was and this was a knock on the knuckles to remind me not to lower my guards.

And above all was I still so fragile that the slightest change in my routine could lead to a meltdown.

These need be answered, and answered fast.

I cannot live with a mask 24/365. I need my few stolen moments to retain my sanity.

Monday, 12 May 2014

TO EAT NOR NOT TO EAT

To eat or not to eat, that is question or rather I should say what to eat and what not to eat that is the question. For the past few months I have been trying to find an answer to this question that may to some seem futile. Not quite as I am now truly convince of the fact that food can make or break us. As Hippocrates said: *Let food be thy medicine and medicine be thy food*, and he was spot on. I have by now read a plethora of books on the subject of nutrition - The China Study, Forks over Knives - and more recently an interesting book by Michael Pollan called In Defence of Food[209] making you wonder why food needs to be defended.

This whole saga began with R's cancer. Being a child of parents who both lost the battle to cancer and thus being, according to modern medicine, a high risk person I had over the years tried to find out ways to beat the beast unconventionally and met many years back a survivor who was vegan and told me about the rainbow diet. This was way before Internet Times and my research, if one can call it so, was limited to articles and books on the subject. And also one must admit as the danger was not real, the research was that of a dilettante. When the beast struck again and mercilessly, the gloves were out and I was ready for battle.

Much of this battle I have shared with all of you in this blog. From my research I have worked out a diet cum alternative medicine cum supplements

---

[209] http://en.wikipedia.org/wiki/In_Defense_of_Food

regimen for R based mostly on common sense and intuition, as that seems to have worked over the years. The diet is quite rigid and almost vegan and has really taken off the diner table many of his 'fav' foods! As R is getting better the question I hear far too often and chose not to answer is: when can I eat cheese/foie gras/ etc.

On the other hand my research has been an eye opener. It has revealed that a change of diet is necessary not only for R but for anyone who wants to live a healthy life till curtain time. Most of what I have read has propounded the importance of vegetables and fruits, grains in some instances but all have condemned milk and dairy products and animal proteins with some acceptance for grass fed cattle! Of course one and all ask you to eat organically. Ouch! That pinches the pocket.

So how do you find your way in all this? In his In Defence of Food, Pollan states the following: *Eat Food. Not too much. Mostly plants*. Does this make sense? Not quite as we all eat food don't we? Not quite.

Pollan gives you some rules to follow which I found quite fascinating. In the last chapter he elucidates what food means and outlines those rules. I would like to share some here.

Don't eat anything your great grandmother wouldn't recognize as food - Imagine your great grandmother in a super market today in front of cartons, tubes, and cans! In India we are lucky as we still eat much of what our ancestors did. Dal, roti and a vegetable curry still look familiar.

Avoid food products containing ingredients that are: a) unfamiliar, b) unpronounceable, c) more than five in number, or that include d) high-fructose corn syrup - This is something we do not do when we buy a pack of chips or a bottle of cola! The example he gives is shocking. There is a bread called *Sara Lee's Soft and Smooth Whole Grain White Bread*[210] - though how can it be whole grain and white beats me. Normally bread has 4 ingredients: flour, water, yeast and salt (our chapatis have just 2 flour and water). Now hold your breath here is the list of ingredients in this bread: *Enriched Bleached Flour [Wheat Flour, Malted Barley Flour, Niacin, Iron, Thiamin Mononitrate (Vitamin B1), Riboflavin (Vitamin B2), Folic Acid], Water, Whole*

---

[210] http://blog.fooducate.com/2009/06/08/
inside-the-label-sara-lee-soft-and-smooth-whole-grain-white-bread/

Grain [Whole Wheat Flour, Brown Rice Flour (Rice Flour, Rice Bran)], Wheat Gluten, Skim Milk, High Fructose Corn Syrup, Sugar, Yeast, Butter (Cream, Salt), Contains 2% or Less of Each of the Following: Calcium Sulfate, Salt, Dough Conditioners (May Contain One or More of the Following: Mono- and Diglycerides, Ethoxylated Mono- and Diglycerides, Sodium Stearoyl Lactylate, Calcium Peroxide, Datem, Ascorbic Acid, Azodicarbonamide, Enzymes), Guar Gum, Calcium Propionate (Preservative), Distilled Vinegar, Yeast Nutrients (Monocalcium Phosphate, Calcium Sulfate, Ammonium Sulfate and /or Calcium Carbonate), Corn Starch, Vitamin D3, Soy Lecithin, Soy Flour. Get the picture. And never, ever buy anything that has corn syrup! It is a killer.

Avoid food products that make health claims. These are always processed foods and thus not good for us.

So I guess what we need to do is eat regular food cooked at home. In India it is still possible and that is a true blessing. It is sad that the 'western' diet of packaged and enriched cereals and fast food has insidiously made its way into our lives, or at least that of our young ones. A fresh lime drink is so much better than a Coke but who can explain that to our kids. I guess one would be on the hit list of many.

Wednesday, 14 May 2014

ALONE WELL

I recently realised how crucial my alone time is to keep me sane. I also realised how vulnerable I am when deprived of my ME time. Till now I had not really identified these moments as no one had ever violated them. Today I know what they are: the early morning hours and my treadmill time when blasting music shuts the world. The former happens when everyone is asleep and during the other the decibels take care of any possible intruders. Yesterday as I trained for my 5km run one of the songs that played on my iPod was White Rabbit by Jefferson Airplane[211]. I must have been 15 when I purchased the album Surrealistic Pillow and at that time when sound was not clear and Google inexistent, the words were sometimes not quite decipherable. It is only yesterday that I finally understood the final line of the song, which is *Feed your Head*. To me it had always sounded like: we are dead! Interesting thought feeding your head and maybe that is just what I do in my alone time.

Anyway alone time is necessary for everyone, more so for a person like me whose mind is always in hyper mode. Many think that being alone is negative or even depressing. I found this wonderful quote[212] that says: *Being solitary is being alone well: being alone luxuriously immersed in doings of your*

---

[211] Jefferson Airplane; White Rabbit, Grace Slick, Album: Surrealistic Pillow; 1967

[212] Alice Koller, the Stations of Solitude, 1990

own choice, aware of the fullness of your own presence rather than of the absence of others. Because solitude is an achievement. What a like in this quote is the bit about *being alone well.* This is something I mastered long ago and somehow never gave up. I realise now that no matter what, I always sneaked out a moment where I was with myself. Maybe, more than imaginary friends only children often conjure, the true best friend you have is you.

It is sad that we have forgotten to love ourselves the way we ought to, love every wrinkle on your face, every laugh line, every hair that has greyed. Each one has a story to tell, a story only we know, a story only you can laugh or cry at. Every morning when we look at ourselves in the mirror we are wiser by a day and a different person that we need to fall in love with. But sadly we have forgotten that art and only look at our defects, because that is what we see them to be, and set off finding ways to efface them not realising that you cannot obliterate who you are. It is only when you accept yourself as you are that you set yourself free. But all this can truly be done when you learn to be alone well.

I need those moments just a others need fresh air or a vacation. How lovely it is to be able to take time off without stepping out of your door. When I am alone well, I find myself laughing, smiling or even crying at times but it feels so terribly right. You have over the years earned yourself the privilege to claim your entitlement to solitude, it is an achievement you have worked hard for and earned. You have the prerogative to take time off from being a wife, a mother, a boss, a grandmother, a mentor, a guardian a anything and shut that door to savour some time with yourself. It is the best anti depressant, pick me up, glass of wine or bowl of fresh air in the world and it is free.

I know I could not have gone through many difficult times in my life and particularly through the past months if without the trysts with myself. I remember the evening of the 16th of July when I got the news of R's cancer. Blissfully I was alone and could indulge in some alone time before I faced the world. I now realise that it is these very moments that have enabled me to keep my sanity and smile.

I guess I need to *feed my head*, and can only do so when I am *alone well*.

Wednesday, 14 May 2014

MY NEW NORMAL

I have written innumerable posts about the 'new normal' - the word use for patients in cancer remission - R and I are slowly crafting ours, one day at a time. Whereas it is almost what our BC (before cancer) life was for R, it is not quite the same for me. Let me explain why. First of all when R's cancer was detected and several options were available to us, my man entrusted all decisions to me and followed them to the T. The decisions I took were those that were suggested and debated by and with people I trust and who are knowledgeable in the matter. The only condition I followed was that I would not accept anything blindly and bless Aunt Google, would research everything myself and then I would trust my intuition. It was a heavy cross to bear as much of what I chose to do was against the conventional ways of dealing with cancer and should things not work out as hoped, the world would descend on me and I would have no one else to blame but me. As my knowledge increased I added several elements to the therapy and to the uninitiated it would look like a Pandora's Box of nonsense. But it has worked. And the reason why I state this with utmost confidence is that for some time now our friend R has been resisting some of the brews - quite foul I agree - and dodging them in subtle ways like fixing appointments in such a manner that he would have to miss his green juice scheduled for 11am! When he was still unwell he did not utter a murmur of dissent.

Talking of the new normal, well as I said it is back to the good old days for R who has taken off for a 5-day jaunt to Thailand with on the menu golf games, fancy meals and sightseeing. I did a double take when I saw the programme as he was landing at 6 am after a sleepless night and heading for a golf game. I just hope he rests and listens to his body. I do not know how vegan he will be. I guess it will be 5 cheat days. So if it is back to old times for R but not for me. I have to keep surreptitious vigil and watch him like a hawk ready to punch when needed. Not a pleasant task I must admit as you are like the proverbial nagging wife getting in the way of the good things of life: Scottish water, Cuban smokes, French pâté, etc. It takes me extra alone time to be ready for these battles with my temper in control.

But it is not all fights. There are tender moments when he tells me that his trust is complete and unequivocal and that he is well today thanks to me. I am at a loss of words at such times as the responsibility is huge and I feel terrified. So whereas R is living a new normal quite akin to the one he knew in old times, my new normal is quite different as I have to keep a watchful eye as discreetly as possible and be the bad cop when needed. It is a role I do not like one bit.

I could go by to the Project more often, but the few times I have been have brought to fore the fact that they too have worked out their new normal - without me - and are doing extremely well, if not better than before. Their boat does not need to be rocked because Anou Ma'am is in need of positive stroking. Quite frankly I feel myself in the way and somewhat superfluous.

Alone time is good but there also there is a limit. Of course I have my day-to-day work for the project as well as the urgent need to work out future plans. And maybe I will get back to writing Dear Popples II - the Project Why story of which 100+ pages sit quietly on my computer waiting for me.

Friday, 23 May 2014

NO NEWS IS....

It has been a long time since I gave an update about R. You guessed right: no news is good news! So why am I writing today. Simply because yesterday we got some blood work done and got the results which are good. The haemoglobin is up, the platelets and WBC abundant and the kidney and liver are both going great shakes. Now we need an ultrasound done which I hope will confirm the trend. Not writing did not mean that I had stopped worrying. Far from that. The difference was that I worried in silence and surreptitiously. Not easy I must confess.

R has just come back from a 5-day golfing trip to Thailand and in spite of the hectic schedule and lots of cheat food days he seems fit. It will now be harder to convince him to strict to his regimen. I guess he will have more ammunition and precedents to cite. But I have mine and am ready to take on the cudgels for this fight that means more than life to me.

Soon my grandson will be here so we all will get our feel good shots and will overdose with alacrity and impunity.

Thursday, 29 May 2014

ONE MORE COMMENT...

On a hospital bed, thousands of miles away, a man is fighting for his life. The doctors have given up on him. Isn't this the pet phrase they spur when they have messed you up to the point of no return. He has cancer, an illness that I seem to symbiotically linked to and that over the years I have learnt to stop fearing and now learning to conquer. Sadly in his case I was unable to win him to my side. I guess it was because I was still a neophyte in alternative options. It was before cancer hit R. I remember having taken him to my Tibetan Doctor and got him medicine. He so trusted allopathy that he 'checked' with his oncologist who of course told him to not have the medication. That was more than five years ago. By the time I became an 'expert', the allopathic treatment of cutting, burning and poisoning (surgery-radiotherapy-chemotherapy) had done its ravage and the cancer had spread to every part of his body. The pain is excruciating and he has been robbed of his dignity as normally happens with such treatment. It was the same with papa.

The person I am talking about is my uncle-in-law. He is the first member of the 'in-law' gang I met, months before my marriage. I remember how nervous I felt and probably must have babbled my way through lunch and looked silly to say the least; meeting an in-law for the first time is traumatising. I liked him instantly but life was to play a devious game before we really came to know and love each other. For reasons still unknown to me, his part of the family was kept at bay so our interactions were few and far apart. But everything was to change when a horrifying incident happened in my life and I was declared guilty and culpable without being given the benefit of the doubt. It suited everyone, as I was the weakest link.

These are the times when your character and your sum and substance are put to test; this is when you are faced with a true Cornelian dilemma and have to make the right decision, and the 'right' decision is often not the easiest one. I remember him being the only one who gave me a patient and honest hearing and believed me even if it meant alienating people that were close to him in terms of relationships. But he stood strong and gave me the love and support I would have got from my parents had they been alive. He did not hesitate crossing the line and standing by me and still stands by me today. Rare are those who have that courage. He is one of them.

When R's cancer hit, he was there by my side and gave me the courage and strength I so needed. And even if he did not quite accept alternative therapies for himself, he encouraged me in my venture of treating R with brews that would make anyone shudder. Though we lived in different cities, he never missed a blog and never forgot to leave a heart warming comment to my ramblings.

For the past two weeks or so my blogs look orphaned and I feel the same. Somehow, he has taken a very special place in my heart, one that had lain empty since my parents moved on.

Today I feel helpless and lost. That is when you turn to the God you believe in. But today I will go a step further and petition all the Gods of the Heavens to conjure that one miracle that will bring him home and give him quietude and peace with those he loves most. I implore them to let him be surrounded by the music he so loves and be with his books and writings where he truly belongs. He more than anyone else deserves his dignity restored.

Please grant me at least one more comment on my orphaned blog.

Wednesday, 4 June 2014

IF I LET IN THE LAUGHTER, THE TEARS WILL FOLLOW

It has been more than a week since my darling grandson landed once again in my arms, and yet I have not written a single blog about him. Rest assured he has not lost his incredible ways - granny speak - and has come up with loads of moments that can only been described as pure unadulterated joy. No, it is Nani who seems to have changed. She has become numb and frightened of opening the little door in her heart that leads to laughter but also tears.

That door was shut tight and double locked in July 2013 when she heard the word lymphoma appended to the name R. She knew that if she was to leave even the smallest of interstices, the floodgates would open and that was something she could not have happen.

What she did not realise was that there would be a huge price to pay.

Today I am so numbed that I have become impervious to the joys of life, even the ones as precious as those that I am being smothered with for the past days: the little and tight hugs, the kisses, the endearing eyes, the welcomed manipulations. Don't think I do not answer with the right responses, far from that! But I realise that everything stops at the shut door and what I say, do, get manipulated into doing is part of the act I had to master to deal with R's cancer.

It is not a happy situation. But I am terrified of letting down my well-honed armour as I know that it cannot be selective. If I let in the laughter, the tears will follow.

Monday, 9 June 2014

I DO NOT LIKE YOUR SMELL

I do not like your smell Nani, is what my little grandson told me recently. I normally do not 'smell'. On the contrary I am quite fond of Parisian fragrances and my lovely man always make sure that I am never in want. I guess there must have been some odour that he did not quite appreciate. I just laughed the comment away but it set me thinking, not about any unsettling stench but about life in general. Maybe I was just smelling 'old'!

I wanted to hold my little bundle of joy and tell him about the 'smell' but how do you tell a five year old that the redolence that emanates from you is the sum of your entire existence, an eclectic mix of good and bad that makes you that sixty two year old woman who was grown from being a baby to today via being a daughter, a friend, a wife, a mother and now a grand mother, not to forget a working woman and even a boss.

But the 'smell' he pointed out is one I wear with pride. I am glad my bonny boy reminded me of this 'smell' as I now recall a blog post I had written almost two years ago when I felt the need to go and get rid of the little red shoes and finally make my scapeCoat. These are images from the incredible book titled Women who run with the Wolves[213] by Clarissa Pinkola-Estes, a book all women should read. The 'smell' is my scapeCoat and I need not be ashamed of it at all.

---

[213] Women Who Run with the Wolves; Clarissa Pinkola Estes, 1991, Barnes & Noble

The famous scapeCoat is a coat on which a woman stitches [214]*details in painting, writing and with all manners of things pinned and stitched to it all the name-calling a women has endured I her life, all the insults, all the slurs, all the traumas, all the wounds, all the scars. It is her statement of her experience of being scapegoated* and instead of burning it you hang it where you can see it everyday and pat yourself in the back for having borne all this with a smile and are still there to tell the tale.

I had forgotten this and the candid remark from the smiling boy brought back a promise I had made to myself two years ago.

I love my 'smell' and now it is time everyone else learns got love it too!

214 http://www.in-vesica.com/Women_1.html

Wednesday, 11 June 2014

YOU DO NOT GET A SECOND CHANCE

There is one thing you do not get a second chance at and that is motherhood. And yet it is a unique experience no woman should be deprived of. The magic of holding your baby and counting her toes to make sure they are all there is indescribable. You fall in love for the length of a life time.

Laura Schlessinger[215] said that *children are our second chance to have a great parent-child relationship*. At first you would tend to agree but in hindsight it is not quite true. You see your idea of having a great parent-child relationship would be to do exactly the opposite of what you have experienced as a child, sort of throwing the baby with the bathwater. What you miss is all the good things that your parents taught you but you were unable to appreciate. Every parent does what she or he thinks is the best at the given moment it is just time that changes and brings new realities. I wonder how my mom and pa would have reacted to TV, screen time and social networking. I guess they would have set boundaries as they did with outings and parties. Deadline was 10 pm! Today parties do not begin before 11pm and I remember how shocked my daughter was when I suggested a 10 pm deadline. One learns along the way.

This was just an intro to some much deeper feelings triggered by the 'second chance' thought and the experience of more than six decades. It has been 24 years since I lost my mom and it has taken me that much time

---

[215] Laura Schlessinger, American talk radio host and author

to realise how much I owe her and I believe there is more soul searching ahead. I am who I am because of who she was. Today I wish I could tell her how sorry I am for the times I hurt her because of my foolishness and lack of sensitivity.

True you do not get a second chance but what children need understand is that you always do what you think best for them within your limitations and even beyond. When I see either of my girls sad, upset, faltering or lost, I ask myself whether it is something I did that brought them to this point. And as I go back in time and do some harsh soul-searching, I do feel that I could have done better. It is a painful ordeal and yes you do find faults that you could have avoided, but then you also realise that it is you today with the experience garnered over the years that makes this judgement. You need to try and sit in judgement of yourself at the age when you took that supposedly faulty decision.

You cannot and should not beat yourself but you still do and that is because you love your children so much that you would want them never to stumble let alone fall. Your child is now an adult but you are still a mother who feels responsible for every moment of her child's life. You simply learn to control your emotions and actions and keep quiet.

Children do not come with an instruction book. You have to make one along the way. You have 20 years to do so and the rest of your life to wonder where you went wrong.

Friday, 27 June 2014

STOP BREAKING MY BRAIN

Yesterday my darling boy Agastya was engrossed in a game of Temple Run on my mobile. Normally 'video games' are a big no-no with his parents who are away at this moment and quite surreptitiously as I still do not know who is the 'culprit', could even be his aunt, he discovered the world of Temple Run and now is always after my phone. I am amazed at how quickly kids as young as him master the nuances and techniques of these games in no time. I have still do get past the first step! Anyway here was Agastya sprawled on the bed in a position most kids playing such games opt for, in deep concentration trying to keep his virtual pal on track. The husband chose this moment to pat his head and of course the little fellow's concentration was disturbed and he 'crashed'! He looked at his grandpa and said: *Stop breaking my brain*!

I guess the word concentration has still not become part of his lexicon and breaking the brain was the best he could come up with. Needless to say both husband and I burst out laughing.

Children come up with such powerful images expressed in the simplest and endearing turn of phrase. *Breaking my brain* was just that. Needless to say it is going to be an expression we are bound to use starting now.

Anecdote apart, imagine how many times our brain is 'broken' and how we always find an inadequate way of expressing ourselves. From the mere headache to a break in concentration at an inopportune moment, it is a brain break!

Thursday, 3 July 2014

THE WADDLING DUCK

There is probably only one picture of me in a swimsuit. It was taken, if I am not mistaken circa 1968 in Pamukkale in Turkey. I guess it is the mandatory shower before entering the wonderful hot springs. In those days Turkey was still not a tourist destination and Papa and I were the two lone swimmers in the hot spring pools. It was a magical and unique experience. No one could have it today. Surf Google for Pammukkale and you have images of crowds in the once pristine wonderland. I feel privileged having known the White Castle or Cotton land as it is known in early times. But this post is not about Pammukkale or Turkey but about swimming! Till the ripe age of 62 my swimming ventures were far and few and across the globe: beaches we visited, hotel we stayed in and unexpected treats like the one mentioned. My swimming talents are basic: I keep afloat and can do an approximation of what is known as breaststroke. When I look back at gone times, I cannot even remember the last time I swam or waddled!

My elder daughter is in India on holidays and though she is a woman of few words, she has a huge caring heart and shows her concern in rather unexpected and sometimes almost infuriating ways. She knows how tense and stressed I am - I guess it shows more than I would like to believe - and she got after my life to go the pool with her. I finally relented and accompanied her and even got into the pool. It was a very soothing and calming experience, and P had guessed right, it was what the doctor would prescribe!

I did not say anything to anyone but decided in my mind to at least learn to swim instead of waddling before I die. So believe it or not I signed up for swimming classes and now go thrice a week to learn how to swim. I would like to be able to swim as gracefully as possible and will give it my best shot. I did 15 laps today. Quite proud of it. But whether I learn to swim like a pro or not, this will still be the only swimsuit shot of mine. When I look at it now, I would say I was fat, but believe me in those days the canons of beauty were different and I found myself confident and even pretty and was never uncomfortable in my skin. I wish girls today understood that beauty comes from within and each one of us is beautiful because God made us unique.

Will the duck turn into an swan. Only time will tell.

Saturday, 5 July 2014

A TRIBUTE TO MY ANCESTORS

I stumbled upon a picture of my ancestor. It is what one would call the 'memorial' of my ancestors who landed in Mauritius on November 2^(nd), 1871 as indentured labour. Their son was my paternal grandfather. Though our surname should have been Singh, the officer who noted out the details of their arrival was too lazy to write the whole name and just wrote my ancestor's first name that became our surname, that to with a strange spelling. I cannot begin to imagine how life must have been for these 'slaves' but I know it was not easy. I also know that my ancestor chose this to escape the gallows, as he was deeply involved in the 1857 rising. Two swords belonging to British officers are witness to this fact.

Leaving your home, however poverty stricken is no easy task, any one who has migrated is an 'exile' of sorts. The longing for the motherland remains generation after generation and manifest itself by an almost irrational attachment for traditions. I wonder how the couple, who landed one fine day on an alien land felt. They toiled hard for the contracted period that was of five year and many chose to stay, eking out a living from the modest amount they had saved.

It is said that the working conditions of these indentured labourers was repressive and their plight terrible. Corporal punishment was frequent. I wonder how many blows my Baba and his wife received on their tired backs, how many tears of rage, of despair and of longing for their homeland they shed. I know that things got get better and their descendants of which I am a proud progeny became one of the leading families of the Island, but do we not owe our freedom and privileges to these two brave hearts; Goburdhun Singh and his wife Kawallee. Every breath we take bears the pain of the blows and misery they suffered. How can I forget that and what can I do to honour their sacrifices and their courage.

In the list of people who made me who I am these two wonderful souls find their place right above all others. Had they not stepped on a ship and ventured into the unknown, my life would have been that of a simple village girl.

God bless their souls. I want them to know, that even if no one remembers them, I do and always will.

Sunday, 6 July 2014

BYE BYE BAPU

Children sometimes have the ability to tug at your heartstrings in the most unexpected ways and before you know it, your throat is constricted, your eyes well up and your vision blurs. This happened to me yesterday night. My son-in-law who has been on a short visit to India interspersed with work visits to Afghanistan was back in Delhi for a day and leaving again for the US last night. So Sunday was to be a long play day for Agastya and his Bapu, a day where Bapu would not switch on his computer - something of a miracle as my son-in-law is a workaholic and his computer is almost an extension of him! But he kept his promise and barring a few phone calls, Agy and Bapu spent the day together. There were motorcycle rides and games of all sorts. My drawing room was rearranged, as furniture was needed to make a 'house' with the help of most of my bedcovers! Agy knows where the linen cupboard is. In the afternoon we all went to visit Utpal and Agastya had a ball jumping in all the puddles left by the afternoon rain. He, who normally wants to change his clothes should the tiniest spot appear on it, was quite happy romping about in his mud stained track pants. Late in the evening the boys played with cars on all fours and the ground shook so much that I thought there was an earthquake.

But all things have to come to an end. It was past bedtime and close to departure time. Bapu read Agy a story and then after brushing the teeth and the last wee, it was time to say goodbye.

My brave little Angel hugged his father and said: *Bye bye Bapu.* It was heart wrenching. You can imagine my state but I lay on the bed stoically watching the scene that was playing in front of my eyes. No camera, however sophisticated, or lens man however proficient, could have captured that moment. There were so many emotions at play that only someone who has mastered the art of seeing with his heart could feel the intensity of the moment and that too second hand. The moment passed and normalcy returned when Agy asked his grandpa to change the channel to his favourite Doreamon. You guessed right. He did without hesitation even though the Wimbledon finals were on.

Agy settled himself and after a moment turned to me and said: *I hope he has a nice flight.*

I do not have the words to express how I felt. I simply said: *Yes he will.*

Tuesday, 8 July 2014

BATTLESCARS

Ok, Ok. This blog was started to follow the peregrinations of Sir Hodgkin who had dared enter our home and lives. It is almost a year since that fateful day and for those of you who have been faithful followers, we went through some tough times. It has also been a journey of discovery and understanding of cancer itself and the multitude of 'cures' proffered and their true worth. I have shared all this in this blog. As writing is a catharsis for me, I also shared many personal events and non-events and thank you all for bearing with me.

What I realise today is somewhere along the way the overbearing and frightening presence of the lymphoma was not only cut to size but somewhat vanished from every one's minds as R grew healthier and better by the day! And more so after we stopped the chemo nightmare we switched to a mix of approaches based on my intuition. So his treatment includes Tibetan medicine, a vegan organic diet, cannabis leaves and seed oil, apricot kernels and soursop tea. I guess that is about it but it could change should I stumble upon some new element. I do think I have become quite an expert at cancer and the treatments offered as I have crawled the web better than any search engine! We also have added coconut oil for the brain and super foods like chia seeds, quinoa, goji berries, hemp milk (home made) and more.

So as I was saying almost everyone seems to have forgotten the bad times, except me who still watches for signs should Sir Hodgkin decide to sneak in any crevice that may have been left unplugged.

You guessed right. R is back to his normal activities, which include golf jet setting. He is out again in August to Thailand.

The only thing I have to pick with him is that he has become lazy and hence put on weight and has not got back to a healthy exercise pattern. I have been trying to explain to him that exercise is as much part of the protocol as food. So the big guns are out and the yoga teacher will come from tomorrow and we will have some serious breathing exercises as well as yoga.

There are other battle scars and those are mine, the one who waged her biggest battle against an enemy that had taken away too many loved ones. These scars will never leave as they ensure my constant vigil and my ultimate victory. So help me God!

Wednesday, 9 July 2014

IF I CAN'T BE BEAUTIFUL, I WANT TO BE INVISIBLE

If I can't be beautiful, I want to be invisible wrote Chuck Palahniuk[216]. I would mend the quote and write: If I can't be heard, loved, appreciated and respected, I want to be invisible. Just like the kid who covers his face and thinks the whole world cannot see him. Just like wearing coloured glasses and believing the world to have turned another hue. I guess being a mix of a control freak and a bit of a mama bear I do tend to try and make everyone happy but do it all wrong and then feel all upset when someone says something totally logical but that becomes hurtful in the context. So it is time for inventing coping strategies that would be workable and not rock the boat. Hiding in my den and resorting to my no fail catharsis: writing. Does not seem to do the trick so it was time to resort to the big guns. At first I did not quite know what the best option(s) would be till I had an epiphany! To become invisible to others I should simply become visible to myself and spend quality time with me. But there was a problem. The recluse cloak needed to be taken off at least for some time. No easy task but had to be tried just like the golden rule my daughter has for my son: try it once and if

---

[216] Charles Michael; Invisible Monsters; "Chuck" Palahniuk is an American novelist and freelance journalist,

you do not like it then do not eat/do etc. it! I guess I could at least do what a 5 year old accepted to do.

I signed up for Pilates classes. Thankfully they are held at a short walking distance. The big question was to get myself to accept being in a class with others whom I knew would be years younger than me. Normally I like exercising alone or at best with a trainer. But I did make the effort to go and sign up and found myself with a group of young mothers and a very nice trainer. The first class was a bit awkward I must admit but soon I got into the groove and am proud to say that I am as good as most of them and even more flexible than some! I now look forward to the three mornings when the classes are held and feel good. That was step one in my visibility to myself programme.

Step two was even bolder. Signing up for swimming classes. Now the lady cannot have a private pool so there was not only the fact of having others around but of getting in front of them in a swimsuit with all the sixty two years old battle scars: flabby skin et al! Here it was again my first born who pushed me to come once, and then the next step were easier. Once the stage fright of swimsuit appearance dealt with it was getting in the pool with my trainer and his other pupils most of them closer to my grandson's age than mine. I remember the first day when the young trainer asked me to make bubbles next to a frightened little girl. I did my best. Thankfully the next lesson was with an older trainer whom I felt more comfortable with. Now I can swim lengths on my own and even keep my head under water. We are still at the breast stroke and there is a long way to go but you cannot imagine how good I feel when I am in the water and swimming. This certainly was a giant leap in my visibility to myself journey.

What happens next is any one's guess. If things fall in place I may just retreat into my comfort zone and go back to being a recluse. On the other hand if I like this visibility trip then who knows I may learn to drive, travel beyond a radius of 3 km from my house or even get over my fear of packing a bag and walking out of the gate of my house for more than the usual hour of so. Only time will tell.

Thursday, 10 July 2014

MY MOBILE READING ROOM

I love reading. I have always loved reading. I presume it is the happy fate of only children with older and busy parents and nomadic lives. I cannot remember a time when books were not a part of my life. Without them, I feel lost. Even today I have a pile of unread books as a security blanket. They are sustainment as well as therapy. In yore time, when I was still travelling I needed a couple of books in my hand luggage should one not fulfil the need of the moment and in spite of having them, I would also drop by the airport bookshop and pick one or two up. In communist Prague where we were posted in the 80s there were no English bookshops so when I came home for a visit my main shopping consisted of books. Prague had one English library run by the British Embassy and within a year I had read every book they had.

I often read more than a book at a time. There is one at my bedside, which is often a thriller, and another lies on my office table and could be anything, from a serious book on Economics to the latest Booker or other Literary Price. The first thing I read in a magazine is the book reviews and should one catch my fancy I am at the bookstore at opening time to buy it and if they have not received it yet, then to order it. I am not comfortable with on line bookstores and use them only when I cannot find the book I want.

My all time treat is to go to the bookstore and look at books, feel them, smell them and feast all my senses. Choosing a book is a sensuous experience, at least for me. The eyes get attracted by the look of the cover, the title that often echoes something familiar, then touching the book gratifies you in another way, its feel, its weight, its volume before you turn to the back cover and read the summary or the reviews before making a final decision. I normally go to one bookshop and the staffs knows my taste by now. Soon after walking in numerous books are proffered and I find a place to sit and chose the ones I may buy keeping in mind the weight of the wallet. I linger on, chatting with the manager who has become a friend by now. I seem to have digressed from the topic I set out to write about: my reading room.

For the past few years now I have mastered the art of reading in my three-wheeler. This at first was a coping strategy to taken on Delhi's nightmarish traffic. Lost in my book, I felt safe and was often surprised at how quickly I reached my destination. Those were the days when I travelled far more than today as I visited my various centres and went to meet people. All that changed when R fell ill and my going out was terribly restricted. I felt I was missing something and it took me a while to realise that I missed my reading room a.k.a the three wheeler!

You may wonder why a person who lives in a huge rambling house with nooks and corners and all kind of seating options chooses to read in a three wheeler whatever the weather and notwithstanding the bumps. I guess once again this is a very precious and unique alone time that is a lifeline and an oxygen shot. So the recluse does take her time off in her mobile reading room everyday. The husband things I am a shopaholic, as I need to find a reason to move and the answer to the *where are you going* is undoubtedly *to the market*. How does one say to anyone: *I am off on my mobile reading room!*

Sunday, 13 July 2014

LET ME FINISH MY DREAM

I love kids. They can make the darkest cloud lift in the batting of an eye! Yesterday my little grandson who sleeps with us woke up when his aunt came and after playing with her a little and realising that there was nothing great planned for the moment declared: *I am going back to sleep to finish my dream.* And he promptly lay down and closed his eyes tight. Sleep was nowhere in sight and after a while I asked him if the dream was finished. *Yes* he replied, *now I am making another*!

You guessed the right, the other dream was made and dreamt in a jiffy and the little chap was all set to go for the day but his words lingered in my mind for long. Dreams are of great importance to me. I conjure them all the times as what else would you call the quasi-impossible challenges I set for myself time and again. Alas, though some come true, many remain unfulfilled, leaving me somewhat helpless. I so wish I could go back to sleep to finish my on going dream and make another!

Agastya is a master of words and can come up with the most amazing retorts that leave you kind of speechless and totally zapped. Wanting to go straight to play outside by passing his breakfast he had to come up with something that would shut the old badgering granny down. When I asked him for the umpteenth time I guess what he wanted for breakfast, proffering all his favourites, he looked back and told me: *I do not want breakfast Nani, it gives me too much energy*! I wonder how he came up with that one. Anyway all the old biddy could do was beat a meek retreat.

Come to think of it I would like to be able to say the same words some day!

Saturday, 19 July 2014

DAMASK

Damask is a fabric using basic weaving techniques of the Byzantine and Islamic weaving centre of the early Middle Ages and derives its name from the city of Damascus, a city that is sadly torn and destroyed by conflict today and where one hears the jarring sounds of rockets and missiles instead of the soothing sounds of weaving looms. As Damascenes say: *we don't know what tomorrow will bring*.

This post however is not on the war in the Middle East but on the fabric damask in one of its favoured avatars: tablecloths.

Yesterday in one of the sporadic cleaning sprees that happen in this house, two rather used and yellowed plastic bags were discovered in the linen cupboard. They were stuffed with ma's old damask tablecloths and napkins. For those who did not know their story, they were good for the recycling bin. I was not party to the cleaning spree and happened to see the two bags in time. I guess my extreme reaction to the idea of throwing them away was incomprehensible to all present but I was in no mood to explain and say more than: you can throw them after I die!

They will once again take the place they have occupied in the cupboard and wait till my time comes. I guess I should have explained my feelings and thoughts but somehow I knew that no one would be able to understand them truly. If you open and look at them, they are a far cry from the beautiful pieces lovingly purchased by my mother. Today they have stains and even tears and have lost their sheen. But every stain and tear holds a childhood memory and I am sure many forgotten ones too.

I guess some of them must be almost 50 year old and it is a tribute to Ma's skills that they have survived in such a good condition. I remember how each stain was first handled and how each piece was hand washed under her supervision. Ma did not like cooking and I think the God's played their cards well when they selected her husband as Pa's passion was food and cooking. Mama's forte was the table decor and she did a great job. These yellowed pieces of cloth remind me of how well my parents dovetailed their talents.

It is around these now ugly tablecloths that my parents entertained what one may call the rich and famous but also a bunch of eclectic people that could range from painters, to poets and writers; royalty and nobility from many lands; diplomats and politicians but also the humblest of people that they met along the way. Around their table everyone was treated equally and probably that is one of the lessons their only child learnt very early: all humans are equal and need to treated and respected in the same way. I have never allowed myself to forget this lesson.

I also remember the number of times I was awoken hastily from my sleep by mama and asked to put on my best party dress and come down to the dining room as a guest had dropped out and there would be 13 at the table so I was to be the 14th guest. For a 7 or 8 or even 10 year old it was exciting beyond words. Never mind if I had already had dinner and had school the next morning. I could eat a meal all over again and loved the fact that I was doing so at the beautifully laid table talking to adults and important people. Being an only child born to middle aged parents, the adult world was a familiar one and somehow I liked talking to grown ups. My parents often told me that I could hold an intelligent conversation. I do not know if they were indulging me or whether it was the innumerable number of books I consumed. But sitting at a table with big people was as close to a fairy tale I could get. It was on these worn out tablecloths that these fairy tales were unfolded. I cannot recount each of them as there are hidden in deep and almost unreachable recesses of my memory, but the sight of these pieces of cloth bring forth collective memories that fill me with warm and happy feelings. How can one throw such memories in a trashcan!

I know they will remain in their ungainly plastic bags, but the memories tucked within their folds make them precious and unique. Once I am no more around, then I guess they will just metamorphose into yards of tattered cloth fit for the dustbin!

THE BEFORE IT'S TOO LATE CRUSADE

I do not know what is the right age to start making a bucket list as we all know that the word 'bucket' in this case comes from the expression: kick the bucket! Now that is if the bucket list is yours. However I guess there must be the ones of 'others' who are connected to you and that is when things become difficult. Ones own list often consists of finishing pending agendas, making wills, clearing debts - the financial ones - if any, ensuring to the best of your ability that things you have begun carry on smoothly if possible but here I think there is a tinge of hubris as how can one forget the age old adage: the King is dead; long live the King. It is us foolish humans who believe that we are essential to the game called life. The other extreme is the course followed by the likes of my father who believed that nothing happens without the will of the almighty. In that situation bucket lists seem quite futile.

However a list can be fun if it includes things like learn swimming, driving, flying should you make it in your sixties and such an exercise could add some spice in your life when your bones creak louder by the day. By the way swimming was NOT on my bucket list

When I look at a bucket list I made in 2010 I cannot but smile! Then came another one in 2013 after R's cancer that I still stand by and guess will, adding to it whatever else should come my way. This I presume will go on till exit time.

There is another list however which is not easy if not impossible to make and that is the one when your loved ones asks you to heal supposed past hurts. Easier said than done. As a dear and wise friend says: *complicated lives are not always open to retro-fitting.* That is the part of your life that you have locked forever as should you find the key, the result may be more devastating than silence. Our lives are filled with coping strategies that we have evolved along the way and made so much part of our lives, that trying to find your way back may just be impossible. We are no Penelope and have not mastered the art of unravelling to perfection the piece we have woven through our lives to protect ourselves from hurt. The process of trying to do so may result in more hurt than healing.

Things have to be heard at the appropriate time and rather than play God, let us leave it to his wisdom. I remember how I found a diary written by Kamala my mother a year before her death and found by me 15 years after her death at a time when I was going through a rough patch and needed most of all my mama's lap to put me back on track. It was not her lap, but pages written in a yellowed diary that had survived many a spring cleaning waiting to be picked up when the time was right. How she had seen what lay ahead was uncanny and comforting at the same time. But more than that, she revealed a part of herself she had held carefully concealed as it might have rocked my boat and shattered the image of the perfect life she had conjured for me. At the same time, I guess she felt the need of sharing her pain with her only child and must have hoped that I would find these pages when I was strong enough to read them.

Mothers do want the best for their children but often fall short not because they lack love but because they are so blinded by it that they are unable to see what is right.

Friday, 25 July 2014

A SELF TO SUIT SOCIETY

I guess we all along our lives have to create a self or many selves to suit circumstances. They could be family circumstances or social ones. To survive you need to adapt even if what you are compelled to create is someone you do not like. Survival of the fittest said Darwin, and here the fittest means the one that is the most compliant. But there comes a time when you can, if you so wish, abandon that self and try to go back to the real one. It is not easy believe me and can have calamitous consequences that can hurt you and your loved ones beyond repair.

I found a picture of my second birthday in Peking. The girl in the picture feels like a princess thanks to doting parents who love her unconditionally. She will live in the warmth of this love for some time till the first hurt that cannot be wished away by a gentle kiss from her mom or a hug from her pa. Sooner or later she will learn that she has to bear the brunt of blows and work her own solutions, some of which necessitate altering her self. This is a survival lesson she will need to accept but what she does not know yet is that there may come a time when the multitude of band aids and masks that she has been compelled to place on herself will render her unrecognisable. That is when she will wonder whether there are still some pieces of the little girl left in some crevice of the mind that can help her retrace the journey she had to travel. The catch is that if she decides to do so, she may open old wounds and create new ones that may never be healed.

I would have never thought of all this and gone happily to my grave were it not for the insistence of a loved one to get answers to some things that I agree look incomprehensible if not placed in a proper context. I have spent some sleepless nights trying to make some forays down memory lane and ask myself what the consequences of airing the past at this moment would be and it did not take me long to realise that no matter how much I am badgered to reveal my reasons, I would not succumb as it will bring more hurt than healing. So I may for my own self unravel the knots but simply to assuage my conscience and see whether I could have done a better job. Life as we know gives us one chance at a time, and a lifetime to regret it.

I have an example that would validate my point of view and it comes from no less than my mother. For the less than 4 decades I spent with my parents, my strength came from the knowledge that my mother and father were happy as that is what they both seemed to be to me in my childhood, teenage and adulthood. I basked in that warm feeling and could live my life with ease and insouciance. Had I tried to delve deeper and found the reality, my life would have been shattered. But my mother must have felt the need to share her pain with her only child as she wrote a rambling diary in the penultimate year of her life, before she lost a part of a memory. In those pages she shared her innermost feelings.

I found that diary more than fifteen years after they both died and by that time I was mellowed and matured and could look at things with a distance and with my heart. Had I read that diary when I was not ripe for it, I could have even hated one of them. But far from that. What I read in those lines was how much my two parents loved each other but how inept and clumsy they were at showing their feelings. I will not say more.

The point I am trying to make is that every action we take has a reason that needs to be respected. When the time is right, in some serendipitous way, truth will be revealed and will be a healing experience.

Saturday, 2 August 2014

MY HEART IS COVERED

My heart is covered! Agastya my grandson flew away two hours ago after two joyful months with us. You may wonder what the expression 'my heart is covered' means and where it originates. Let me elucidate. This expression is part of my grandson's delightful lexicon that never ceases to amuse and amaze me and that I gleefully appropriate. He used it first about a week or so ago when he fell ill and nauseous. *My heart is covered with the rice* is what he stated and believe you me, we all understood what he meant. The ensuing days were terrible as the poor boy went through the nightmare of the famed Delhi belly!

Today my heart is covered not with rice or pasta, but with an indescribable medley of feelings ranging from melancholy to acceptance laced with a tinge of fear as well as forbearance and even an imbue of unease. The fear of course is transient but will choke the covered heart till all the planes land safely till their final destination. In the present scenario this means 6 unending days and nights as they break journey in Paris.

This bundle of joy has for the past 70 days and nights ruled my heart and my life and I have complied unabashedly. He slept with us - Nanou and I - as he has always done for the past 5 years irrespective of all the canons of child rearing and the initial barely expressed resentment of his parents were soon set aside as he was the one who decided on the matter.

My heart is covered by the emptiness that greeted me this morning when in my half sleep, I extended my hand in search of my little foot. You

ANOURADHA BAKSHI

see even the hands and feet are divided: one set being mine and the other his nanou's. I cannot tell you how empty the world felt for that instant before the heart was assuaged by reason and the emptiness translated into the realisation that he was gone! It had been just a few hours but they felt like eternity.

As I crept down the stairs to my burrow, the silence was palpable and overpowering, even for one who revels in solitude. My eyes refused to stray on the tiny objects left behind - a bright pair of crocs, some cars his Mom refused to put in the suitcase and a T-shirt hung on the banister presumably for drying and presumably conveniently forgotten for want of space again. I know that as the day enfolds there will be innumerable reminders of the little fellow's stay at home. My heart is covered by this deafening silence that will become louder and louder as I miss my agyTalk!

TWO MEN

2014 - 103, 65, 62, 40 and 40! Wonder what these numbers are. The first goes without explanation. The other two are a riddle no one but me can solve. 103 is the age my father would have been today; 65 is R's - the husband - age today, 62+ some months is how old I am today and 40 and 40 are the number of years I have spent with the two men I love most. Papa and R share a birthday or almost: the former was born on August 15th and the later on August 14.

These two men undoubtedly made me who I am even if it took me long years to realise this and learn not only to accept it but to celebrate it as though they outwardly are as different as chalk and cheese, their heart and spirits are almost clones of each other. And today I realise that I have spent exactly the same amount of years with each of them with a few of them overlapping of course. Those would amount to 22 years!

As I said these two men have a lot more in common than you may want to believe. First of all they both fell in love with me almost instantly. It took R a week to propose! And in spite of lots of ups and downs they never wavered no matter how many doors I banged or tears I shed, they waited unobtrusively for the brat to come to her senses. Papa or Tatu as I called him, made me from a crying lump of flesh to a caring and erudite human being. He patiently and lovingly moulded the raw material and taught me right from wrong as well as the courage to walk the road less travelled. He let me make my mistakes and get hurt, sometimes deeply but was always there to wipe the tears, tender to the wounds and help me get up and run again. The day he left the world I think he, more than anyone else and most of all me knew that I was ready to jump without the parachute he had been.

But none of this would have been possible without another man who gave me the total freedom to walk all the less travelled roads and also stood in the wings lest I fall, and fall I did. He simply picked me up without a single word of retribution or even counsel and set me on another course. If one moulded the raw material, the other allowed it to grow and bloom the way I wanted it to. And I would be unethical if I did not say that the road(s) I chose went against all the conventions and mores that we are meant to live by. He defended me like a knight in shining armour at every moment of my life. I must admit that I now realise that it must not have been easy for him but he never uttered a word. Just like Pa, I think he was and is proud of the person I am. It is now my turn to prove to him that he was right.

Today I want to tell both these incredible human beings that I love them and always will. May God bless them.

Happy birthday R and Ram.

Monday, 8 September 2014

24 HOURS

The last 24 hours have been the longest in my entire existence. R is in Srinagar with a group of golfers and what was meant to be a nice holiday has turned out to be a nightmare as the river broke its dyke and the city is flooded. I last spoke to R exactly 24 hours ago and his words were: we are in dire straits and need help. It is an SOS. Then silence. The network died and I have been unable to establish direct contact and if one is to believe the news, connectivity will be resumed in 48 to 72 hours. The last I heard was that R was in his hotel that was relatively safe as on a higher point but part of his group was in a hotel situated at a lower level and its two floors had been flooded. He was feeling helpless as there was no way he could reach out to them and worried as they were now without food or water as kitchen and stores are rarely on upper floors. I wonder if they have run out of provisions in his hotel by now. I hope not. I also realise that I will not know if and when they are rescued because of the communication breakdown. I have never felt so helpless.

For a control freak like me this is a nightmare. Helplessness is the sworn enemy of control freaks and I have been turning like a lion in a cage the whole day. Finally here I am resorting to the only known catharsis for me: writing. Wonder how I spent the day. True to my control freak persona I had to find 'things' to do and I did. I tried all the helplines I could find on news channel and on the net but NONE worked. So I sent Dharmendra, my colleague and strong support, to Jammu and Kashmir House and he was able to give the details and seek help. He saw the names been loaded on a computer but only God knows what would have happened to the list. It may be still sitting on the hard disk of the said computer. Then I wrecked my brain to find out at whose door I could knock and remembered and old friend who is a senior officer in the Intelligence Bureau and contacted him. I presumed he would have some mean of communication. He promised to see what could he do and informed me that he had sent a rescue request. Not knowing whether it was acted upon is again nothing short of killing. I hope it has reached the right place and some action has been taken. I then turned to FB more to get some support and was overwhelmed by all the positive vibes that were sent to me. There were a few suggestions and I complied immediately.

But came the time when I knew I could do nothing else. And that is when I knew I had to 'write' as otherwise I would go insane. Writing helps me get rid of my angst and put things in perspective. Last year at about this time, I was battling R's cancer but I was in charge and that made things easier. I use to write everyday to share every aspect of my battle with all at large. Somehow putting it out there on the web helped in some strange way. It also helped me voicing the concerns and worries and that made addressing them a little easier. My main worry is of course R's health as much of his recovery is based on him following a healthy and strict regimen. I have been wondering about his food and water and the quality of the two, the later being more critical. The helplessness is at its zenith as I have no way of knowing and even less of helping. Even if I found my way to Srinagar there is little I could do.

I am also concerned about the stress R is going through as he is accompanied by a group of 50 golfers, some with spouses and I know how helpless he is feeling as knowing him I know he feels responsible for each of them and will not budge unless all of them are safe. Part if his group is from Lahore and unfortunately they are in the hotel that is most affected. Now stress is cancer's worst enemy and I am keeping my fingers crossed hoping that the adrenaline rush he must be feeling, keeps him safe. I guess I will only know what is happening when he lands home after making sure his brood has landed home too.

As I write these words, I also realise how selfish one can be when a loved one is in trouble. This tragedy is huge and R and his pals will come back to safety once they are rescued. But what about the local people who have lost everything they own; the children in flooded hospitals, the elderly who cannot move on their own. When will they come home, if home they have! My heart goes out to them and I feel a little guilty not having thought of them earlier. This is how writing helps me: to put things in perspective and take a little distance from my own limited concerns.

SOMETIMES THERE IS NOTHING YOU CAN DO

It has been almost two days since I have heard R's voice. Since then, silence, a silence so deafening that it devours you. And in that silence your mind works over time building scenarios that would put Oscar winning storywriters to shame. Your imagination runs wild more so as it is helped in ample measure by the feeling of helplessness that engulfs you. More than that, when your loved one is in danger of any kind and you cannot be of help, a sense of guilt pervades you. This guilt is insidious and has no real ground and you know it, but in those moments only the heart rules.

I do not know why I cancelled all my appointments but it felt the right thing to do. Somehow the idea of exercising or going for a meditation class or even a work meeting seem anathema. So what do you do? You sit in front of the box that shows you in a loop the same images of the place your loved one is and maybe in doing that you feel, quite erroneously, that you are with your loved one in spirit. I know it sounds stupid. I know that R will laugh when I tell him that. But at this moment, sitting in front of the screen and staring at the images without quite seeing them, holding on to the phone in the hope that it will ring whilst knowing that it cannot be, as all lines are down, writing a message on FB just to feel you are not alone, wrecking your brain to find anyone who could maybe help, hunting for your prayer beads and praying, taking a break while walking aimlessly in the house before starting all over again. That has been my regimen, as I need one to keep thoughts in check, the stop my mind from wandering too much.

Everyone is worried. My firstborn calls from the US frequently. Friends call or send text messages all wanting to know as soon as I get news. Maybe I should start making a list of all those I need to contact when I finally get news. It will take care of some of the time that is ticking at a snail's pace in true Bergsonian style.

Think positive is what everyone is saying and I am trying to do just that. So let me end by saying that Agastya is waiting for his Nanou for their next game of golf!

Monday, 8 September 2014

WE WON

I need to fill my mind with happy and positive thoughts and who else can provide these but my darling grandson! In a recent Skype call he announced with great aplomb that his soccer team had won 8-2. Yes the bloke is now on a soccer trip with a game each weekend. While he was telling me all about his winning, his mom was making strange faces. It transpired that his team had lost 8-2. But Agastya had his logic. The ball entered his goal and thus he won. It will take him time to understand the true rules of the game.

For the match he had his gear and was over the moon. The gear was the most exciting thing of the day. He was playing defence with his pal but they were too busy comparing their gear and the T-shirt was more important than the ball. Anyway what lay behind them was 'their' goal so what was the fuss about. His father and his coach could scream what they wanted; the two boys had better things to do.

They have time to grow up. For now let them play by their rules. It is what makes children so special and brings a big smile on Nani's face making her forget, albeit for a few minutes, all her worries.

Tuesday, 9 September 2014

I AM BUSY BEING GRATEFUL

I am busy being grateful are words I chose to append to my signature in my email account. I did this many years ago when I was overwhelmed with gratitude at everything I had been given in life. Then somehow I forgot about them though they sat at the bottom of each and every email waiting to be acknowledged again. I do not know why, but as I sat to write a quick mail to my daughter telling her that her Papa was safe, the words stared at me and their deafening silence was full of reproach. I stood exposed as I am guilty of having forgotten for far too long how indebted I am for having been given so much. Even if I spent all the hours I have left, be they day or night, thanking God and all those who have sprinkled my life with miracles, big and small, I would still not be able to express my gratitude. Today is a wake up call.

R is safe. It took those terrible hours to bring me back to earth and to realise how infinitesimal we are in the face of Nature and God. We may fall prey to the most exalted hubris but are brought back to earth with a bang in no time. Nature is a great leveller. It makes no difference who and what you are. I wish we understand this better. As for God he has a plan that only he knows; we as humans can only bow to His Will and understand that his plan is better than ours. I thank the Almighty for the grace he has blessed me with.

But that is not where it ends. I could not have survived this ordeal if it were not for a multitude of people, known and unknown, who reached out to me. Every word of comfort that was sent to me helped me immensely and I am deeply grateful for all who took time to write a few words. Those who know me well knew in what state I was. To all of you a big Thank You!

Then there are those who helped me trace R: a long time friend now in an important position who used his network to send rescue appeals; my colleague who went to the local Kashmir office to send a message through their wireless and even spoke to an army officer who confirmed that the group had been rescued; friends who used their connections to send messages and all those who sent their suggestions that I have dutifully followed. I do not know which one worked. For me each and everyone did.

But there are some others I need to thank: the reporters of all the news channels who continued reporting even when they had no news of their own loved ones and helped us have a connection, however tenuous, with our loved ones; the people who are working day and night, in dangerous conditions, to bring our loved ones home; the staff of the hotels who must be doing everything in their power to make our loved ones comfortable. I can only fold my hands in gratitude and say: thank you.

Yes I am busy being grateful!

Tuesday, 23 September 2014

WITHOUT LEAVING FOOTSTEPS

Had gone to visit the family astrologer for a friend and could not resist asking where I was heading. Wish I had not, as he told me that my 18 years of Rahu were beginning in January 2015. 63 + 18 takes me to the ripe age of 81. I guess exit time will be under the Rahu spell. Rahu[217] is also known as the dragon's head. Dragon is my Chinese astrological sign! But Rahu is a severed head that swallows the sun causing eclipses and *is depicted in art as a serpent with no body riding a chariot drawn by eight black horses.* Not the best image to lead you through 18 years and I believe that it all depends on where the planet is placed in your chart. I do not know the details but hope it is not too bad as *Rahu dasha can either be the best time of any person's life or plunge him into deep trouble depending on which planet is controlling him.* There seems to be no middle path so let us hope for the best. It is also said that Rahu *dasha gives immense scope for obtaining spectacular results from worship or dhyana. Worship of Goddess Durga pleases Rahu the most and he confers immense benefits to the worshipper. Rahu is seen as an asura or demon who does his best to plunge any area of life he controls into chaos.* Guess who is going to worship Durga unabashedly. Let us say in all honesty that I am truly worried as my life is linked to too many others and thus I maybe need to hand over to someone with good planets! Chaos is not what I wish for transition and/or

---

[217] http://en.wikipedia.org/wiki/Rahu

ANOURADHA BAKSHI

mutation time at Project Why. And yet it will all have to be done under the watchful eye of Rahu as will my bucket lists and last hurrah!

Did a bit of research - bless Aunt Google - and discovered that my Rahu is in Aquarius. What I found in one of the pages was quite amusing and spot on if it works. It says that Rahu in Aquarius is an excellent placement for; hold your breath; *professional labour union organiser, leader of regulated lawful social-change movements; orchestrator of rallies and gatherings; fund-raisers!* That sounds great for one who is looking for donors! If what is written is correct than Rahu gets ahead via large-scale networks. Of course before I could rejoice tool much another article provided the tempering needed, talking about worries and troubles and over confidence. When Rahu is in Aquarius then Ketu, the tail of the severed head is in Leo and it is said that *these Nodes represent the struggle between the personal life and an impersonal dedication to humanity. The Leo Ketu symbolises prior lives where much revolved around the self. The Rahu in Aquarius points to a future of service for mankind, where the individual will assume the role of the 'water bearer', so that he may be an instrument in the crusade for world evolution. Before he can do this, the enormous power of the Leo Ketu must be dealt with.* What it means is that one was very self centred in ones past life and it's payback time. Sounds spot on again. The line I like best was the following: *His karma now is to learn how to walk lightly, without leaving footsteps, for in essence he is the ruler making ready to abdicate his throne.*

How true. Time has come to make myself so tiny that my footsteps become invisible and I can hand over the mantle and move on.

This is what awaits....

A VERY SPECIAL BIRTHDAY WISH

Today is my mother's Kamala's birthday, a blessed day in more ways than one. At the crack of dawn I got my almost daily Skype call from my grandson. He is now old enough to call himself. He was keen to show me his 'new' computer - actually his father's old laptop! He was over the moon as he could now imitate his Bapu and type on the keyboard even if the computer did not work. Children have their unique make believe world, and only children excel at that. Ask me! I am an only child too! After typing his name, and mine he suddenly asked me a word beginning with K. Serendipitous to say the least as Ma's name begins with a K. I spelt it out and told him it was my Mama's name and that today was her birthday. His hands immediately flew on the keyboard as he told me he was sending her a message. He was quick to tell me what he was writing: *happy birthday; though I do not know you, I love you.*

It was a magical moment. I gently told him that she loved him too and even if one could not see her, she saw us and specially him and always showered him with love and blessings.

The moment ended as the little fellow chased another thought yet in filled me with immense joy and I knew that Kamala was smiling!

WHAT'S IN A NUMBER

OK so yesterday was our fortieth wedding anniversary. Why is the fortieth more important than the fourty ninth or the forty first? To me each anniversary from the very first has been a cause to celebrate. Yet someone somewhere decided that some are better than others: the twenty fifth, the fiftieth or the sixtieth! Come to think of it every day of togetherness is sufficient cause to celebrate. The success of a marriage is to be able to fall in love every morning with the same person as everyone of us changes as time goes by and we need to accept and embrace the changes. If we are wise enough to understand that our love is safe.

Many people have huge parties to celebrate the social milestones of a marriage. I have never been one to do so. On those days I have wanted to be with those I love and be able to spend quality time. I recoil at the idea of dressing as a bride or renewing my vows. I renew them each day and more than never when faced with a challenge. That is when love is put to the test.

Marriage is a series of relationships that you stumble upon as you travel the journey of life. It often starts with that woolly feeling of falling in love, when the world is viewed through rose coloured glasses and everything seems right. But those glasses come off and you need to conjure the ones suitable for the moment you are living. And as you trudge along, your relationship takes on many hues: you are friend, philosopher, guide, partner, companion and much more. You are the shoulder to cry on, the patient listener, the cheerleader, the devil's advocate and above all the honest critic even when it hurts. It is in being each of these and more that you secure your love and can move into the twilight years.

After forty years, I guess one has been all of the above as best one can. Today our love is bathed in comfortable quietude and often we do not even need word to comfort each other or to convey what needs to be said. One knows when to hold a hand or give a hug and when to remain mute. From the passion of the first moments one has moved into a comfortable zone when the yore years have found their place and only the future remains.

It is a blessed feeling that needs no loud revelry. Come to think of it every moment is a celebration

Monday, 15 December 2014

A FEW GOOD MEN

A gentle soul breathed his last yesterday night after a long and valiant battle with the unrelenting crab. My relationship with him was unique. He was the first 'in-law' I met before my marriage. I was nervous like hell as I walked the stairs leading to the Chinese restaurant where we were to meet. The question in my mind was: would he approve of me. But the moment I met him, all doubts flew away as his charm and kind ways worked wonders and all tabs were soon castaway. He was an amazing erudite and I found myself mesmerised by his knowledge. The much-feared lunch ended too soon with a warm hug and words of blessing.

Then life tools its twist and turns and sadly the note we had struck while enjoying noodles and Manchurians vanished altogether. We met a few times, as niece and uncle in-law, the equation that never seems to balance.

It was a few years back that our paths would cross again. This time it was a terrible challenge that would bring us together, one that would test the mettle we were made of. He would stand tall, like few do and take the road less travelled even if it led to difficult choices. But he took them with courage and conviction. He filled a space in my heart that had laid empty for far too long. I felt blessed. Thus began a new relationship, one that defies all definition and obliterates all tags and labels.

We enjoyed talking about any and everything. His massive erudition and wisdom never failed to amaze me and I learnt more at his proverbial knee that I would in books. We shared a passion for reading and writing and he never failed to comment on my blogs. The have lain orphaned for the past months as he lay in a hospital bed, his body wrecked but his spirit soaring.

Good men are few. He was one of them. The world will never look the same after his demise.

May his soul rest in peace.

Monday, 29 December 2014

BICEPS AND BHAI SAHIBS

Being a recluse, I have my evolved my own ways to de-stressing, taking time off or even traveling to strange lands without having to go further than a few minutes walk. For me these are ways of getting of the spinning world and catching my breath and even recharging my batteries. My latest travel is to the gym located ten minutes walk from my home. For an hour or so I am transported on to another planet I have fondly named - Biceps and Bhai Sahibs! As I walk down the steps of this strange world, I feel a different person. I am in alien world and make sure to embrace its ways. So off comes the jacket and scarf, and with a wave to the burly trainers I get on to the treadmill, set my speed at 6km and take off. The blaring music, the kind I normally shun, sets the rhythm of my walk and I find myself enjoying the mix of house music, Hindi pop, Punjabi rock that hits my ears through a speaker located just next to my treadmill. I catch some words but mostly it is just the beat that gets me going. Before I know it, my 30 minutes are over. Strangely these are the only 30 minutes where I find myself not thinking or anything at all. Maybe this is a form of meditation.

Often the treadmills next to mine have bhai sahibs with large biceps running at high speed. Most are young men eager to get the beloved 6 0r 8 or whatever packs. Some of them grunt while they run. Actually there is a lot of grunting, mostly with the lads doing weight training. It is funny, but somehow I feel quite comfortable amidst them. They sometimes smile at me, but are mostly serious trying to impress one and all.

After my walk, it is time to train and all the young trainers are most eager and ready to 'train' me. I think they are quite amused at the old biddy wanting to build her body! So it is one machine after the other and repetitions laded with encouraging words. I somehow don't feel ridiculous even though in most machines I can only lift the minimum weight of 5 kilos though I have reached 15 kilos in some.

I am like a child trying to concentrate and do my best. Lower body, upper body, abs.. the whole enchilada. And all through the show my mind does not stray in any direction: no Project Why, no family, no home. Just me and my training.

I am glad I found the world of biceps and bhai sahibs. It gives me the breath of fresh air I need, in spite of the grunts, the sweat and the loud music!

Tuesday, 6 January 2015

NOT BAD LUCK

A new study doing the virtual rounds of the World Wide Web wants us to believe that most cancers are caused by bad luck[218]! I guess this is the easiest answer a doctor can provide a patient when he has nothing else to proffer. All patients want to know what caused their cancer and the doctors do not have any answer in spite of the gazillions spent on cancer research. So the medical fraternity must be thrilled and relieved at now having a study emanating from none other than John Hopkins giving them an answer that fits all, satisfies all and needs no further explanation. Come on if you have bad luck mutations then what can anyone say, bar God I guess! That makes the big C beyond any ones control and bad luck a scientific phenomenon. I wonder whose agendas are being met by such a study.

In a hard hitting rebuttal cancer survivor Chris Wark makes some interesting remarks. This study seems to suggest that if you have cancer, you drew the bad lot and lost the lottery. Simplistic? Not quite as if we were to accept this rather absurd view then changing your lifestyle and eating habits may not help; the only thing that will help is to find out as early as possible whether you are in the lucky lot or the unlucky one. And how do you do that? By early detection and more research. And whose pockets are filled: research and conventional and expensive investigations

---

[218] http://www.hopkinsmedicine.org/news/media/releases/bad_luck_of_
random_mutations_plays_predominant_role_in_cancer_study_shows

and treatment. Luck cannot be changed by eating broccoli or giving up sugar. Accepting this study would actually push you to eat, drink and be merry as if you are lucky nothing will happen to you, but if you are unlucky then why not live recklessly. This study, if it were to be believed, sweeps all other options away.

I have had cancer in my life since 1958 when I was just 6. My grandma died of liver cancer. Then four decades later it took my mom and pa away. At that time I knew nothing of alternative therapies and other options. In 1993 when I net to Paris a month after my father's demise and had to visit a doctor for some minor problem, I was asked my medical history and when the doctor realised that both my parents had cancer, it was suggested that I have a detection test every year. Mercifully for me, I never do anything without thinking and I decided I did not want to live a life of yearly remission. I would wait for my body to send me a signal and then decide. When I came back to India I met my Tibetan doctor and since have been taking Tibetan medicine.

I however also took the decision of finding out more about cancer and even though the Internet had not arrived in our lived I did find books and articles that talked of diets, and life style and alternative therapies. I made some radical lifestyle and dietary changes and am still going strong.

Two years ago Cancer came into my like in the worst way possible. My husband wad diagnosed with Hodgkin's Lymphoma. But I was ready and bad luck was not one of the things on my check list. As the Internet has arrived in our lives, I spend days and nights looking for information and making informed choices to prepare my own protocol. I only agreed to chemotherapy because my Tibetan doctor told me that Hodgkin's was one of the three cancers that responded well to chemotherapy. She gave medication to keep the immune system going and also to soften the side effects of the lethal and legal poisoning. My husband had no side effects. When I felt that he was saturated I bullied the oncologist to agree to stop the chemos.

I have shared my battle with Hodgkin's in this blog. My protocol for R was a mix of dietary changes, supplements, cannabis leaves, soursop tea, and more. Even today, he follows that protocol. R is golfing, and even jet setting and is off to Helsinki in a few days and then to a gourmet weekend in Paris with his best friend. I do not know where luck stands in all this.

Coming back to the study and to Chris Wark's rebuttal[219], I agree with him when he states: *Bad luck is perhaps the most dangerous idea to permeate the cancer community because it renders the patient powerless. Nothing you did caused cancer; therefore nothing you can do will make any difference in healing it. Now you are completely dependent on early detection to prevent cancer, and if that doesn't work, your only hope is surgery, chemo and radiation to save you. There's no use in changing your diet or lifestyle.* This is absurd. Only by changing your like style and even jumping on a trampoline you can beat the big C!

There are innumerable studies that show that you can reverse your cancer. Chris Wark mentions some in his article should you be interested in knowing more and as he also says: *There are 21 African nations with less than 1/3 of the cancer rates of the United States. Niger has 1/5th, but their starchy plant-based diet and physical activity has nothing to do with it. They are just 80% luckier.*

Changing your life style, exercising and thinking positive can reverse your cancer. I speak from experience.

---

[219] http://www.chrisbeatcancer.com/study-claims-65-of-cancers-are-caused-by-bad-luck/

Friday, 9 January 2015

FROM 7 TO 16. BOOTING THE ELEPHANT OUT OF THE ROOM AND OUT OF OUR LIVES

For all those who love my better half and have been following our battle with Sir Hodgkin, here is an update and good news. R's last reports are A+! All parameters are good and the haemoglobin which at one time had reaches its nadir: 7, has now shot up to 16! This could only have happened with the guidance of two exceptional doctors, my GP and my Tibetan doctor and the unstinted support of all my friends from the world over. But above all it is because R trusted me implicitly and agreed to swallow all the potions and brews I made for him. Not to forget the Internet that allowed me to get all the information I needed. I so wish I could have done the same for my parents. I know have a greater admiration for my mother who refused all conventional treatment. Sadly I could offer her nothing in lieu.

We did have 11 chemo sessions but again with the approval of my two doctors. The oncologist wanted 12 more but I decided to stop when I realised that R was saturated with the poisoning. All along my Tibetan doctor and I prayed that his immune system would remain intact and it has.

I did not follow any protocol. I trusted my intuition and made choices when I felt them to be right. I would call it the Anou Protocol, which was a medley of diet changes, supplements, jumping of the trampoline, exercising and above all not accepting to live in 'survival' mode. We just lived as we had when he was well. We absolutely did not return to the conventional options of post chemo tests and scans and all else. We booted the elephant out of the room and of our lives.

I recently read two articles on cancer. The first[220] is about a doctor profiting from selling toxic chemotherapy. It is only the tip of the iceberg. The second article[221] is about the lifting of the hold on a breakthrough cancer treatment by the FDA. Dr Burzynski[222] does not believe in 'one size fits all' and offers personalised care. This is a point I had raised with R's oncologist when I insisted that he did not need the last 2 chemos that were part of the 'protocol'.

What modern medicine or let us rather call it bizMedicine is an almost total corruption and manipulation of the Hippocratic oath, and we are falling for it. I am reading a fascinating book by Rana Dasgupta entitled Capital,[223] and urge you to read Chapter Five to see what is happening in our city. It is terrifying.

We all need to make the right choices, to inform ourselves before rushing into treatments proffered with alacrity and impunity, to listen to our body and above all to keep positive. Laughter is indeed the best medicine!

---

[220] http://www.naturalnews.com/048239_cancer_doctors_false_positive_health_care_fraud.html

[221] http://www.examiner.com/article/feds-finally-release-burzynski-cancer-cure-treatment

[222] http://www.burzynskiclinic.com

[223] http://www.nytimes.com/2014/05/11/books/review/capital-by-rana-dasgupta.html?_r=2

Tuesday, 13 January 2015

BLESSED

You may wonder what makes a seemingly intelligent, reasonable and sensible person perform an act that would be deemed demeaning and even repulsive to some. And yet despite the Cartesian principles I live by, I crawled yesterday from the entrance of the Kalkaji temple to the shrine. For those of you who have never been to this temple, the half a mile or so walk is along an over crowded path littered with every kind of dirt and muck that man and beast can create. To the scientific mind this stretch of partly cemented partly tiled expanse would be home to every bacteria, germs, bacilli and pathogens under the sun. People walk on it, spit on it, dogs poo and pee on it and I presume children too! It is supposedly cleaned twice a day but in a perfunctory manner. And yet I crawled all the way, to the feet of Goddess Kalka to redeem a pledge I had made in July 2013 when I performed a 'challisa', which means going for 40 days to the shrine. You maybe wondering why!

That was the time when R was very sick and we had not been able to get a diagnosis. His blood counts were taking a free fall, he was melting away and I was helpless and powerless. Everything that I could have done had been done. Every test and investigation had been performed and gave no incline. I had knocked at the door of every kind of doctor possible and come empty handed. I had prayed and prayed but God remained mute. But one thing I did not lose was my Faith. And it those times of despair, it was the only rock I could hold on to. I knew my faith was being tested and I was ready for the test.

One the last day of my 40 day pilgrimage, I had pledged that I would come crawling to the Goddess is she were to show me the way and the day R's haemoglobin would touch 13. Actually the reason I knew about this 40-day pilgrimage and the crawling pledge was because many in the slums perform it. I guess on the other side of the fence it remains unknown! On that side God is propitiated in lavish ways that can be bought through money. Not so with the poor.

When I took that pledge, I was in the deepest of despair and this pledge was my way of accepting defeat in front of God. It was the undoing of all my hubris, and megalomania as well as my firm belief that God would not let me down. I simply needed to find what God wanted from me and to acknowledge how far I was prepared to go to save R. The pact was sealed. The fact that I had been heard was revealed a few days later when we got a diagnosis and I felt in charge again.

It would take 17 months for the haemoglobin to cross the 13 mark. It did last week and I was ready to fulfil my part. I must admit that I was a little scared as the ritual requires you standing than lying and extending your hands and then standing again from the point your hands were and lying again to be repeated for the whole distance. At 62, with ageing knees and stiff back it is no mean task. Add to it the filth, the damp and even wet patches make it even harder.

I did it yesterday, and it went like a dream. The filth did not matter; it was as if it did not exist. Once I began, it was as if I was transposed to another realm and that the God I held on to was by my side all the time. I did the run in 15 minutes and for those 15 minutes I felt in deep communion with my God.

It was a humbling and yet uplifting experience that filled me with hope and joy.

I felt blessed.

EVERYONE HAS CANCER

It has been long since I wrote on this blog, as it is an actual case of 'no news is good news'! However I pick up my virtual pen again because of a very scary trend I am seeing around me that may become fashion and then routine as it suits vested interests and fills greedy pockets. I am talking about the second elective surgery that a famous actress has chosen to have.[224] After opting for a double mastectomy, she has undergone surgery to remove her ovaries and fallopian tubes again to ward off a risk of getting ovarian cancer. This is something I cannot understand and accept. I speak with responsibility because after having lost my parents to cancer, and having my husband diagnosed for Stage II lymphoma, I have spent all my waking hours finding about what we know as cancer and the findings have demystified the rogue and turned the elephant in a room to at most a fly! What is even more disturbing is a medical advertisement on Indian TV propagating the option of elective prophylactic surgery to ward off cancer. When a celebrity endorses something, it catches the eye of predators who set to work. So if we were to take this idea to the absurd why not remove stomach, liver, lungs and anything else that may become home to cancer cells. And let me tell you something should any one of us take certain tests, we would all be detected with cancer, as each one of us has cancer cells in us and thus is predisposed to cancer. As conventional medicine has ensured

---

[224] http://hereandnow.wbur.org/2015/03/24/angelina-jolie-cancer-surgery

that many of us are kept in the dark about alternative therapies that range from diet and lifestyle change to herbs and potions, we can be duped into taking extreme measures that will do us more harm than good.

Everyone literally has cancer[225]! Our cells make mistakes and these mistakes make the cells look like cancer. Mercifully we have been gifted an extraordinary body that has the capacity of correcting its mistakes and cells are known to commit suicide when needed. Sometimes it does not happen and that is when cancer has we know it occurs.

What I discovered while dealing with R's cancer is that cancer is caused by lifestyle and deep emotional stress and thus can be reversed by changes in these. Every one of us has more than 3000 cancer cells growing in our body. Cancer need not be feared[226] and our immune system, provided it is healthy and spot on, is the best arsenal to deal with these cells. We must ensure that our immune system is intact and change our diets and lifestyle. It has now been proven that a three-day fast can reboot the immune system[227].

I am often asked about how R is feeling and find myself wondering why I am being asked this question over and over again. And then the penny drops: he had/has cancer. And cancer is the big C, the one everyone fears or is made to fear for rather dubious reasons. I too once feared the beast as it took away those I most love, my mama and papa and then had the audacity to strike again. But this time I was ready to meet it head on. I was not going to fall for all this fear business. The so-called big C was no more than the big F (flu) or the big I (infection)! In order to that I had to arm myself if as much knowledge as I could lay my hands on, particularly the ones that are purposely hidden from us. Luck was on my side this time as the Internet had shattered all barriers to knowledge.

---

[225] Paul S. Knoepfler ; American biologist, writer, and blogger. He is an associate professor in the Department of Cell Biology and Human Anatomy, the Genome Center, and the Comprehensive Cancer Center, http://www.science20.com/confessions_stem_cell_scientist/why_literally_everyone_has_cancer_and_what_means_you-81937

[226] http://www.bio-mats.com/the-fourth-treatment-for-medical-refugees/chapter-2

[227] https://news.usc.edu/63669/fasting-triggers-stem-cell-regeneration-of-damaged-old-immune-system/

To the question how is R, the answer is great and he is in..... fill in the blank! R has never been travelling so much for business and pleasure. As I write these words he is with his best buddy in Melbourne ready to watch the World Cup Finals; he was in Mauritius last week and went on a submarine dive, in Thailand the week before playing Golf, and will be in Indonesia next month then in the US and then I have lost count. It is impossible for a recluse like me to keep up with him. I am constantly packing his suitcase and medicine packets as he tends to be forgetful like all men are.

After the last chemo/PETscan combo in January 2013, we opted out of the one size fit all protocol that is the best on offer by the medical fraternity who has arbitrarily decided that it takes 5 years for them to declare you cured. For five years you have to be subjected to scans and tests and to living in the state called 'remission'. Having cancer in my genes, I was offered this remission business 20 years ago when I was told to have check ups every year. I refused and here I am hale, hearty and kicking. The only thing I did 20 years ago is change my diet.

For me Ranjan is cured of whatever he had. We do occasional blood work to keep a check. He has his Tibetan medicine to keep his immune system spot on, we eat healthy and almost vegan and have some supplements. That is it.

I just wanted to share this as I think it is time we realised what is causing our immune system to break down and avoiding the possible causes. Most of them are related to the food industry and the chemical load we ingest. Add to this lack of exercise and you have a recipe for disaster. Stay away from them and you are on the road to good health.

EPILOGUE

July 2014 came and went. We were all busy as July is the month Agastya is with us and sets the mood for each one of us. It is playfulness, hugs galore and laughter. The existential questions are whether one puts on Doreamon or Chota Bheem; how does one sneak out to the toyshop or convince mom to agree to an ice cream. The elephant in the room is the rapidly decreasing number of sleepies that Agastya has left with us. All else is banned. No wonder then that the supposed PET that loomed large post the last chemo and was supposed to tell us where Mr H stood was conveniently forgotten. Our new oncologist was a spunky and adorable 5 year old who decreed that his Nanou was well. He was aptly seconded by both my doctors, who felt that a simple blood test was as good as the invasive and hated PET! The rule of thumb was how Ranjan felt and he was top of the world.

When I look back at the few blogs dated July 2014, they seem to be more about walks down memory lane and the Agastya speak. The elephant had been booted out and so it should be as living in the state called remission with well engineered protocols that never let you forget the dreaded presence are a sure recipe for disaster and keep the Damocles sword hanging on your head. Listening to your body and living life to its fullest were better indicators and we follow just this protocol. Mercifully things have been good.

For me R is cancer free. I of course continue all the support therapies that make sense. Our life style has changed and we follow the regimen as best we can I still jump out of my skin when a fever or cough appears and rush to the doctor for advice.

I still fight a somewhat losing battle with the Scots and the Cubans. I have given in to a few raclette evenings and I accepted many more cheat days.

Our new normal looks quite unique as it is devoid of any visit to hospitals and oncologists. I still scour the net for more information on alternative therapies, which is now far greater than it was when this battle began. If I feel convinced I find myself adding elements to smoothies and salads, fine tuning the menu and ordering supplements that I feel would help.

My life has definitely changed after Mr Hodgkin's uninvited stay but even if it sounds ludicrous, it has changed for the better. I have given up as much negativity as possible. I have stopped looking at the past and learnt to live in the moment

But must of all I have learnt to petition the Gods for smaller and simpler things, taking care of wording my entreaties carefully without ambiguity.

I have buried my hubris in the deep recesses of my mind and lost the key. I have fully accepted my limitations and learnt to be grateful for everything that comes my way.

I try and live each day as if it was the last one.

ACKNOWLEDGMENTS

I could not have fought this battle without:

Ranjan who trusted me and believed in me

Agastya my grandson who can make his Nani laugh even at the worst times and who was and is my partner in crime making sure his Nanou 'jump jumps'[228], eats healthy and exercises every day

Parul for her wise counsel and silent but unflinching support

Shamika for taking over the house responsibilities so I could take care of R

Jef my son-in-law who stood by me

Utpal taught me what hope was

P & R for the morning mail ritual that was my lifeline

To Bisham Chachaji who was like a rock, reading my blogs, calling without fail, and supporting me all the way. Unfortunately he lost his battle to cancer in early 2015

Satish Chandra for making all the trips to the airport, being there whenever needed and making sure the project had all the resources

Dharmendra who stood by me like a son and was by my side any time I needed him even if it meant bone- chilling rides on a bike before dawn cracked

Doc Ravi Paul for the shoulder I could lean on

Doc Dolkar for her never give up shot

Rani and the Project Why team who kept the ship sailing

---

[228] jumps on his trampoline

Xavier for his trust and love

Harriet for conjuring a miracle

Debra for finding me after half a century and being there for me

Cat for taking time to come and see her Indian pop and mom

Emily and Alan for their support and for their ability to make the world a better place

Emily for all the hugs and much needed words

Julia for her love and support and medicine vials

Claudia for the chocolates and the kisses

Deepak, Gita and the house staff for catering to my every demand, no matter how infuriating

Radhey for never refusing to take me anywhere come rain, heat or cold and for providing me my mobile reading room

Irene for being a die-hard reader of my blogs and leaving regular comments to lift me up

My family members who ALL came to see R and give their support.

Vaibhav for all the advice and the bottles of laetrile

Melissa for her sound advice on nutrition and for validating my approach

Saras for making me look at my house with my heart

Jennie, Barbara, Jon, Jhoomur, Damynati, Sabrina, Steve, Enrico, Abhigyan, Anand, Kashmira, Joseph, Vikas, Audrey, Kannan Heather, Shagun, Susmita, Anita, Aparajita, Sheetal, Madhu, Sabine, Tom, Sophie, Veena, Sarah, Mrinal, Meg, Hans, Catherine, Guriya, Lukas, Sunil, Nina, Sanjay, Angelique, Kishan, Ritu, Sonal, Devu, Jamuna, Chandan, Clare, Naoko, Saras, Katia, Mathieu, Nandini, Karuna, Dawn, Abha, Sabrina, Christian and all my virtual friends who stood by me in this journey.

To all a big Thank You!

New Delhi June 2105

Printed in the United States
By Bookmasters